THE PUTIN PAR

THE PUTIN PARADOX

Richard Sakwa

I.B. TAURIS
LONDON • NEW YORK • OXFORD • NEW DELHI • SYDNEY

I.B. TAURIS
Bloomsbury Publishing Plc
50 Bedford Square, London, WC1B 3DP, UK
1385 Broadway, New York, NY 10018, USA

BLOOMSBURY, I.B. TAURIS and the I.B. Tauris logo are trademarks of
Bloomsbury Publishing Plc

First published in Great Britain 2020
Reprinted 2020

Copyright © Richard Sakwa, 2020

Richard Sakwa has asserted his right under the Copyright, Designs and Patents Act, 1988, to be identified as Author of this work.

For legal purposes the Acknowledgements on p. xiv constitute an extension of this copyright page.

Cover design by Liron Gilenberg

All rights reserved. No part of this publication may be reproduced or transmitted in any form or by any means, electronic or mechanical, including photocopying, recording, or any information storage or retrieval system, without prior permission in writing from the publishers.

Bloomsbury Publishing Plc does not have any control over, or responsibility for, any third-party websites referred to or in this book. All internet addresses given in this book were correct at the time of going to press. The author and publisher regret any inconvenience caused if addresses have changed or sites have ceased to exist, but can accept no responsibility for any such changes.

A catalogue record for this book is available from the British Library.

A catalog record for this book is available from the Library of Congress.

ISBN: HB: 978-1-7883-1830-3
PB: 978-1-8386-0127-0
ePDF: 978-1-8386-0372-4
eBook: 978-1-8386-0371-7

Typeset by Newgen KnowledgeWorks Pvt. Ltd., Chennai, India
Printed and bound in Great Britain

To find out more about our authors and books visit www.bloomsbury.com and sign up for our newsletters.

Dedicated to the memory of Anastasia Baburova,
Stanislav Markelov and Natalya Estemirova

CONTENTS

List of Tables ix
Preface x
Acknowledgements xiv
List of Abbreviations xv

1   PUTIN AND HIS TIMES 1
  From *kommunalka* to the Kremlin 1
  The many Putins 6
  The post-Cold War context 12
  The democracy paradox 16

2   STATE, SOCIETY AND REGIME 23
  The birth of the regime-state 24
  The meta-factions of Russian society 29
  The dual state and neo-patrimonialism 44
  Reform, transition and beyond 51

3   PUTIN AND POLITICS 59
  The state of exception and regionalism 59
  Putin and the past 65
  Anti-revolution as a political practice 70
  Putin's statecraft 76
  Stasis, or the developmental impasse 81

4   POLITICS AND THE THIRD STATE 85
  Regime reset 85
  The third state and meta-corruption 92
  The third state and micro-factionalism 100

5 MANAGED CAPITALISM 113
State and market 114
Economic performance and plans 123
Powering Putinism 132
Sanctions and their effect 138

6 FROM PARTNER TO ADVERSARY: RUSSIA AND THE WEST 145
The clash of post-Cold War world orders 146
The logic of Russian foreign policy 152
A new era of confrontation 158

7 RECREATING THE HEARTLAND: EURASIAN PARTNERSHIPS 167
Eurasian integration in perspective 168
The post-Atlantic world 175
Putin's Asian gambit: Escape from confrontation? 180
Global Russia 185

8 THE WINDS OF CHANGE 189
Towards Putin's fourth term 189
The return of politics 195
The 2018 presidential election 198
Challenges of Putin's fourth term 206

9 THE PUTIN PHENOMENON 215
Putin's people and power 215
Is Putin an ism? 220
Putin's grand strategy 229

10 PARADOXES OF PUTINISM 233
When success means failure 234
Towards the succession 236
Russia without Putin 242

Notes 247
Bibliography 283
Index 307

TABLES

4.1 State Duma election, 18 September 2016 90
7.1 The EEU in figures 170
8.1 Presidential election of 18 March 2018 205

PREFACE

Vladimir Putin is one of the most important leaders of our era. He is in equal measure misunderstood and condemned. He has been at the helm of the world's largest country since late 1999, and his decisions have shaped not only Russia but also some of the key issues in world politics. It is therefore crucial to understand what motivates the man, what shapes his policies and what the consequences have been. This study is an exploration of these issues, focused on explaining the Putin phenomenon through the prism of 'paradox'. A paradox is something that at first appearance appears absurd or untrue, yet the contradiction ultimately makes sense. A paradox appears to deny the truth, yet the implied meaning reveals some deeper truth. In practical terms, the duality of meaning reflects a particular type of politics, as in George Orwell's 'war is peace'. It was indeed Orwell who coined the term 'cold war', and the world stumbled into a Second Cold War from 2014. Equally, Russia formally remains committed to the principles of the 'democratic revolution' that gave birth to the independent country as it emerged from the Soviet Union in 1991, yet from early on it became a 'managed democracy'. Democracy by definition requires the open-endedness of outcomes and the firmness of rules, yet in post-communist Russia it is the rules that are flexible and the outcomes predetermined. Can a managed democracy be a democracy at all? Who does the managing, and with what justification? These are the issues explored in this work.

The Putin phenomenon is a response to the challenges facing Russia, but it is also the outcome of the complex reaction between the man and the system. Putin reflects the contradictions and paradoxes of contemporary Russia, but he is also a unique leader who is both more and less than the country that he rules. He is more, because of the extraordinary powers vested in the presidency by the December 1993 constitution. The president is designated as the 'guarantor of the constitution' (Art. 80.2), suggesting that they stand outside of the constitution in order to protect it, a paradox of power that cuts through the whole system. This helps explain the emergence from the very early days of a self-designated power system focused on the presidency but not limited to it, which effectively claimed supervisory or tutelary rights over the management of public affairs. The administrative regime derives its power and legitimacy from the constitution, but it is not effectively constrained by it. A 'dual state' emerged, in which administrative and democratic rationality are entwined. This is why it is misleading to call Russia an 'autocracy'. The authoritarian features are rooted in a non-democratic technocratic appeal to the pursuit of the public good. The priority under Boris Yeltsin in the 1990s was economic and political reform, and then under Putin from 2000 as economic development, state sovereignty, national unity and international status. Putin's ability to articulate an agenda of progress, although in contrast to the Soviet years no longer embedded in a coherent vision of the future, helps explain his extraordinary and enduring popularity, which with some ups and downs has been maintained at levels far exceeding those normally found in liberal democracies.

Putin is also less than the country, in the sense that his rule, as we shall see, draws its power from most of the main political and ideological constituencies, but he allows none full rein. Putin is a brilliant 'faction manager', maintaining the stability of the dual system by playing off the various groups against each other but allowing none to assert its dominance over the others. This means that policymaking is often fragmented and incoherent, representing the lowest common denominator by not threatening vested interests. It also means that policies are often contradictory and go round in circles, endowing the system with the air of stagnation and suffocation. The Putin system is efficient to the degree that government is ordered and strategies, plans and policies are adopted; but much of this 'efficiency' is devoted to perpetuating the system itself rather than to the development of the country. Paradoxically, the greater the managerial efficiency of the administrative system, the less the potential of the country is released. Putin is genuinely appealing to the country that exists, but he has not been able to articulate a vision of the Russia of the future.

As always, the context is crucial, and this applies no less to my attempts to get to grips with the phenomenon. This is my fourth book devoted to the study of Putin's rule, and it may well not be the last if Putin remains leader until 2024, as he is constitutionally mandated to do following his re-election for a fourth term in March 2018. He may even find a way to stay in power for longer. Each book has been different. The first, *Putin: Russia's Choice*, was published in 2004, with a revised version issued in 2008, and focused on Putin's development as a man and as a political leader, and it traced how he came to power then consolidated his rule. The book considered the ideational framework in which Putin operated as well as the key features of Putin's statecraft, including an aversion to revolution accompanied by political managerialism and statism. It also examined the main policy areas, including changes to the federal system, economic reform and foreign policy. The second book, *The Crisis of Russian Democracy*, came out in 2011 and examined the tension within the power system in the transition from Putin to his temporary successor Dmitry Medvedev in 2008. The constitution (Art. 81.3) limits the Russian president to no more than two *consecutive* terms. First elected in March 2000 and again for a second four-year term in March 2004, Putin was faced with the choice of either changing the constitution to remove term limits or declaring himself some sort of 'national leader', as many of his supporters at the time urged him to do. Putin refused to take this path, thus distinguishing himself from the standard pattern of authoritarian leaders. Putin chose to obey the letter of the law and, in a 'managed succession', arranged for Medvedev to be elected, while he became prime minister. The so-called tandem was created. Putin scrupulously held to the black letter of the law, while Medvedev represented the most liberal of the possible choices. Medvedev advanced plans for the modernisation of the country accompanied by a 'reset' in relations with the United States. Not much was achieved, but liberal reform and international engagement were placed on the agenda.

The third book, *Putin Redux*, published in 2014 after Putin's return to power in 2012, described how the modernisation agenda was derailed, as so often, by the onset of the global financial crisis (GFC) in 2008 and foreign developments, notably the war in Georgia in August 2008 and then the Libyan crisis in 2011. Medvedev was not allowed a second run at the presidency, and the modernisation and democratisation rhetoric associated with his rule came to a juddering end. Putin's return to the presidency was announced with clinical brutality at a congress of the ruling United Russia party on 24 September 2011. There was to be a reverse castling move (*rokirovka*), undoing the tandem arrangement of 2008. Putin would return to the presidency, while Medvedev would become prime minister. This was declared to have been the plan all along. This may or may not have been the case, but either way the cynicism of the move appalled the intelligentsia and ordinary citizens. There were rumblings of discontent culminating later that autumn in the emergence of the 'white ribbon' democracy movement. Widespread electoral fraud in the parliamentary elections of 4 December provoked the greatest upsurge of political activism since 2000. The regime responded with a combination of concessions and repression. This is what I call the 'regime reset': it was not liberalisation, but it did involve some deconcentration of political management, including the return of gubernatorial elections and reforms to the party and electoral systems. The regime had no intention of giving up control, but it understood the need to ensure credibility and legitimacy by granting some concessions.

In March 2012, Putin was elected to what had become, following the adoption of constitutional amendments in December 2008, a six-year presidential term. Putin returned to the Kremlin convinced that the West was an untrustworthy partner. The attempt to establish a viable relationship with the West through the 'new realism' between 2000 and 2012 had run into the sand, and now Putin advanced a neo-revisionist strategy that sought to advance Eurasian integration as the counterpart of the European Union (EU), accompanied by a significant deepening of the relationship with China and with Asia as a whole. His ambitious programme to restore Russia's great power status (*derzhavnost'*) had mixed results. Relations with the Atlantic system deteriorated, provoking a direct confrontation over Ukraine in 2014 and the seizure of Crimea. Sanctions were imposed, exacerbating what was already an economic slowdown. Putin's popularity soared as a result of the return of Crimea and the Sevastopol naval base, but there were soon signs of 'Putin fatigue', especially among young people who had grown up knowing no other leader. By the time that Putin came to run for his fourth, and if he stuck to the constitution, his last term in March 2018, the economy was pulling out of recession, although growth remained sluggish and living standards depressed. The administration used its resources to ensure a high turnout, and Putin, not surprisingly, won decisively. As Putin returned to the Kremlin, the foundations of his rule changed as society and elites began to think of Russia after Putin.

This book takes up the story to cover recent developments and places the larger Putin phenomenon in context. It covers its historical origins, makes comparisons with earlier periods of Russian and Soviet history, and draws on cross-national studies. Putin's return to power in 2012 inaugurated a new and more decisive era in Russian foreign policy. His more assertive neo-revisionist foreign policy sought not to destroy the international system but to modify the way that it worked. As far as Moscow was concerned, a more assertive foreign policy would create the conditions for a more equitable and peaceful system of international politics, but the effect was the opposite. The paradoxical approach allows the close integration of domestic, ideational and foreign policy factors in the Putin era. The work ends with an evaluation of the Putin phenomenon, one of the great political curiosities of our era.

Canterbury, April 2019

ACKNOWLEDGEMENTS

I am grateful to Joanna Godfrey at I.B. Tauris (Bloomsbury) for her unstinting support for this work, and I greatly treasure our long-term collaboration. When we began the project, relations between Russia and the West were strained, but few would have predicted that they would become so toxic. Russia was accused of 'meddling' in the US presidential election in 2016, and the stated aspiration of the new president, Donald J. Trump, to 'get along' with Russia was stymied by the extraordinary 'Russiagate' allegations of Russian interference. Instead of the anticipated improved relations, Russia was subjected to wave upon wave of sanctions. In all of this it has been hard to maintain a balanced and analytical approach. In this endeavour I have been greatly helped by my comrades in the field, notably my friends and colleagues at the Faculty of World Economy and International Affairs, National Research University – Higher School of Economics in Moscow, where I am a senior research fellow in our International Laboratory on World Order Studies and the New Regionalism; the Faculty of Political Science at Moscow State University, where I serve as an honorary professor; long-term associates at the Centre for Russian, European and Eurasian Studies (CREES) at the University of Birmingham, where I am an honorary senior research fellow; my confederates in the Valdai International Discussion Club; my coadjutors in the Russia and Eurasia Programme at Chatham House, where I am an associate fellow; and above all my friends and colleagues in the School of Politics and International Relations at the University of Kent. This book is the result of hundreds, if not thousands, of hours of conversations, presentations, discussions and debates in Moscow, St Petersburg, Sochi and Tomsk; Beijing, Shanghai and Ningbo; Washington, San Francisco and New York; Berlin, Brussels, Rhodes and Sicily; and, of course, London and environs. Many people have helped shape my thinking on the paradoxes of Putinism and the Putin phenomenon, but responsibility for the views expressed in this book is mine alone.

ABBREVIATIONS

ABM	Anti-Ballistic Missile treaty (1972)
AIIB	Asian Infrastructure Investment Bank
APEC	Asia-Pacific Economic Cooperation (forum)
Apparatchik	Worker in the Communist Party's Central Committee apparatus
ASEAN	Association of South-East Asian Nations
bcm	billion cubic metres
BMD	Ballistic missile defence
BRI	Belt and Road Initiative
BRICS	Brazil, Russia, India, China, South Africa
CAATSA	Countering America's Adversaries through Sanctions Act
CBR	Central Bank of Russia
CC	Central Committee
CEC	Central Electoral Commission
CEE	Central and Eastern Europe
CFDP	Council for Foreign and Defence Policy (in Russian: SVOP)
CFE	Conventional Forces in Europe treaty (1990)
CFSP	Common Foreign and Security Policy
Cheka	*Chrezvychainaya Komissiya*, Extraordinary Commission, Soviet security organ 1918–22, although the name lived on to describe the various Soviet security agencies
Chinovnik	(Tsarist) civil servant
CIS	Commonwealth of Independent States
CoE	Council of Europe
CPC	Communist Party of China
CPD	Congress of People's Deputies
CPRF	Communist Party of the Russian Federation
CPSU	Communist Party of the Soviet Union
CSCE	Conference on Security and Cooperation in Europe, established in Helsinki in 1975 (see also OSCE)
CSTO	Collective Security Treaty Organisation

DASKAA	Defending American Security from Kremlin Aggression Act
DDoS	Distributed Denial of Service (computer) attacks
ECHR	European Convention on Human Rights and Fundamental Freedoms
ECtHR	European Court of Human Rights
EDB	Eurasian Development Bank
EEU	Eurasian Economic Union
EU	European Union
FC	Federation Council
FCS	Federal Customs Service
FD	Federal district
FDI	Foreign Direct Investment
FSB	*Federal'naya sluzhba bezopasnosti*, Federal Security Service
FSIN	Federal Penitentiary Service
FTA	Free trade area
GDP	Gross domestic product
GDR	German Democratic Republic
GEP	Greater Eurasian Partnership
GFC	Global financial crisis (of 2008–9)
GUEBiPK	Main Directorate for Economic Security and Countering Corruption
ICT	Information and communication technology
IMF	International Monetary Fund
INF	Intermediate-range Nuclear Forces (treaty, 1987–2019)
INSOR	*Institut sovremmennogo razvitiya*, Institute of Contemporary Development
ISP	Internet service provider
JR	*Spravedlivaya Rossiya*, Just Russia (political party)
KGB	*Komitet gosudarstvennogo bezopasnosti*, Committee of State Security
Komsomol	*Kommunisticheskii soyuz molodezhi*, Young Communist League
krai	Territory, province
LDPR	Liberal Democratic Party of Russia
LNG	Liquefied natural gas
MFA	Ministry of Foreign Affairs (see also MID)
MID	*Ministerstvo inostrannykh del*, Ministry of Foreign Affairs
MVD	*Ministerstvo vnutrennykh del*, Ministry of Internal Affairs
NACC	North Atlantic Cooperation Council
NAM	Non-Aligned Movement
NATO	North Atlantic Treaty Organisation
NDB	New Development Bank

NDR	*Nash dom –Rossiya*
NG	*Rosgvardiya*, National Guard
NKVD	People's Commissariat of Internal Affairs
Nomenklatura	The Communist system of political appointments, came to designate the class of office holders
NPT	New political thinking
NPT	Non-Proliferation Treaty (1968)
NRC	NATO–Russia Council
Oblast	Region
OCG	Organised criminal group
OECD	Organisation for Economic Cooperation and Development
OMON	Special-purpose riot police
ONF	*Obshcherossiiskii narodnyi front*, Russian Popular Front
OSCE	Organisation for Security and Cooperation in Europe (the name for the CSCE from December 1994)
OVR	*Otechestvo-Vsya Rossiya*, Fatherland–All Russia electoral bloc
PA	Presidential Administration
PACE	Parliamentary Assembly of the Council of Europe
PCA	Partnership and Cooperation Agreement
Perestroika	Restructuring
PfP	Partnership for Peace
PGO	Prosecutor General's Office
PJC	Permanent Joint Council
PL	Party list
Postanovlenie	Directive
Raion	District, borough
Rasporyazhenie	Executive order
RIC	Russian Investigative Committee
RF	Russian Federation
RNE	*Russkoe natsional'noe edinstvo*, Russian National Unity
ROC	Russian Orthodox Church
Rossiyanin	Russian (in the civic sense)
RPF	Russian Pension Fund
RSFSR	Russian Soviet Federative Socialist Republic
Russkii	Russian (in the ethnic sense, although now used more broadly)
SALT	Strategic Arms Limitation (Talks) Treaty
SCO	Shanghai Cooperation Organisation
SEB	Economic Security Service
SMD	Single-member districts in elections
Sootechestvenniki	Compatriots
SPIEF	St Petersburg International Economic Forum

SREB	Silk Road Economic Belt
START	Strategic Arms Reduction Treaty
SVR	*Sluzhba vneshnoi razvedky*, Foreign Intelligence Service
TEP	Third Energy Package
UN	United Nations
UNSC	United Nations Security Council
UR	United Russia
USSR	Union of Soviet Socialist Republics
VAT	Value-added tax
VKP(b)	All-Union Communist Party (Bolsheviks)
VPN	Virtual private network
VTsIOM	All-Russian Centre for the Study of Public Opinion
WTO	Warsaw Treaty Organisation, Warsaw Pact
WTO	World Trade Organisation
Zastoi	Stagnation

1 PUTIN AND HIS TIMES

The question facing Putin when he assumed power in 2000 is the same one that faced Yeltsin as the first Russian president between 1991 and 1999 and the one which shaped Mikhail Gorbachev's reform efforts as the last Soviet leader between March 1985 and his departure from office in December 1991. The problem is a simple one, but Russia's destiny is to be found within its endless ramifications. The issue can be formulated as follows: Would Russia join the existing US-led liberal international order, adapt to its norms, conventions and power hierarchy, or would it try to maintain its autonomy as a great power and separate political civilisation, even if this generated conflict with the dominant power system? Gorbachev's response was to 'leap forwards': formulating a new model of world order in which he hoped the question would become irrelevant. Gorbachev sought to transcend what he came to see as the sterile divisions of the Cold War to create a transformed inclusive and cooperative world order in which the West and the Soviet Union would be co-creators and become partners. Instead of this new world order based on *transformation*, an alternative post-Cold War system was proposed based on the logic of *enlargement* of the existing Atlantic system, or more broadly, the expansion of the historical West. The tension between adaptation to the norms and institutions of the historical West, and the attempt to forge a model that was perceived to correspond better to Russia's traditions and national interests, has shaped post-communist Russia and after an early honeymoon period determined the character of Putin's leadership. His Soviet upbringing and work in its security forces was only one factor shaping his complex political personality.

From *kommunalka* to the Kremlin

Putin's background before assuming the presidency in December 1999 is both unusual and typical. It is unusual because of Putin's multifaceted past, comprising a number of elements that together constitute a striking biography for a world leader. It is typical in that Putin in several respects epitomises Russia's fragmented, tragic and disjointed recent history. Putin's complex biography reflects the contradictions of Russia itself. The several facets of his character represent the pluralism now deeply embedded in society.[1] Surveys suggest that about a fifth of the population, or some twenty-five million people, adhere to the democratic values as formulated by the West, but various strands of neo-traditional and other critical thought, often deeply antithetical to Western values, maintain a powerful hold. The cosmopolitan urban and well-educated classes are balanced by millions who live in small towns and the countryside, with values that tend to be more insular and traditional. Thus, when Vyacheslav Volodin, at the time the deputy head of the Presidential Administration (PA) responsible for domestic political affairs, declared at the Valdai Discussion Club on 22 October 2014 that 'Putin is Russia, and there can be no Russia without Putin',[2] he was making a political declaration, but this notorious formulation also captures something of the complex bond between Putin and the country. The denial of complexity too often leads to one-sided or distorted portrayals of Putin's leadership. Without an understanding of the context, there can be no understanding of the personality, policies and processes.[3]

Putin was born in Leningrad (as St Petersburg was then known) on 7 October 1952.[4] He was the youngest of three children, with his older siblings born in the mid-1930s: Albert died in infancy, and Viktor died of diphtheria during the 872-day siege of Leningrad. His mother, Maria Ivanovna Putina, was a factory worker, while his father Vladimir Spiridonovich Putin was a conscript in the Soviet Navy, serving in the submarine fleet in the early 1930s and then in the NKVD's destruction battalion before joining the regular forces, where he was severely wounded in November 1941. He later worked in the Yegorov wagon-building plant, where he was secretary of the workshop communist cell. Putin started School No. 193 on 1 September 1960 in Baskov Lane, in the street where his family lived in a communal apartment (*kommunalka*) with two other families. Putin notes in a recent film, 'We lived in one room, in a communal flat, on the fourth, the top floor. Sometimes the roof would leak.'[5] He was an unruly child and one of the few in his class who refused (or was refused) to join the Young Pioneer organisation. At the age of 12, he took up sambo, a Soviet martial and combat sport, and went on become a judo black belt, instilling in him a new sense of discipline. Putin studied German at High School No. 281 and now speaks the language fluently.

He entered the Law Faculty of Leningrad State University in September 1970 and joined the Communist Party of the Soviet Union (CPSU) before graduating in 1975. He had long wanted to join the Committee for State Security (KGB), and this influenced his choice of what to study at university. His early years in the KGB up to 1985 were uneventful in career terms. Putin served initially in the Second Chief Directorate (Counter-Intelligence) and then in the First Chief Directorate (PGU), where he monitored foreigners and consular officials in Leningrad. Putin ended up working in the most sensitive department of the PGU, Department S, requiring a high level of expertise and skill from its officers. These were peak years for the 'stagnation' associated with Leonid Brezhnev, but they were also the years when some sort of Soviet 'normality' became established. Even today, many in Russia regard this period of peace, stability, modest but tangible development and high prestige as one of the two superpowers as the best of times.

In August 1985, Putin's career took a sharp turn when at the age of 32 he was posted to Dresden in the German Democratic Republic (GDR). He moved there with his wife Ludmila and daughter Maria, and his younger daughter Ekaterina was born in Dresden in 1986. He worked as a senior case officer, although the precise details of his activities remain vague. It appears that Putin worked as a Department S officer working with 'illegals', deep cover intelligence assets.[6] Putin described his work as 'pretty routine', including recruiting informants, information gathering and transferring the material to Moscow.[7] Working abroad, Putin missed the excitement of Gorbachev's great reforms: *perestroika* (restructuring), *glasnost'* (openness) and *demokratizatsiya* (democratisation). Gorbachev had been elected in March 1985 as a representative of the younger generation of Soviet leaders, and his six years in power saw the communist system dismantled and the staging of the most open and honestly counted elections in Russia's history. By 1989, the structures of communist power had gone, and the new political thinking (NPT) in foreign policy brought the Cold War to an end. Gorbachev's initial aspiration to modernise socialism through 'reform communism' were soon dashed; but he also failed to effect a Chinese-style manoeuvre of creating a 'communism of reform', whereby the party puts itself at the head of the movement to restore a market economy. As Putin felt even in distant Dresden, the whole system of governance was dismantled with nothing effective put in its place. The Berlin Wall was breached on 9 November 1989, and in a famous incident on 5 December, Putin telephoned Moscow for orders as a crowd prepared to storm the KGB residence, but 'Moscow was silent'.[8] Soviet power was crumbling and it would soon disappear.

Although not a participant of the domestic turbulence, Putin recognised that East Germany's political system was even more repressive than the Soviet Union's. In his four-hour series of interviews with Oliver Stone aired in June 2017, Putin described the GDR as entirely lacking 'the spirit of innovation' and noted that it was a 'society frozen in the 1950s'. Stone conducted more than a dozen interviews with Putin over a two-year period, with no subject off-limits, and the series provides a fascinating insight into Putin's thinking.[9] Putin made the same point in his book of interviews published as he assumed power in early 2000: 'It [the GDR] was a harshly totalitarian country, similar to the Soviet Union, only 30 years earlier.' He noted, 'The tragedy is that many people sincerely believed in all those Communist ideals',[10] implying that he was not one of them. There is no evidence that Putin was ever a committed communist in ideological terms, although he was a fierce patriot. The point is important, since it indicates a pragmatic cast of mind, a trait that characterises his leadership. Although Putin was distant from the hopes and expectations of *perestroika*, he was witness to its consequences, above all the weakening of state capacity and the accompanying social disorder. Putin is critical of revolution and spontaneous social activism, but while alert to the negative consequences of autonomous social and political activism, he appears blind to its potential for emancipation and renewal. The concepts of 'reform' and 'modernisation' are absent from his lexicon.

Putin returned to Russia in January 1990 with not much to show for his efforts in East Germany and with an uncertain future. In June, he was appointed to the International Affairs department of Leningrad University. At the same time, in May 1990, Putin became an international affairs advisor to one of his former professors, Anatoly Sobchak. In March 1989, Sobchak had been elected an independent to the new Congress of People's Deputies (CPD), where he became co-chair of the Inter-Regional Group of Deputies, which provided support for Yeltsin's political ambitions. In April 1990, Sobchak was elected a member of the Leningrad City Council, and in May, he became chair. From the first, Sobchak demonstrated authoritarian inclinations, although couched in the language of democracy and reform. He pushed through proposals to create a directly elected chief executive and won the subsequent mayoral election in June 1991 (accompanied by a plebiscite on restoring the city's original name). On 28 June 1991, Putin became head of the Committee for External Relations in the St Petersburg mayor's office, responsible for international contacts and attracting inward investment. On the second day of the coup against Gorbachev's federal reform plans, on 20 August 1991, Putin resigned from the KGB with the rank of lieutenant colonel. Putin later commented, 'As soon as the coup began, I immediately decided which side I was on',[11] although the choice was not an easy one since he had spent his career in 'the organs'. The CPSU was disbanded soon after, although Putin appears never to have renounced his party membership.[12] Faced with the coup, Stone asked Putin whether he still believed in communism, in the system, to which Putin responded, 'No, certainly not, But at the beginning I believed it ... and I wanted to implement it.' So, when did he change? 'You know, regrettably, my views are not changed when I am exposed to new ideas, but only when I'm exposed to new circumstances.' This was Putin the arch-pragmatist. He was also the realist who understood that 'the political system was stagnating ... it was frozen, it was not capable of any development', and drawing on the experience of the GDR, he concluded that 'the monopoly of one political force, of one party, is pernicious to the country'.

Sobchak served as mayor from 1991 to 1996, with Putin in March 1994 becoming one of the deputy mayors, while the other, Vladimir Yakovlev, in the end challenged his patron. In these years, St Petersburg hosted several major cultural and sporting events, but the infrastructure degraded and the city was engulfed by criminality and poverty. In an attempt to alleviate food shortages in late 1991, Putin authorised the export of metals and other goods worth $93 million in exchange for food, but while the goods were exported, very little, if any, food aid arrived.[13] An investigation led by Marina Salye, a member of the city legislature, recommended that Putin be dismissed for inappropriately licensing the deal and then failing to monitor it adequately.[14] Accusations of corruption were used by both sides in the struggle between the mayor's office and the city soviet for power in the city, a microcosm of the struggle between Yeltsin and the Russian CPD, which ended in the bloodshed of October 1993. Despite the serious charges against him, Putin thrived and became acquainted with some high-profile foreign visitors to the city, including Henry Kissinger. All this came to a crunching halt with Sobchak's defeat in the election against Yakovlev in June 1996, with Putin refusing to serve under the new mayor, whom he accused of treachery.[15]

Putin moved to Moscow, and in August 1996, he became a deputy head under Pavel Borodin of the Presidential General Affairs Department, responsible for Russian property abroad. This was the beginning of Putin's vertiginous rise. On 26 March 1997, Yeltsin appointed him a deputy head of the PA, a post he retained until May 1998, and head of the Main Control Directorate (until June 1998), a job that involved monitoring expenditure. On 27 June 1997, Putin defended his doctoral (*kandidatskaya*) dissertation at the St Petersburg Mining Institute, supervised by the rector Vladimir Litvinenko, on the subject of *The Strategic Planning of Regional Resources during the Formation of Market Relations*. Putin argued that the state had an important part to play in maximising natural resources to advance national developmental goals, a principle that he implemented as president. In an associated article, Putin argued that Russia's mineral resources, and in particular hydrocarbons, would be central to the country's economic development for the foreseeable future. To achieve the most effective exploitation of these resources, the state would have to take the lead in regulating and developing the resource sector, although using 'purely market methods'.[16] Typically, Putin favoured the market but not market *forces*. The resource sector became the prime example of a managed market. As president, Putin relied on a set of 'national champions', taking the form of Gazprom for gas and Rosneft for oil. Gazprom in particular became an instrument of state policy, and although condemned as a distortion of market forces and an avenue for corruption, this form of state capitalism built on the Soviet legacy and comparative developmental experience.[17]

On 25 May 1998, Putin was appointed first deputy head of the PA responsible for regional affairs and on 15 July became head of the commission responsible for the bilateral 'treaties' between Moscow and the regions. Putin now oversaw the work of regional administrations and clearly opposed the ad hoc rather than constitutional character of the agreements. His predecessor, Sergei Shakhrai, had signed forty-six agreements with forty-four regions, but Putin halted the process, and when he became president he allowed them all to lapse, except the one with Tatarstan which was renewed in 2007 (but which finally ended on 26 June 2017). Putin was not long in this post. On 25 June 1998, he was appointed director of the Federal Security Service (FSB), the successor to the KGB, where he conducted a radical purge and reassignment of staff. Putin once again soon moved on, this time to become prime minister. He was nominated on 9 August and confirmed by parliament on 16 August 1999. Yeltsin made clear that he considered Putin his designated successor. This was an even more difficult period than usual, with Russia suffering from endemic fiscal crisis which culminated in the partial default of August 1998 and persistent political instability as Yeltsin's health failed.

There was also renewed turmoil in Chechnya. The first war was launched in December 1994 and ground on until August 1996, when the Khasavyurt agreement granted the republic a five-year interim period of self-rule that could well have ended in independence for 'Ichkeria'. Instead, the republic descended into internecine conflict, the imposition of harsh elements of Sharia law, public executions, hostage taking and killings. In the summer of 1999, armed incursions into neighbouring Dagestan and the creation of radical Islamist enclaves there created a security threat of the first order. The still-unexplained explosions in two Moscow apartment blocks and one in Volgodonsk took a heavy toll of lives. The Chechens were held responsible, although the precise circumstances remain a mystery. In September, Putin launched what was to become the second Chechen war, which in the end defeated the radical Islamic authorities while co-opting Chechen forces defending traditional representations of Chechen nationalism. The second war, like the first, was accompanied by the terrible loss of life and material destruction. Putin's defence of the territorial integrity of Russia and dynamic personality, especially compared to the years of rule by a debilitated Yeltsin, prompted a sharp rise in his popularity. Putin's endorsement of the new political party called Unity gave it a surprise success in the December 1999 parliamentary election, winning the second largest share of the vote (23.3 per cent) – the Communist Party of the Russian Federation (CPRF) came first with 24.3 per cent.

Conditions were now in place for the first of Russia's managed successions. On 31 December 1999, Yeltsin addressed the nation to announce his resignation and, as stipulated by the constitution, Putin as prime minister became acting president. Putin's first decree that day provided immunity for Yeltsin and his family. Preterm elections were held on 26 March 2000, in which Putin won in the first round with 53 per cent of the vote, with the CPRF leader since 1993, Gennady Zyuganov, coming second with 29 per cent. Putin was formally inaugurated on 7 May, and he appointed the former finance minister, Mikhail Kasyanov, as prime minister. The Putin era had begun.

The many Putins

Putin's precipitous ascent led to much speculation about 'who is Mr Putin?'. This question is not susceptible to any simple answer, since Putin remains a protean figure onto which people project their own prejudices, ambitions, aspirations and hopes. No single element in his biography or career shapes his political preferences. The Hill and Gaddy biography does a good job in identifying the various facets of Putin's political personality, but it fails to integrate them into a dynamic or convincing portrait of the man or the system. Lacking a broader analysis of the political context of his work or a conceptual framework for the analysis of his rule, the work arbitrarily (in methodological terms) draws on one aspect (Putin as a KGB 'case officer') to explain the onset of a period of confrontation with the West in his third term after 2012.[18] Putin's ambition to join the Soviet security service and his subsequent employment by the KGB and the FSB no doubt contributed to his understanding of politics, but other experiences also shaped his views.[19] As deputy mayor in St Petersburg in the early 1990s, Putin was responsible for the liberal transformation of the city's economy, seeking to harness the power of the market and international capital to create a capitalist economy. This required many insalubrious deals with organised interests, some of which may have been criminal, but this was the only way to get things done in the chaotic conditions of Russia's 'primary accumulation of capital' phase of development.

Corners were undoubtedly cut, reinforcing what became Putin's goal-oriented managerial strategy: processes and institutions were subordinated to the achievement of defined ends. Even this result-focused approach is tempered by Putin's legal training, so even if ends shape means, formal adherence to the law and regulations remain paramount in his statecraft. Although the foundations of a capitalist democracy were established in the 1990s, the Putin years saw the development of the legal and regulatory framework for a market economy and a liberal democracy. However, when we come to discuss the dual (and possibly even triple) state, we shall see how contradictory elements were embedded in Russian state development in the Yeltsin years, which became more deeply entrenched after 2000. Condemnation of the 'chaotic 1990s' is one of the founding myths of Putin's rule, but his system owes much to the principles of statecraft and political economy laid down in that decade, reinforcing the multiple and contradictory features of Putin's leadership. In the Stone interviews, Putin insists that he favours private property and privatisation but opposes the way that the oligarchs in the 1990s exploited their ties to the state apparatus to grab whole industries on the cheap. Putin also revealed that he had been subject to five assassination attempts, and contrary to the view that he was anti-American, he emerges as someone ready to do business with the West, if the terms are right.

Two historical events shape Putin's political character. First, the influence of what in Russia is called the Great Patriotic War, the terrible conflict unleashed by Nazi Germany's invasion of the Soviet Union on 22 June 1941. By then the Second World War had been raging for nearly two years, with France and the western part of continental Europe occupied by Germany but with Britain standing alone and defiant. Poland and much of Eastern Europe had been delivered to

Germany in the Nazi-Soviet Pact of 23 August 1939 and its subsequent (secret) Protocols. Following the failure to create an effective collective defence alliance against Hitler, Joseph Stalin sought to buy time and turn the German war machine against the Union of Soviet Socialist Republics (USSR)'s capitalist enemies in the West. This may well have been a rational policy, but the savage character of the Soviet occupation of eastern Poland and other territories, accompanied by mass deportations, the slaughter of some twenty-two thousand Polish officers at Katyn and elsewhere, the failure to build adequate defences along the new border and the obsequious character of the relationship with Hitler, was not. Stalin refused to acknowledge the many warnings of the impending German attack and was shocked when it came. Entire Soviet armies were destroyed, and Moscow barely escaped capture in the winter of 1941–2. The blockade of Leningrad from 8 September 1941 to 27 January 1944 was one of the longest and most savage sieges in history, accompanied by mass starvation and over half a million deaths. Putin's mother only survived because of the rations given to her husband as a soldier. Putin grew up in the war's long shadow, and to this day victory in that struggle remains the foundational moment of Russian national identity. Some twenty-seven million Soviet people were killed in the titanic struggle, which brought the country's armed forces to Berlin. Victory endowed the Soviet Union with a great power status, consolidated in the Yalta and Potsdam agreements of 1945. This is tempered by Stalin's horrific collectivisation of agriculture in the early 1930s, which provoked a widespread famine (called in Ukraine the *Holodomor*), the murderous purges of the 1930s and his costly wartime mistakes. Nevertheless, the country's heroic sacrifice garnered the laurels of victory, the consolidation of a security zone in Eastern Europe, the status of a founding member of the post-war order and the validation of the achievements of the Soviet system combine to make the war one of the foundations of national identity today.

The second major event is the self-dissolution of the communist system and the subsequent disintegration of the USSR. In 1988, the major instruments of CPSU rule were dismantled, including the whole *apparat* of the Central Committee and its agencies. In March 1989, elections were held to a newly empowered CPD, and this ballot (along with the election to the Russian CPD a year later) was the freest and fairest Russia has seen. By 1989, the Soviet Union was no longer recognisably communist, and in the autumn, most countries in the Soviet bloc shook off communist rule through 'velvet revolutions' and began what was described at the time as the 'return to Europe'. The CPSU in February 1990 was stripped off its 'leading and guiding role', and power shifted to the newly established presidency and a newly empowered parliament. In foreign affairs, by 1989 the Cold War was over, and the country looked to a new era of transformed relations with the Western powers. However, powerful national movements gathered force in the union republics, with Russia under Yeltsin in the lead. The Russian Declaration of State Sovereignty of 12 June 1990 marked the moment when Russia defected from the country whose heart it had been for over half a millennium. A cascade of sovereignty declarations gave way to declarations of independence, despite Gorbachev's attempts to negotiate a new 'union treaty' to hold the country together. On 7–8 December 1991 at Belovezhskaya Pushcha in what was then Belarussia, the Soviet Union was abolished by the leaders of Russia, Belarus and Ukraine, and the Commonwealth of Independent States (CIS) was created. Russia became the 'continuer state', assuming the Soviet Union's legal and treaty obligations, as well as its debts, but above all its permanent United Nations Security Council (UNSC) seat.

The Great Patriotic War and the Soviet collapse haunt Russian history. The first reinforces Putin's belief that Russia has to defend its sovereignty diplomatically and militarily, and the second that centrifugal trends have to be curbed. This gives rise to Putin's enduring commitment to 'stability'. He saw the consequences of wartime destruction and the ill-thought-out reforms in the Gorbachev years, which provoked the dissolution of the communist system (which does not seem to have bothered Putin very much), and the disintegration of the Soviet Union and the weakening of the state (which worried him very much). Although Putin in April 2005 talked about the collapse (*krushenie*) of the Soviet Union as 'a major geopolitical catastrophe of the [twentieth] century', he certainly did not mean that the USSR could be recreated. The phrase has been misinterpreted and taken out of context.[20] Putin explained that he considered the event so catastrophic because millions of members of the Russian nation suddenly found themselves outside of the Russian Federation's borders, and the Soviet downfall opened the door to oligarch power and mass poverty. He went on to insist that Russia's development as a democratic state was 'the main political-ideological task', but Russia had come to democracy by 'the hard path', and thus democracy was especially valued in the country. He declared that democracy was something that Russia had itself chosen and that it was not something imposed from outside, and hence the country would do it on its own terms and in its own way.[21] Political shocks, irresponsible mobilisation and the imposition of 'reforms' in his view precipitated revolution and collapse. As he put it in his landmark statement on the eve of taking power, *Russia at the Turn of the Millennium* (known hereafter as his *Millennium Manifesto*), 'Russia has reached its limit for political and socio-economic upheavals, cataclysms, and radical reforms. ... Be it under communist, national patriotic, or radical-liberal slogans, our country and our people will not withstand a new radical break-up.'[22] His response was to limit the autonomous mobilisation of political interests, intensify the monitoring of NGOs and curb external financing and influence on political actors in Russia.

While Russia remains an intensely pluralistic country, the political representation of contending views has been stifled. As in the Soviet years, everything is political, but not at the level of 'the political' – the agonistic formal and institutionalised contention between deeply held views on a nation's destiny and policies. In this sense, Putin depoliticised the policy process, the counterpart of pragmatic policymaking. Technocratic rationality claims to be superior (and may well be in certain limited respects) to the short-termism of democratic contestation and governmental turnover. It allows longer time horizons and the implementation of long-term strategies. However, sovereignty is shifted from the democratic citizenry to administrative elites and specialists (the technical intelligentsia). This displacement reproduced the 'stability system' that predominated in the late Soviet years, although in conditions of greater openness and exposure to foreign influences. A stability system is one in which the political regime monitors and controls social and political forces, and thus stands outside of politics. Putin's 'stabilocracy' is embodied in the tutelary role of the administrative regime, claiming to know better than the views expressed by democratic majorities and insulated from the emotions of the democratic masses. This is a technocratic understanding of the political sphere and inevitably raises fundamental questions about political legitimacy. By what right does a self-constituted regime close itself off from popular accountability? The unstable foundation of the semantic shift in the meaning of stability from a technical term to an ideological principle, paradoxically, generates instability.[23]

This is the paradox that ultimately undermined the legitimacy, and hence durability, of the Soviet Union. In the late Soviet years, the earlier mobilising belief in world revolution, industrialisation and modernisation eroded, and instead regime legitimacy was based on 'eudaemonic' performance; that is, the ability to deliver tangible public goods, rising living standards and stability. This represented a 'social contract': in exchange for limitations on public autonomous political participation, the regime would deliver improved prosperity and security. In its final years, the regime could no longer keep its end of the bargain, especially when the privileges and corruption of the elite became known, provoking the people to demand more meaningful political participation. This burst out in the wave of civic activism during perestroika, including the creation of a vibrant network of *neformaly* (informal associations) as well as the beginnings of a reborn competitive party system. This democratic wave soon ebbed, although Yeltsin rode on it to take power in an independent Russia. Once in the Kremlin, he no longer needed popular mobilisation and political pluralism, and instead relied on the administrative system. In this way, post-communist Russia recreated a stability system. A new 'social contract' also promises to raise living standards in exchange for political passivity. Equally, the Putin system is in danger of being caught in the 'eudaemonic trap', when a regime is unable to deliver on its promises. In Putin's case, the basis for legitimation is broader than that of the earlier system but nevertheless relies on performance criteria that erode popular support when not fulfilled.

Coming after jarring shocks to society and the political system, the promise of stability was certainly attractive for large parts of society. Putin's administration positioned itself as both the heir and repudiator of three earlier systems: the Imperial, the Soviet and the liberal 1990s. The first two collapsed and the third ended in chaos, although all three had notable achievements to their credit. Putin sought to exploit the accomplishments, in terms of domestic development and status abroad, while repudiating the failings. This is the classic task of a restoration period, selecting what useful elements from the revolutionary period to incorporate into the new order. This renders Putin's rule an eclectic mix of systems and histories, incorporating elements of all preceding orders but not fully articulating their individual purpose and logic. This is the trademark characteristic of the Putin phenomenon: taking a little from each historical era but allowing none to become dominant. This makes it difficult for the Putin system to articulate its own meaning and purpose other than stability itself. This entails the danger of repeating the mistakes that destroyed the earlier regimes, including political closure and, in the case of the Soviet regime, social, political and economic stagnation.

Awareness of Russia's historic vulnerability and the concomitant emphasis on stability are the foundations of Putin's leadership, and it is in this context that his achievements have to be assessed. Putin's rule has been extraordinary, and he joins the ranks as one of Russia's longest serving leaders. Leonid Brezhnev came to power as part of a collective leadership in 1964, and the latter part of his eighteen years in power are known as the era of stagnation (*zastoi*). Putin joins an illustrious and sometimes less-than-distinguished grand pageant of Russian leaders. As an avid amateur historian, he is well aware of the succession of heroes, reformers, misfits and mass murderers who have preceded him at the helm of the country's destiny. Opinions are divided over which category Putin will join, and this very divergence of views is a characteristic feature of the Putin phenomenon. For some, he is the man who presided over the degradation of Russian democracy and who became the sponsor of attempts to subvert the West.[24] For others, he is the leader who stabilised the country and provided a framework for development while asserting Russia's sovereignty at home and abroad, an act of defiance that brought down the wrath of the Atlantic power system on his head.[25]

The religious side of Putin's personality is undoubtedly important and has probably been underestimated in the various biographies. Putin was baptised into the Russian Orthodox Church (ROC) as a child, and there are indications that his spiritual advisor is Bishop Tikhon (Shevkunov), formerly Archimandrite at the rebuilt Sretensky Monastery in central Moscow and the author of the bestselling *Everyday Saints and Other Stories*. At the same time, Putin entertains a utilitarian view of organised religion as one of the pillars of his vaunted 'stability'. During the 2012 presidential election, the close link between Putin and Patriarch Kirill was stressed, but they appear to have drifted apart as a result of the Ukraine crisis. For Putin, organised religion (and not just the ROC) is one of the main supports of the regime in inculcating patriotic sentiments in the population and the source of spiritual values and ethical values compared to the amoral West. By contrast,

Patriarch Kirill criticises the state's historical influence on the church. Whereas Putin wanted Kirill to condemn the Ukrainian authorities after 2014, the ROC was cautious since the Moscow Patriarchate is head of some two-thirds of Orthodox parishes in Ukraine, who find themselves under intense pressure to subordinate themselves to the Kiev Patriarchate.[26] At the same time, Putin is always respectful of the other 'traditional' religions in Russia: Judaism, Islam and Buddhism. Putin himself is a philo-Semite, attributed to friendship with his Jewish neighbours in his childhood *kommunalka*, and he has gone out of his way to forge a strong relationship with Israel and to respect its security interests. The support of local authorities in the construction of churches and the general encroachment of the church into matters of morality and education provokes resistance in society, especially since the constitution stipulates the separation of church and state.

The Putin system is trapped in a liminal space between democracy and authoritarianism. It has elements of both, but the logic of neither is given free rein. This is not a no man's land, since the country is living and developing in that space, but it is one where different rationalities of governance compete, accompanied by contesting ideological orientations and appreciations of the past. None is 'hegemonic', that is, no single vision of the public good and vision of the future predominate. Instead, competing interpretations of Russia's destiny and place in the world coexist.

The post-Cold War context

The post-Cold War era has been shaped by the tension between transformation of the European security order and the enlargement of the Atlantic system. Yeltsin tried to finesse the question and do both. However, as it became clear that enthusiasm to adapt to Western modernity entailed acquiescence to the logic of enlargement, a powerful head of resistance built up within the country. An oscillating pattern of cooperation and conflict between Russia and the West was established, and this was the situation inherited by Putin. As the most European leader Russia has ever had, he tried to negotiate a way out of the impasse. This involved attempts to forge a closer relationship with the European Union (EU), and he even suggested membership of the North Atlantic Treaty Organisation (NATO), a strategy that could be called *transformation from within*. For various reasons (explored in Chapter 6), this failed in the most spectacular manner. By the time Putin returned to office for his fourth presidential term in 2018, the pendulum had swung firmly towards a position of entrenched conflict. This is the Second Cold War: as different from the first as the Second World War differs from the first. All three leaders – Gorbachev, Yeltsin and Putin – believed that there was some sort of Russian third way between subordination to the logic of US-led liberal order enlargement and outright resistance.[27] This larger logic of international relations in the post-Cold

War years since 1989 is the matrix within which Russian domestic politics were shaped and the paradoxes of the Putin phenomenon developed.

There could be no straightforward 'return to Europe' for the newly independent Russia. By then the liberal international order in Europe was made up of two key components: NATO and what was soon to become (as a result of the Treaty of Maastricht) the EU. NATO was created in 1949 as a way of containing the USSR as well as of ensuring the continued commitment of the United States to West European security. In 1990, the Soviet equivalent of NATO, the Warsaw Treaty Organisation (WTO), was disbanded, but NATO not only continued but after some hesitation in the early 1990s (aware of the alienating effect that expansion would have on Russo-Western relations) also began a process of *enlargement*. This represented the augmentation not only of a security organisation but also of a whole ramified power system, accompanied by forceful ideological and normative claims. Post-communist Russia to a degree shared these normative principles because the country became an independent state through what was considered at the time to be a 'democratic revolution', albeit 'unfinished'.[28]

The problem was that Russia could not be a passive recipient of a transformation based on models generated elsewhere. Just as the country sought to become the co-creator of a new world order, its whole history militated against simple adaptation to patterns devised elsewhere. Russia sought solutions to historical problems within the framework of its own cultural traditions. This is why Russia's 'democratic revolution' always looked anomalous from the perspective of classic theories of democratisation and included elements that were far from democratic. The popular movement was led by a former communist regional boss, and the popular movement never gained a solid independent basis. These contradictions were exacerbated by the perceived threat of the Western enlargement agenda. At the time of German unification in 1990, there were heated discussions about whether the united country would be a NATO member and whether in return for Soviet acquiescence for unification a pledge had been given not to enlarge NATO beyond the united Germany. Although not all scholars agree, the general consensus is that repeated verbal promises were given to that effect.[29] Today, the majority of former Soviet bloc East European states are members of NATO, as well as the three Baltic republics (Estonia, Latvia and Lithuania). In April 2007, Georgia and Ukraine were promised membership at some point in the future, a commitment that provoked a serious deterioration in Russo-Atlantic relations. With Montenegro's accession in 2017, total NATO membership rose to twenty-nine.

Thus, the fundamental process at the end of the Cold War became enlargement of the Atlantic community. By contrast, Gorbachev and his successors in Russia sought *transformation*, a negotiated end to the institutional and ideational structures of the Cold War in which Russia would become a founder member of a new political community. Instead, all that was on offer (and as far as the Western powers were concerned, it was quite a lot) was associate membership in an existing concern. No one really believed that Russia could join NATO without changing the character of the organisation and of the whole Atlantic system. There were understandable fears that Russia's membership would lead to normative dilution, institutional incoherence and, above all, a weakening of US leadership. Fully fledged Russian membership would mean that it would have constituent authority and veto powers. In the post-Cold War era, there were simply not enough Western leaders, let alone military planners, ready to take the risk and weaken (from their perspective) a functioning enterprise in favour of an uncertain and possibly dangerous alliance with Russia. This was certainly something vigorously opposed by most former Soviet bloc countries in Eastern Europe. In addition, as the country plunged into the chaos of the 1990s, Russia was a much weakened power, and its voice could be safely ignored. The resurgence of powerful neo-traditionalist and security (*silovik*) forces further justified the enlargement of the Atlantic system while the going was good. The start of the first Chechen war in December 1994, accompanied by the savage bombing of civilian objects and brutal attempts at pacification, only confirmed the fears of a nationalist backlash.

It seemed reasonable to ask why the Atlantic powers should make concessions and transform themselves, when Russia hardly seemed an attractive and desirable partner. In any case, the offer was on the table for Russia to establish a 'strategic partnership' with the enlarging system. This was formulated in 1997 through the creation of a NATO–Russia Permanent Joint Council (PJC). NATO promised not to station forces in Eastern Europe on a permanent basis, not to place nuclear weapons on the territory of new members, and to work on adapting the Conventional Forces in Europe (CFE) treaty.[30] The PJC format proved inadequate, and following the 9/11 attack on New York and Washington and Putin's support in the struggle against terrorism, including intelligence sharing and opening up bases in Central Asia for the war in Afghanistan, enhanced cooperation and a more equal partnership was on the agenda. On 28 May 2002, the NATO–Russia Council (NRC) was established at a summit in Rome as 'a mechanism for consultation, consensus-building, cooperation, joint decision and joint action in which the individual NATO member states and Russia work as equal partners on a wide spectrum of security issues of common interest'.[31] Russia's status was enhanced from one against the others to what was intended to be a higher degree of partnership as part of an expanded security community. However, the agreement avoided giving Russia a 'veto' in any shape or form on NATO security issues.[32] Neither side pursued a zero-sum strategy, yet in the end without a structural transformation, aspirations for genuine partnership proved nugatory. NATO continued to hedge against Russia's possible resurgence as a security threat (prompted in particular by the concerns of East European countries), but hedging inevitably represented a lack of trust and inhibited even small steps towards 'transformation from within'. Despite endless statements of good will by both sides, the estrangement intensified.

Much the same logic applied to Russia's relations with the EU. It was initially assumed that in the civilian sphere there were greater opportunities for deep engagement. A Partnership and Cooperation Agreement (PCA) was signed in 1994, although it only came into effect in December 1997 because of the Chechen war. At the St Petersburg summit in May 2003, it was agreed to develop four common spaces in the framework of the PCA: economy and environment; freedom, security and justice; external security; and research, education and culture. At the EU–Russia summit (the PCA stipulated biannual meetings, alternately one in Russia and one in the EU) in Rostov-on-Don in mid-2010, a Partnership for Modernisation was signed, which attempted to reset relations, but such a rebooting signalled the deeper exhaustion of the relationship. The foundations for an enduring partnership based on trust and mutual respect were missing. The original PCA came to an end after ten years, and although renewed annually, no new framework agreement has been devised. After 2014, the biannual summits have been abandoned. Each side blames the other for the deterioration, and both sides are right. The problem lies in a different plane, the very basis of post-Cold War international politics. The politics of enlargement by definition assumes a linear and, ultimately, teleological view of political change – that the end point is known and all that has to be done is get there. Russia was to adapt to the existing norms and values of the predominant liberal order. This would undoubtedly have provided a framework for Russia to transform itself into a more liberal, a more democratic and a more compliant state.

Instead, the Moscow leadership already under Yeltsin argued that Russia would transform itself into a liberal and market democracy, but it would do so in its own way and at its own pace. Above all, it argued that the transformation should be mutual, including a transformation of the system of European international relations and, above all, of European security. The West insisted that Russia had to transform itself, while Russia asserted that it would do so, but as part of a broader transformation. Russia hoped that its membership would transform the historical West (with the Atlantic powers and institutions at its core) into a 'greater West' in which Russia would be a constituent member and thus with all the rights of a co-founder. The same applies to Europe where Gorbachev in a landmark speech in Strasbourg in July 1989 had proclaimed a 'common European home'. Russia sought to transform the single-minded axiological logic of EU enlargement into a more dialogical process – in which all are transformed as a result of interaction with each other. Instead, Russia was offered a 'strategic partnership' with the smaller or core Europe, as institutionalised in the EU, in which the norms and institutions of the EU would predominate. By contrast, Russia favoured the transformative and pluralistic creation of a greater Europe (the current term for common European home), in which it would be a founder and core member. The idea of a greater Europe displaces the monist idea of the EU as the sole representative of Europe in favour of a more plural model, in which the EU would be part of a broader pan-European community. Both the greater West and greater Europe ideas are based on a dialogical approach to politics – the view that engagement transforms both subjects. Instead, the West tried to stay the same and enlarge; while Russia was to change and assume a new power and normative identity.

This, then, is the fundamental question. Once it became clear that there would be no transformational politics at the end of the Cold War, and instead the logic of enlargement would prevail, what should Russia do? Should it associate itself with the historical West and the smaller Europe as a subaltern and adapt to the existing institutions and norms, or should it assert its own autonomous great power and normative identity? Yeltsin and Putin, as noted, tried to finesse the question by finding some sort of middle course, but both failed in this endeavour. By the time he returned to power in 2012, Putin had given up the search and now unequivocally advanced the view that Russia would be an independent source of sovereign power in the international system. This gave rise to a neo-revisionist foreign policy: one that remained committed on the vertical axis to the institutions of international law and governance, above all the UN, but in horizontal relations with other states would challenge the hegemony of the US-led liberal order. This inevitably brought Russia into confrontation with the Atlantic system. This was balanced by the creation of an anti-hegemonic alignment with China and some other states.

This was the framework in which Russian politics developed in the post-Cold War era, and in which Putin devised his policies. Foreign policy in this account is not something external but at the heart of Russia's identity and civilisational character, and the central facet of Putin's rule. Russia is far from unique in this respect, but given its size, history and vulnerable geographical location, the interaction of domestic and foreign policy in Russia is exceptionally close. Putin devised his own specific formulation of the challenges. The external threats reinforced the power and legitimacy of the regime at home, but this does not mean that the fundamental structural dilemmas facing post-communist Russia were imagined. In the absence of benign and transformed European international relations, the move from 'strategic partnership' to open confrontation was, if not inevitable, certainly likely. In that context, Putin's statecraft is only the latest manifestation of enduring themes in Russian politics and his leadership only a small chapter in Russia's history of resistance and adaptation to external developmental and security challenges.

The democracy paradox

The Putin project is predicated on maintaining differentiation and pluralism in the international system, while at home it seeks to depoliticise differences and manage contestation between social groups and elite interests. The standard narrative would suggest that as the contradictions of the Putin system accumulated, the role of scapegoating would intensify. This meant identifying the West as the source and the inspirer of Russia's problems, a feature accentuated at times of political stress. Thus, the flawed December 2011 parliamentary elections, followed by the largest political demonstrations of Putin's tenure, were accompanied by a virulent response to alleged Western 'interference'. This was not without some substance, since the US secretary of state at the time, Hillary Clinton, is recognised for her interventionist approach in international affairs; yet the campaign clearly had an instrumental purpose, to mobilise core supporters against the 'other', both internal and abroad. The Putinite system of internal political management recognises the political subjectivity of other political actors as long as they are ready to sacrifice their autonomy. The strategy of depoliticised state management delivers a certain type of stability but requires intense 'manual management' to achieve its goals. Managed democracy stifles genuine dialogical politics, but by the same token, it attempts to build consensus from the centre and avoids extreme forms of axiology.

Putin is often accused of destroying Russia, but film director Andrei Konchalovsky argues instead that 'Russia has destroyed Putin'. Like previous Russian leaders, he finds it hard to 'rule a state whose population has no idea about democracy … and according to inviolable tradition voluntarily delegates all power to one single individual'. In Konchalovsky's view, the Russians were an archaic nation, even though they used iPhones, with a system of values still rooted in the eleventh or twelfth century, before the creation of a bourgeoisie or citizenry. The absence of defensible property rights, a Manichaean way of thinking in which there is only light or darkness, and where reforms always run into the sand shape the destiny of the nation. It also makes the country remarkably resilient, and sanctions have little effect because Russians are used to endurance and in case of conflict will rally round the Kremlin.[33] This characterisation is misleading, since numerous studies reveal a sophisticated understanding and desire for democracy in Russia, accompanied by an awareness of how far the existing system falls short.[34] But there are cultural and historical differences. For the West, democracy is the only political form relevant to the modern world; for Russia, however, the concept is in danger of joining the ranks of failed experiments, alongside fascism and socialism. The experience of near state collapse in the 1990s, accompanied by the enrichment of a small group of oligarchs, traumatised the nation and shapes perceptions to this day. Historical experience determines views, reinforced today by the structure of post-Cold War international politics. While for the West liberalism has become the ideology of modernity, in Russia it is widely perceived to be the creed of an expansive (and quite often hostile) power system.

Post-communist Russia has suffered from a particularly sharp form of what can be called the 'democracy paradox', where majorities may elect a government that threatens the democratic process that brought it to power. The vote in July 1932, in which the Nazis won 37 per cent of the vote, propelled Adolf Hitler to power and can be considered a tragic instance of the problem. The paradox was reflected in the way that the 'democratic' forces, with the help of American advisors, manipulated the 1996 presidential election to get Yeltsin re-elected for a second term, even though his health had collapsed.[35] In a closed-door meeting with oppositionists in February 2012, Medvedev apparently conceded that the result had been rigged: 'There is hardly any doubt who won [the election]. It was not Boris Nikolaevich Yeltsin.'[36] If there had been a genuinely free and fair contest, the communist leader Zyuganov would probably have won. This would have provided Russia with the experience of a competitive transfer of power, something the country still lacks. The manipulative techniques of electoral management were forged in the 1990s in conditions of genuine political pluralism, and they were then honed by Putin in a more managerial environment. His co-optation strategy drastically reduces the competitive character of political pluralism and delivers votes to what has now become a complaisant parliament and for his (or his surrogate's) repeated election to the presidency.

The democracy paradox is far from unique to Russia, and although it is repeatedly used by authoritarian leaders to justify their hold on power, it highlights genuine dilemmas. These were identified by Samuel Huntington in 1968 in his exploration of the political conditions for successful modernisation. Huntington looked at what political institutions would be able to deliver both stability and development, and controversially asserted that order itself was a crucial quality, irrespective of what would nowadays be called 'regime type' at the political level: democratic, authoritarian or something else; or free market or socialist at the economic level. He argued that economic development and political stability were two separate things and that it was a mistake to conflate them.[37] These arguments have lost traction in the post-communist era, and instead the emphasis has been on democratisation as the supreme value. As a pragmatic developmentalist, it is hardly surprising that Putin has returned to Huntingtonian themes in his politics of stability, and these are embedded in the character of Russia's post-communist transformation as a whole.

All Kremlin leaders since 1991 have tried to insulate themselves from social pressures. The political basis of this gulf between the regime and society is that the regime constituted itself consciously as the bearer of a certain set of goals, which lacked an autonomous social basis, and hence had to be created from above – a rerun in reverse of the Bolshevik revolution. In the 1991–3 period, this took the form of a political conflict between the presidency and parliament. After the violent denouement of October 1993 and the adoption of the new constitution in December 1993, the terms of the relationship changed. The regime now had the institutions of a modern liberal democracy to work with and over the years became increasingly adept at manipulating the required outcomes through the formal institutions of constitutional democracy. This gave rise to the dual state. In the Yeltsin years, the manipulations were relatively crude, notably in the 1996 presidential election, when Yeltsin forced his way back into the Kremlin for a second term through flooding the electoral market with perhaps up to $500 million (way above anything permitted by electoral law) and whipping up fear of a 'communist *revanche*'. There were also attempts to create a pro-regime party. In the first instance, this was Yegor Gaidar's Russia's Democratic Choice, but following its disappointing performance in the December 1993 election, the plan shifted towards a 'two-wing' strategy: a centre-left party headed by Ivan Rybkin and a centre-right grouping that in the end took the form of Our Home is Russia (*Nash Dom Rossii*, NDR), headed by the prime minister, Viktor Chernomyrdin.

However, when Chernomyrdin showed signs of harbouring presidential ambitions, he was summarily dismissed in March 1998, and his party dissolved. The initiative passed to the opposition. In late 1998, the mayor of Moscow, Yuri Luzhkov, and some regional leaders, including the president of Tatarstan, Mintimir Shaimiev, created the Fatherland (*Otechestvo*) party. Another potential presidential candidate, Evgeny Primakov, created his own party, All Russia (*Vsya Rossiya*). The two allied in the Duma election of December 1999, merging to create *Otechestvo-Vsya Rossiya* (OVR), and rallied behind Primakov's candidature in the anticipated June 2000 presidential election. For the first time in post-communist Russia, it looked as if there would be democratic leadership rotation. Instead, Putin was appointed prime minister in August 1999 as the regime candidate, and thereafter the Kremlin's political technologists set to work to create a new political party, *Edinstvo* (Unity). Established only in September 1999, against the background of war in Chechnya, a vicious media campaign against Primakov, Putin's soaring popularity and selective incentives to bring over wavering governors, Unity did remarkably well in the December 1999 Duma election. It came second, after the CPRF, with 23 per cent of the party list vote and with 73 members of parliament. Yeltsin resigned on 31 December, and acting president Putin waged a 'non-political' campaign for the pre-term presidential election of 26 March 2000. He presented himself as the voice of reason, far above petty party politics and personality conflicts. This was an enduring trait in which he viewed the public as less than an electorate that had to be won over but as assumed supporters who, if they had any sense, would vote for him.

This was the first national experience of a distinctive sort of Putinite rationality, and one that had profound resonance among the Russia public. Putin easily won in the first round with 53 per cent of the vote, with Zyuganov trailing far behind in second place with 29 per cent. Putin's victory was helped by a sympathetic media and the structural conditions of pre-term elections, but he also tapped into a deep well of popular sympathy for his style and policies. In other words, Putinite rationality was congruent with popular policy and political preferences. This was a type of centrist pragmatism, seeking to take 'the political' out of politics, presenting a set of 'common sense' policies that avoided extremes while offering a way out of crisis. Given the degradation of the political process in the Soviet years, the short-lived and ultimately catastrophic character of the outburst of genuinely competitive political life during perestroika, and then the shabby political conflicts and manipulations of the Yeltsin years, release from that sort of 'politics' represented an undoubted relief for a large part of society in the early 2000s.

Putin then went on to shape the institutional conditions for his representation of political rationality. This included the absorption of the former oppositional parties. In 2001, OVR joined *Edinstvo* to create United Russia (UR), with the top officials of both taking leading positions in the new political formation. Over time, UR became the genuine 'party of power' to which NDR and the other regime parties of the 1990s had aspired.[38] In the end, most governors joined the new party, and it became something analogous to the old CPSU, replicating its practices in appointments, influence networks and privileges; and also by the 2010s generating the same sort of public hostility and contempt. Putin also went on to create a number of para-constitutional institutions (discussed below). All this reflected what can be called the 'post-communist syndrome', in which attempts to replicate the institutions and ideas of European modernity in postmodern conditions, leavened in the Russian case by some pre-modern prejudices, inevitably generates tensions. According to the commentator Vladimir Pastukhov, Russia cannot have a political ideology along the lines of the classic left–right division of the modern era, since Russia remains a pre-political society that has failed to separate property from power.[39] Governance in contemporary Russia is in part based on the circulation of rents, in which businesses are vulnerable to 'raids' by more powerful competitors, in league with the legal and security apparatus (where many of the raids originate in the first place).

The political consequence of the failure to separate power and property, according to the political scientist Alexei Zudin, led to what he calls 'monocentrism', a term that avoids the normative baggage associated with such terms as 'democracy' and 'authoritarianism'. In Zudin's view, Putin created a strong centre of power focused on the presidency around which the political system was reconstructed. This is in contrast to the system under Yeltsin, which Zudin characterises as 'polycentric', with numerous independent centres of power and influence, notably the governors and the oligarchs as well as the mass media. Through various strategies of co-optation and penalties, the system by 2004 had been refashioned.[40] Thereafter, a Soviet-style 'circular flow of power' was restored, in which regional and other elites owe their positions to Putin, who in turn relies on them for support. Although the administrative regime undoubtedly aims to be monocentric, there are powerful horizontal forces which the Putin system has to take into account. The so-called Putinite 'vertical of power' is greatly tempered by the power of horizontal forces at all levels.

Such a system has little to do with democracy, but at the same time there remains tension between authoritarian practices and democratic legitimation. The problem existed in a different way in the Soviet years but could be resolved by various ideological contortions, above all, derived from the foundational Stalinist idea of 'socialism in one country'. In post-communist Russia, the legitimacy of the system is derived from the democratic principles embodied in the constitutional state, and the machinations of the regime are denied rather than justified. There is no sustained ideological justification for the monocentric practices of the administrative regime. There is therefore an absence rather than a presence in the ideational field, which is filled by the administrative rationality of the regime itself. This accentuates technocratic managerialism and reflects Putin's profound aversion to the restoration in Russia of anything resembling 'an official state ideology in any form'.[41] It also entails depoliticisation of the system of regime rule – since if it became the subject of politics, it would then be contested through the democratic process itself. There have been various attempts to fill the ensuing vacuum in ideological orientation. Vladislav Surkov, the head of the domestic politics department of the PA between 2000 and 2011, outlined the idea of 'sovereign democracy' as a way of providing 'basic ideological theses' for the country.[42] Characteristically, Putin was sceptical, while Medvedev was outright dismissive.

In his third term from 2012, however, Putin sought to shift the ideational basis of his rule from technocracy to culture and argued that 'conservatism' would be the ideology of the ruling party, UR. In his speeches of this period, he defended traditional values against the West's alleged betrayal of its own cultural foundations. Although Putin remains a pragmatist rather than an ideologue at heart, there are certain principles that remain consistent throughout his rule. This includes an outcome-oriented approach to politics, an unwillingness to risk the fate of the country to the vicissitudes of unconstrained electoral competition (a characteristic he shared with Yeltsin), a strong sense of destiny and duty (although he seldom speaks of these things), and a contempt for demagogic populism other than his own formulation of them. Putin's centrism is derived not only from the sociological and historical realities of the country but also from his own inherent caution and repudiation of ideological certainties. This explains why there is so little of Soviet or liberal certainty in Putin's thinking. Putin is sceptical that the market on its own can advance development, hence the emphasis on the state in modernisation, but his economic statism is embedded in classical, even rigid, macroeconomic orthodoxy.

This comes through in his assessment of democracy. Putin is never one to be constrained by institutions or the uncertainty generated by genuinely competitive elections. This does not mean that Putin rejects democracy, but he has a distinctive understanding of how it should work. First, his consistent belief is that coherent public policy (as interpreted by him and his team) is a value higher than the pure chance embedded in the unfettered electoral process. Just as in the economy he favours the market but seeks to limit market forces, so in the political realm he practices a form of *dirigiste* democracy: elections are fine as long as they do not give power to a demagogue, a Russian ethnonationalist, a neo-communist or even a radical liberal who would destabilise society by imposing structural reforms and undermine long-term development plans. This model is certainly elitist, in the belief that the ruling group better understands the needs of society than a randomly selected politician, who has to promise the earth before the election and whose horizons by definition stretch no further than the next election. However, and this is the second strand, this elitism is grounded in a populist understanding of democracy – the belief that the 'will of the majority' can be understood and articulated in an unmediated way. In his address to the Federal Assembly in December 2013, Putin argued,

> Today, many nations are revising their moral values and ethical norms, eroding ethnic traditions and differences between peoples and cultures. Society is now required not only to recognise everyone's right to the freedom of consciousness, political views and privacy, but also to accept without question the equality of good and evil, strange as it seems, concepts that are opposite in meaning. This destruction of traditional values from above not only leads to negative consequences for society, but is also essentially anti-democratic, since it is carried out on the basis of abstract, speculative ideas, contrary to the will of the majority, which does not accept the changes occurring or the proposed revision of values.[43]

In other words, the regime can speak on behalf of the true interests of the people. Just as Russia posited itself at this time (as it had done in the late nineteenth century) as the 'true Europe', as opposed to the actual Europe which seemed to be denying its own values, so Putin here suggests that there is a true democracy that stands outside mere electoralism, and he is its truest representative.

2 STATE, SOCIETY AND REGIME

Russia continues to suffer from the 'long hangover' of the dissolution of the Soviet system and the disintegration of the Soviet Union.[1] The Soviet Union reformed itself out of existence, and Putin vowed that this would not happen to Russia. A party state ruled the USSR, although the balance of power between the party and the state varied. During Stalin's long pre-eminence, the All-Union Communist Party (Bolsheviks) (VKP(b)) became the instrument through which Stalin ruled and was itself purged repeatedly. In 1952, the name was changed to the Communist Party of the Soviet Union (CPSU), and Article 6 of the 1977 Soviet constitution finally recognised that the party exerted a 'leading and guiding role' in the state and society. Up to then, the party had retained an ambiguous constitutional position – all-pervasive but not formally recognised. In post-communist Russia, the functional analogue of the party is the administrative regime, giving rise to a regime-state. Although the regime lacks the CPSU's formal institutional framework, with party cells in every Soviet factory and institutions all the way up to the Central Committee and the Politburo, in structural terms it is comparable. A power system stands outside of constitutional institutions and processes, governed by its own rules and understandings (*ponyatiya*, a code of mutual comprehension) which together comprise an 'informal constitution'. The administrative regime exercises a pervasive influence over political processes and society. Parties are shaped, elections are managed and the normative framework of political life is constantly modified in response to evolving challenges but governed by one constant principle – to ensure the autonomy of the regime, to ensure that it is not swallowed by society on the one side or forced to abide by constitutional rules on the other. The system is not foolproof, and each electoral cycle is something of a trial for the managerial capacities of the regime. As little as possible is left to chance, but because of the dualism inherent in the system – the tension between constitutionally mandated competitiveness and regime-driven managerialism – there are always opportunities for acts of resistance and unexpected events. This is a dynamic model of Russian politics, which recognises that the legitimacy of the administrative regime is dependent on its formal compliance with the norms of the constitutional state. There is permanent, although seldom creative, tension between authoritarianism and constitutionalism.

The birth of the regime-state

This system is far more complex and sophisticated than a simple one-man personal dictatorship. The president in post-communist Russia is less constrained by checks and balances than post-Stalin Soviet leaders, yet even the 'super-presidential' powers enjoyed by the office are limited by horizontal restraints. The system is not a simple top-down power *vertikal*, to use the common Russian term, but is constrained by powerful 'horizontal' forces, various interest groups representing deeply entrenched factional communities. Putin is by far the most authoritative and pre-eminent element in the regime-state, but he also has to ensure that the various horizontal pressures remain balanced and that constitutional norms retain vitality. If he infringed the unwritten rules, then the system would be destabilised and his power would be jeopardised. He could of course repudiate the constraints and openly rule as a dictator, in which case any pretence of balance between democratic principles and authoritarian practices would be jettisoned. The other alternative would be to subordinate the leadership, and the regime as a whole, to the unconstrained operation of constitutional norms. The road to a functioning democracy would be open, and the regime-state would wither away. For this to happen, the conditions that gave rise to the predominance of the administrative regime and its associated managerial rationality would have to be overcome.

The regime-state was not Putin's invention but was formed in the 1990s. It emerged as a distinct type of governance in the Yeltsin period but achieved a peak of functional efficiency under Putin. Putin did not create what Russians call the *sistema*, the interlocking network of rules, practices and institutions that make up the Russian polity. In fact, as Grigory Yavlinsky (one of the major political leaders in the 1990s and still at the head of the Yabloko party) argues, Putin is a product of the system that he inherited, created in part with Western help when in 1996 they ensured Yeltsin's re-election and with it the Kremlin-oligarch alliance, which in the end delivered Putin.[2] There could be no 'democratic backsliding' under Putin since the system in the 1990s was far from democratic. He calls the system 'peripheral authoritarianism': it is peripheral because it lacks innovative industries than can generate domestic growth and instead relies on raw material exports; and it is authoritarian because of the control over institutions exercised by the ruling elite led by one man. As he puts it, 'the entire period since the collapse of the Soviet state has seen a continuous consolidation of the authoritarian power of the bureaucracy, operating under the distinctive conditions of Russia's peripheral capitalism'.[3] The system reproduced not only the flaws of the Soviet period but also those of imperial Russia, including over-centralisation, lack of balance between governance institutions, weakness of feedback loops from society and weak parliamentary oversight over executive authorities.[4] The key point is to prevent any 'significant concentration of political resources in the hands of any other group'.[5] To this end, media resources, non-governmental organizations (NGOs) and elections are managed. However, with the old growth model exhausted by 2012, Putin turned to a conservative ideology to shield Russia from the West, guaranteeing a breakdown in relations. Yavlinsky is right about the origins of the system and some of its features, but his model of peripheral authoritarianism fails to capture the dynamics of Russia's domestic politics or the logic of relations with the world outside. He is, nevertheless, right to stress that Russia's monopolistic state-centred economic system fosters the tightening of authoritarianism.

Post-communist Russia is distinctive in several respects. Most remarkable is the speed with which a power complex emerged, separate and distinct from the constitutional system. In part, this is because of the extended deadlock over adopting a new constitution.[6] The Russian Soviet Federative Socialist Republic (RSFSR) adopted its last constitution in 1978, a modified version of the 1977 Soviet constitution. Both underwent significant changes during perestroika. One of Gorbachev's major institutional innovations was the creation of what were intended to be more powerful legislatures, to counter the CPSU's power and to provide a new source of legitimacy for government. In Russia, the new CPD was elected in March 1990 in a remarkably free election. Although Communists still predominated and there was no competitive party system, dynamic associations and groups rooted in civil society participated in the campaign, the votes were counted fairly and in parliament the debates were open and covered comprehensively by the media. However, the new CPD was a travesty of effective parliamentarianism. It had over a thousand members and it was poorly structured into stable political groups. It was in effect a permanently sitting constituent assembly, able to change the constitution by a simple majority. To allow the system to work, a two-hundred-strong Supreme Soviet was carved out from the larger CPD. By any definition, this was a constitutional monstrosity and generated permanent instability. It was not able to assume the burden of governance after the banning of the Communist Party in Russia after the failed coup of August 1991.

When Russia officially became an independent country on 1 January 1992, instead of holding new elections, the Yeltsin administration focused on the economy. The country was in a desperate situation, with food supplies running low and economic linkages snapping.[7] The old command planning system disintegrated but regulated market mechanisms were absent. The vacuum allowed a predatory class of capitalist entrepreneurs to emerge, combining the illegal earnings of underground operators, the bank capital of the late perestroika years and administrative capital in the form of links to governmental agencies. A distinctive type of political capitalism was established, which flourished in the form of the 'oligarchs'. These were years of permanent crisis. On the one side, Yeltsin was elected president of Russia on 12 June 1991 with 57 per cent of the vote, trouncing his five opponents. This gave him a convincing source of popular legitimacy, which allowed him to face down the putschists in August 1991. On the other side, the Russian CPD had also gained democratic legitimacy through election. The fundamental question needed to be resolved: Would Russia be a presidential or a parliamentary republic, or some semi-presidential combination of the two? The only way the question could be resolved peacefully was through the adoption of a new constitution, but that would mean the premature termination of the authority of the CPD, which its members were reluctant to do. The country entered a period of extended constitutional crisis (defined as a contest over the principles of governance), accompanied by a deep political crisis – a struggle for power between Yeltsin as the incumbent president and the speaker of the CPD, Ruslan Khasbulatov, later joined by the vice president, Alexander Rutskoi. These two crises were exacerbated by intense ideological conflict between the so-called democrats (as they were termed at the time) and neo-traditionalists of various stripes, ranging from Russian nationalists to neo-Stalinists, as well as Eurasianists, who were sceptical about the whole idea of Western-style democracy. Lurking in the wings were the security agencies, devastated by the collapse of the Soviet order and ready to recreate Russia in their image.

On 25 April 1993, Yeltsin held a referendum in an attempt to break the deadlock, followed by the convocation of a Constitutional Assembly, but the impasse remained. The crisis was resolved by Yeltsin's 'constitutional coup'. On 21 September 1993, he issued decree No. 1400 dissolving the CPD and announcing elections to a new assembly. The CPD dug in, appointing Rutskoi president and on 3 October launched a violent assault against the Moscow mayor's office and the Ostankino TV building. Yeltsin finally persuaded military leaders to act, and early on 4 October, tanks fired on the White House, the seat of the CPD, and by the end of the day, the rebel parliamentary forces surrendered. Yeltsin then rammed home his victory by amending the draft constitution to increase the powers of the presidency. The Russian constitution was adopted in a referendum on 12 December 1993, in a vote that was tainted by fraud in an attempt to ensure the required minimum turnout of 50 per cent and the 50 per cent vote in support. The new constitution was approved by 58.4 per cent on a turnout of 54.8 per cent of the registered electorate but only 30.7 per cent of the total electorate. On the same day, elections were held to a new slimmed-down State Duma of 450 members, a parliament that could only exist if the constitution was adopted. Half of the new assembly was elected through proportional representation on party lists (PLs), and half in single-member constituency seats. Russia's Choice, the party of the 'democrats', won only 15.5 per cent of the PL vote (although with the addition of the thirty single-member seats it became the largest party in the Duma with seventy seats), while Vladimir Zhirinovsky's Liberal Democratic Party of Russia (LDPR), a populist-nationalist party, came out on top with 22.9 per cent (but with only five single-member seats), with the revived CPRF coming third with 12.4 per cent. Against the background of mass poverty and devastating social dislocation, the weakness of the organised democratic forces was exposed.

The December 1993 constitution is a liberal and democratic document. Its first two chapters, drafted before the events of autumn 1993, enshrine an extensive range of liberal and human rights, as well as social benefits, but the later chapter on the executive is unbalanced and grants excessive powers to the presidency. However, the main problem is not with the black letter of the basic law but the absence of the spirit of constitutionalism, where the law is obeyed and conflicts adjudicated by an independent Constitutional Court. Compliance problems are compounded by the vagueness of many of the constitution's provisions. Although powerful in its declaration of liberal principles and human rights, the mechanisms for their implementation, above all in matters of accountability, are not specified. This vagueness in constitutional provisions has allowed the mechanisms to select membership of the upper house, the Federation Council (FC), to be changed several times, for the voting system to become the subject of endless major revisions, for the manner of choosing regional governors to move from direct election to appointment and back, and for independent local government to be radically weakened by the 2014 municipal reform. The list could be extended but this instability in part is derived from the hurried and ultimately un-negotiated way the constitution emerged out of the political crisis in late 1993. The constitution was written for Yeltsin's convenience, allowing the presidency to overshadow parliament and to rule without effective accountability mechanisms.

By the time of the second State Duma elections on 17 December 1995, the CPRF had consolidated its position as the main opposition party, and it came out on top of the party list vote with 22.3 per cent. The LDPR came second with 11.2 per cent, while the new centrist official party, NDR, trailed in third place with 10.1 per cent (but won ten single-member seats to become the second-largest group, after the communists, in parliament), while the social liberal party Yabloko came fourth with 6.9 per cent. It was clear that what was termed Russia's 'democratic revolution' lacked substantive public backing. This further widened the growing gap between the power system centred on the Kremlin (the administrative regime) and the constitutional provisions for free and fair elections. This was evident, as noted, in Yeltsin's bid for a second term in 1996. In ailing health, his standing in opinion polls at the beginning of the year was in the low single digits, yet through massive spending, a virulent press campaign against Zyuganov and the application of 'political technologies' (including the hiring of American political consultants), and what would later be described as 'administrative resources', Yeltsin made it through to the second round. In the first ballot on 16 June, he won 35 per cent of the vote to Zyuganov's 32 per cent, and after promising third-placed Alexander Lebed a post in the administration, Yeltsin went on to win the run-off vote on 3 July with 53.8 per cent to Zyuganov's 40.3 per cent. Between the two rounds Yeltsin suffered a heart attack, although this was hidden from the public, and for the next several months he largely disappeared from view as he underwent a multiple heart-bypass operation.

It was not only Yeltsin's health that was failing. The 1996 election is often considered the moment when Russian democracy died. The massive abuse of the privileges of incumbency, accompanied by the fear that a Zyuganov victory would halt Russia's move towards the market and liberal democracy, meant that the self-defined democratic forces intervened to ensure an outcome that would allow the continuation of reforms. The dilemma was a real one, described as the 'democracy paradox' above, and the issue still divides Russian opinion to this day. Was it right for administrative resources to be used to save market democracy, even if their use undermined the principles of liberal democracy? Did the alleged rightness of the cause justify underhand means to defend that cause? At the same time, just as the Bolsheviks made a socialist revolution in a country lacking a developed working class, the democrats in power argued that the social base for democracy in Russia was lacking. For this reason, reformers sought to privatise as quickly as possible, believing that the disbursement of formerly socialist property to a new class of capitalists would create the social basis for the new order. As in 1917, the political revolution preceded the social conditions required to ensure its fulfilment. Anatoly Chubais devised a system of coupon privatisation intended to give the whole population a stake in the new economy, but these 'talons' were bought up by those with capital, and very few citizens were ever paid dividends on their share of privatised property. Equally, on the eve of the presidential election, the cash-strapped government agreed to the 'loans-for-shares' scheme, whereby the government received loans from some leading oligarchs in exchange for shares in major companies. Everyone understood that the government would not be in a position to repay the loans, and thus some major enterprises were gained on the cheap. This also applies to the fire sale of state property, which allowed leading oligarchs to amass major industrial empires in auctions which they typically organised to exclude competitors. This is how the major Yukos oil company fell into the hands of Mikhail Khodorkovsky.

This was political capitalism of the classic sort. In both the political and economic spheres, there was no spontaneous evolution of the social forces and institutions underpinning democracy, or of market players constrained by law and generating resources through entrepreneurship. Instead, the power system intervened to manage not just administration but also political competition itself, while in the economic sphere the business tycoons were in effect state-appointed oligarchs. The constitutional crisis of 1991–3, the electoral setbacks to the ruling group, the strongly presidential constitution, the challenge from the revived CPRF and the nationalist-populist LDPR, the weakness of the social base for democracy, the intense ideological divisions and the fear of some sort of Soviet restoration through the ballot box, all encouraged the formation of a 'regime' separate from constitutional constraints. This reinforced the social division identified by the sociologist Simon Kordonsky, in which millions of people live outside the realm of law and government institutions:

> We have two normative systems: the official one, which is built around the written law, and the second one, which is informed by the quasi-law [mutual understandings] called *ponyatiya*. The two systems operate within the same space, within the same people. People are split within themselves: they live according to the *ponyatiya*, but interpret other people's behaviour according to the law.[8]

This applies as much to the regime as to society.

The meta-factions of Russian society

A powerful presidency is the heart of a regime system of rule that eclipses the constitutionalism in which it is embedded. This reflects an enduring culture of power that has been superimposed over the new democratic institutions and normative order.[9] Post-communist practices reproduced elements of communist and pre-communist political cultures. For those who believe in path dependency, deep patterns were reasserted. Many countries are described as having 'hybrid' political systems, combining elements of democratic principle with authoritarian practices, and Russia is certainly one of them. Even the most consolidated of liberal democracies contain hybridity, otherwise they would be impossible to govern, and across the world there has been a creeping increase in unaccountable executive power accompanied by societal illiberalism. In such a system, 'the main benefit of controlling a modern bureaucratic state is not the power to persecute the innocent. It is the power to protect the guilty.'[10] Administration of public affairs invariably requires a combination of authoritative leadership and accountability. Although such a spectrum exists, there is a qualitative difference between a consolidated liberal democracy, where the courts are substantively independent, where property rights are defensible and where elections are genuinely competitive, fairly contested and accurately counted, and systems where these qualities are in one way or another diminished. On this spectrum, Russia lies towards the latter end.

The question is why. The answer lies not in Putin's imputed malevolence and hunger for power but in the character of the dual power system that he inherited and then honed, as well as in the political and sociological character of the elite structure and political economy. About two hundred thousand people make up the political elite, including local and regional politicians and up to the great mass of elected and appointed officials in Moscow, as well as the leading figures in the plethora of think tanks and analytical centres.[11] Running in parallel are the various relevant institutions of the Russian Academy of Sciences and universities. Media institutions, print and electronic, as well as social media sites play an influential part in shaping popular attitudes. Above all, the military and security apparatus, as well as the judicial organs, act as major constituencies in structuring elite politics. Britain is considered to have a self-reproducing elite structure that is far from hermetically sealed yet which replicates certain structures of thought and political preferences.[12] The existence of an 'establishment' is contested, yet the idea can be also applied to Russia.

A relatively small group shapes the country's destiny. Some are holdovers from the Soviet period, notably in the military and security apparatus and academic establishments, whose political views were shaped by the 'long 1970s', the years between the destruction of the 'Prague Spring' in 1968 and the appointment of Gorbachev in 1985. Putin is very much of this generation, no longer imbued with the idealism of the 1960s and the belief in 'socialism with a human face' but not yet enthused and then disillusioned by Gorbachev's perestroika. A new elite generation is emerging, but it was only as he entered into his fourth term that Putin started appointing them in significant numbers as he tried to avoid the sclerosis that characterised the stagnation of the late Brezhnev years. However, one of the most consistent sociological findings is that in substantive political orientations there is not much difference in world views between elite generations in Russia, with the new cohort having been thoroughly socialised into traditional views on domestic order and Russia's great power role in the world. There had been an expectation that as the Soviet generation passed away, a more pro-Western group would take their place. In fact, the older generation had been inclined to take a more positive view of the West, but the younger generation has lost that starry-eyed idealisation.

Russian political thinking is typically divided into three great trends: the Westernisers, Slavophiles and Eurasianists. While catching something of the main trends, such a categorisation does not capture the complexity of contemporary Russia. Instead, we can represent the Russian 'establishment' as structured into four great factions, each of which cuts across the generations. A faction is here defined as a sociological-ideational formation that does not take the form of a political party and is broader than any ethnically or family-based clan but represents an enduring national political viewpoint or constituency.[13] They can be defined as epistemic-interest groups, combining ideational preferences with socio-professional affiliations. The factional model provides the key to understanding the character of Putin's leadership. The supreme form of Putin's managerial role is as faction manager, ensuring that incompatible groups and ideas are kept in permanent balance. The regime draws on these forces but is not dominated by them. Putin's statecraft is based on his ability to ensure that all main factions have enough of a stake in the system so as not to defect, but not enough to allow any faction to dominate or to become so powerful as to threaten his political independence or the fundamental interests of other elite and establishment groups.

None are able to impose the entirety of their political agenda, but each contributes to policy formulation. In some areas, one faction shapes policy rather more, while in another, an opposing faction has a greater voice. Thus, the economic liberals shape macroeconomic policy, the neo-traditionalists the cultural sphere, the security agencies foreign policy (although not unchallenged) and the Eurasianists Eastern policy. This is a recipe for a politics of consensus and 'centrism', but since no policy is pursued with consistency and to the full extent of its logical development, this is also a recipe for policy confusion, stagnation and stasis. These ideological trends are more than permitted discourse within an overarching Putinite narrative of Russia's resurgence as a great power but reflect genuine differences rooted in the intellectual history of the nation and the sociological realities of the country. It is not a question of the regime allowing some tonal variation to a central narrative but the fragmented character of the mainstream itself. The Soviet era had extirpated a genuinely hegemonic class-based power system, and in its stead the post-communist 'establishment' is ideationally divided. There is only one point on which most are agreed, and that is the idea of an independent and strong Russia; but when it comes to a more fine-grained definition of what Russia should be, the consensus breaks down. In its absence, the regime seeks to co-opt as much as possible from contending narratives but does not allow any to predominate or to potentially frame a new hegemonic historic bloc.

The political-interest factional spectrum can be cut in many different ways. Marlene Laruelle identifies three 'ideological ecosystems': the military-industrial complex, encompassing all of the power agencies; the Orthodox realm, including the Russian Orthodox Church, some business-people closely aligned with it such as the former head of Russian Railways, Vladimir Yakunin, and the businessman Konstantin Malofeev, the head of the St Basil the Great Charitable Foundation, and various conservative politicians; and the PA, which under Surkov generated the idea of 'sovereign democracy' and throughout sought to shape the country's ideological terrain by advancing the idea of state-centred development and Russia as a multinational great power.[14] Instead, I identify four ideational-factional blocs, which represent the main sociological classes and groups as well as the main ideational matrices.[15] The four factions are far from internally coherent, let alone monolithic, and there is a great deal of overlap in personnel and ideas. Each of the factions is divided into endlessly quarrelling and contesting subgroups. Putin exploits this characteristic to ensure that none of the blocs consolidates to represent an alternative hegemonic and power constellation. As noted, one or another faction has more influence in certain policy areas, but each has a stake in the system. Their leaders are part of the Russian establishment, but the roots of the factions reach deep into society. They run in parallel and intersect with the classic sociological categories of class, profession, gender, region, ethnicity and religion, and they aggregate political preferences from across these divides. In conditions of post-communist societal fragmentation, it has been impossible to recreate a classic party system, at a time when even in some mature capitalist democracies party systems have been fragmenting, leading to a range of 'party substitutes' acting as the functional equivalents.[16] Political preferences are aggregated in a fluid manner, with 'networks' substituting for political parties.[17]

The liberals make up the first group, divided in turn between legal constitutionalists, economic liberals, liberal statists, social liberals and radicals.[18] The divisions are real, but mostly far from decisive, and in the main this faction can be likened to the 'national liberals' of the Bismarck-era Kaisserreich, supporting a strong Russia with a liberal economy. The legal liberals seek to complete Russia's long revolution of constitutionalism by ensuring the rule of law and the better functioning of the judicial system. They draw in particular on the tradition of statist liberalism advanced by Boris Chicherin to argue that a strong state is one that not only works through law but which is also constrained by a genuine spirit of constitutionalism.[19] In other words, the legal liberals seek to close the gap between the two wings of the dual state by bringing regime practices into closer conformity with constitutional principles. This was the aspiration of the Medvedev presidency between 2008 and 2012, and was given expression in the various publications of the think tank charged with devising a programme to fulfil this goal, the Institute of Contemporary Development (*Institut sovremmennogo razvitiya*, INSOR). It published a series of studies that pushed the Medvedevite reforms to their limits. Its first major report in 2008, *Democracy: Development of the Russian Model*, examined Russian political institutions and conditions for the development of a free society.[20] Its major report, *21st Century Russia: The Shape of a Desirable Future*, called for Russian politics to be thoroughly democratised, the drive for market relations to be completed and for Russia to work towards eventual NATO membership and partnership relations with the West.[21] Its last major publication in 2011 set the agenda for a putative second Medvedev term, warning in desperate tones that the choice facing Russia was not between detailed policies but rather 'between the country's future and the absence of such a future'.[22]

Economic liberals dominated macroeconomic policy throughout the Putin era. Alexei Kudrin served as finance minister from 2000 to 2011 and in those years stabilised the rouble and finances. He introduced the countercyclical strategy of investing oil rents in a Stabilisation Fund in the good years to finance deficits in harder times. The national wealth fund saved the country from excess borrowing in the financial crisis of 2008–9 and again in 2014–16. Kudrin is a classic national liberal, supporting the attack against Khodorkovsky and Yukos in 2004 for financial reasons, yet in 2011 he came out strongly for more democratic and competitive elections. He opposed the diversion of scarce resources to military needs, and it was over this issue that he was publicly sacked by Medvedev on 25 September

2011. Kudrin spoke at the protest rallies at the end of the year and later established the Centre for Strategic Research (CSR), an analytical group drafting economic reform ideas. The economic liberals were dominant in Medvedev's cabinet when he took over as prime minister in 2012 and again when he formed a new government in 2018, much to the chagrin of the other factions. The economic liberals pursue an orthodox macroeconomic policy seeking to achieve balanced budgets and low inflation through tight credit and a reduced national debt, accompanied by a diversification strategy to reduce dependency on energy rents.

Russian liberals across the spectrum tend to assume a statist inflexion. This, for example, was the case with Khodorkovsky, who always acknowledged the need for a strong but constitutionally constrained state.[23] On his release from jail in 2013, Khodorkovsky settled in London and sponsored the Open Russia Foundation, which works for the creation of a law-based constitutional state with competitive and free elections. Khodorkovsky feared that the emergence of another insurgent politician on the model of Yeltsin's populism during perestroika, which condemned the alleged slowness of Gorbachev's reforms, would simply reproduce authoritarianism in new forms. Hence, Khodorkovsky called for a constitutional reform that would abolish the strong executive presidency and create a parliamentary republic.[24] Medvedev is also a liberal statist, as demonstrated in his period as president between 2008 and 2012. Although later his status and authority was reduced, he continued to exercise a moderating influence on policy. Apparently the price for his agreement to the 'castling' manoeuvre in 2011 was that he would remain prime minister until the end of Putin's third term; but in recognition of his loyalty and hard work he was reappointed in 2018. Overall, there is a broad category of 'regime liberals', willing to work within the system for their own benefit and out of concern for the fate of the country. These 'systemic liberals' are the subject of particular critique by radical liberals, many of whom launched their broadsides from abroad.[25]

The social liberals are represented by the Yabloko party headed since its foundation in late 1993 by Yavlinsky. Social liberals condemn the excesses of the privatisation of the 1990s, which allowed productive capital to be concentrated in the hands of what are conventionally called the 'oligarchs', and later fought for redistributive policies. Their goal, in short, was some sort of social capitalism.[26] Many of these positions were adopted, in a rather more dynamic and populist format, by Alexei Navalny, the firebrand anti-corruption campaigner at the head of the Foundation for the Struggle against Corruption (FBK). Navalny had, in fact, been a member of Yabloko before he was expelled in 2007 for 'causing political damage to the party; in particular, for nationalist activities'. Having once described himself as a 'nationalist democrat', in recent years he has stressed the latter while downplaying his ethnic Russian nationalism. His social and political programme remains close to that of Yabloko, although on the Crimean question he is more 'patriotic'.

The only major exception to the statist or social orientation are the radical liberals, who tend to adopt Hayekian positions (neo-liberalism) regarding the dangers of excessive statism in economics and politics, and are more ready to leave matters to unrestrained market forces. Coming out of the excessively statist Soviet system, the attractions of minimal statism are understandable, but in the 1990s, the country veered from one extreme to another. Putin's centrism is an unstable combination of these positions, with the strong reassertion of state power, creating a type of state capitalism in industry and manufacturing, accompanied by elements of neo-liberal marketisation in areas such as healthcare and education. Radical liberals tend to assume that there is a single appropriate response to complex policy questions, which can move into a monism that repudiates the pluralism that has traditionally been the core of liberalism. It is also often coloured by arrogant elitism. For example, the journalist Dmitry Travin notes that with the stifling of the opposition, 'ordinary Russians have no one to tell them how miserable their lives are becoming'.[27] In foreign policy, the radical liberals tend to follow the Atlanticist line and uncritically accept the rationality of Western positions. An extreme example is the former chess champion Garry Kasparov, who called on the West to declare 'war' against Putin's regime. He argued that 'the mantra of engagement' is no more than a synonym for appeasement and that 'dictators only stop when they are stopped'.[28] In his view, 'Russia's descent back into totalitarianism can be traced to the West doing too much to respect the legacy of the USSR as a great power, not too little'.[29] In other words, the West was too soft on Russia after the fall of communism and should have humiliated and marginalised the country even more. It is not clear how this policy could serve Russian national interests, but not surprisingly, it was taken up enthusiastically in Washington. Equally unsurprising, such a radically negative stance (unfairly) discredited liberals as a whole in Russia.

The second group is the *okhraniteli-silovik* bloc. It is hard to translate the term *okhranitel'*, but the word defines a political trend since the late nineteenth century to assume some sort of 'guardianship' role over the Russian state. The *siloviki* represent the security apparatus and their associates, focused in particular on the main bodies such as the FSB as well as the Russian Investigative Committee (RIC), hived off in 2011 from the Prosecutor General's Office (PGO). Together, they comprise the security bloc (in the broadest terms), who consider themselves part of Russia's long 'guardianship' tradition (*okhraniteli*) but who as a self-identified caste exploit their position for economic advantage. The first incarnation of the *siloviki* took the form of the Alexander Korzhakov, Mikhail Barsukov and Oleg Soskovets group, who launched the first Chechen war in December 1994 and then called for the 1996 presidential election to be cancelled. In between the two rounds of the 1996 presidential election, the liberal-oligarch group led by Chubais seized the initiative and dismissed their rivals, and opened up the golden, although short-lived, age of oligarch power. The late 1990s saw elements of 'state capture' by the oligarchs, accompanied by the consolidation of what was called 'the family'.

This group at various times included Yeltsin's daughter Tatyana, her husband Valentin Yumashev (who later went on to head the PA), Oleg Deripaska (who was married to Yumashev's daughter from his first marriage), the chief of staff Alexander Voloshin, the head of security Alexander Korzhakov, and the oligarchs Boris Berezovsky (who later discovered a passion for democracy) and Roman Abramovich. The family stepped in to fill the vacuum as Yeltsin's physical capacities waned. Chubais took over as head of the PA and together with Kudrin sponsored Putin's move to Moscow in 1996 and helped smooth the ascent of the 'enlightened securocrats' later in the decade. This era lasted until Putin consolidated his power in the early 2000s.

Under Putin, the *siloviki* flaunted themselves as the guardians of Russian state interests, and their influence seeped out of narrowly defined security matters into business relations and the information sphere, as well as into foreign policy.[30] Viktor Cherkesov, the veteran security official at the head of the Federal Anti-Narcotics Service, in 2004 published the manifesto of contemporary 'Chekism' (from *Cheka*, the original name for what later became the KGB and FSB). He asserted that their duty was to prevent the disintegration of the country, hailing their role in defending the country from internal and external 'enemies', and in a postscript argued that 'there is no such thing as a former Chekist'. He asserted that it was not their fault that 'history ordered that the burden of maintaining order fell mainly on our shoulders'. He described the Chekists as the 'hook' that had stopped Russia's fall.[31] Russia spends some $60 billion a year, about 3 per cent of the gross domestic product (GDP), on the security services, and roughly the same amount in addition on regular military forces. The overblown security apparatus generates interests of its own, with department piled upon section, each of which fights for its own perpetuation, slice of the budgetary pie, access to the rent management system, ability to intercept cash flows and its perceived right to advance its vision of the world.

The regular military has long resisted becoming politicised, especially after the bitter experience of being drawn into political battles in 1991 (the attempted coup against Gorbachev) and 1993 (Yeltsin's shelling of the parliamentary insurgency in the Russian White House). Today, the armed forces have regained respect and professionalism, and following the major reforms launched in late 2008 have been re-equipped and reorganised. This counts as one of Putin's major achievements. However, typical of his rule, the regular armed forces are complemented by other military structures. The Ministry of Internal Affairs (MVD) and other security agencies have armies of their own who act as the praetorian guard of the regime. The creation of the National Guard (NG, *Rosgvardiya*) in April 2016 represented a further step in the creation of armed forces under the direct control of the president. The NG combined several paramilitary units to create a massive new force numbering some 350,000, with the bulk of the MVD's armed forces (including the special-purpose riot police, OMON) transferred to the new body. It was formed to deal with possible internal dissent and public unrest, but it was also an attempt to bring the irregular forces in Chechnya under national command. This is another act of balancing under Putin intended, according to one analyst, '[not only to] be a force to keep the masses in check, but also the elite'.[32] Putin appointed his trusted chief of security (2000–13) Viktor Zolotov, who since May 2014 had commanded the MVD's internal troops, to head the NG. Zolotov was at the centre of factional intrigue in the Putin years, consolidating the power of his group and the institutions with which he has been associated within the *siloviki*. His appointment signalled that his power and that of his group was on the rise.

Nikolai Patrushev is one of the leading figures of this sub-faction. He took over as FSB director from Putin in 1999 and served until 2008, after which he became head of the Security Council. He is one of the inner group of Putin confidants who authorised the action in Crimea in early 2014 and remains one of Putin's key associates. His views are representative of the *siloviki* as a whole, believing that Russia is locked in an existential struggle for survival, with the West intent on reducing Russia's status and power in the world. In his view,

> The Ukraine crisis was an entirely predictable outcome of the systematic activity by the United States and its closest allies. For the past quarter century this activity has been directed towards completely separating Ukraine and the other former Soviet republics from Russia and totally reformatting the post-Soviet space to suit American interests. The conditions and pretexts were created for colour revolutions, supported by generous state funding.[33]

The *siloviki* are obsessed about the need to avert a 'colour revolution' in Russia. The term comes from the sequence of popular uprisings in the former communist world against corrupt and repressive regimes, notably the November 2003 Rose Revolution in Georgia, the Orange Revolution in Ukraine in the autumn of 2004 and the Tulip Revolution in Kyrgyzstan in the spring of 2005. Rather than seeing them as genuine movements for civic dignity and governance renewal, they are perceived as US-supported attempts to overthrow regimes not to Washington's liking. This is how Putin interpreted the December 2011 'white ribbon' protests against electoral fraud. He accused Secretary of State Hillary Clinton of setting 'the tone for some actors in our country and gave them a signal. They heard the signal and with the support of the US State Department set to work.'[34] In Patrushev's view, the 'coup d'etat' in Kiev in February 2014 followed the classical pattern of US interventions in Latin America.[35] Patrushev went so far as to claim that the United States sought to dismember Russia 'to open up access to rich resources that they think Russia unfairly controls'. He warned against the increasingly aggressive behaviour of NATO and claimed that the EU's foreign policy was dictated from Washington. Russia's alarm about NATO's push into the Balkans (Montenegro joined NATO in 2017) is revealed by Patrushev's informal assignment to deal with the region, amid which he warned that NATO was looking to persuade Bosnia as well as what is now called the Republic of North Macedonia to join the bloc.[36]

Alexander Bortnikov took over from Patrushev as head of the FSB. In an interview in December 2017, he reported that since 2012, the FSB had convicted 137 foreign intelligence agents, and the work of 120 foreign and international NGOs had been halted. He stressed that a central part of the agency's work was the struggle against terrorism. The joint work of the National Antiterrorist Committee and the Federal Operations Staff led to a ten-fold fall in the number of terror crimes after 2011, and in 2017 alone they prevented twenty-three acts of terrorism, and since 2012, 9,500 people had been convicted of crimes associated with terrorism and extremism. Some 4,500 Russians who had gone abroad to take part in insurgent activities had been identified. This work was accompanied by the struggle against economic crimes and corruption, and over the course of the previous five years, nearly thirteen thousand people had been convicted. Since 2012, some three hundred organised crime groups, some headed by high-ranking officials, had been broken up and over seven thousand drug traffickers convicted. The protection of cyberspace was now one of the FSB's main priorities. Since 2013, what the Russians call 'information security' had been managed by the FSB's State System for the Detection, Prevention and Elimination of the Consequences of Computer Attacks (GosSOPKA), which had proved its worth during the massive distributed (DDoS) attacks in 2016 and the large-scale virus infection in May 2017. Every year, there are tens of thousands of targeted attacks on official websites and the IT systems of state agencies, including the presidential website. Amid all this work, Bortnikov was proud of the traditions of the Russian secret services and insisted that although there was 'massive fabrication of accusations' under Stalin, there really were active conspiracies (led by Trotskyists) designed to overthrow the country's leadership.[37] The report identified the genuine threats facing the country, but it also revealed a security apparatus steeped in Soviet attitudes that were both cause and consequence of the new era of confrontation with the West.

This group dominates domestic security policy, although in keeping with the factional model, it does not entirely own it. Thus, plans to impose harsh controls on the internet have been blocked, although a range of restrictive measures – usually couched in terms of the struggle against terrorism and child abuse – have been adopted. In July 2017, a law banned the use of any technology or software that allowed access to websites that had been officially blocked on Russian territory, targeting in particular so-called web anonymisers and virtual private networks (VPN).[38] The goal was access to extremist or dangerous information, and although the law allowed operators to contest the ban in court and did not apply to corporate users if they needed VPN services for their work, the law was yet another brick in the information wall. In Putin's third term, the *siloviki* enjoyed increased influence over foreign policy but only because Putin allowed them to do so as his own views moved towards neo-revisionism. The assertive shift was accompanied by condemnation of the cultural degradation of the West, above all defined by its alleged repudiation of traditional values (the family and traditional gender patterns). In terms of policy and political development, the *siloviki* are a two-edged sword: they give muscle to Putin's vision of statehood, eradicating alternative sources of criminal power and combating external enemies; but at the same time are themselves a factor in the degradation of the constitutional order to something even worse than a regime system, namely a semi-criminalised kleptocracy. Although there is much talk of the militarisation of the Russian elite (or, more precisely, its 'securitisation'), the evidence is, at best, weak. Although those with a security background are prominent among the Russian leadership, the professional career patterns are diverse, and the 'militocracy' paradigm simply does not stand up to scrutiny.[39]

The cultural and political struggle against the West is the concern of the third faction, a diverse bloc of neo-traditionalist conservatives ranging from monarchists, neo-Stalinists to Russian nationalists. Monarchist groups look to the tsarist era for inspiration, others defend the perceived glory of the Stalinist years, while some are simply neo-imperialists, who believe that the whole Russian nation (and often quite a lot more) should be reunited under Moscow's stern but supranational rule.[40] In the immediate aftermath of the Soviet collapse, this group constituted itself as a major actor in Russian politics and were known as 'national patriots'. They combined a double rejection of Soviet 'totalitarianism' (although not all shared this view) and of Western-style liberal democracy. In his study of what he called the 'Russian new right', Thomas Parland stressed the deep historical roots and anti-Semitic character of much neo-traditional thinking.[41] In the confrontation with Yeltsin in 1993, the 'red-brown' alliance, bringing together neo-communists and nationalists, used the CPD as the base for their resistance to Yeltsin's 'shock therapy' and his plans for constitutional change. The CPRF was reconstituted in February 1993, and its surprisingly strong showing in the first elections to the State Duma in December 1993 (in which they won 11.6 per cent of the vote), together with the 21.4 per cent won by Zhirinovsky's populist-nationalist LDPR, indicated the deep social roots of neo-traditionalism. In the second parliamentary election in December 1995, the CPRF took first place with 22.3 per cent of the vote. By contrast, the liberal vote was never able to come close to a plurality, let alone a majority, winning some 22 per cent in 1993 and declined to half of that in 1995. The creation of United Russia (UR) in 2001 allowed this centrist formation to absorb and tame much of the soft neo-traditionalist vote, winning an astonishing 37.6 per cent in 2003, and since then it has been the hegemonic regime party, although the CPRF and LDPR continue to enjoy representation in parliament.

Beyond the party system, there is a roiling neo-traditionalist public sphere, with a strong media and public policy presence. Alexander Prokhanov initially edited a neo-traditionalist weekly paper called *Den'* (*The Day*), which was closed down after the October 1993 confrontation but was reborn as *Zavtra* (*Tomorrow*), warning of things to come. The paper continues to provide a platform for national patriotic sentiments. To challenge the liberal-statist Valdai Discussion Club, established in 2004, the neo-traditionalists in 2012 founded the Izborsky Club to preserve Russia's 'national and spiritual identity' and to provide an intellectual alternative to liberalism.[42] The club brought together a broad range of neo-traditionalist thinking, not only encompassing Prokhanov but also stretching as far as the Eurasianist Alexander Dugin as well as the economist Mikhail Delyagin and the scientist Sergei Kurginyan, and media commentators Mikhail Leontiev (strongly pro-Putin) and Maksim Shevchenko (advancing a critique of Putinism from the left) together with the neo-Stalinist publisher Nikolai Starikov and other critics of liberalism. They draw on the thinking of 'new right' thinkers such as Alain de Benoist to press home the attack. Their website carries the eponymous near-monthly 'thick' journal *Izborskii Klub*, as well as a rich range of interviews and discussions.[43] In January 2018, for example, Delyagin, the head of the Institute of Globalisation Problems, provided an interview under the title 'The Liberal Elite [meaning the group of socio-economic ministers in Medvedev's government] Is Destroying Russia for the Benefit of the West'.[44]

The fourth and final epistemic-interest faction is made up of Eurasianists. Its members are as divided as the others, but all believe that there is a fundamental incompatibility between Russia and the West.[45] This draws on the tradition inaugurated by Nikolai Danilevsky in his book *Russia and Europe* (1869), which argued that Romano-Germanic culture would inevitably be opposed to Russia's Slavic civilisation. Danilevsky outlined issues of universalism, particularism and geopolitical thinking that have an enduring relevance to this day.[46] Following the Bolshevik revolution, Eurasianism underwent significant intellectual development. Nikolai Trubetskoi had been a professor at Moscow State University and a strong critic of Eurocentrism, which he denounced in his book *Europe and Humanity* (1920). His condemnation of European universalism and defence of a 'multiplicity of civilisations' has strong resonance in Russia today. This diversity of cultures meant that attempts to 'catch up' with the West would entail borrowing elements that were incompatible with Russian culture. In their 1921 manifesto *Exodus to the East*, the Eurasianists argued that the centre of cultural gravity had moved to the East, and this would give Russia a special place in the new order, neither European nor Asian but Eurasian. The colonised people of the East, dubbed 'real humanity', would rise up against the European colonisers, supported by the Bolsheviks as the defenders of 'national liberation'.

Geopolitical thinking enjoyed a renaissance in Russia after 1991 to replace Marxist-Leninist universalism. Issues of Russia's civilisational identity, the relationship between competing world orders and the importance of space and territoriality came to the fore. This faction has extensive links with groups across Europe with similar sentiments, although couched in national idioms, but it is an exaggeration to suggest that the links between Russian Eurasianists and the European far right is reframing the entire relationship between Russia and Europe.[47] There have long been links between the Russian (and, before that, Soviet) authorities with West European right-wing movements, but these are typically instrumental rather than based on ideological contiguity.[48] They share a common concern for sovereignty and tend to oppose Atlantic integration, but Moscow's policy appears to be to ally with friends wherever they can be found, and this includes numerous leftist groups, notably Die Linke in Germany.

The Eurasianist tradition is capacious and not a little contradictory, with four main streams giving rather different answers to questions of identity and development.[49] The first is the classic Eurasianism of the 1920s, with roots stretching back into the nineteenth century to encompass Danilevsky as well as the conservative monarchist Konstantin Leontyev. This is the Eurasianism developed by Russian émigré writers in the 1920s and 1930s, stressing Russia's combined European and Asian identity that created a new social formation distinct from Europe. Lev Gumilev (1912-92) has become part of the classical tradition, even though he was writing in a later period and responding to different challenges.[50] Gumilev argued that the Mongol invasions, the mixture of peoples and the distinctive pattern of cultural development meant that 'ethnogenesis' had created a new people, in which Russia as a nation was effectively dissolved. In his view, Eurasia represented a distinct civilisation, sharply delineated from the West.[51] Russian nationalism from this perspective is a Western import, and a pan-Eurasian supranational civilisational identity is advanced instead.

The second group comprises the neo-Eurasianists, who emerged in the wake of the Soviet collapse and who were strongly represented in Russian public life in the 1990s.[52] The president of Kazakhstan, Nursultan Nazarbayev, spoke favourably of Gumilev's ideas about the geographical and cultural-historical ties that bring together the peoples in northern and central Eurasia. As for Putin, even though he mentioned Gumilev at the 26 August 2005 celebration of the city of Kazan's millenary anniversary, this does not make Putin a neo-Eurasianist. In numerous speeches and writings, Putin pronounced Russia a Eurasian power, but this usually meant that Russia should diversify its foreign policy orientations by turning towards Asia and the Pacific region. Putin's Eurasianism is of a severely pragmatic geographical sort, although this is necessarily tinged with geopolitics. He does not share the transnational inflexion and virulent anti-Westernism that is characteristic of classical Eurasianism. For Putin, Russia comprises many different and separate nations, which together represent the larger Russian nation as a cultural formation rather than an ethnic category. Thus, Putin eschews the civic term *Rossiiskii*, favoured by Yeltsin, and instead advances a denationalised formulation of the term *Russkii*. As for ethnic Russians, who now make up 80 per cent of the total population, Putin, like Yeltsin before him, is torn between 'nationalist' formulations that would make Russians the 'system-forming' nation and pluralist representations of Russia as a pluricultural community comprising 146 autochthonous peoples.

New Eurasianists make up the third group. They assume a strongly geopolitical reading of the concept that ties in with various anti-liberal movements across the continent. The leading exponent of this current is Alexander Dugin, who has recently become more of a Russian nationalist than a genuine partisan of pan-Eurasianism. His complex mix of metaphysics, geopolitical analysis and Fourth Political Theory should be distinguished from the bulk of contemporary neo-Eurasianism and thus deserves a category of its own.[53] Dugin's best-known work is *Foundations of Geopolitics* (*Osnovy geopolitika*), written in 1996–7 and thereafter published in numerous editions, in which he argues that geopolitics is the supreme methodology and that Russia is the natural hegemon in Eurasia. New Eurasianism repudiates the rather more pluralistic and Westphalian approach of most neo-Eurasants and instead advances nationalist themes. To counter Atlanticism, Dugin proposes making Eurasia an alternative *Grossraum* (greater space, using the term popularised by Carl Schmitt), which envisages some sort of 'strategic centre' accompanied by a number of 'autonomies'. Dugin's Fourth Political Theory connects him to some of the radical currents in twentieth-century European political philosophy. He draws on Martin Heidegger's argument that 'modernity is a kind of scientific objectification of the world which only accepts cultural or traditional knowledge as long as it remains secondary to any objective enquiry', a paradigm which in Heidegger's view is central to the three great insurgent creeds of modernity: communism, fascism and liberalism.[54] He rejected all three in favour of his Eurasianist philosophy, but they each contribute something, hence the Fourth Political Theory.

Dugin saw Putin's Russia as the natural leader of the recreated Eurasian *Grossraum*, challenging the hegemony of Atlanticism, although that does not make Putin a Duginite, let alone render Dugin 'Putin's brain'.[55] Putin did not move into Crimea in 2014 because of Eurasianist ideas but because of the structural failures of the European security system. He certainly sought to imbue the action with larger cultural significance, above all the sacralisation of the contested territory as part of the reunification of a divided people, the *Russkii Mir* (Russian World), but this sort of myth-making usually left Putin cold – it was used to justify an action that was prompted by structural factors and security concerns.[56] It can be questioned whether Dugin is a Eurasianist at all, since Eurasianism is a philosophy of isolationism, whereas Dugin's thinking, although radically anti-Western, is 'not an adaptation of classical Eurasianism to the post-Soviet period, but rather a peculiarly post-Soviet and essentially European "new right" ideology of its own'.[57] In other words, it is not neo-Eurasianism but a new Eurasianism.

The fourth model of Eurasianism is the one that was adopted by the Putinite elite, namely pragmatic Eurasian integration. This is often accompanied by the rhetoric of neo-Eurasianism and even absorbed some of the themes of the new Eurasianism, notably in the speeches and writings of Putin's advisor on international cooperation, Sergei Glazyev, but this only obscured the rational and pragmatic core of the project. At the heart of the current Eurasian integration drive is the belief that at some profound level, a number of post-Soviet countries form a natural economic, and potentially political, community separate and distinct from the EU and other comparable integration projects. At the same time, Eurasian integration was proposed not simply to counter the advance of the EU but was intended to act as a mode of advancing the greater Europe project that would ultimately encompass the EU while allowing the various parts of Europe to retain their identity. The claim that there is some sort of pre-political unity to much of the Eurasian land mass is an important one and is typically rooted in some combination of the first three variants of Eurasianism, with the crucial addition of a strictly economic rationale. This is why the very notion of 'Eurasia' is considered a backward-looking and repressive ideology in much of the post-Soviet world, and represents the dark opposite of the progressivism associated with 'Europe'. Classical Eurasianism had always advocated the need to create suprastate institutions, but this was combined with a *dirigiste* inflexion that strove to regulate all of social life. It is this mix of motives and intellectual tributaries that alarms those who argue that Eurasian integration is an anti-liberal geopolitical project that would restore Russian hegemony over the region. In practice, defenders of the project argue that the Eurasian Economic Union (EEU) is the functional equivalent of the EU, is not incompatible with liberal economies and responds to the needs and traditions of the region.

Putin himself is not recognisably Eurasianist in any of its ideological guises, even in its democratic neo-Eurasian form, but he is a pragmatist in international affairs and a (statist) liberal in economic matters. It is for this reason that new Eurasianists criticise him for his *Realpolitik* approach to international affairs, his excessive liberalism in economic matters and for his continued commitment to the liberal transformation of the Russian economy and society (to be achieved through the *dirigiste* monopoly over the polity). Putin's support for Eurasian integration is in part a response to the failure of pan-European unification (the greater European idea) and the stalemate in Russo-EU relations, although despite the setbacks, the regime does not repudiate its European and pan-continental aspirations. Putin's pragmatic Eurasianism stresses the economic functionality of integration, and while he refers to the common cultural legacy, only rarely does he mention civilisational factors. However, his 'cultural turn' after 2012 accentuated some Eurasianist themes, notably the need for spiritual renewal and the alleged exhaustion of the civilisational values on which the West had once been built. The ideology of Russia's 'special path' (*Sonderweg*) began to be smuggled back in, although now framed in terms of the West having repudiated its own values. From this perspective, the 'true West' has now moved to the East, and its values are being defended by Russia's conservative elite.[58]

In sum, Russian public life is divided into four major epistemic meta-factions, each of which has social and institutional roots. Putin's genius as leader is to draw strength from them all but to become dependent on none. This meta-factional model confirms the argument advanced by Elena Chebankova that Russia has 'paradigmatic pluralism'.[59] None of the groups or political tendencies can become hegemonic, rendering Russian politics fundamentally pluralist. To use Gramsci's term, there is no 'historic bloc', the basis of consent to a given social order. The absence of societal or policy consensus gives Putin scope for manoeuvre, while limiting his ability to shift the country decisively in one direction or another. The administrative regime compensates for the absence of a hegemonic social formation. It also limits the need for coercion since Putinite statecraft ensures that these elite groupings, each with deep societal roots, retain a stake in the system. Coercion in that context is selective and limited.

Each of the meta-factions is torn by internal factionalism, and micro-factionalism is characteristic of post-communist Russia. The *siloviki* bloc is particularly prone to such rivalry, since they are the ones closest to the struggles for ownership and access to resources. This means that far from being monolithic, the Putinite system is the composite of the four great meta-factions and the shifting tides of the battles between micro-factions. Mikhail Zygar's account of the Putin years does a good job in describing the various shifts, as allies and officials are brought in to the core and then shuffled out.[60] Zygar confirms the view outlined in this book that Putin is a broker, balancing the interests not only of rival 'clans', including business oligarchs, security officials, regional bosses and ministries, but also of the major ideational-sociological 'factions' structuring the country. The shifting fortunes of the meta-blocs determine the overall direction of policy. At the same time, there is a generational aspect to the factionalism. Zygar shows how three generations of Russian politicians interact and compete. The vestiges of the Soviet generation still cling on to power, in particular among the *siloviki* and neo-traditionalists, while the liberal camp is strongly represented by the Yeltsin generation, with Putin's own group of leaders, many of whom initially began their careers in Putin's native St Petersburg, spanning the generations. As Putin came to the end of his third term, there was an active attempt to rejuvenate the elite by creating a younger fourth generation of Putinite technocrats, and to this end there was a major reshuffle of regional leaders. In ideational terms, the Putin system is predicated on a cross-generational discourse and the assimilation of the various periods of Russian history into a single narrative of endurance, although not unified into a single model of power or development.

Serhii Plokhy is wrong to argue that Putin is attached to some sort of conservative nationalist utopia through the imperial reconstitution of the various East Slavic nations (Russia, Ukraine and Belarus).[61] Equally, it would be going too far to suggest the formation of some sort of 'collective Putin', since Putin's political personality is far from dissolved into any amorphous entity, although there is a shifting collective face to the regime. The former Kremlin spin doctor, Gleb Pavlovsky, argues that the hundred or so strong group around Putin use the term to describe the Kremlin's decisions, and Zygar's study confirmed the element of collective decision-making. The predominance of the 'family' in the late Yeltsin years gave way to a disparate group of St Petersburgers in the early Putin years. Some of the more hard-line figures from this group, in turn, gave way to liberal modernisers in the Medvedev years. With Putin's return to the presidency in 2012, the foreign policy hawks and statist developmentalists regained the upper hand. In all of this, Putin remained the central decision maker. Within the regime, he is referred to as 'the body', the informing spirit that animates the whole collective. The collective in turn seeks to anticipate the direction that Putin will take. This was vividly in evidence when the Kremlin was planning its response to the Magnitsky Act, a bipartisan bill passed by Congress in December 2012 that banned entry into the United States and the use of the US banking system by listed Russian officials held responsible for the death of the tax accountant working for Bill Browder's Hermitage Capital, Sergei Magnitsky, in November 2009. Vyacheslav Volodin, the deputy head of the PA responsible for domestic political affairs, prepared two versions of a bill regulating American adoptions of Russian children, one taking a hard line with a ban and one only imposing greater restrictions. Putin was taken ill, and with him out of circulation, the framers of the legislation prepared the two versions, with Putin finally deciding on the outright ban.[62]

The dual state and neo-patrimonialism

Duality is a feature of all political systems, but as a recent study of Silvio Berlusconi's Italy suggests, the question of degree is crucial: 'All Western governments, more or less, are marked by the gap between the poetry of constitutions and the prose of power as it is exercised. What is decisive, however, is precisely the degree of this "more or less." '[63] Italy from this perspective has endured a long-term creeping coup that subverts the independent functioning of institutions, and the response lay between the radicalisation of democracy and the imposition of technocratic rule. In Russia, Putin's administration claims to stand above the historic divisions of the modern era and seeks to reconcile the forces that tore Russia apart in the twentieth century. The democratic process is managed by a force standing outside democracy, co-opting elements of political society willing to compromise and marginalising the rest. This is a type of passive revolution, which for Antonio Gramsci entailed 'an abortive or incomplete transformation of society'. This can take a number of forms, including one where an external force provokes change, but this lacks a sufficiently strong domestic constituency and runs into the resistance of entrenched interests. When the forces are equally balanced, a stalemate emerges, giving rise to a situation of 'revolution/restoration'.[64] In contemporary Russia, there is a neo-Bonapartist situation where class forces are equally balanced, with the entrenched bureaucracy of the administrative regime resisting the rise of an independent bourgeoisie or middle class. This provides space for the regime to act as the supreme balancer, the essence of my factional model of Russian politics.

The 'dual state' model is at the heart of the analysis presented in this book.[65] In contemporary state theory, the constitutional state exists separate from the government and the ruler of the time, and endures beyond the lifespan of a particular administration. The constitutional state is rooted in defending law and statute to advance a certain idea of the general public good. It is regulated by impartial norms of law and managed by a disinterested bureaucracy. In Russia, this Weberian ideal has been subverted by the emergence of an administrative regime, which draws its legitimacy from claiming to apply the principles of the constitutional state and derives its authority from its representation of the common good but in practice exercises power in ways that subvert the impartial and universal application of constitutional rules. The polity and the state effectively became the property of the regime and increasingly of the leader himself – the classic definition of patrimonialism. In this context, the rhetoric of strengthening the state effectively means enhancing the prerogative powers of the regime. In other words, a new type of neo-patrimonialism was consolidated – a system in which the political authorities stand outside the constraints of the constitutional state, although drawing on its legal, coercive and disciplinary resources to maintain their rule.[66] Neo-patrimonialism combines patrimonial and legal-rational bureaucracy. Put differently, Walter Bagehot's theory of dual institutions can be applied with particular force here. Bagehot, the mid-nineteenth century commentator on the British constitution, distinguished between 'efficient' institutions, those which actually run a country, and 'dignified' institutions, which are largely decorative when it comes to making the hard choices.[67] This is the 'double government' of the dual state that is at the centre of my analysis of the Putin phenomenon.[68]

Already under Yeltsin there was a divergence between the culture of power of the administrative regime and the rules-based constitutional state. Instead of consolidating the rule of law, the authority of constitutional institutions such as parliament and the formal procedures of modern governance, 'regime' practices predominated, characterised by arbitrary interventions, the management of elections (notably Yeltsin's re-election campaign in 1996) and in his later years by the direct influence of economic magnates (known colloquially as oligarchs), who had made their billions through access to political influence. The presidency emerged to dominate all other institutions and gained unprecedented authority to intervene and manage political process. This is what Henry Hale calls 'patronal politics', a social equilibrium in which people pursue their collective and economic goals mainly through concrete, personalised rewards or punishments achieved through extended personal networks rather than impersonal institutions.[69] Hale provides the example of a local official seeking to entice a hospital to locate in their area and, thus, authorises 'facilitation' payments. This is corruption by any other name, but if the official takes the moral high ground, another district would get the hospital. This self-reinforcing system is what constitutes the equilibrium.[70] However, while this sort of behaviour is prevalent across Eurasia, it operates in Russia in distinctive ways because of the counterbalancing effect of the legal and behavioural norms embedded in the constitutional state. The corruption is systemic (in other words, it is 'meta-corruption') but at the same time (in this case at least) developmental.

The overall model is that of a reinvented 'enlightened despotism', with an administrative rationality endowing the moving force in the state (the presidency and its support mechanisms in the administrative regime) with the power to achieve 'reform' in the Yeltsin years; and to restore 'order' and 'stability' in the Putin period. The cultural practices of pragmatic goal-oriented rationalism run against the nascent culture of constitutionalism, with its rule-oriented legalism and accountability mechanisms. Another way of formulating the dual state paradigm is to apply Irvin Studin's distinction between two paradigms of governance. On the one hand, there is the democratic tradition, which represents what he calls 'argumentative governance', and on the other hand, there are various types of managed systems, which he calls 'algorithmic governance'.[71] The administrative regime became more sophisticated under Putin, and its 'despotic' features were tempered by the 'enlightened' incorporation of elements of the constitutional culture, although subordinated to the 'algorithmic' logic of regime survival. This can be couched in Weberian terms as the distinction between formal and substantive rationality. The primary concern of formal rationality is to achieve outcomes within the rules determined by the logic of profitability (of whatever sort), whereas in substantive rationality, the choice of means is guided by a set of human values, which in our case are the principles enunciated by the constitutional state.

Weber also wrote about the bureaucratic apparatus, and Putin is the perfect product of such a system. There is no need for charisma or exceptional talents, but mastery of departmental intrigue is essential. Personnel appointments are made to ensure factional balance, and policy is tailored to satisfy the needs of the administrative system. The institutional innovations of the Putin period reinforced the technocratic rationality of apparently enlightened governance, and that was why they encountered so little resistance from the existing elites. The creation of para-constitutional bodies, such as the seven (later eight) federal districts, the State Council and the Civic Chamber, did not repudiate the formal framework of the constitution but weakened public accountability mechanisms in favour of administrative rationality. The sphere of executive discretion exists in all political systems (discussed in Chapter 3), but in Putinite Russia, it became extraordinarily wide. This encouraged the practice of what is called 'legal populism', the pursuit of political goals through judicial means. The notable example of this was the prosecution of Khodorkovsky, who had turned the Yukos oil company into one of the most dynamic corporations in the country. Khodorkovsky nursed the ambition to transform the buccaneering capitalists of the 1990s into an independent bourgeoisie, who would defend the nascent capitalist order from becoming subject to what he considered were the whims, venality and corruption of the administrative regime, the so-called *sistema*. Following his arrest in October 2003, Yukos was effectively expropriated through the use of legal and exaggerated tax recovery measures, and Khodorkovsky spent ten years in jail.[72]

Two political systems operate in parallel. Because the administrative regime is embedded in the constitutional state, direct extrajudicial coercion is kept to a minimum. The law is used to advance regime policies, which in many cases while not formally in contravention of the constitution run counter to the spirit of genuine constitutionalism. The legal system is subordinated to political authority and in certain cases, such as in the Yukos prosecutions, undermines independent courts and the rule of law in general. The result is an erosion of trust in the institutions of the constitutional state. These include the conventions and instruments of public politics encompassing political parties, elections and parliamentary politics. Components of the constitutional state neither form nor control the administrative regime, which stands outside of and above public political institutions. This is a parapolitical sphere based on informal groups, factions and personal networks. This is the world based on the inner court of the presidency, over which Putin rules not as a dictator but as arbiter. This second level is more than simply 'virtual' politics, the manipulation of public opinion and the shaping of electoral outcomes through manipulative techniques and *dramaturgiya*.[73] The institutions of the constitutional state are real and work with regular precision, and thus the notion of 'virtual politics' is misleading. Instead, the parapolitical sphere acts as a substantive alternative arena of policy contestation where the interest groups and epistemic communities structuring Russian society and thinking feed into the policy process. The presidency acts as the essential link between the two levels, exercising a whole range of 'patronal' techniques to maintain both the public and factional sphere in balance.

The administrative regime takes the form of a dominant power system but is balanced by the constitutional state. The administrative regime is careful not to step outside the bounds of the formal letter of the constitution but constantly presses against its spirit. The para-constitutional institutions undermine the formal constitutional body designated to fulfil that role. Para-constitutionalism refers to the creation of institutions that are not specifically anti-constitutional but which are not mentioned in the constitution.[74] Thus, the Civic Chamber duplicates in certain respects the consultative work of the State Duma, while the State Council complements the work of the upper house, the FC. The seven (now eight) federal districts established in May 2000 were designed to monitor the work of regional authorities but undermine federalism, and the creation of the State Council later that year brings together regional leaders on a selective and partial basis. The Civic Chamber was formally established on 1 July 2005 as a type of 'collective ombudsman' with purely consultative powers.[75] Its duties include the review of draft legislation and the work of parliament, and the monitoring of federal and regional administrations. It offers non-binding recommendations to parliament and the government on domestic issues, comments on legislation, instigates investigations into possible breaches of the law and requests information from state agencies.[76] The first Chamber had 126 members: one-third was selected by the president, intended to be authoritative individuals who would be neither politicians nor business people; the second group was nominated by the first from national civic and voluntary associations; and once in office, these two groups in turn chose the remaining third, representing regional NGOs. The body's funding and offices are allocated by the PA. By the time the sixth convocation was selected in 2017, the body had grown in size. Forty members were chosen by the Kremlin, 84 were delegated by regional civic chambers and 43 were selected in a vote from 403 NGO nominations. The chair to 2020 was the journalist and public activist Valery Fadaev. At its first meeting, Putin insisted that the Civic Chamber 'should not replace the government or parliament' but should find a niche of its own including 'public oversight over executive and representative bodies of authority, expert analysis of immediate and more distant plans, assessing how these plans are implemented, and directly communicate with the people who are on the receiving end of the authority's efforts to improve life in our country'.[77] Hearings are live-streamed on the chamber's website, and witnesses have overwhelmingly been experts in their respective fields and are far from toadies. Some of the Duma's more outlandish legislative ideas, such as the plan to create a cyber militia to control illegal and extremist activity on the web, were subject to severe criticism, although a law blocking untrue or distorting information ('fake news') was adopted in March 2019.

Para-constitutionalism is accompanied by the development of a range of parapolitical bodies. Parapolitics is the process whereby entities are created in the public realm to stymie and shape the conduct of free and open pluralistic politics but which lack the autonomy to act as independent subjects of a competitive political sphere. Following the Orange Revolution in Ukraine in the autumn of 2004, the creation of the Nashi youth organisation was an exemplary case, designed to occupy the streets to prevent colour-style popular rallies against the regime.[78] Later, faced by sustained attack and irredeemably tarnished by the moniker 'party of thieves and swindlers', the regime looked to an alternative instrument to UR, its pedestal party, to mobilise the electorate and to associate its supporters. Instead of allowing UR to develop as an autonomous political force, facing up to its own weaknesses, lack of coherent programmatic development and overwhelmingly bureaucratic character, Putin in May 2011 created the Russian Popular Front (*Obshcherossiiskii narodnyi front*, ONF) as a popular vehicle for Putin's re-election bid. It was registered as a public movement in June 2013, and at its inaugural congress in that month, Putin was elected its head. Thereafter,

ONF acted as an auxiliary parapolitical organisation in the various campaigns launched by the regime. Putin's statecraft creates para-constitutional bodies subordinate to the regime to constrain and compensate for the shortcomings of official constitutional bodies, which his own policies had eviscerated. The ONF was designed to broaden the flagging appeal of UR by co-opting civic associations, and some 185 Front members were included on UR's 600-strong candidate list for the December 2011 Duma election to increase parliamentary turnover.[79] This was also the case in the September 2016 Duma elections, in which ONF members competed in primaries against more established UR nominees. Putin reviewed the various activities at the ONF Action Forum on 19 December 2016. There was the ONF Cleaning Project, dealing with the problem of illegal landfills, and the ONF Youth Project which participated in Russia's Future Image project in the run-up to the 2018 presidential election.[80] This is a classic instance of the bifurcation between official government bodies and the formalised voluntary work of para-constitutional bodies. Formal channels were both undermined and transcended by this parapolitical form of civic engagement.

At the same time, the regime assiduously manages the informational sphere, especially the electronic mass media, but in keeping with its dual character, the system did not restore anything like the Soviet system of censorship. The internet is increasingly monitored by the security services but by and large remains free. Equally, the regime monitors the pulse of public opinion and is careful to remain within the bounds of its preferences, although tempering some of its more extreme and vengeful moods. This has been called an 'informational autocracy', although the term 'autocracy' exaggerates the despotic elements in what is a sophisticated managerial model. This alleged autocracy uses traditional methods of informational manipulation (propaganda) as well as the new social media in which 'fake news', hackers and trolls seek to shape debates.[81] The view that Russian public discourse is substantively shaped by fake media troll farms and manipulation is exaggerated.[82] Political institutions are far more than an arena for bargaining between elites, and the public sphere is more autonomous than the 'informational autocracy' model would suggest. Institutions and the public sphere work in interaction with the technocratic rationality of the regime (mostly within the framework of presidential power) and, thus, remain limited, and they are also subverted more fundamentally when it comes to elections and practices of accountability; yet both have a life and dynamism of their own based on a vitality derived from the normativity of the constitutional state.

The dual state model and neo-patrimonialism both examine the dynamics of regime-society relations, although the dual state approach has a greater emphasis on institutions, in particular those associated with the constitutional and legal order. The neo-patrimonial approach moves away from the largely personal ties of the classic patrimonial model, with the focus on the bureaucratic structures that endow power relations with a degree of anonymity and permanence. It is in the realm of political economy, however, that neo-patrimonialism comes into its own, with its examination of the formal and informal ties between power and property, intended to create a system in which the dominant regime can perpetuate itself. As in the dual state model, two operative systems of domination and rule combine, imbuing the whole edifice with uncertainty as to which system will apply at any particular time. As in the dual state model, there is constant tension in the triangular relationship between the regime, the state and society. This gives rise to an inherent instability, which in the dual state system in countered by a whole range of specially designed stability mechanisms. In fact, as Neil Robinson points out in his discussion of neo-patrimonialism, 'regime stability has been able to pose as a substitute for state building'.[83] This is precisely the point at the heart of the dual state model. In the Putin years, the strengthening of the regime has been taken as synonymous with rehabilitating the state, but in fact these are two parallel, although deeply interconnected, processes. The situation is paradoxical, because in the Putin years the state has been consolidated, the institutions function as prescribed, new courthouses have been built and democratic politics is formally practiced through a competitive party system and elections. However, the autonomous functioning of these institutions is circumscribed by the tutelary powers arrogated by the regime. In this second system, relations are fluid and unregulated, although the operative norms are filtered through various cultural practices, including the Russian notion of 'understanding' (*ponyatie*) itself. It is the regime that manages elite relations, although the legitimating discourse of restoring effective governance and pursuing rational public policy concerns at home and abroad is couched in the language of state power.

The regime governs by exploiting uncertainty, since at any particular time it is unclear whether the routines of the constitutional state or the exceptional politics of the administrative regime will be applied. In such a system, there tends to be few permanent winners or losers, since all are subject to the arbitrariness of the administrative system, although this arbitrariness is limited by formal allegiance to the constitutional state. The dual character of the system is more than the 'hybridity' characteristic of political systems in post-Soviet Eurasia but represents a 'historic bloc' that is unique to Russia and which reflects its social structure, political economy and legacy features from the Soviet and even the imperial past. Putin's authority derives from his ability to keep the various historical manifestations of Russia and the factions balanced against each other while drawing on each to the degree that they all have a stake in the system but not to the extent that any one of them can eclipse the others. Putin's statecraft deftly mediates between the constitutional state and the administrative system, drawing normative authority from the former while gaining real power from the latter. This endless balancing and counterbalancing reproduced elements of the old Soviet 'stability system'. As in the earlier period, the permanent politics of stabilisation leaves little room for radical innovation and, thus, encourages political stalemate and inhibits dynamic economic development.[84] Political stasis prevents Russia becoming an outright dictatorship, but it also blocks moves towards greater democratisation. Experience suggests that such stalemates or blockages are overcome either by revolution or collapse. However, the distinctive features of Russia's dual state may allow an evolutionary transcendence of the stalemate by strengthening the constitutional state; but by contrast, if the more authoritarian elements are consolidated, then the compromises and balances of the dual state will give way to a more overtly autocratic system.

Reform, transition and beyond

Reform denotes dissatisfaction with the existing order of things and suggests ameliorative improvements, while reform delayed too long, as Russian experience repeatedly demonstrates, can precipitate revolution and systemic collapse. Reform induced the end of the Soviet Union, and this is why the concept is anathema in Russia today, yet reform necessarily remains on the agenda. The newly independent country had to create a new polity, fundamentally reshape the economy, recast the contours of national identity and find a new place in the world. Equally, commentators on Russia are faced by some very hard methodological choices – how do you study a country that is so different, yet which aspired to become part of the existing 'historical West'? The classic language of transitology barely begins to grasp the multiple layers of Russia's 'transition', yet what other language is there to analyse the complexity of Russia's attempt to 'modernise' its economy and polity? The Russian political system is indeed unique, but so are all the others. Even countries that share the same basic political institutions differ widely in the ways that they operate. Edwin Bacon is right to question the 'othering' of Russia, the idea 'that Russia somehow defies logic', and insists that neither the people nor the country should be constructed as a 'country and people whose actions and attitudes are too alien to ours to warrant considered analysis'.[85] Instead, he stresses that there is no great chasm between the attitudes of people in Russia and the West, and that Russia's international behaviour is neither uniquely disruptive nor exceptionally unusual but fits into the logic of Russian history and normal patterns of international relations. This is true, but the problem in studying the country is how universal categories can be applied in a manner sensitive to Russia's uniqueness.

An example of this is the idea of 'civil society'. The twilight period of the Soviet system was accompanied by an extraordinary focus on the concept. The fundamental argument was that the Soviet system had become its own gravedigger by modernising society and creating a nascent middle class (or bourgeoisie), demanding civil rights and equal citizenship.[86] Civil society was considered the foundation for democratisation and a way of embedding constitutionalism into societal mores.[87] This Tocquevillian view is challenged by those who argue that the fall of communism represented not the triumphant upwelling of a society in waiting, ready to assume the task of state-building and modernisation, but in fact reflected little more than the implosion of an exhausted and increasingly ineffectual communist establishment. Rather than representing the victory of a nascent civic society and the maturation of a responsible citizenry, the anti-communist revolutions expressed unsatisfied consumerist demands (dubbed by Stephen Kotkin as an 'uncivil society').[88] The collapse of communism was followed not by the emergence of an active citizenry and responsible market players but by the rampant manifestation of society's own pathologies. In the semi-anarchic 1990s, citizens forfeited a number of social rights and above all the right to security, while in the 2000s Putin delivered basic social rights (including getting paid on time) and restored elementary security to the streets, for which he received the thanks of a grateful population. But what he was not able to do was to create the conditions for the exercise of democratic rationality, in which diverse and conflicting popular interests and preferences are mediated through representative institutions. Liberal democratic theory suggests that this should result in good government, where corruption is low and public servants act with probity for the public good.

The regime system, already under Yeltsin and intensified by Putin, operates according to an algorithmic managerial and technocratic rationality. Both derived their legitimacy from the formal application of democratic procedures within the framework of a liberal constitution but increasingly carved out a sphere of political action free from constraints within the framework of the dual state. To explain this unexpected outcome of Russia's 'transition', discourse shifted from civil society to social capital theory. Robert Putnam's landmark study of Italian regional government identified certain forms of social solidarity and effective governance in the north of the country, drawing on traditions of civic governance in the city states of the medieval and early modern periods, whereas in the south, he argued, 'amoral familism' predominated, accompanied by poor governance and a fragmented society.[89] The term 'amoral familism' comes from Edward Banfield's famous study of an Italian village in the 1950s.[90] Although the forms of civic alienation may not take such culturally determined forms in post-communist Russia (and the Italian findings, not surprisingly, have also been hotly contested), the relationship between civic subjectivity and political outcomes is clearly an important one. Harry Eckstein devoted his long academic career to studying the relationship between societal mores and political democracy. Although he gave a convincing explanation about why democracy flourished in Norway's isolated and self-governing fishing and farming communities, there were less convincing answers about why the long tradition of popular participation in village communities in tsarist Russia, in soviets, trade unions and other social organisations in the Soviet Union, and the upsurge in civic engagement during perestroika, ended up reproducing an authoritarian system in the post-communist period.[91]

The concept of *anomie* helps chart aspects of Russia's post-communist mentality. The sociological concept of anomie describes disorientation and alienation from one's surroundings. The phenomenon today shapes the political culture of the elite, with shallow loyalties to institutions and even the ruling regime, although balanced by perhaps an exaggerated veneration of the past and traditional cultural patterns. In a country where three regimes have crashed in less than a century, it is hardly surprising that there is greater affiliation with what is enduring and timeless, rather than a political construction that may prove as ephemeral as its predecessors.

Others talk in terms of path dependency, the view that earlier institutional or political choices foreclose later options. There is a long tradition in Russian academic writing (itself probably path-dependent) arguing that a so-called Russian system (*Russkaya sistema*) reproduces itself in different formats but with the consistent exaggeration of the prerogatives of an insulated and demanding power system, accompanied by the acquiescence of a passive citizenry.[92] Stefan Hedlund frames the argument in terms of socio-economic structural constraints.[93] There is also a version of path dependency based on cultural factors. Alexander Yanov argued that the West would have to move fast to support Russian democracy after the change from the Soviet system, but the window of opportunity would soon snap shut. His analysis of the cycles of reform and counter-reform in Russian history led him to predict that unless strongly supported by the West, the period of liberalisation would be short.[94] By the 1990s, he was already talking of 'Weimar Russia', thereby suggesting that post-communist Russia was comparable to pre-Nazi Germany, ripe for some virulent new authoritarian consolidation. Putin's critics argue that this is indeed the case, but at most Russia remains stuck in an extended Weimar syndrome where democracy is not consolidated but so far no outright revanchist and revisionist power has been established. Putinite Russia is not out to destroy the foundations of the liberal constitutional state or to subvert the existing world order. This misunderstanding provoked Putin's demonization.[95]

It is too easy to blame the people for the sins of their leaders. Russian civil society from the first took distinctive forms. As Chebankova convincingly argues, observers tend to look for Western patterns of citizen engagement and participation, whereas in Russia, civic activity takes specific forms.[96] The state typically exercises close supervision, but this does not mean that voluntary civic activism and engagement does not exist.[97] This is certainly the case when it comes to the work of the Civic Chamber, which although detracting from what should properly be the monitoring work of elected representative bodies nevertheless contributes to the exercise of accountability over regional and central executive bodies. This public control body is in keeping with the Soviet tradition of social *kontrol'* (supervision) bodies.[98] More broadly, although the foreign agents law of July 2012 restricted the

Western funding of Russian civil society, most Russian NGOs had never received such support, peaking at about 7 per cent in 2009. Since 2012, Russian NGOs have to register as foreign agents if they receive overseas funding, forcing the closure of many organisations. The 162 organisations registered as foreign agents by 2017 have to submit detailed financial accounts and undergo frequent review, and are prevented from pursuing activities that are considered political, such as election monitoring. Environmental groups have been the prime casualties of the law, forcing at least a dozen to close.[99]

The decline in foreign funding is offset by an enormous expansion in the sources of domestic funding. These include federal and regional grant-awarding bodies, as well as corporate donors and private foundations, notably the Potanin Foundation, the Sistema Foundation and the Timchenko Foundation, as well as direct awards by such companies as Norilsk Nickel, Gazpromneft and Metalloinvest. Although foreign sources of funding have decreased sharply (although it still continues despite the bureaucratic hurdles), 'the bigger story, however, is that Russian civil society has persevered with the growth and diversification of indigenous funding sources'.[100] In fact, according to one civil society activist, the Western narrative that Russia is unfree is far from the whole truth.[101] However, the character of this freedom is ambivalent, and some of the anarchic elements of the 1990s have been incorporated into the Putinite system of rule. The view of an all-seeing and all-powerful Putin presiding over a well-oiled power *vertikal* is nonsense. Instead, 'the proliferation of grey zones that are neither totally grassroots nor state-sponsored should be comprehended as a fundamental feature of the regime and its adaptive nature', as in the emergence of various militia groups.[102] In fact, adaptation was a dual process – not only to the exigencies of the law and international norms but also to the needs of the regime and the pressures of society.

The Soviet system created a distinctive pattern of class and social power, as well as a specific form of relationship between intellectuals and the power system. Not surprisingly, society responded to the challenge of 'transition' to capitalist modernity in unique ways. The engagement of social groups in the structures of authority and the power system was shaped not only by Soviet legacies but also by some pre-Soviet traditions and post-communist realities.[103] The Tocquevillean myth of a beneficent civil society ready to take advantage of the anti-communist revolution proved to be false. Instead, the more appropriate model appeared to be the Hobbesian one describing the brutality of the state of nature. If that is indeed the case, then Putin's creation of a Leviathan state makes theoretical sense. The Hobbesian model of just authority lies at the heart of modern liberal democracy (although tempered by Lockean legalism and pluralism) and is ultimately concerned with the pacification of social conflict and pathologies through the establishment of a dominant power system. The Hobbesian 'social contract' can be terminated if the power system fails to deliver what it promises in terms of security and, today, in social welfare, and thus is not outright despotism. Writing during the English Civil War, Hobbes was obsessed by security and the fear of disorder, and these concerns became paramount in post-communist Russia.[104] It is striking how the dilemmas of early modern state-building in England have been repeated in post-communist Russia, confirming the view that Russia's historical time is not necessarily synchronised with others.

Whereas the contemporary West stresses Lockean liberty, Russia highlights Hobbesian security. The Leviathan emerges as the benevolent despot who can restore order and stability but whose power is far from unlimited and is bound by a new 'social contract': in the Soviet and Russian cases, security and rising prosperity in exchange for political passivity. More than that, in contemporary Russia, neo-traditionalists endow authority with a sacred dimension, seeing it as the *katechon*, a power keeping at bay the destructive forces of the Antichrist. Moscow is considered the Third Rome, imposing order on a sea of chaos and holding back the apocalypse. Thus, the Leviathan is endowed with a sacral aspect, reinforced by close alignment with organised religion. The ideology of 'normality' espoused by Putin, in fact, has many layers, reaching deep into the spiritual heart of the nation. This is why Putin, who is a far from a charismatic personality and who deliberately understates his rhetoric (apart from the occasional verbal flourish), has become structurally charismatic. This in part is derived from his institutional position, as president of a country with a neo-monarchical constitution. As in the United States, the president is both head of state and chief executive at the same time, but there is more to it than this. The culture of power in Russia tends towards personalisation, a feature that despite its grounding in Marxist materialism reached delirious heights in the Stalin years.

Putin's persona is a pragmatic one, and despite certain pictorial excesses (for example, horse-riding bare-chested and diving for amphorae in the Black Sea), the overwhelming portrait presented in countless press conferences and meetings is that of the efficient and authoritative chief executive. The historian in Putin understands that the greatest victim of a 'cult of personality' is the personality itself. The sad end of most modern tyrants remains a salutary warning. The strutting and posturing of a Napoleon III or Benito Mussolini would be quickly lampooned in the age of the internet. Putin is thin-skinned and intolerant of the cruel satire that characterised his portrayal in the *Kukly* political puppet show on NTV in the early 2000s (the latex representations of politicians similar to the *Spitting Image* programme in the UK), and the programme was duly taken off air. Putin has a rather prim 1950s view of the dignity of political office, but there is no shortage of public criticism of his policies in the serious press and some radio stations, although none is shown on the main nightly TV news programmes and the Sunday evening political chat shows (although some of the weekday ones can contain some sharply critical discussion).

Strong leadership remains in demand in Russia but is framed in a particular way. Putin's model of cultivated modesty reflects his personality, but it is also a requirement of the character of his leadership. Putin is a broker between the various entrenched factional blocs, and his power derives from his ability to achieve consensus within the elite while satisfying basic social demands. This gave rise to the 'stability system' described above, in which stability became the overriding concern, suppressing organised political struggle between different visions and models of national development and reducing party and electoral competitiveness. This was mechanical (imposed) rather than organic self-sustaining stability. Democracy became the legitimating ideology, but already under Yeltsin it assumed features of what the Russian political scientist Dmitry Furman called 'imitation democracy', copying the forms of a democracy such as regular elections, a parliament with competing parties, and a free press, but these institutions reproduced the form, not the spirit, of their models.[105] Democracy is 'managed' by the administrative regime, the power system standing outside of democratic competition, creating what was very quickly dubbed 'managed democracy'. Managerial practices very soon gained a high degree of autonomy. In the mid-2000s, the deputy head of the PA responsible for political affairs, Surkov, as noted, devised the term 'sovereign democracy' to describe the phenomenon.[106] For him, sovereignty was the central political value, providing a framework to resist the normative hegemony of the West and to allow Russia to become more competitive in the global competition of ideas and values – as well as to compete more effectively in the global market.[107] Surkov was associated with a 'democratic statist' orientation, in which sovereign democracy sought to combine the universals of democracy (as they understood the term) and the particular challenges facing Russia.

Surkov and his allies argue that 'normality' in Russia cannot simply adopt the institutional and cultural experience of the West but instead requires a new synthesis of Russian traditionalism with the norms of modernity. Contradiction and competition are not suppressed, as would be the case with the formal imposition of a state of emergency or martial law, described by the notion of 'autocracy' in the democratisation literature to denote non-democracies. Instead, the Putinite system seeks to manage these contradictions while constraining competition. The electoral and party systems in mature democracies are also tailored to achieve certain desired outcomes, such as parliamentary majorities to provide stable government. In post-communist Russia, these constraints inhibited the emergence of a genuinely pluralistic system that could give voice to political contradictions and substantive alternative programmes. It is not so much that alternatives are not on offer – they are, with the CPRF and the LDPR at the neo-traditionalist end of the spectrum, and the Yabloko party offering a social liberal perspective – but a variety of manipulative techniques reduce their impact, ranging from outright electoral fraud and ballot stuffing to the exclusion of candidates. Democratic theory suggests that by containing contradiction within the formal rules of political competition, with political parties acting as the aggregators of social interests accompanied by the free expression of civil society, societal tensions lose some of their system-destroying potential. By contrast, Putin appears to have been haunted by the fear of systemic breakdown and the potential for democracy to spawn forces that would destroy even the freedoms available within the framework of the managed system. This is the heart of the Putin paradox: a system that derives its legitimacy from democracy is unable to allow the free exercise of democracy for fear that democracy will destroy itself. The democracy paradox and Weimar Germany haunt post-communist Russia.

3 PUTIN AND POLITICS

The 1993 constitution explicitly repudiated Soviet principles and practices, but in the end, a monist power system was reproduced – that is, a system that is concentrated rather than internally pluralist, in which competitive elections are managed by a force standing outside of the elections themselves and in which exceptional and arbitrary authority can be exercised. These processes are governed by a single implacable rationality – an idealised and reified notion of 'stability'. This is a stability generated not by the relatively harmonious interactions between political institutions and society, regulated by the law and norms enshrined in the constitutional order – what we call organic stability – but through the managerial capacities of an agency exogenous to that constitutional system – which can be called mechanical stability. This is the great paradox of the Putinite dual state: the administrative regime is committed to the perpetuation of its power as a way of maintaining the constitutional order, but the preservation of the power of the regime does not allow constitutional order to become endogenous (organic), a self-controlling and regulating mechanism of governance. The neo-patrimonial features of the system allowed a range of extraconstitutional forces and 'factions' to structure political space. When it came to the reform of the federal system, the struggle to overcome the segmented regionalism that had developed in the 1990s employed a range of administrative measures. Instead of using law to deal with the problems of legal deviance, managerial or administrative methods were applied. This is characteristic of the paradoxes of the dual state: attempts to strengthen the constitutional state end up only reinforcing the administrative character of the regime.

The state of exception and regionalism

Putinism is the politics of the exception and thereby in Schmittean terms reasserts its fundamentally political character. Carl Schmitt argued that sovereignty is the prerogative of the authority to decide on the exception. As he famously put it, 'The specific political distinction to which political actions and motives can be reduced is that between friend and enemy.'[1] Schmitt tied the concept of the 'sovereign' to the state of emergency; with the sovereign determining whether there was an emergency situation allowing the authorities to govern outside of the rules. In his *Political Theology*, he argued that 'the exception is more interesting than the rule'. 'The rule proves nothing, the exception proves everything; it not only confirms the rule, the rule itself exists only thanks to the exception.'[2] The sovereign acts outside of constitutional constraints in response to existential threats. In Russia, the permanent state of emergency has become the standard for post-communist normality, while normality is imbued with a permanent sense of the exceptional where it is never clear whether constitutional or regime rules will apply. This logic informs the dual state.

The Putin synthesis represents a distinctive reformulation of the political, in which the state of exception becomes permanent. The regime absorbs the entirety of the political, removing agonistic choices from society and resolving them within the regime. This reduces elections to little more than choices between different facets of the hegemonic regime bloc (whether these are called UR, the CPRF or LDPR). Genuinely independent forces were effectively neutralised in the early 2000s, either by co-optation or by depriving them of political space to develop. For example, the Yabloko party and its counterparts enjoy political and ideational independence, but the all-encompassing character of the Putin hegemonic system deprives them of political oxygen and resources. The characteristic squabbling and factionalism of the opposition is epiphenomenal to the broader context in which they work. It would take a monumental act of leadership to exercise independent agency in a system designed to stifle such independence.

Naomi Klein argues that the destabilisation, disorientation and economic disaster of shock therapy in the early 1990s was exploited to force Russia's turn towards neoliberal capitalism, one that undermined organised social interests (such as trade unions) and opened the Russian economy to predatory forms of international capitalism.[3] In a later work, she describes how the politics of the exception, what she calls the 'shock doctrine', especially in the wake of natural disasters such as Hurricane Katrina in New Orleans and environs, weakened resistance to urban displacement and the lucrative gentrification of what had previously been low-income neighbourhoods.[4] Klein's work roots the politics of the exception in the use of crises to transform social relations and economic power. The Putin system is, thus, part of Russia's extended social and political post-communist social transformation, and there are deep continuities between the Yeltsin and Putin years. The year 2000 did not represent a major turning point. The difference is that what was immanent in the 1990s became real in the 2000s. With remarkable speed Putin eliminated genuine sources of autonomy in society: the governors in Russia's regions, the 'oligarchs' in the economy and independent parties with the capacity to achieve governmental turnover in political society.

The politics of exception is particularly stark in the sphere of human rights. The category of 'political prisoner' is obviously contentious, but Russia today is alleged to hold some 300 political and religious prisoners. Political activists or others who have fallen foul of the system tend to be prosecuted for criminal offences, unlike in the Soviet period where the criminal code contained at least two overtly 'political' crimes, including the catch-all category of 'anti-Soviet activity'. One of the longest-serving prisoners in this category is Alexei Pichugin, a mid-level security official in Yukos who was the first to be arrested in connection with the attack on the oil company. He was arrested on 19 June 2003 and after a series of trials was given a life sentence for 'organising murders', although the evidence is deeply flawed. The European Court of Human Rights (ECtHR) has twice ruled that the Russian authorities have violated Pichugin's right to a fair trial and his presumption of innocence.

The main target of oppression, contrary to the mainstream Western view, is not the liberals but radical Russian nationalists (as opposed to Putin-style moderate nationalism, which is better described as state patriotism). In the 1990s, Alexander Barkashov led the 15,000-strong far-right Russian National Unity (*Russkoe natsional'noe edinstvo*, RNE) militia, but it was closed down by Putin (although remnants fought in the Donbas in 2014). The nationalist Ivan Mironov was accused of an assassination attempt against Chubais, and he vividly describes his time in jail.[5] Members of the far-right RNE were regularly jailed, while the Movement Against Illegal Immigration, who advanced the slogan 'Russia for Russians', was regularly condemned. Russian ethnic nationalism has the potential to mobilise popular opinion in a fundamentally anti-regime direction, above all by tapping into the powerful currents of neo-traditional and Eurasianist thinking. Russian ethnic nationalism has the power to destroy the state. This is why it is a mistake to call Putin a nationalist, if that is meant to be a commitment to ethnic Russians over those of the other people constituting Russia. He is instead a *derzhavnik* (great power defender), with legitimacy derived not from the ethnic nation but the state.[6] Putin is a statist rather than a nationalist. This entails the supremacy of the state over citizens, from whence in part the authoritarianism of the system is derived; however, typical of the Putinite paradoxes, it also guarantees relative interethnic peace and social inclusivity.

As for the regions, on coming to power, Putin launched a drive to reduce anti-constitutional diversity but at the same time undercut the independence of regional executives. Many had adopted charters or constitutions that in one way or another breached the provisions of the 1993 national constitution. Some republics declared the right to declare war, to change the conditions for military service, to establish their own procedures for declaring a state of emergency, to conclude international treaties or to declare ownership over the natural resources in the region. They were now forced to bring these documents into conformity with the federal constitution and to ensure that regional legislation was in accord with national provisions.

Putin terminated the forty-six bilateral treaties signed between Moscow and the regions between 1994 and 1998, forty-two of which contained provisions contrary to the constitution. The one signed with Tatarstan in February 1994, for example, granted the republic economic and political sovereignty, including control over foreign trade and foreign policy. Yeltsin in June 1999 already issued a decree calling for these treaties to be brought into conformity with national norms, but it had little effect until Putin enforced the policy.

Putin's strategy is based on 'desegmentation' – the attempt to introduce legal uniformity across the country and to enhance the authority of the central authorities. In a typically paradoxical fashion, Putin reasserted the power of the constitution by introducing a range of para-constitutional bodies and practices, ones which did not infringe the letter of the constitution but which were not specified in the text, and thus established a set of governance practices that ran alongside it. Putin's first major institutional innovation was the creation of seven federal districts (one of the para-constitutional institutions discussed above), each headed by a presidential envoy, with the task of imposing legal uniformity. The envoys reimposed central control over federal ministries and agencies in the regions, and monitored (the word *kontrol'* in Russian means supervision rather than control) the work of regional governors and republican presidents. A second innovation was the reform of the upper chamber of Russia's bicameral parliament, the FC. The constitution stipulates that each subject of the federation sends two members, one from the legislative and one from the executive branch, but the method of selection is not specified. In the first convocation, senators were elected, but from 1995, the heads of the regional executive and legislative branches personally attended the FC. Putin removed *ex officio* membership, and each branch delegated someone to represent them. At a stroke, the status of the regional heads was reduced and the FC became a forum for placemen and women. The third reform compensated regional leaders for their loss of status by creating a State Council (for the governors) in September 2000 and a Council of Legislators the following year for the heads of regional legislatures. Both bodies are advisory and lack constitutional authority but allow governors and legislators to deliberate on matters of national policy. These changes were accompanied by fiscal centralisation and federal interventions in regional affairs.[7]

The abolition of the direct election of governors in December 2004 was perhaps the most radical of all Putin's federal reforms. Already in May 2000 the president had been granted the right to dismiss governors and disperse regional assemblies, although these powers were very hard to implement. Now, the president was granted the right to appoint governors, and thus one of the foundational principles of federal autonomy was breached. Regional assemblies were to vote on the presidential nominee, but if rejected twice the regional assembly could be dissolved. An amendment of December 2005 allowed the party that won most seats in regional assemblies to nominate candidates, a measure that was implemented during

Medvedev's presidency, by which time UR enjoyed a majority in most regional assemblies. The struggle against regional segmentation constrained the autonomy of the subjects to the point that it became common to talk of defederalisation. This view is exaggerated, since the federal system remains in place and the centre cannot govern by fiat as in a unitary state but has to engage in permanent negotiation as part of a two-level system of governance. Nevertheless, the federal system moved from one extreme to another, from segmentation to centralisation, and a genuine balance incorporating the spirit of federalism is still to be established. This was in part rectified by the restoration of gubernatorial elections following the resurgence of contentious politics in 2011. An unprecedented protest movement demanded political reform, to which Medvedev responded in his annual address to the Federal Assembly on 24 December by promising a broad package of political reform (see 'regime reset' in Chapter 4).

The politics of the exception was practiced most spectacularly in Chechnya. Following the break-up of the Soviet Union, the republic had ambitions to become a sovereign state like the other fifteen former Soviet Republics, but its status as an autonomous republic in the old federal system did not allow this. Instead, the republic granted itself unconstitutional powers and swiftly descended into civil conflict, banditry and financial manipulations, including raids on the federal treasury. A negotiated solution may well have been possible, but urged on by hardliners in December 1994, Yeltsin launched a military operation that turned out to be disastrous for the republic and for Russia. After two years of war, in which the capital, Grozny, was turned into rubble, a peace agreement was finally achieved at Khasavyurt in August 1996. A five-year transition period was agreed, after which the republic's final status would be decided. Chechnya had achieved de facto independence, but instead of building a stable state, the republic, as we have seen, descended into lawlessness accompanied by the imposition of harsh Sharia laws and became a threat to its neighbours. By 1999, the situation was spinning out of control, and following two armed incursions into neighbouring Dagestan in August and the apartment bombings in Moscow and elsewhere, with responsibility attributed to Chechens, Putin in late September launched a second war. Learning from the disastrous experience of the first, the military campaign was more successful, although attended once again by massive destruction and death.

By 2001, the worst of the fighting was over, and a political settlement was imposed in which one of the insurgent leaders of the first war, the chief mufti of the so-called Republic of Ichkeria, Akhmad Kadyrov, took over and formally became president in October 2003. He was assassinated in May 2004, and when he became eligible, on reaching the age of 30, his son Ramzan became president. The Chechen compromise is a classic case of Putinite exceptionalism. The region formally remains part of the Russian Federation, but the policy of 'Chechenisation' created a constitutional and political black hole in which Kadyrov exercises almost unchecked power.[8] Federal agencies provide the bulk of funds for the republic, but even the security agencies exercise little authority. Kadyrov expresses virulent loyalty to Putin personally but not to the Russian state. At the same time, Kadyrov sent his armed forces to Georgia in 2008, the Donbas in 2014 and Syria from 2015. It is alleged that Kadyrov's forces were responsible for the murder of the investigative journalist Anna Politkovskaya on 7 October 2006 (Putin's birthday), the human rights activist and board member of the human rights organisation Memorial, Natalia Estemirova, on 15 July 2009 and the leading oppositional politician Boris Nemtsov on 27 February 2015. Following the latter murder, Putin disappeared for two weeks, and (as Gleb Pavlovsky notes) 'he spoke about how we in the future will heroically overcome the difficulties which we ourselves have created', representing 'a public rebuke [to those who had killed Nemtsov]: you perhaps had state goals but you did not please me'. As Pavlovsky, a presidential advisor in Putin's first presidential decade and head of the Effective Politics Foundation, notes, 'it became clear that the system was not completely under control', with more indications of that sort ever since.[9] In other words, Putin's permanent state of exception became victim to exceptional acts.

There remains a high level of state repression in the republic, and contrary to the Russian constitution's defence of religious freedom, women have to cover their heads in public with hijabs, a rule enforced with characteristic brutality by Kadyrov's militia, while men have to wear beards. The application of Sharia law defies Russia's secular constitutional order. In the spring of 2017, it was reported that Kadyrov had launched a pogrom against gays, with over a hundred allegedly arrested, tortured or killed.[10] The repression continues. Kadyrov also had ambitions to conduct an independent foreign policy, especially in the Islamic world, where he considered himself the leader of Russian Muslims far beyond the Caucasus. Kadyrov pacified Chechnya through the destruction of international radical Islamic forces, and the republic has now been rebuilt, with the help of generous funds from Moscow. There are even plans to turn Chechnya into a tourist destination, with a ski resort being built not far from Shatoi, a highland town that was repeatedly the site of terrible fighting in the two wars.[11] Kadyrovite Chechnya exposed the harsh limits of the Putinite stability system. Where the constitutional order gives way to personalism and even to sultanism, the situation becomes anything but stable and ultimately undermines the coherence of Russia.[12] Kadyrov remains defiantly independent of Russia's constitutional state, but his loud loyalty to Putin damages the integrity of the regime of which Putin is head. In the post-Putin era, this personalistic semi-feudal construct may well give way to renewed conflict.

The Chechen case is exemplary when analysing Putin's politics of exceptionalism. Although calling for uniformity and subordination to the constitution, Chechnya represents an extreme case of deviation from these principles. The long-term goal of Moscow is to 'normalise' Chechnya and to make it just another region, but as long as Kadyrov rules, there is little prospect of this being achieved.[13]

Russian security services had long sought to cut Kadyrov down to size, but the cost would be exorbitant. After a confrontation between federal agency officials and Kadyrov's forces in early 2015, Putin came under enormous pressure to put an end to Chechnya's 'legal separatism'. As Amy Knight notes in her study of 'Putin's monster', 'If Putin moved against the Chechen leader he would have to eliminate Kadyrov's large extended family and the loyal troops who form part of his notorious private army, the so-called Kadyrovtsy.'[14] In effect, he would have to launch another Chechen war. Instead, it is argued that Nemtsov's assassination – on the Bolshoi Moskvoretsky Bridge at its closest point to the Kremlin walls – on 27 February 2015 was designed to warn Putin of the consequences. Following the killing, Putin cancelled all meetings, and it is assumed that during his absence, Putin was considering the options: to launch what would in effect be the third Chechen war, with all of its destructive consequences, or to acquiesce in Kadryov's anomalous status. In the end, Putin opted to maintain the status quo. Both options were invidious (as Russians say, *obe khuzhe*) and reflect the harsh realities of trying to manage Russia's unruly regions and fragmented political sphere.

Putin and the past

The Putin phenomenon represents a distinctive response to the problem of 1917 and Marxism–Leninism in the country. While Gorbachev initially tried to salvage something from Leninism, and Yeltsin simply denounced the whole communist experiment, Putin forged a new synthesis that recognised the modernising impulse of the Soviet experiment, although acknowledging the enormous price that was paid. At no time has Putin evinced any sympathy whatsoever for Lenin and has indeed accused him of having placed an 'atomic bomb' under Russian statehood by devising the system of ethno-federalism with arbitrary borders. He cited the example of the Donbas, which in his view had been transferred to Ukrainian jurisdiction to increase the proportion of proletarians in the country, a decision that Putin categorised as 'delirious'.[15] In his view, Lenin's creation of a federal state in which the entities enjoyed the right to secede provoked the disintegration of the Soviet Union in 1991.

Putin draws on an heterogeneous range of ideas, and the synthesis modifies over time to reflect changes in society and the factional balance. As noted, Putin in 2005 lamented the break-up of the Soviet Union, but this did not mean that he sought to recreate the USSR. Putin's repertoire of historical figures has changed over time but indicates an eclectic list of incompatible elements. Putin rehabilitated the religious philosopher Ivan Ilyin, deported by the Soviet Union in 1922, but this does not make him 'Putin's philosopher of Russian fascism'.[16] Ilyin believed that Russia was naturally Orthodox and authoritarian, with a destiny separate from the West, which he saw as dangerous and out to destroy

Russia's Orthodox civilisation. The sentiment is widely shared in post-communist Russia, but this is far from fascism. There remains an enormous well of imperial resentment, born of the dissolution of the powerful communist system in 1989 and the disintegration of the country in 1991. Unlike the other Soviet republics, Russia did not gain independence from an alien empire but from its other self. Not surprisingly, the 'transition' to democracy in these circumstances was traumatic, and the two Russias – the old imperial power with global reach and the representative of a universal ideology, and the slimmed-down post-imperial democratising country in search of adequate forms to institutionalise its cultural and historical specificity – are not easily reconciled.[17]

Putin's strategy when it comes to history is the same as in politics: to draw on all historical epochs but to let none dominate. In his annual address to the Federal Assembly in 2012, Putin argued,

> To revive national consciousness, we need to link historical eras and get back to understanding the simple truth that Russia did not begin in 1917, or even in 1991, but rather, that we have a common, continuous history spanning over one thousand years, and we must rely on it to find inner strength and purpose in our national development.[18]

The issue of historical appraisal came to a head when it came to mark the hundredth anniversary of the Bolshevik revolution in 2017. In the end, the event was acknowledged rather than commemorated.[19] For liberals, the communist seizure of power in October 1917 represented the repudiation of everything that the 'Russian revolution' had aspired to ever since the Decembrists went on to Senate Square in St Petersburg in 1825 calling for a constitution and accountable government. The 1905 revolution finally gave birth to a constitutional monarchy of sorts, although Nicholas II never fully reconciled himself to parliamentary democracy. Following his abdication in February 1917, for a time it looked as if the Provisional Government would finally give constitutional form to democratic aspirations, and hence the plans for a Constituent Assembly to hammer out the details. These plans were overwhelmed by the continuing war, the dynamics of 'dual power' as workers and peasants organised in 'soviets' (councils), and then the overthrow of the Provisional Government in what some now call a 'coup' by the Bolsheviks in October.[20] When it came to the centenary, not only was there very little official commemoration but also the broader debate among public intellectuals was remarkably muted. Discussion of historical issues has long been a surrogate for political debate in Russia, but the enormity of the Soviet revolution and its complex legacies in conditions of renewed conflict with the West undermined the foundations for such a discussion. The old certainties had gone, and official discourse lacked a master narrative to provide a framework for new orientations. Putin's convictions are anti-revolutionary, and this set the tone for the year. Apart from some academic conferences and minor events, the anniversary passed unmarked and largely unlamented.

As early as 1996, the post-communist authorities distanced themselves from 1917, renaming what had earlier been the 7 November (25 October in the Old-Style Julian calendar) Day of Accord and Reconciliation, and in 2004 it was renamed Unity Day and shifted to 4 November, the day of Moscow's liberation from the Poles in 1612. Despite calls for unity, there remain passionate contending views. For the Russian Orthodox Church, the Bolshevik revolution is an unmitigated evil. The tsar himself suffered before being murdered, along with his family and retainers, in Ekaterinburg on the night of 16–17 July 2018. Nicholas II was canonised by the Russian Orthodox Church Abroad (ROCA) in 1981 and by the Moscow Patriarchate in 2000. For the CPRF and its supporters, the events of the fateful years are still described as the 'Great October Socialist Revolution', and hymns are sung in its praise. For the people, the memory of the Bolshevik repressions is now remembered in the Immortal Regiment movement. This began in Tomsk in 2011 where citizen investigators discovered the names of the People's Commissariat of Internal Affairs (NKVD) operatives who had killed their family. The movement has grown, and now millions march on 9 May (Victory Day), holding portraits of grandparents and relatives who had suffered in one way or another.[21] This is part of a living history in which people immortalise the suffering of previous generations. It also humanises what has become pompous Victory Day celebrations over Nazi Germany. It is worth remembering that following the first Victory Parade in 1945, the second only took place in 1965, the third in 1985 and the fourth in 1990, and the parade only became an annual event and a public holiday in 1995, at the nadir of Russia's fortunes and in some way compensating for current failures. There remains the problem of distinguishing between the people's triumph over Hitler and Stalin's role in that victory. The path to historical reconciliation, in this and the revolution as a whole, remains contested. Some recent publications suggest that the enduring divisions of the revolutionary era are being transcended. As the Russian historian Alexei Miller puts it, 'The point is not that we need to find out which side was right or wrong in the revolutionary conflict. Rather, we must accept that remaining humane is much more important than being red or white.'[22]

Like his predecessors since Stalin's death in 1953, Putin has faced the challenge of coming to terms with the enormity of the phenomenon of mass terror. Since the perestroika years and the establishment of Memorial, created in the heat of perestroika in January 1989 by Arseny Roginsky, Lev Ponomarev and others to preserve the memory of the victims of Stalinist repression and to conduct research, activists have been working to rediscover the historical truth, including the discovery of burial sites and who was buried in them. One of them, Yuri Dmitriev, discovered the Sandarmokh site in northwest Russia by the White Sea canal. He was explicit about the political significance of his work: 'For our government to become … accountable, we need to educate the people.' This maxim was particularly true in his case, because in December 2016, he was arrested and accused of taking indecent pictures of his 12-year-old adopted daughter, when in fact he had been recording her development since he and his wife had taken her into their family as a malnourished child of 3. For a brief period in the early 1990s, the secret police archives had been open, and Dmitriev read thousands of execution orders into his tape recorder, which he then used to match with the skeletons he unearthed. In January 2018, Dmitriev was released from detention, and in April, he was acquitted by the Petrozavodsk District Court, a decision overturned in June by the regional Supreme Court and new charges were brought.[23] Memorial has also come under attack, with several of its branches being declared 'foreign agents'.[24] Nevertheless, Memorial fights on to record the repressions of the Soviet years and to monitor the abuses in Chechnya and elsewhere in Russia today. As long as it survives, the spirit of freedom and genuine democracy, long nurtured in the recesses of Russian and Soviet society and which flowered in the perestroika years, will remain alive. Memorial is a living monument to the hopes of the Soviet underground and the optimism of the perestroika years.

Evaluation of Stalin is a surrogate debate over Russia's past and a struggle over models of the future. The fundamental divide is between those who consider Russia, in broad terms, part of Western modernity and those who would like it to become the rampart of a struggle for civilisational alternatives.[25] The contest is fought over the terrain of liberal values, tolerance and inclusivity, which too often in Russian parlance are dismissed as no more than 'political correctness'. The 'cultural turn' in Russian politics after 2012 was accompanied by a hardening of attitudes against human rights campaigners in general and Memorial activists in particular. Russian TV attacked Memorial in November 2016 after it published information on forty thousand Soviet secret police officials, accusing it of helping 'those who aim to destroy the Russian state'. Earlier that year, in June, Putin warned that the 'excessive demonisation' of Stalin was a 'means of attacking the Soviet Union and Russia'.[26] There are reports that statues of Stalin have been erected in some towns. However, all this does not mean the rehabilitation of Stalin. The regime has refused to adopt a policy of historical homogeneity and instead has allowed alternative narratives to compete. This is a politics of *bricolage*, bringing together incompatible elements.[27] This fragmented approach to history is in keeping with the generally ideologically eclectic character of the regime, which itself reflects the moods and concerns of society.

The hybrid approach applies to the study of Stalinism and above all to the teaching of history. Although one notorious textbook by Alexander Filippov, *A History of Russia 1945–2006*, published in 2007, argued that Stalin was an 'effective manager' and emphasised his role as a war leader, other texts have been approved for use in schools that take a more critical stance. A condensed version of Alexander Solzhenitsyn's *The Gulag Archipelago* remains compulsory reading for secondary school pupils. Although some influential officials have favoured relatively positive evaluations of Stalin, notably the Minister of Education Olga Vasileva and the Minister of Culture Vladimir Medinsky, their views are not dominant or uncontested. As a recent study argues,

> Despite the behaviour and statements of Medinsky and frequent efforts by the regime to ignore the crimes of Stalin, the assessment that the Kremlin uniformly burnishes and simplifies the Soviet past is itself a simplification. Although Medinsky clearly enjoys support among various strata of incumbent elites, his statements do not command *ex cathedra* status; his perspective on the Soviet past is far from hegemonic, whether in the ranks of the regime or in Russian society.[28]

The evaluation of Stalin, like the assessment of the Bolshevik revolution itself, remains the subject of bitter controversy, and the issue divides the regime as much as society. While Stalin statues have been erected, an impressive Gulag museum has been opened in Moscow, a monument to the victims of the Gulag was unveiled by the Admiralty building in St Petersburg and the former Gulag camp Perm-36 has become a museum of Stalinist repression.

Memorial came under sporadic attack by the *siloviki* and in 2014 was forced to register as a 'foreign agent'. In 1991, Memorial succeeded in replacing the statue of Felix Dzerzhinsky, the founder of the Cheka (the precursor to the KGB and FSB), outside the Lubyanka (the headquarters of Russia's police from its foundation in December 1918) with a massive stone from the Solovetsky Islands, the site of the first Soviet prison camps established by Lenin. Memorial's attempt to establish a publicly funded library and archive of state repression and the secret police failed. In 1998, Roginsky became the head of the Memorial board and remained a symbol of integrity and steadfastness. Despite criticism from some human rights activists, he joined the presidential commission overseeing the building of the Wall of Sorrow, arguing that 'a monument on behalf of the state is necessary because the state must clearly say terror is a crime'.[29] The wall joined other monuments to the terror inaugurated in 2017. A wall bearing the names of about twenty thousand victims opened in September at the Butovo firing range, and a memorial at the Sretensky Monastery commemorates the 750,000 people executed during the Great Terror in 1937–8. The Gulag Museum moved into larger premises and presents moving testimony to the crimes of the Soviet regime.

It is important to distinguish between decommunisation and destalinisation. The former rejects the whole legacy of the Soviet period, including its social and modernisation achievements, whereas the latter focuses on the crimes of the political system. Conflation of the two has provoked an upsurge in grass-roots Stalinism, which typically has little to do with the man himself but seeks to defend the gains of the Soviet period. Indeed, in certain respects, decommunisation has impeded effective destalinisation.[30] As far as Tony Wood is concerned, the survival of Soviet welfare institutions provided Russians with some sort of a social safety net after the fall of communism, including low rents, free medicine, the pension system and access to free healthcare. The attempt to dismantle the Soviet social security legacy by liberal reformers provoked sustained resistance.[31]

As for Putin himself, as in so many issues, his views are as divided as those of the country. He acknowledged the achievements of the Soviet period (in particular, through the sacrifices of the Second World War, in which his parents had nearly died) while decrying the savagery. Putin condemned the superfluous sacrifices in the name of a flawed modernisation project, although he recognised the achievements of the period. Opening the Wall of Sorrow (located, appropriately, on Sakharov Prospect) on 30 October 2017 (the national Day of Remembrance of Victims of Political Repression), he argued,

> It is very important that we all and future generations – this is of great significance – know about, and remember this tragic period in our history when entire social groups and entire peoples were cruelly persecuted, including workers, peasants, engineers, military commanders, clergy, government employees, scientists and cultural figures. Neither talent, nor services to the Motherland, nor sincere devotion to it could help avoid repression, because unwarranted and absolutely absurd charges could be brought against anyone. Millions of people were declared 'enemies of the people', shot or mutilated, or suffered in prisons, labour camps or exile. This terrifying past cannot be deleted from national memory or, all the more so, be justified by any references to the so-called best interests of the people.[32]

This was an unambiguous condemnation of Stalinism, while hinting at the achievements of the Soviet period.

Anti-revolution as a political practice

Contrary to the common assertion that he is a 'counter-revolutionary',[33] Putin, in fact, is 'anti-revolutionary', condemning not just the Bolshevik revolution but also the idea of revolution as a form of political change. He argued, 'We did not need a global revolution', referring to 1917, but is consistent in his view that revolutions inflict more damage than good.[34] He applies this not only to perceived Western attempts to achieve regime change through 'colour revolutions' in post-Soviet Eurasia but also to what Moscow came to see as Western 'revisionist' attempts to reshape the global order in its image. This stance is obviously generated by concerns over regime preservation, but it is also rooted in the perceived deleterious consequences of revolutions in general and most immediately by the revolutionary although relatively peaceful 'bourgeois democratic' revolution of 1991, which precipitated the disintegration of the USSR and inaugurated a decade of social and economic cataclysms and perceived national humiliation.

Although he is an anti-revolutionary, Putin has accepted regime change when it does not challenge the geopolitical balance. This was the case repeatedly in Kyrgyzstan, in Armenia in mid-2018, and Moscow even brokered Eduard Shevardnadze's removal in the Rose Revolution in Georgia in December 2003 when it looked as if Mikheil Saakashvili was amenable to a deal with the Kremlin. When it came to Ukraine, however, every change of government became bound up with a senseless and ultimately catastrophic struggle between Eastern and Western geopolitical orientations. The standard liberal view here has matters precisely upside down: a democratic, thriving and Europe-associated Ukraine poses no threat to Russia or even 'Putin's regime' and would even be welcomed, but the radicalism of the Atlanticist geopolitical reorientation and the monist interpretation of Ukrainian history did represent a threat to established ties and to Russian security. Successive post-communist Russian leaders sought to obviate the potential conflict through the creation of sturdy and independent pan-European structures. Instead, enlargement of the Atlantic system denoted the expansion not only of a normative and economic order, which Putin initially was ready to embrace, but also of a power system, which Putin again was initially ready to accept, albeit reluctantly, until the price of that acceptance was perceived to be too high.

Despite his anti-revolutionary beliefs, Putin is cautious in criticising Soviet leaders, for fear of alienating the older generation. Although a consistent critic of Lenin, he left Lenin's body in the mausoleum on Red Square, well aware that his removal would provoke conflict and divide society. As for Stalin, Putin, as we have seen, is as torn as the rest of society, with some 54 per cent in March 2016 considering that the Soviet leader had played at least a somewhat positive role in history. The percentage believing that Stalin's cruelty was 'historically justified' and his repressions were a 'political necessity' rose from 9 per cent in August 2007 to 26 per cent in March 2016, while over the same time period, those condemning his political crimes fell from 72 per cent to 45 per cent.[35] Putin acknowledges that in the Soviet years, the country was transformed as it industrialised, urbanised, became more literate, educated and defeated Nazi Germany in the terrible war between June 1941 and May 1945, exploded its first atomic device in August 1948, launched the first sputnik to orbit the earth with the dog Laika in November 1957, put the first man in space (Yuri Gagarin) in April 1961 and the first woman (Valentina Tereshkova) in June 1963, and went on to become a nuclear superpower. Equally, the cost in human lives and the stifling of autonomous creativity was enormous.

Putin is an organic traditionalist, understanding that the broad river of Russian experience, both good and ill, cannot be simply repudiated or stopped; but neither can it form the basis of contemporary government or policy, as demanded by an assorted phalanx of neo-traditionalists and *okhraniteli*. Putin sought to devise a new synthesis, finding elements of a 'useable' past, while condemning the excesses. This, of course, satisfied neither extreme and left the problem of Stalinism unresolved. The victims of communist repression have been memorialised and Stalin has not been rehabilitated, but Soviet-style authoritarianism still taints the body politic and social life. Stalin's achievements as a 'good manager' in industrialisation and in presiding over the Soviet victory in the Great Patriotic War are recognised, but the mass repressions are no longer centre stage in official representations of the Soviet past. This is why the regime found it so difficult to shape a coherent narrative on the hundredth anniversary of the Bolshevik revolution.

In October 2017, Putin summed up his negative view of revolution as a way of resolving social and political contradictions. At the Valdai Club gathering, he noted the effects of technological change and the costs of not responding adequately in a timely manner:

> Successful technological, industrial breakthroughs were followed by dramatic upheavals and revolutionary disruptions. It all happened because the country failed to address social discord and overcome the clear anachronisms in society in time. Revolution is always the result of an accountability deficit in both those who would like to conserve, to freeze in place the outdated order of things that clearly needs to be changed, and those who aspire to speed the changes up, resorting to civil conflict and destructive resistance.

He then made the crucial argument that in many ways lies at the heart of the Putin phenomenon:

> Today, as we turn to the lessons of a century ago, namely, the Russian Revolution of 1917, we see how ambiguous its results were, how closely the negative and, we must acknowledge, the positive consequences of those events are intertwined. Let us ask ourselves: was it not possible to follow an evolutionary path rather than go through a revolution? Could we not have evolved by way of gradual and consistent forward movement rather than at a cost of destroying our statehood and the ruthless fracturing of millions of human lives. However, the largely utopian social model and ideology, which the newly formed state tried to implement initially following the 1917 revolution, was a powerful driver of transformations across the globe (this is quite clear and must also be acknowledged), caused a major revaluation of development models, and gave rise to rivalry and competition, the benefits of which, I would say, were mostly reaped by the West.[36]

Putin's condemnation of Stalinism here came close to decommunisation as a whole. It certainly represented strong condemnation of revolution as a mode of political change.

Revolution means public activism and mobilisation, whereas depoliticisation is at the heart of the Putinite culture of power. The system demobilised spontaneous and independent political activity, but at moments of stress it called on the people. This was the case in the mid-2000s when a number of youth groups (notably, *Nashi* and *Molodaya Gvardiya* – Young Guard) were mobilised against 'colour revolution' and again in early 2012 in response to the protests against electoral fraud. A mass meeting was held on Poklonnaya Hill on the eve of the March presidential ballot. Putin for a time licenced the neo-traditionalists to mobilise, and they did so with gusto. With the election out of the way, the regime once again clamped down. Similarly, in 2014 during the Ukraine crisis, Putin once again allowed neo-traditionalists, and in particular Russian nationalists, to become politically (and even militarily) active, but once the crisis had passed, the genie of Russian ethnonationalism was firmly returned to the bottle.[37] While the West complains about the liberal political prisoners in Russia, the great majority, as mentioned, throughout Putin's rule have come from the nationalist wing. Any attempt to impose a liberal order on Russia through 'regime change' would be met by a hard nationalist response, including the unleashing of modern-day Black Hundreds amid renewed pogroms and purges. This is why the Putinite stabilisation, while entirely satisfying few, is recognised by the great majority as a lesser evil than renewed revolutionary convulsions.[38] Putin understood that the greatest danger to the regime comes from the nationalist and neo-communist right rather than the liberal 'left'.

This is why the bounds of 'permitted dissent' (to use the Soviet-era term) are drawn so tightly. Putin has an abiding fear of popular mobilisation and, thus, sought to ensure control of the streets and squares. The 'anti-Maidan' groups include the National Liberation Movement (NOD), the revival of the Young Guard from 2018 and the creation of the Young Army, a military-patriotic movement for schoolchildren.[39] While Putinism is not a coherent ideology, it does represent a consistent set of political practices. Earlier, we discussed the concept of a 'stability system', and the defence of this stability was maintained by a range of 'manual' interventions into political processes. Putin's authoritarianism sacrificed institutional checks and balances enshrined in the constitutional order on the altar of political expediency and political stability. This generated a set of political practices, which we will now examine.

First, the struggle against external and domestic enemies, real and imagined, and threats to political stability underpinned and justified the regime system of power. External threats were designated as 'colour revolutions'. This was reinforced by the struggle against democracy promotion, which was considered little more than a synonym for attempts to delegitimate the administration and ultimately to achieve 'regime change', in the parlance of Anglo-American interventionism of the 2000s. The foreign agents' law of 2012 clamped down on foreign funding for broadly defined political activities, with repression strengthened following the

Ukraine crisis. One of the most prominent critics of the annexation of Crimea, the philosophy professor Andrei Zubov, lost his position at the MGIMO University, while the head of the state archive service, Sergei Mironenko, was also dismissed. The director of INION (a social sciences research institute), Yuri Pivovarov, was subject to legal trials. In 2016, a number of institutions were categorised as 'foreign agents', including the Levada Centre for public opinion research, the Centre for Independent Social Research in St Petersburg, the Saratov Centre for Gender Studies and, as noted, the human rights organisation Memorial. The autonomy of higher education institutions was undermined by restrictions on the election of rectors, and they became in effect appointees of the education ministry.

While repression is relatively soft, it is real and highly destructive of Russia's aspirations to become a dynamic modern and open society. An example of the porosity of the system was the repeated attempts to close the European University in St Petersburg (EUSP). This is a private independent postgraduate institution with 100 staff and 260 students initially established with foreign funding. The EUSP quickly established itself as one of the best social science and humanities universities in the city with a world-class research record. The university survived several attempts to close it down, notably after it received a €700,000 grant from the European Commission in 2007 to fund election monitoring, when it was charged with infringing fire code regulations. The attack was renewed in 2016, with accusations of up to 120 infringements, including the absence of adequate sporting facilities. Kudrin, one of the patrons of the university, repeatedly spoke with Putin about the attack, and Putin apparently ordered that the matter be resolved positively, that is, in favour of the university. Despite this, the attack continued, and on 28 September 2017, the university's educational licence was withdrawn.[40] It was not clear at what level in St Petersburg the assault was launched and what the motives were: Was it an ideological attack on a known and respected centre of Western educational norms; a conservative backlash against liberal ideas, with the St Petersburg UR deputy Vitaly Milonov complaining about the teaching of gender studies at the institution; about property, with the university occupying the highly desirable and centrally located Small Marble Palace; or far more petty, with neighbours fearing the noise and disturbance that would accompany the planned modernisation of the building? It could have been some or all of the above, but it is clear that some sort of coalition came together to crush the university, despite Putin's ostensible attempts to save the institution. The university was subject to a procession of inspections by state control agencies, and in the end, it was forced to close its doors to new students and become a research-only institution.[41] However, in August 2018, the EUSP received a new educational licence and reopened in a different premises soon after for a new cohort of taught students. The incident exposed the ability of 'horizontal' forces to stymie the presidential 'vertical'.

This testifies not to the strength of the system but to its weakness. The institutions of the constitutional state, even when mobilised by the president, appeared powerless in the face of spontaneous arbitrariness. This was given legislative form in the 'patriotic' legislation adopted by parliament, which in many cases was too restrictive even for the Kremlin. This is why Volodin was despatched to the Duma following the September 2016 election. He swiftly introduced new rules designed to stifle independent legislative initiative, which at first sight appears as an infringement on the rights of parliament, but its deeper purpose was to constrain the flood of restrictive and ideologically motivated repressive measures – to turn off the 'mad printing press'. Volodin aimed to reinvigorate the Duma and to enhance its prestige while improving its internal procedures.[42] Volodin hosted the first International Forum on Parliamentarism on 4–5 June 2018, which later became an annual event. Delegations attended from around the world, although notably very few from the West. Irina Olimpieva correctly notes the paradox: 'The increasingly common injection of "political logic" into governance processes in fact works against the state's own agenda of improving the situation in science and education, resulting in a policymaking process that is inefficient and contradictory.'[43]

Second, the maintenance of a dominant political party marginalised other organised political forces. UR dominates the party, electoral and legislative spheres, and although other parties survive, the 'systemic opposition' is effectively forced to align with UR. Like Mexico's Partido Revolucionario Institucional (PRI) between 1929 and 2000, UR unites the various elite factions and aggregates their interests. The party also became the vehicle for bureaucrats and the channel for advancement. Even Putin was aware of the party's limitations, and this is why in 2011 he created the ONF to act as a check on the bureaucratic degeneration of the pedestal party and as an alternative vehicle for monitoring the bureaucracy and for political mobility. UR is not the ruling party but the dominant party, a very different political model. The experience of Armenia in 2018 shows how quickly such a pedestal party can evaporate (see below).

Third, unlike in the Soviet years, there is no need for total media control, and, thus, websites and newspapers are largely left alone. Derk Sauer, the head of Sanoma Independent Media which owns 60 per cent of the Russian magazine market, argued that Putin modelled himself not on Brezhnev but on Silvio Berlusconi: 'It's not for nothing that they are such good friends. They understand that if you control the main TV stations and make propaganda there, you'll go far.' This led to the paradoxical outcome that 'there's complete press freedom for the informed but none for the uninformed'.[44] State-owned or supported publications have deep pockets and continue to operate in a Soviet-style manner, although they have adapted now to the advertising market while wishing to be seen as serving the public. The overweening presence of the government in the media sphere is a Soviet legacy. 'But it's also the result of creative engineering by Putin-era authorities, aimed at stimulating the growth of a broad spectrum of media voices while also keeping them all on a leash.'[45] On 15 November 2017, the State Duma adopted a new media law that forced foreign media to register as 'foreign agents', a response to a similar law which forced the RT (formerly Russia Today) TV station in the United States to register as a foreign agent.

Fourth, student activism in Russia is very weak, reflecting the state-dependent structure of the higher education sector as well as the general scepticism of radical engagement in a society still in the throes of post-revolutionary demobilisation, although that is weakening. Demobilisation is not the same as apathy, and is reinforced by complex structures of coercion, including disciplinary practices within institutions and the threat of expulsion. Some institutions still practice Soviet-style exercises in getting out the student vote at election time. Tomsk State University has been in the forefront of such practices, accompanied by threats against student participation in anti-corruption protests. Local FSB officials returned to the personnel department, effectively recreating the old Soviet 'first department', the KGB office overseeing personnel matters. There was considerable passive resistance among staff and students to the recreation of Soviet-style surveillance and mobilisation, as well as open condemnation of attempts to monitor staff travelling abroad for conferences and research. An order issued by the education ministry in February 2019 urged scientists to inform their superiors five days in advance of any plans to meet foreign colleagues, a move that, if implemented, would kill the internationalization aspirations of Russian research institutions. Already Putin's goal set in 2012 to get at least five Russian universities into the top-100 lists by 2020 was far from being achieved. It was this sort of Soviet-style repressions that brought tens of thousands of young people onto the streets in the summer of 2019 to protest against the exclusion of opposition candidates from the Moscow Duma elections of 8 September. The era of demobilisation appeared to be over.

Putin's statecraft

In his 2008 press conference, Putin assessed his performance: 'I have worked like a galley slave throughout these eight years, morning till night, and I have given all I could to this work.'[46] He was ready for the 'opportunity to be useful' to his country in another post, and for the next four years, he served as prime minister before returning in 2012. The time horizon now shifted to 2024 when Russia would possibly have to learn to live without Putin. A long era in Russia's history is associated with his name and his unique style. Putin became a consummate politician, although he never hid his contempt for competitive politics. Already in March 2000 Putin said, 'All these modern election technologies are a pretty dishonest thing. They always involve looking into the eyes of millions of people and giving promises you know are impossible to fulfil. I cannot bring myself to do that. And I am very glad that so far I have not had to.' This later bloomed into a general policy of non-committal, in which he rarely pins himself down with specific promises.[47] This signals a deeper issue. In his 'Politics as a Vocation', Max Weber argued that leadership requires the acceptance of 'ethical paradoxes', compromises that allow a leader to bend with the wind rather than break in the storm. The 'ethics of responsibility' recognises the dangers inherent in 'a pure ethic of absolute ends'.[48] However, there has to be a balance between compromise and principle (what Weber calls 'the ethics of conviction', enduring core beliefs). The Putinite leadership strategy of permanent compromise eroded the enunciation and implementation of long-term objectives based on convictions.

These are important facets of Putin's statecraft, a concept rather different from the broader notion of leadership. Statecraft refers specifically to the discourse and practices of managing the affairs of state, whereas leadership encompasses the many facets of the activity of a leader.[49] The greatest manual on statecraft is provided by Niccolo Machiavelli's *The Prince*, where he outlines alternative strategies for a leader to achieve their goals. Machiavelli's name is now associated with a distinctive form of cynical statecraft and raises the question of whether Putin's leadership style can be so designated. The style of rule is only part of the question, since Machiavelli stressed a rational and pragmatic approach to deciding fundamental questions, and in substance, this is Putin's approach. Machiavelli distinguished between *fortuna*, which in common parlance is called luck, and *virtù*, the qualities of leadership emanating from character and ability 'to achieve great things'. Putin was certainly 'fortunate' for a large part of his period in office, with rising commodity prices in his first two terms and with his bold moves in his third term achieving remarkable success, like the retrocession of Crimea and the intervention in Syria, although such moves came with enormous costs. Putin's obfuscations if not outright lies in denying the presence of Russian forces (the 'little green men' without insignia) in the takeover of the peninsula in the spring of 2014 are frequently cited against his bona fides.[50] As for *virtù*, this for Machiavelli had nothing to do with virtue as conventionally understood but was connected with raison d'état: what is good for the state in this definition is virtuous. But who is to decide what is in the long-term interests of state, and how can these interests be separated from the mere survival of the regime?

These questions become sharper in light of Putin's role as the great faction manager. At the metalevel, Putin draws on the four great factions but allows none to dominate, while giving each a stake in the system. This is the definition of Putinite centrism, but it is a centre that changes with the ebb and flow of factional strength, which in turn reflects popular attitudes and the international situation. While the regime tries to shape popular sentiments, there are natural limits to how far state-sponsored propaganda (put out above all through the main TV channels) can shape the views of its audience. It is relatively easy to change popular opinions, but it is much harder to change views, let alone attitudes. Thus, Putin's statecraft requires permanent engagement with its fundamental constituencies. Putin is the ultimate decider, but decisions are not taken in a vacuum, and regime survival means that he cannot consistently go against the majority. This inevitably means that Putin's leadership – irrespective of its durability and impressive ability to maintain consensus for so long – is ultimately transactional rather than transformative. Horizontal pressures push in at all levels, from the great meta-factions to the micro-factionalism that swirls around the towers of the Kremlin. Policymaking in the Putin court has been likened to Byzantine intrigues and Game of Thrones back-stabbing.

The 'postmodern' image-making of Putin's personality cult predominated when Surkov was responsible for domestic political affairs, with Putin shaped as a 'celebrity and cultural icon'.[51] The Kremlin spin doctors bear much responsibility for some ill-judged public relations (PR) stunts. While flying with cranes may have some justification and satisfied Putin's hankering for adventure and ostensibly burnished his environmental credentials, some of the other stunts were poorly judged. A dive in the Black Sea to find Greek amphorae was obviously staged, but to what purpose it is not clear. Above all, the pictures of a bare-chested Putin riding a horse, fishing and climbing trees have launched an avalanche of commentaries about 'Putin's macho personality cult'. This is mostly well observed, since Putin does assert a particular type of traditional masculinity. As Sperling notes, 'While some of Putin's displays of muscles and bravery may have been intended to appeal to the female population, a male politician's "manly" image can also be enhanced by portrayals of attractive young women's support for him.'[52] However, when this is taken as a driver for foreign policy, the links become rather more tenuous. Putin acted decisively in the autumn of 1999 when he launched the second Chechen war and in approving the assault against Yukos in the autumn of 2003, and then in intervening in Ukraine in 2014. It is far-fetched to suggest that these decisions were in some way 'gendered', and to suggest that Russian foreign policy is driven by 'macho' braggadocio is just another way of denigrating what may well have been legitimate concerns (whether they were the right policies or not is another issue). With Surkov's departure from the PA in December 2011 and replacement by the dour Volodin, the macho stunts mostly disappeared, a policy of reticence that continued when Sergei Kirienko took over the management of domestic politics in September 2016. Nevertheless, Putin did emerge as a cultural icon, and inevitably the Kremlin has been concerned to portray certain images of him, notably as a wise, thoughtful and resolute leader.[53] This helps explain his extraordinary and enduring popularity, although his popularity cannot be reduced to PR manipulations.

The typical vagueness of Putin's rhetoric reflects the broader developmental impasse in which the country finds itself. Although the Kremlin spin doctors carefully nurture an image of Putin as decisive and resolute, in the normal course of events, he is cautious and consensual. Factional balance inevitably means that on mundane issues Putin seeks to maintain the broadest consensus. The aim is to ensure that none of the main factions are alienated, while all can acquiesce to the policy. This is a recipe for policy stagnation, although it does avert some of the worst excesses of short-term decision-making governed by the electoral cycle. The Putin system, however, cannot stand outside of its era, and the absence of a deep commitment to any particular programme, other than the general ambition to restore Russian greatness and its status as a great power, means that it can be shaped by prevailing forces. Three key issues are relevant here.

The first deals with the problem of ideology, and in particular the degree to which the Putin system applies neoliberal economic policies. The Putin system eschews grand ideological formulations, but in the end, its pedestal party, UR, explicitly declared itself a conservative party. This was in keeping with the broad social conservatism of the Putin system, rejecting the social liberalism sweeping the West. When it comes to social policy, the administration supported traditional social democratic welfare policies – an extensive welfare state, a state-sponsored pension system (which as the population aged became increasingly stretched) and the provision of public goods such as further and higher education and support for the Russian Academy of Sciences and its regional affiliates. Some of these functions were devolved to the regions, where there was also a crisis due to increased responsibilities without an adequate tax base, except in the dozen resource-rich regions and the big cities. But even Russia was not immune to neoliberal solutions, meaning the marketisation and consumerisation of hitherto freely available public goods. In education, this means that salaries in many cases are tied to performance indicators, while institutions as a whole have to adapt to the stringencies of international league tables and the like. In education, health and other fields, a commercialised sector operates alongside the state-subsidised part. The result has been dubbed 'authoritarian neoliberalism'.[54] This combines heavy-handed political management, with the market penetrating into areas where other rationalities, such as altruism and public service, have traditionally predominated. The outsourcing phenomenon, in which various layers of administration take their cut while those actually delivering the goods see their salaries and employment conditions eroded, began to displace neo-Soviet practices of direct employment and guaranteed conditions. One of Putin's first acts was a new labour law which weakened trade union rights and restricted labour activism.

The second and associated issue is Putin understanding of politics. 'The political' is defined as the agonistic and open-ended debate over issues of public concern. From his very first activities in public administration, Putin demonstrated a proclivity for a technocratic and non-transparent managerial style. This is evident in his work in the St Petersburg mayor's office in the Sobchak years, and his experience of competitive elections was rather painful. He headed the staff for Sobchak's re-election in 1996 and lost out to the challenge from the other vice-mayor, Yakovlev. The experience seems to have traumatised Putin and turned him against elections in which the outcome is not known in advance. Discretion was part of the job descriptions in the various posts he held in the late 1990s in Moscow, notably when he headed the FSB. He took this closed attitude with him when he fought his first presidential campaign in early 2000. Instead of participating in public debates, he preferred to issue missives from on high, notably a campaign article in *Izvestiya*.[55] In the 2012 campaign, Putin issued half a dozen articles on fundamental issues such as nationality, economic or foreign policy. Each represented a fascinating dissection of the issues, but in his typical manner he stayed in control, and the public debate on the issues was very limited and there was little follow-up.

The technocratic style is accompanied by a brisk and businesslike way of dealing with subordinates, officials and citizens. His typical style is to be well informed on any particular issue while issuing *ratio decidendi*, as in the English common law tradition. In other words, instead of parliament and public forums deciding, Putin set himself up as the supreme judge, issuing judgements, leavened by *obiter dicta*, but focused on his personal preferences and inclinations. A large proportion of the population clearly approves of his judgements, but this has nothing to do with 'the political' and clearly undermines the essence of democracy, in which the people are assumed to exercise free choice to decide on who will decide for them (except in the case of referendums, where the decision is direct-acting unless clearly stated to be consultative). Democracy assumed personified forms: Putin was elected directly by the people, and he then acted in the classic democratic manner in judging according to his own conscience about what was in the best interests of Russia. But democracy also entails a certain quality to 'the political', a conversation with and between the people, and it is this quality that is lacking. The system with justification has been called 'post-political'.[56]

The third issue returns us to the paradoxes of the stability system, which has – paradoxically – destabilising effects. This is reminiscent of the Brezhnev years, when mobilisation gave way to stabilisation and then stagnation. The more a regime mechanically tries to impose stability, the more the factors contributing to long-term organic stability are eroded. The conservative-guardianship strategy undermines what in contemporary neo-liberal parlance is known as 'resilience': the ability of a system to withstand shocks and to manage periods of turbulence. The stability system in Russia today reflects Putin's preferences, but these preferences in turn are generated by the profound sociological and political reality of four roughly balanced epistemic-interest groups, none of which is 'hegemonic' but each of which is exploited by Putin for ideas and personnel. The ideology of stability is also a generational issue, with those who endured and lost so much in the transition from communism unwilling to countenance another period of turbulence inevitably generated by proposals for structural reform.

Stasis, or the developmental impasse

There is a profound *stasis* in Russian political and economic development. Stasis is defined as a state of equilibrium or inactivity caused by opposing equal forces. The concept of stasis is more than a synonym for stagnation but contains the potential for a 'sudden interruption of the hectic inertial motion, in a move of reflection and contestation'.[57] As my factional model suggests, the four great factions in contemporary Russia balance each other, and each has a stake in the present system, but none can predominate. The four great 'blocs' have entrenched their position in the polity, but none can establish its hegemony over society as a whole. Each has a sufficient stake in the situation to ensure its loyalty, but fear of defection remains an abiding concern of the power centre. The liberals remain responsible for overall macroeconomic policy, but state capitalist, if not outright corporatist, concerns typically prevail when it comes to industrial policy and support for the state corporations and leading enterprises. The *siloviki* are oriented towards security and in domestic affairs stress the need for the maintenance of Cold War-style controls and in foreign policy have never entirely given up on the Soviet conception of the West as a threatening and dangerous force, and hence are ready once again to take up the cudgels (like their counterparts in the Atlantic system) to renew Cold War policies and practices. The heterogeneous bloc of neo-traditionalists, encompassing monarchists, neo-Stalinist communists, neo-Soviet imperialists and Russian nationalists, are united by little other than their tradition-based reading of Russian exceptionalism. For them, the West represents as much a danger of cultural degradation as it does a security threat. The final group, the Eurasianists, despite their many divisions, are united in their view that there is a fundamental and irreconcilable gulf between 'Romano-Germanic' (as they put it) civilisation of the West and Russia.

This is a position of radical uncertainty, in which any one of these positions could make a break and try to impose hegemony over the others. There is a lot of hectic activity, but 'inertial motion' predominates. This is the key to the Putin system, where the energy is drawn from others while Putinism itself represents an inert centre. Its appeal is precisely as the counter of the untrammelled predominance of one of the substantive factions, where real constituencies and passionate ideologies are to be found. This is anti-politics with a vengeance. Putinism is the negation of this passion and works by limiting the sociological predominance of a single group. Part of Putinism's attraction is that it represents an external limitation on the potential radicalisation of the factions and is indeed in part welcomed by most of the groups as a way of limiting the potential damage that would be caused by the predominance of another group. Just as in international affairs a multipolar system keeps the ambitions of each of the states in check, so too in domestic politics the system of internal factionalism acts as a system of para-constitutional checks and balances. The difference is that in domestic affairs, the system is not anarchic, but there is a force standing above the constellation of individual powers to act as the integrator and suppressor, namely the state. In the Russian context, the dual state means that two operative codes manage factional conflict at the same time, the impartial rule-governed principles of the constitutional state and the arbitrary and selective practices of the regime. There is stasis at three levels: the basic 'social contract' between the state and society, which in the Putin years meant ensuring relatively stable living standards and social security; keeping the various factions in rough balance; and maintaining a relatively stable equilibrium between the two wings of the dual state. In such a construct, there is not much room for radical reform, let alone of a government committed to revolutionising the social order. The Putinite political platform is conservative in both the direct sense of the word and also in its ideological manifestation, aiming to preserve not so much the status quo as the complex political construct that underlies the status quo. The merits of such a system can hardly be presented to the public in political terms, and instead the symbolic level is accentuated, including the notion of Russia as a great power, as the defender of traditional values and, paradoxically, as the defender of the international status quo and international law against the revisionism of the West.

Putin avoids the use of words such as 'reform' and 'modernisation', both of which are drenched in ideological baggage. 'Reform' is what Gorbachev did, and the result, from Putin's perspective, was disastrous. Thus, he was sceptical about those who tried to resurrect the concept and the idea of 'modernisation' in the Medvedev years. Instead, the supreme form of Putin's managerial role is as faction manager. This is a recipe for a politics of consensus, but since no single policy is pursued with consistency and to the full extent of its logical development, it becomes a recipe for policy stagnation. While a breakthrough to a genuinely competitive democratic system is impeded, the consolidation of an outright authoritarian system is also inhibited. The factional model helps explain the character of Putin's centrism. Putin positions himself at the centre of the factional network, and, thus, it is not so much the hierarchical verticality of his position as president that shapes policy but the horizontal structuring of the political field. The so-called vertical of power is blunted by powerful horizontal networks and remains more a metaphor than an accurate representation of how the system really works.[58] Although the centre generates policy initiatives and provide leadership, in domestic politics, any radical departure from centrist positions threatens factional balance and with it the stability of the entire political system. In the United States, a comparable framework operates, in the sense that the constitution has established a system of checks and balances designed to temper extremes but which also makes domestic policy innovation, except in times of crises, exceptionally hard. In both the United States and Russia, the executive has much greater leeway and room for manoeuvre in foreign policy, although in both cases the presidencies usually seek to act within the framework of the domestic consensus. In Russia, perhaps also as in United States, the overall outcome is stasis.

The concept of stasis helps delineate the social roots of the situation, indicating the equilibrium between relatively equal contending forces. Joel Hellman in 1998 identified the 'partial reform equilibrium', where the winners in the early stages of the transition from communism lock in their gains to prevent further reform that could threaten their position.[59] In the 2000s, Putin broke the independent power and authority of the early winners (oligarchs and red directors), notably in the Yukos affair, and created a dual economy where market relations operate in certain sectors while in others a state corporatist model was developed in which market forces are trumped by administrative interventions.[60] As in the political sphere, two orders operate simultaneously, the profit-seeking and the rent-extraction models. These are analogous to what have been described as open-access orders and limited-access orders (see below). It is tension along this spectrum that shapes the current Russian political economy. A complex rent-management system has been created that circulates resources across the population as part of the 'social contract'. Economic stasis is reinforced by political considerations. In an era where the great structuring ideologies of the past have dissolved, political formlessness is filled by an accentuation of identity politics. Fear that identitarianism, in particular, ideas advanced by the nationalist part of the neo-traditionalist bloc would fragment society and intensify antagonisms in public discourse reinforces the regime's justification for its own predominance. Its goal is to pacify social, class and ethnic divisions, while ensuring a modicum of co-optive representation. Pacification, of course, is not the same as resolution. The regime's efforts created a 'stability system' rather than one in which some sort of democratic consensus has been achieved on the basis of law and constitutional regulation.

The prevalence of stasis and stabilisation politics does not mean that there is no change in politics or that the economy has not registered some notable achievements. However, economic growth rates and the structure of the economy as a whole lack the dynamism expected of a country at Russia's level of development (a variant of the World Bank's 'middle income trap'). The tutelary system and the stabilocracy's fears that radical policies could provoke instability through extensive job turnover and unemployment inhibited structural reform. Instead, it maintains elements of the Soviet social contract, whereby basic social welfare, job security and public infrastructure are provided in exchange for constraints on political expression and social contestation. Russia finds itself in a developmental impasse.[61]

The power of the horizontal in domestic affairs tempers the regime's ability to launch radical policy initiatives. The system expends great efforts to maintain its power, while in international affairs the regime also seeks to reproduce a horizontal structure to international politics through multipolarity and the creation of an anti-hegemonic alignment. In domestic politics, stasis is maintained by the balance between the epistemic-interest blocs described above, and this generates an inherent pluralism in which no developmental programme can become hegemonic. Zweynert and Boldyrev describe the 'relative failure of Russia's transition' as a 'failure of ideas', although it was not so much an ideational failure as the inability of any one to become hegemonic. As they argue, 'the main problem lies in the fact that elites still seem to be vacillating between conflicting patterns of thought'.[62] They are right to note the parallels with the Brezhnev years, with analysts and scholars agreeing that 'fundamental change is needed to prevent a further breakdown of the Russian economy', but the entrenched elite structure, as in the 1960s' and 1970s' Soviet Union, means the leadership groups are 'not interested in fundamental change which would endanger their power positions and the rents based on these'.[63] They characterise post-Soviet Russian debates about economic reform as trapped by tensions between 'two opposing camps, liberals and "*gosudarstvenniki*"', the statists.[64] In fact, there are more players, and each of the four blocs has more liberal elements and those who believe in an activist state. Nevertheless, they are right to argue that overwhelmingly the various factions regard modernisation as a means to an end and not an end in itself; thus, Russian debates have an instrumental character that undermines the possibility of a coherent policy outcome.[65] While there may be a consensus on the need for change, there is no agreement on the necessary changes.

4 POLITICS AND THE THIRD STATE

Rising commodity prices in the 2000s allowed Russia to strengthen its positions. Putin restored the autonomy of the state, but within the state, the regime centred on his personal networks became relatively independent of the constraints of the constitutional order. The dissatisfaction that Yeltsin had articulated earlier now became the predominant mode of interaction with the West. The post-Cold War international order did not suit Russia, but its attempts to revise it were inchoate and inconsistent. Russia had a weak material basis to sustain its ambition to become a separate power in the multipolar international system. At home, although Medvedev may not have achieved much, he nevertheless defined an intra-systemic alternative and indicated an evolutionary path away from managed democracy and towards a more open and competitive system. The 24 September 2011 *rokirovka* (swap or castling move) between Putin and Medvedev delivered a shock to elites and the political society as a whole. The ensuing mass protest exposed not only the vulnerability of the regime but also its ability to recover.

Regime reset

Medvedev's team at INSOR issued a range of papers and ideas about how to make the system more competitive and open. Medvedev and Putin openly clashed over the West's intervention in Libya in 2011, but even then some in the elite believed that Medvedev could run for a second term. Gleb Pavlovsky, Igor Jurgens and even, apparently, the arch-manipulator, Surkov, aligned with the Medvedev second-term project despite the threat that this could have on their careers. This was the first indication of intra-elite splits that could lead to regime change. However, Putin appears to have come under pressure from the guardianship-security bloc to foreclose what they feared was Medvedev's excessive liberalism at home, neo-Gorbachevite complaisance abroad and lack of political gravitas. This group was apparently spearheaded (as in 2007–8) by Igor Sechin, a deputy head of the PA to 2008 and then a deputy prime minister, who warned Putin of the dangerous consequences of a potential second perestroika. The original had reformed the Soviet system out of existence, and the 'securocrats' were intent on preventing this happening again. On a famous fishing trip to Siberia in August 2011, Putin allegedly told Medvedev that he planned to return to the presidency. By all accounts, Medvedev bargained hard and in the end was assured that if he acquiesced, then he could become prime minister and hold this post until the end of Putin's third presidential term. This is what was announced in brutal terms on 24 September; and to add insult to injury, Medvedev declared that this is what had been decided when Medvedev assumed the presidency in 2008. The managed and manipulative character of the system was laid bare.

This was the period of the 'Arab Spring', with regime change in Tunisia, Egypt, Libya, Yemen, and the disturbances in Syria that burgeoned into outright civil war. There was also a spirit of protest in the air that betokened what some called a 'Russian spring'. The white ribbon became the symbol of aspirations for a more open and law-bound system, in which corruption would be exposed, the arbitrariness of the regime would be constrained and the pressure on businesses from administrative bodies (as well as corrupt law enforcement agencies) would ease. Even some officials took to wearing the ribbon as a sign of a nascent intra-elite split between those aligned with the aspirations vested in the Medvedev programme of moderate reform (if not in the man himself) and the partisans of the restoration of Putinite order and stability. There were also signs that the population was restive, with Putin openly booed at a sporting event and some leading cultural figures speaking out in favour of change. The plan by Gazprom to build a giant skyscraper in the centre of St Petersburg mobilised broad opposition, a struggle that was ultimately successful. The Lakhta Centre in the end was built on the city's north-western outskirts, and at 462 meters (1516 feet) became Europe's tallest building.

Even before the Duma election on 4 December, the country was stirring. In the event, clumsy mismanagement and the widespread fraud and ballot stuffing provoked the largest political protests of Putin's time in office.[1] The cack-handed *rokirovka* followed by heavy-handed electoral interventions when political society was demanding free and fair elections brought tens of thousands onto the streets. Some 60,000 took part in the demonstration in Bolotnaya Square on 10 December and up to 120,000 on Sakharov Prospekt on 24 December. The 'democratic opposition' in Russia has exhibited a persistent inability to unite, but the protests brought together disparate movements allied in their condemnation of electoral fraud. However, when it came to advancing a programme of substantial political change, other than 'down with Putin' and 'for fair elections', they were divided between liberal, statist populist and nationalist positions. The regime quickly regained the initiative, and already in his final state-of-the-nation speech on 22 December, Medvedev outlined a programme of political reform, including the restoration of gubernatorial elections and changes to the party and electoral systems.[2] These reforms were implemented in the following year with various modifications.

The unprecedented political mobilisation provoked a combination of concessions and coercion accompanied by changes to the regime itself. Putin's return to the presidency proved a watershed moment in Russian political development. On the one side, contentious politics returned with a vengeance, although that particular wave of mobilisation soon ebbed. On the other side, the regime sought new forms of legitimacy, and to this end a number of stratagems were adopted. First, politics underwent a 'cultural turn', with a greater emphasis on identity issues and conservative social motifs. It was in this period that the Duma adopted a range of repressive and socially conservative legislation, including the ban in 2013 on homosexual propaganda among minors. Although homosexuality remains legal and a lively gay scene continues, the legislation encouraged homophobic attitudes. Discussions of LGBT issues tend to impose Western temporalities on Russian problems, and as Dan Healey notes in his sophisticated study of Russian homophobia, 'our own histories cannot dictate pathways to progress elsewhere'.[3] This cannot disguise the intolerance manifested by the neo-traditionalist part of the Putinite elite, reflected in the condemnation of the social liberalism of the West, including the tired trope of 'gayropa'. A law protecting the dignity of religious feeling was also adopted, apparently at the prompting of the Russian Orthodox Church. This was the period when parliament acted as a 'crazy printing press', rushing out ill-considered and intolerant laws, not all sponsored by the Kremlin but reflecting the empowered conservative sentiments of the assembly.

Second, the concessions included a range of political reforms, which can be described as a 'regime reset' rather than democratisation. Voting was made, literally, more transparent with the installation of cameras in polling stations and the introduction of clear plastic ballot boxes, but this was balanced by the introduction of various 'filters' for the nomination of candidates. The political reforms outlined by Medvedev were largely implemented, including the restoration of gubernatorial elections, the return of a dual election system to select the 450 members of the State Duma: half by first-past-the post constituency elections and half by proportional PLs. This was the electoral system in operation until 2003, but the 2007 and 2011 Duma elections had been purely proportional. It now became easier to register a new political party, and existing ones had less stringent requirements imposed on them in terms of minimum membership requirements. Legislation was changed to make it easier for parties to register for elections. Typical of Putinite statecraft, what was given with one hand was taken away with the other. Tight requirements were imposed on potential gubernatorial candidates, including what came to be called the 'presidential filter' (the ultimate power of the president to choose who could run) as well as the 'municipal filter', the requirement introduced in 2012 for candidates for regional and local leadership posts to be backed by between 5 and 10 per cent of legislators.

The changes were hedged in with limitations and restrictions that blunted their democratising character. The new Kremlin overseer of political matters, Volodin, sought to introduce greater competition into a managed political system as part of his relegitimation strategy. These goals were obviously incompatible yet reflected the Kremlin view that old methods of political management had become counterproductive. The regime was still out to win, but with less blunt – and, thus, delegitimising – instruments. The fear of being swept from office through some sort of popular movement prompted concessions, although accompanied by new forms of control. This was deconcentration rather than liberalisation. The veto powers of the president were regularly exercised to exclude potential challengers. The notable exception was allowing the anti-corruption campaigner and one of the leaders of the 2011–12 protests, Navalny, to stand in the Moscow mayoral election in September 2013. By allowing Navalny to run (by helping him pass the 'municipal filter'), the incumbent, Sergei Sobyanin, sought to endow his victory with greater legitimacy. In the event, Navalny fought a vigorous campaign as the candidate of the Republican Party of Russia-Party of People's Freedom (Parnas) coalition. He applied an innovative crowdfunding and poster strategy, and won an astonishing 27.24 per cent of the vote.

The push for more competition saw the CPRF candidate, Sergei Levchenko, win the gubernatorial election in Irkutsk in September 2015, the first competitive opposition victory since the return of gubernatorial elections, and in Orël, the incumbent CPRF governor, Vadim Potomsky, was re-elected by a large margin in September 2014. Between 2012 and 2014, oppositionists won mayoral elections in a number of cities. In Ekaterinburg in September 2013, Evgeny Roizman, a prominent campaigner against corrupt police and the illegal drug trade, and a practitioner of controversial drug rehabilitation programmes, won the mayoral contest running on Mikhail Prokhorov's Civic Platform ticket. In April 2014, the CPRF candidate Anatoly Lokot became mayor of Novosibirsk, Evgeny Urlashov won in Yaroslavl and Irina Shirshina in Petrozavodsk. In Pskov, the journalist and leading Yabloko member Lev Schlosberg won a seat to the regional legislature in December 2011 before he was thrown out in September 2015 by a court and his fellow deputies. Schlosberg became famous after the publication of a letter on 25 August 2014 about the deaths of soldiers in the 76th Guards Airborne Division, suspected of engagement in the war in the Donbas. Yabloko won 8.5 per cent of the seats in the Pskov City Duma election in July 2017. The patriotic upsurge following the transfer of Crimea (the so-called *Krym Nash* – Crimea Is Ours – movement) did not take the form of ethnic Russian nationalist mobilisation, and at the local level, social and political issues predominated.

The regime reset was limited but serious and provided more opportunity for organised oppositional activity. However, even the modest deconcentration was derailed by the intensification of conflict with the West. The reform of municipal administration passed in May 2014 disempowered local government bodies. Elected mayors were replaced by city managers, chosen by UR-dominated city legislatures with the process overseen by regional governors.[4] In practice, concessions and exceptions were allowed, with Roizman remaining mayor of Ekaterinburg, although he was disqualified from running as the Yabloko nominee for governor in September 2017 because he failed to pass the municipal filter. The incumbent governor, Evgeny Kuivashev, won re-election. This was a typical case in which strong candidates are not allowed to register. Roizman supported Navalny's call for a boycott of the March 2018 presidential election, arguing, 'These are not elections. This is deception of voters and role-playing games. I think honest people should not take part in this. These elections need to be boycotted.'[5] At the governor's bidding, the regional legislature in April 2018 abolished mayoral elections, and Roizman resigned in protest. Even incumbent oppositionists were forced out of office. Soon after announcing that he would run for governor, Urlashov in Yaroslavl was accused of corruption and left office in July 2013, and in August 2016, he was given an extraordinarily harsh twelve-and-a-half-year prison sentence. Shirshina was forced out in December 2015, although she continued to fight against the heavy-handed actions of the governor of Karelia, Alexander Khudilainen. By mid-2018, what had earlier been the norm now became the exception, and only eight of Russia's regional capitals retained directly elected mayors.

The regime tried to find a way out of the political and developmental impasse by introducing elements of competition into a fundamentally uncompetitive system. This is why Navalny was allowed to run and why some other opposition figures won posts in regional mayoral elections. The events in Ukraine, however, stifled the stirrings of intra-systemic political reform. The spectacle of a legitimately elected (although deeply corrupt) president being chased out of office, with Western incitement, alarmed the Kremlin. Nevertheless, the regime reset was not entirely dead, and Volodin sought to make the September 2016 Duma election more competitive and transparent than the one in 2011. The goal was still to win a majority for UR but with less fraud and ballot-rigging. The task set for regional leaderships was to ensure the victory of regime representatives, but by legal means, to prevent another popular mobilisation on the scale of the earlier electoral cycle. In the event, the return to the dual electoral system paid handsome dividends. UR won only 54.2 per cent of the PL vote (giving it 140 seats), but in the single-member districts it won an overwhelming 202 seats, giving it a constitutional majority with 76 per cent of the seats, a total of 343 UR deputies (see Table 4.1). The CPRF ended up with only 42 deputies, the LDPR with 39 and Just Russia (JR) with 23. The representation threshold had been reduced from 7 to 5 percent, but once again none of the liberal parties came close, with Yabloko winning only 2 per cent, while

Table 4.1 State Duma election, 18 September 2016

Party	PL vote% (total vote)	PL seats	Single-member districts (SMDs)	Total% (number)
United Russia (UR)	54.20 (28,527,828)	140	203	76% (343)
Communist Party of the Russian Federation (CPRF)	13.34 (7,019,752)	35	7 (no UR candidate in 3 SMDs)	9% (42)
Liberal Democratic Party of Russia (LDPR)	13.14 (6,917,063)	34	5 (no UR candidate in all of them)	9% (39)
Just Russia (Spravedlivaya Rossiya, JR)	6.22 (3,275,053)	16	7 (no UR candidate in all of them)	5% (23)
Sub-Total		225	222	447
5% Threshold				
Communist Party Communists of Russia	2.27 (1,192,595)	–	–	–
Yabloko	1.99 (1,051,335)	–	–	–
Russian Party of Pensioners for Justice	1.73 (910,848)	–	–	–
Rodina	1.51 (792,226)	–	1 (no UR candidate in SMD)	1
Party of Growth (Partiya Rosta)	1.29 (679,030)	–	–	–

Party	PL vote% (total vote)	PL seats	Single-member districts (SMDs)	Total% (number)
Russian Ecological Party 'Greens'	0.76 (399,429)	–	–	–
Parnas (Party of People's Freedom)	0.73 (384,675)	–	–	–
Patriots of Russia	0.59 (310,015)	–	–	–
Civic Platform (Grazhdanskaya Platforma)	0.22 (115,433)	–	1 (no UR candidate in SMD)	1
Civic Force (Grazhdanskaya Sila)	0.14 (73,971)	–	–	–
Independents	–	–	1 (no UR candidate in SMD)	1 (joined UR faction)
Total electorate	110,061,200			
Total vote	52,631,849 (Valid ballot papers 51,649,253; invalid 982,596)			
Turnout	47.8			
TOTAL	**100**	**225**	**216**	

Source: Central Electoral Commission:
For the list of deputies elected, see http://www.cikrf.ru/law/decree_of_cec/2016/09/23/56-541-7.html. For overall results, see http://www.vybory.izbirkom.ru/region/region/izbirkom?action=show&root=1&tvd=100100067795854&vrn=100100067795849&region=0&global=1&sub_region=0&prver=0&pronetvd=0&vibid=100100067795854&type=233.

Parnas gained less than 1 per cent. The sheer scale of the regime's victory appeared to take it by surprise and undermined its attempts to make elections look fairer and more legitimate. The turnout of only 48 per cent was the lowest of any national election in the post-communist years and eroded the legitimacy of the result.

Gubernatorial elections were restored in 2012, but the various filters meant that the Kremlin remained the decisive voice. The criteria for appointment combined political characteristics, above all loyalty to the regime, as well as administrative competence in delivering political and economic results. A new cycle in gubernatorial appointments began in mid-2017, with changes in fourteen regions in the run-up to the presidential election in March 2018. Most were young technocrats, reflecting a desire by the Kremlin to rejuvenate the system from within. This was not enough to address the deep-seated problems of regime power.

The third state and meta-corruption

The gulf between the visible part of politics and various subterranean processes became apparent from the start of Yeltsin's rule. The 'democratic' revolution of 1991 was quickly captured by the Yeltsin group, which despite, or even because of, its reformist agenda soon became transformed into a 'regime' system of manipulative politics, allied with oligarchs. In addition to the dual state described earlier, there is a subterranean 'deep state', operating according to a separate behavioural code. The journalist Maxim Trudolyubov argues that there are two states in Russia today, the 'ordinary' state and the private, invisible state. He likens the situation to that under Ivan the Terrible, the first Tsar of Russia from 1547 to 1584, when the 'outside' or 'separate' system stemmed from the *oprichnina*, a militarised state outside the ordinary, *zemshchina* state.[6] The *oprichnina*, with its dreaded *oprichniki*, was a militarised formation riding black horses and wearing black uniforms that terrorised the population between 1565 and 1572, receiving wealth and loyalty for service to the tsar. The analogy works only as a metaphor for contemporary Russia. In fact, changes in criminal law sharply reduced the number of prisoners, with the number dropping by 200,000 between 2000 and 2018 to 484,000. In the seven years from 2011, ninety-three prisons were closed and the others reorganised.[7]

Dualism undermines the autonomy of the institutions of the constitutional state and the practices of competitive open politics, but in its Putinite formulation it also articulates an alternative rationality which aspires to transcend the limitations of classic Western practices of capitalist democracy. Para-constitutionalism and its associated parapolitics were already evident in the Yeltsin period through various forms of institutional duplication, although it became more explicit as an instrument of political management in the Putin years. More specifically, the power system that took over the democratic revolution quickly developed needs of its own. Already in the 1990s, the security apparatus, above all the FSB, began to 'feed off the land', in a manner reminiscent of the ancient custom of *kormlenie*, or feeding (tax farming), whereby officials on low salaries extorted resources from the population over which they governed.[8] A quasi-feudal relationship between business and power had taken shape long before Putin came to power.[9] Although he changed the terms of the relationship between the state and the top oligarchs, he inserted himself into the system and was unable, or unwilling, to challenge the underlying archaic culture of power and property driven by codes of loyalty and motives of personal profit. In fact, the security apparatus was emboldened by Putin's accession and considered itself 'the new nobility'.[10]

One of Putin's first moves was to defang the oligarchs and in effect to block their development into an independent bourgeoisie (Khodorkovsky's ambition). Instead, he turned them into a type of service class. In the new 'social contract' imposed at a famous meeting in July 2000, business leaders could keep their wealth, but they were to desist from active intervention into politics and their resources were to be at the service of the state. This is an example of the neo-patrimonial approach, where property and power merge. Early examples of oligarchs who thrived in the new dispensation include Roman Abramovich and Oleg Deripaska, while a large category had always kept out of politics and continued to do so, notably Vagit Alekperov at the head of Lukoil and Alexei Mordashov of Metallinvest, and various other steelmakers. However, in Putin's third term, even loyal servants of the state could be threatened, as Vladimir Yevtushnkov, the head of the AFK Sistema investment conglomerate, discovered when his interests apparently ran athwart those of Sechin, by now head of the largely state-owned Rosneft oil company and historically one of Putin's closest confidants. One of the beneficiaries of the new dispensation was Arkady Rotenberg, one of Putin's childhood friends, who developed the Stroigazmontazh (SGM) construction conglomerate focusing on gas pipelines and electrical power supply cables. His links with Putin served him well but not so much because of corruption – defined as stealing without doing anything – but as part of the system in which companies are granted contracts in a non-competitive manner because they will actually deliver. Rotenburg's company completed some major infrastructural projects before being granted the contract to build the Kerch Strait Bridge from Russia to Crimea, a massive and complex engineering challenge. The project was undoubtedly controversial, but the combined road and rail link was completed on time by early 2019.[11]

Putin is a centrist, balancing the various factions to ensure that they all have a stake in the system but none can dominate. In this context, the idea that 'Putin's cronies' hold some sort of hold over him is mistaken, and 'even Putin's friends cannot always influence decisions'.[12] Putin is also at the centre of another model, balancing the competing demands of the rent consumers (whose top level has been identified by US-sanctioning bodies as a 'kleptocracy'), industrialists, the energy sector and other interest groups. The Soviet legacy of a managed economy has been reproduced in the form of a vast rent management system based on hydrocarbon finances, running through an extended capillary system of dependencies.[13] The whole population gains, but the ruling elite spawned out of the debris of the Soviet system benefits incommensurately. The rent management system insulates itself from popular control and public accountability, and instead the logic of mutual dependency trumps the logic of democracy. This is a distribution system that reinforces the power of the distributor.[14] Kordonsky goes so far as to argue that the whole mechanism, notably in its regional dimension, has reproduced some sort of neo-feudal system.[15] This long predates the present era, but 'Putin, having come from it himself … failed to transcend it'.[16] This is not classic patrimonialism, where political authority and property ownership are entwined and effectively become the same, but a more sophisticated neo-patrimonial system, in which both politics and property are elements in the bargaining between factions and conflicting systemic imperatives. For Putin, development and modernisation remain priorities (derived from the rationality of a developmental constitutional state), but this is tempered by the logic of rent extraction associated with the administrative system. The administrative regime thus also has two faces – the developmental and the exploitative.

The dual state inevitably generates continuous dissonance between its two operative principles, the constitutional and administrative, but in conditions where there are permanent warring factions, this disjunction between principle and practice creates an aporia that ruthless operators exploit. Factional balancing encourages business magnates, ministers and security officials to jostle for access to the leader, but where normal constitutional rules are suspended, this becomes a struggle for access to 'the body' to shape policy as much as to gain property and power. This exposes a dimension that requires further elaboration. This is the socio-economic degradation of the regime-state into various forms of criminality and corruption. The power of the regime (*vlast'*) becomes in certain respects the power of *avtoritety*, the godfathers in the mafia tradition. As Mark Galeotti demonstrates, already in the late Soviet years the *vory v zakone* (thieves in law), the criminal subculture forged in the Stalinist Gulag, had effectively become a 'super mafia', a law unto themselves. In conditions of state weakness in the 1990s, they filled the vacuum with their own codes.[17] Putin pushed back against the *vory*, jailing some of the more prominent ones who challenged the authority of the renascent Putinite state (often by using strong-arm tactics, as in the struggle against the Vladimir Barsukov [Kumarin] Tambov gang in St Petersburg), while incorporating others as economic actors, sometimes working in conjunction with the law enforcement and security establishment. In the process, as Galeotti notes, the boundaries between the underworld and the 'upperworld' became blurred, and it is not clear where the state ends and the criminal underworld begins. A law adopted in March 2019 finally took on this state within a state, making it a crime with harsh penalties to 'hold a top position in a criminal hierarchy'. The simple fact of leading a criminal organisation was enough to convict a crime boss.[18] The super mafia were no longer untouchable.

Thus, the administrative regime and the constitutional state are joined by a third force, which in Italy, Turkey and some other countries is called the 'deep state'. This is a subterranean nexus of bureaucratic power, security services and various types of criminal organisations. In Russia, this dense network of corrupt relationships is variously called 'the mafiya' or some similar designation (such as *vory*), and it is assumed to shape foreign as well as domestic policy.[19] The exit from communism endowed Russia with powerful organised criminal groups (OCGs), who ran rampant in the 1990s. In the Putin era, the most independent and ambitious were destroyed (notably the Tambov gang), while the rest adapted to a new *modus vivendi* with the regime. This does not make Russia a mafia state, as some of the more lurid accounts would have it;[20] but the 'mafia' is part of the complex ecosystem of the Putinite polity. In turn, Russian financial flows became part of the global network of offshores and money-laundering operations.[21] Some of this was legitimate capital looking for a safe haven abroad (capital flight), while the rest was hot money looking to be laundered. Various exposés, notably the Panama Papers of the Mossack Fonseca law firm in 2015 and the Organised Crime and Corruption Reporting Project (OCCRP), revealed how financial 'laundromats' worked.

Russia's economic system is regulated by formal legal relationships, but these are complemented by a network of informal institutions (encompassing norms and informal practices).[22] Business people are vulnerable to officials and competitors acting informally to achieve personal benefits, forcing businesses to adopt a range of defensive practices. The business environment is hostile, but businesses can thrive as long as they take into account the potential predatory behaviour of officials.[23] In normal circumstances, the courts can be used to adjudicate disputes, and in many cases justice can be achieved.[24] Russian law, like the state, is dualistic, with a persistent tension between the law as it is and the law as it should be.[25] This was one of the central concerns of Medvedev during his presidency, and some of the worst abuses by predators of the judicial system were tempered, but ultimately no structural change was achieved. The arbitrariness of the force structures could not be restrained in the absence of a systemic overhaul. Businesses and their legal representatives are forced to exploit divisions between competing groups, finding protection with one against the predation of the other. Putin tolerates the situation not so much because he was a *silovik* himself (despite his professional background in the security system, Putin is a pragmatist exploiting the ideological-interest divisions in society to maintain his supremacy) but because the *siloviki* remain an important constituency and provide a power resource that no other group can.[26]

This third state reaches into the very heart of government and is characterised by two types of corruption. The *venal* sort is focused on classic bribe-taking and bribe-giving, donated in payment for services that are nominally free but which assume a pecuniary character in a system where controls are weak, the public ethos underdeveloped, wages low and the opportunities for rent extraction rife. The scale of this of course is unknown but is reflected in Transparency International's Corruption Perceptions Index (CPI) on which Russia has always scored very low. In the CPI for 2018, Russia continued its downward trend and found itself ranked 138th, below Ukraine in 120th place but above Bangladesh and Nigeria.[27] Whatever the flaws in the methodology (based on perceptions and not empirical data), the result is far from the position in which a highly developed country should find itself. Corruption is widespread and persistent, and according to a recent study is a holdover from the 'Tsarist feudal system and Soviet social order'.[28] In his February 2008 annual press conference, Putin identified corruption as one of the scourges of the country, and Medvedev made the struggle against it one of the cornerstones of his presidency. The problem ran deeper than the bribery of officials but included the coercive and improper use of the judicial and regulatory system against businesses, and Medvedev adopted various measures to protect entrepreneurs, including removing some of the powers of the courts to impose harsh sentences and to reduce the opportunities for regulatory agencies to abuse their position. Medvedev also banned government officials simultaneously serving as directors on the boards of state-owned companies, a move reversed by Putin on his return to the presidency in 2012. Putin had other priorities, including control over officialdom. His 'deoffshorisation' campaign forced bureaucrats and politicians to declare foreign property and bank accounts, and included measures to encourage the repatriation of assets. The campaign against venal corruption was continued. According to the prosecutor general, between 2015 and 2017, corruption cost Russia some $2.5 billion, and in that period 122,000 corruption-related crimes were registered, leading to 45,000 convictions, of whom 4,500 were law-enforcement staff, 400 were politicians and 3,000 were officials.[29] These figures included some oppositional politicians falsely accused of criminal offences, with Navalny often considered one of them as well as some mayors and regional leaders.

There is a second form which I call *meta-corruption*, when the autonomy of the political system is eroded and administration is placed at the service of criminal and inappropriate activities, undermining the independence of the courts and the impartial management of social processes. The judicial system becomes degraded as the state security agencies and the courts merge. Meta-corruption describes the combination of political power and economic interests outside of the bounds of law and constitutional constraints. It describes systemic corruption in a neo-patrimonial system where property rights cannot be adequately defended and, thus, become prey to powerful political or economic interests.[30] This gives rise to raiding (*reiderstvo*), the attack on the property of others by officials, corrupt law-enforcement officers, collusive courts or business rivals working with some of the previous categories.[31] According to Alexander Lukin, the problem of corruption stems from the 'mentality' of the regime, believing that it has a sacred mission to 'save' Russia from disintegration and collapse, and 'saving the country is hard work and so those who carry it out deserve more than other citizens'.[32] This also helps explain the enormous pay differentials between administrative officials, such as hospital directors, and rank-and-file workers (a pervasive feature of neoliberal capitalism). When it comes to politics, the 'rent managers' believe they deserve a generous share of the rents. This endows Russia with the archaic feel of a traditional estate-based society, with two-thirds of the population 'outside of the market and modernity because it is immersed in an economy that is controlled by the state and based on unearned income'.[33] The 5 per cent of the population that distributes the rent takes a generous cut, while two-thirds are dependent in one way or another on the state for their income (earned and unearned), but only 15 per cent are engaged in business or commerce.[34]

The problem of 'administrative rents', as the extortion of bribes and other kickbacks to various inspection officials and corrupt bureaucrats is known, is only one aspect of the persistent pressure on businesses, small and large. Property rights cannot be secure when the rule of law remains weak and the courts can be suborned by powerful political figures.[35] This was recognised by Putin in his annual address to the Federal Assembly on 3 December 2015 when he described the way that business people are persecuted by the courts:

> I would like to cite some figures supplied by one of our business associations. During 2014, the investigative authorities opened nearly 200,000 cases on so-called economic crimes. But only 46,000 of 200,000 cases were actually taken to court, and 15,000 cases were thrown out during the hearings. Simple maths suggests that only 15 percent of all cases ended with a conviction. At the same time, the vast majority, over 80 percent, or specifically, 83 percent of entrepreneurs who faced criminal charges fully or partially lost their business – they got harassed, intimidated, robbed and then released. This certainly isn't what we need in terms of a business climate. This is actually the opposite, the direct destruction of the business climate. I ask the investigative authorities and the prosecutor's office to pay special attention to this.[36]

This was an astonishing admission by the leader of a country who had been its head for so long. He repeated the complaint in his 20 February 2019 address, suggesting that the situation has not improved. The courts almost always sympathise with the prosecutors, with only 0.36 per cent of criminal cases in 2016 ending in acquittal. While there are reckoned to be about 300 political prisoners in Russia today, tens of thousands of business people sit behind bars. The mass abuse of criminal law against business people is now openly admitted.

In his recent study of the phenomenon of raiding, Philip Hanson notes, '*Reiderstvo* means the acquisition of business assets by means that involve manipulation and distortion of the law, albeit often with the active involvement of law-enforcement officers and the courts.' The implication is that this involvement is 'corrupt'. He describes a characteristic case:

> A typical story is that of a businessman who is charged with an 'economic crime', and who is arrested and put in pre-trial detention or at least faces the threat of pre-trial detention. The case may or may not go to trial, but one of two outcomes is likely: a deal is struck, the assets sought by the raider are handed over and the accused is released; or the accused goes to prison and the assets are acquired by the raider while the victim is, for practical purposes, out of action. It appears that only state-controlled entities and companies controlled by close associates of the leadership are safe from this.[37]

As the lawyer and independent scholar Vladimir Pastukhov put it, 'The FSB can dabble in any business it likes, but relies on the police to do the footwork. Serious police reform is therefore impossible if the masters are left alone.'[38] In another study, he argues that Putin did not eliminate arbitrariness but gave it 'a more or less organised character'.[39]

The security forces have a special role, but even their illicit political and economic activities are balanced by other features of the complex organism that is the Russian power system. Unable to act as a state within the state, they operate as a sub-faction within the regime. Although Russia is a rent-based distribution system, this does not necessarily make Russia a rentier state – where the ruling group exists to extract value from the predominant commodity and the financial system with which it is associated. In the neo-patrimonial system, the state remains the largest employer not just in public services but also in the economy, where bonds of mutual self-interest generate patterns of loyalty and dependence, accompanied by the expansion of the semi-authoritarian political sphere based on a dependent middle class and a crypto-bourgeoisie dependent on the state for its survival. In this hybrid system, the elite are allowed to enrich themselves, but the methods used to gain wealth are in turn a stick used to discipline the elite and to ensure their loyalty. As for business leaders, to survive, they become 'stoligarchs' – state oligarchs. The small group of stoligarchs, typically the heads of state-owned companies, control around a fifth of Russian GDP. They include Arkady Rotenberg, the head of Stroigazmontazh, Gennady Timchenko at the top of Gunvor and Novatek, Sechin at Rosneft and Alexei Miller at the head of Gazprom. Most of these have a personal relationship with Putin going back to his St Petersburg days.[40] Putin tamed the nascent bourgeoisie and swashbucklers of the 1990s, but his model of state oligarchs also provoked widespread resentment. The business leaders of the Putin era have to deliver certain public goods as the fee for their enrichment, but this does not mean that their power is not resented.

The *siloviki*, the security services and their allies, have a special place in this story. While their power to shape the regime is exaggerated (they are after all only one of the four major factions in contemporary Russia), they remain a powerful force. Masha Gessen argues that Putin was the spearhead of a group of former security officials who took control of Russia. For Gessen, Putin came to power with a conscious plan to install some sort of dictatorship, a view that ignores any complicating details such as policy conflicts over the economy or external relations and assumes some sort of perfect state of governability.[41] Karen Dawisha presents all the publicly available material on the various businesses and enterprises Putin and his associates have been involved with since the early stages of his career. The story begins with the collapse of the Soviet Union and the attempt by CPSU to prepare for the loss of its monopoly of power by shifting resources abroad and underground, the so-called Party gold. Dawisha traces the story of the alleged hoard and argues that this shift of resources to banks and other institutions outside the Soviet Union really did take place.[42] These are the resources drawn on later by the security apparatus to consolidate its alleged hold on the nascent capitalist economy. Felshtinsky and Pribylovsky eloquently describe the rise of various security-force factions, including the way that the Korzhakov faction provoked the first Chechen war. Putin was appointed head of the FSB on 25 July 1998 to reform the body and not simply as their emissary in the power system.[43] In other words, even in their sensationalist account, a political level remains outside the deep state, which retains decisional autonomy. This is also reflected in the account of the 'new nobility' by Soldatov and Borogan, in which they note, 'Putin opened the door to many dozens of security service agents to move up in the main institutions of the country, perhaps hoping that they would prove a vanguard of stability and order. But once they had tasted the benefits, agents began to struggle amongst themselves for the spoils.'[44] There is no unity of purpose in Russia's third state, and instead a mix of venal- and meta-corruption erodes the quality of governance.

Putin came to power in 2000 promising to strengthen the state, but in the end, the state remained brittle and undeveloped, while the administrative regime consolidated its hold over the constitutional state and society. The neo-patrimonial order brought institutions and political processes under the tutelage of the administrative regime. However, the power system was susceptible to the very forces on which it based its power and to subversion by its own meta-corruption. The old structure of oligarch power at least had the virtue of transparency in its venal corruption, but this was dismantled by Putin and a much more complex and opaque system of meta-corruption installed. The interpenetration of economic and political power means that the boundary between the two is constantly shifting and arbitrary. Raiding is a symptom of this instability, with prosecutions to order and the selective exercise of coercive power stifling the development of an entrepreneurial culture and undermining the development of the economy as a whole. The stability system, as in the Soviet Union, seeks to constrain and control the pathological effects of its own behaviour, but the failure to move away from 'manual control' prevents the emergence of a more self-regulating organic and law-based system. The mechanical approach creates an order that is brittle and susceptible to an escalating breakdown. Dualism is in danger of degenerating into a triple system in which the merger of power and property jeopardises the viability of the system as a whole.[45] Venal corruption in an uncontrolled triple state is in danger of metastising into meta-corruption and the decline of order in its entirety.

The third state and micro-factionalism

The four ideational-interest groups – the liberals, the *siloviki*, the neo-traditionalists and the Eurasianists – structure the political landscape of the country and provide contrasting understandings of Russian national identity and its place in the world. The four groups are abstract representations of what is a complicated and contradictory reality, and each is divided within itself. Given the disparate nature of the groups, the divisions within each operate differently. The liberals engage in debates on economic and foreign policy, as well as discussing the best way to shift towards genuine constitutionalism and more competitive politics. The neo-traditionalists pick their favoured version of the past, which they then project as a possible future. The various trends of Eurasianism enjoy a rare unity in believing that Russia's destiny ultimately lies in the East and that attempts to become European have only undermined the country's unique civilisation while bringing humiliation and an almost permanent regime of sanctions. As for the *siloviki*, the military on the whole keeps out of factional conflicts (other than engaging in classic departmental demands for greater resources and investment), while the security services stress their unique mission to defend the country, even if that means limiting societal freedoms.

The security agencies have been racked by interminable conflicts. The Soviet-era struggle between the KGB (now FSB) and the Ministry of the Interior (the MVD) has been reproduced in new forms, now without the watchful eye of the Politburo. The tension is often provoked by the intersection of the struggle for power and property. This was the case with the Yukos affair, when one of the putative leaders of the 'guardianship' faction resolved not only to destroy what was perceived to be the impertinent political status claimed by the last significant independent oligarch, Khodorkovsky, but also to take over his oil company. Khodorkovsky was arrested in October 2003, and Yukos was hit by escalating tax demands that brought the company to its knees. The appropriation of Yukos assets laid the foundation for the state-owned Rosneft to become Russia's largest oil company and in due course one of the world's top oil majors. Sechin appears to have masterminded the whole operation. In mid-2004, he became head of Rosneft's board of directors (a classic case of the mixing of politics and business), and over the years he steadily built up his power. During the Medvedev presidency, he followed Putin into government and became a deputy prime minister. Soon after Putin's return to the presidency in 2012, Sechin became the managing director of Rosneft, a post he retains to this day. When one day the archives are opened and we discover the inner workings of the Putin elite, we may well discover that the history of the period will have to be rewritten in terms of Sechin's activities and ambitions.[46]

As for the FSB, its Directorates, as in the Soviet period, collect *kompromat* (compromising materials) on federal and regional officials through a network of informants and phone tapping. In fact, the security apparatus acts as a second *vertikal* of power, acting outside of the constitutional state and on occasions even threatening the administrative vertical. The security-judicial apparatus remains a powerful instrument of regime power, but it is as factionalised as the rest of the system.[47] Despite Medvedev's calls for reform, the law enforcement agencies remain a law unto themselves. There are reports that new recruits have bribes pushed on them by their colleagues, as a clean policeman represents a threat to the others. The head of the PGO, Yuri Chaika, was furious when on 1 January 2011 the RIC was removed from the jurisdiction of the Prosecutor's Office. The new free-standing RIC is answerable directly to the president, and the change was just one of the interdepartmental conflicts plaguing the power system. Headed by the pugnacious Mikhail Bastrykin, who became one of the most powerful and independent figures in Putin's power elite, RIC was involved in the prosecution of some high-profile individuals, including Sergei Magnitsky. Bastrykin stresses that one of RIC's main tasks is to fight corruption among the elite.[48]

A regime has emerged that can trump the stipulations of the constitution but which remains constrained by the constitutional framework. Its subversions of legality remain illegitimate as defined by the system itself, and there has been no legal invocation of emergency rule. However, the system of meta-corruption cuts across officialdom, the factions and the security and judicial apparatus. In this third state, the regulatory framework of the constitution is irrelevant and the informal rules and 'understandings' (*ponyatiya*) of the regime do not operate. The enormous financial and coercive power of the third state ultimately threatens both the constitutional state and the administrative regime, while undermining the legitimacy of both. The two have a common systemic interest in limiting corruption, yet the entrenched power of the third state means that that the structural entrenchment of the meta-corruption is hard to extirpate. Putin, unlike Medvedev, has never made the struggle against corruption one of his priorities, although he is well aware of the potentially significant political advantage to be gained by demonstrating that even the elite is not immune to law enforcement.

Some high-profile and sensational corruption prosecutions capable of capturing the public imagination would signal the regime's commitment to the struggle against corruption, but these have been signally lacking. Instead, there have been isolated and instrumental corruption cases, usually the result of intra- and interservice factional conflicts. There has long been an internal power struggle between Directorate M of the Economic Security Service (SEB) of the FSB and the 6th Service of the Interior Security Department (USB) of the FSB. The latter is considered the most secretive section of the FSB and is even referred to as the 'Gestapo' by some within the agency. In early July 2016, the head of Directorate M resigned (as did the head of SEB's Directorate K, which oversees the sector) and Putin appointed the head of the 6th Service as his successor. The 6th service attacked the SEB in an attempt to gain control over the most profitable areas of business, namely the banking and financial sectors.[49] The success of the 6th Service's coup against Directorate M has been attributed to the patronage of General Viktor Zolotov – Putin's long-standing and highly trusted head of security (2000–13). Zolotov is completely loyal to Putin and in spring 2016, as we have seen, was appointed to head the newly formed NG.

The 6th service of the FSB was created by Sechin when he was deputy prime minister, headed by his close associate Oleg Feoktistov. This was one of Sechin's main 'special forces' units. Together, they convinced Putin to dismantle the Federal Service for Drug Control (FSKN), part of the *silovik* wars' that attended the succession from Putin to Medvedev in 2007–8. Feoktistov would go on to be at the centre of major scandals in years to come, although by 2016 his position was weakening because of the many enemies he had created.[50] In February 2014, the 6th Service apparently spearheaded the extraordinary attack on MVD general Denis Sugrobov, the head of the MVD's Main Directorate for Economic Security and Countering Corruption (GUEBiPK), who himself was accused of corruption.[51] In fact, Sugrobov's arrest and that of his deputy Boris Kolesnikov in February 2014 appears to have been part of inter-agency rivalries. In June 2014, Kolesnikov fell out of a window on the sixth floor of RIC's headquarters while undergoing interrogation and died.[52] On 27 April 2017, Sugrobov was convicted of abuse of office and of creating a criminal group allegedly running a protection racket, and was given an extraordinarily harsh sentence of twenty-two years in prison. The Sugrobov case is particularly controversial, since by all accounts he genuinely sought to combat corruption, and for this he was given an exemplary punishment to deter anyone else who would threaten elite interests. The case was presented to the media as an instance of the struggle against corruption but in fact demonstrates the intensity of the various inter-agency and corporate conflicts. The fight against corruption in Russia is as much a political question as it is a legal one. The analysis of the case in the *New Yorker* stressed the 'power struggle between Russia's rival security agencies'.[53]

This is not to say there is not a struggle against corruption. In an extensive interview, Bastrykin noted that since the agency had become independent in 2011, it had launched 3,958 criminal cases for corruption, including against 1,256 heads of municipal agencies and local government bodies, 459 heads of investigative bodies, 369 lawyers, 94 procurators, 73 deputies of regional legislative assemblies and 26 judges. He urged that confiscation be introduced as a penal sanction.[54] He also mentioned the controversial Sugrobov case, which appears to have had little to do with anti-corruption but represented an inter-agency settling of scores. At the same time, there have been some brave social movements established to defend the rights of business people and to help those ensnared, expropriated or incarcerated by raiders. Notable among them is Russia Behind Bars, established by Olga Romanova when her husband's business was stolen and he was jailed. She fought to implement Medvedev's famous injunction of 2008 to 'stop terrorising business'.[55] Romanova describes the Russian law-enforcement agencies (the police, prosecutors and the courts) as 'a single, predatory institution that lives off looting private capital'. During the recession, she argued that the predators had turned against each other as well as against her organisation – she fled to Germany in October 2017.[56]

Anti-corruption issues also serve to set the relationship between the regime and the cultural community. The arrest in August 2017 of the avant-garde theatre director Kirill Serebrennikov on charges of fraud and embezzlement represented a warning that those in receipt of government grants and subsidies were expected to show loyalty to the regime. The case was launched by the FSB's Department for the Defence of Constitutional Order, the successor of the KGB's Fifth Directorate in which Putin had served. This same directorate appears to have taken the lead in trying to close down the Moscow School of Social and Economic Sciences (MSSES), known as the 'Shaninka' after its founder, Soviet-born British sociologist Teodor Shanin. It appears that the regulatory agency, Rosobrnadzor, came under pressure to remove the school's state accreditation, in a case with clear parallels to the earlier one against EUSP. The Serebrennikov affair signalled a growing conflict between the regime and the creative elite, scripted rather like a dramaturgy of the Soviet period.[57] As the minister of culture, Vladimir Medinsky, put it in 2014, 'The one thing I don't see the point of, is making films with [state] funds that not only criticize but vilify the elected government.'[58] In fact, Serebrennikov's arrest represented a major blow to the legitimacy of the government and undermined respect among the intellectual class. The political commentator Yulia Latynina argued that 'nothing in recent times has damaged Putin as the "Serebrennikov affair"'.[59] In April 2019, Serebrennikov was released from house arrest, allowing him to return to work.

Some artists have exploited the contradictions in cultural policy and the porosity of the dual system to produce highly critical and internationally acclaimed work, like Andrei Zvyagintsev's film *Leviathan*. As in Iran and China, there is a constant tension between independent cultural creativity and state controls. Following the release of *Leviathan*, Medinsky devised a new set of guidelines targeting films that 'defile' Russia. Zvyagintsev noted, 'Yes, Mr Medinsky was disappointed by *Leviathan*. But I was being sincere. If I show the mayor to be corrupt, that's because these people exist.'[60] Zvyagintsev's next film, *Nelyubov'* (*Not Love*, 2017), is a complex and bleak meditation on contemporary relationships, and shows how Russian civil society supplements the work of the authorities, in this case the Liza Alert group, who search for a missing boy. Zvyagintsev did not ask for state funding, but it was nevertheless nominated for the Academy Awards by the Russian government.

In an extraordinary turn of events, in the morning of 19 July 2016, officers of Directorate M of the SEB of the FSB burst into the offices of the RIC armed with search warrants. The offices of the department's head, Alexander Drymanov, were searched, and three senior members of RIC were arrested and charged with the abuse of power and bribe-taking. The three RIC members were Denis Nikandrov, who in April 2016 had become deputy head of the Moscow RIC;[61] Mikhail Maksimenko, head of RIC's department of internal security; and Alexander Lamonov, Maksimenko's deputy. Large sums of money were confiscated from the detainees, as well as watches worth half a million euros. The authorities framed the case as part of the battle against corruption, including against its own officials, but it was prompted by the high-profile detention of the well-known alleged organised crime figures Zakhariy Kalashov (known as *Shakro Molodoi*, 'Young Shakro'), Andrei Kochuikov (known as 'The Italian') and the *Solntsevskaya Bratva* (Solntsevo Brotherhood) OCG. Although couched in the language of the struggle against corruption, the case was used by the FSB to demonstrate that it was the real power in the land. RIC's usually pugnacious spokesman, Vladimir Markin, waited twenty-four hours before commenting on the raid on his offices and then uncharacteristically ate humble pie: 'What has happened to our colleagues is shameful and hard to take. This does, of course, cast a shadow over the investigative committee, but our self-purification will continue.'[62] Nikandrov appealed to his boss, Bastrykin, to get the case transferred out of the FSB's hands, arguing that the FSB would 'not be objective'.[63] Nikandrov was certainly in a position to know.

Nikandrov's spectacular rise and fall was indicative not only of the enormous powers granted to security officials in the Putin era but also how these agencies could devour each other. Nikandrov had long been the regime's legal hitman, using political cases to achieve rapid promotion, although many of the cases in which he was involved subsequently fell apart. He is reputed to have been unscrupulous in his methods; with repeated suggestions he pressured people to give evidence. One of his early victims was Yevgeny Ishchenko, the mayor of Volgograd in the mid-2000s, who was battered by accusations by Nikandrov, then a young local investigator, and spent a year in jail before being exonerated by the courts. As Ishchenko chillingly notes, 'He [Nikandrov] was never interested in the truth. He followed a goal – in my case, to remove me from city hall.'[64] Having demonstrated his loyalty, although still only in his late twenties, Nikandrov was promoted to Moscow where he took part in gathering evidence against Khodorkovsky for the second trial against the bankrupted Yukos company executives. In 2008, he then took part in the case against investigator Dmitry Dovgy, who had fallen out with his seniors in the RIC. Dovgy was accused of having accepted a bribe, and most of his colleagues refused to take the case, but Nikandrov, still a rank-and-file investigator, jumped at the chance. Nikandrov pursued the case with typical ruthlessness. Dovgy was thrown in jail in awful conditions, while Nikandrov looked for evidence against him. Although Dovgy was falsely convicted, Nikandrov's career took off. When RIC became a stand-alone agency, Nikandrov became one of Bastrykin's elite investigators. In April 2011, he was appointed senior investigator for particularly important cases.[65]

It was only three months earlier, in January 2011, that RIC had been removed from the jurisdiction of the PGO and given autonomy under Bastrykin. The fury of the Chaika at this drastic reduction in his power, and the enmity that developed thereafter between Chaika and Bastrykin, is well documented.[66] In subsequent years, Nikandrov gained a reputation as Bastrykin's 'attack dog' and was often engaged in open conflict with the PGO.[67] He took part in the casino case, considered a classic instance of inter-agency conflict, but after four years the case fell apart. His remarkable rise culminated in April 2016 when he was appointed deputy head of RIC's Moscow branch, apparently by Putin himself.[68] Nikandrov shows how the security and law-enforcement agencies can become a law unto themselves. The RIC arrests created a media sensation and demonstrated that factional conflict between – and within – Russia's law-enforcement agencies was back with a vengeance. The arrests were clearly a major blow to Bastrykin and RIC. Already in April 2016, two of his subordinates had been sacked by Putin as part of the reorganisation of the power system. Nikandrov and Maksimenko are reputed to have supported Bastrykin in the conflict with one of the two ousted deputies.[69] Factional conflicts between sections of the security apparatus as well as within specific organisations typically involve abusive means of attack including the misuse of the criminal justice system. Those who have fallen foul of these attacks have commonly lost their right to a fair trial, been held arbitrarily for an extended period in pretrial detention, usually in poor conditions, often accompanied by psychological and physical ill-treatment. In systemic terms, factional conflict is a symptom of Putin's balancing strategy to ensure that no single security agency or faction dominates over the others, and, thus, none is able to exert leverage over the president himself.[70]

Other senior figures have also fallen victim to these moves. In 2016, three governors were arrested and several businesses were raided (the most prominent, and visible, being Mikhail Prokhorov).[71] In June 2016, the governor of Kirov Oblast and former head of the liberal Union of Right Forces (SPS) party, Nikita Belykh, was detained as he received $440,000 in marked cash in a Moscow restaurant. The prosecution argued that it was a bribe for him to include two local companies – a ski factory and a forest-management firm – in a federal investment programme as priority projects, whereas Belykh insists the money was a contribution to a charity. Belykh had been appointed in January 2009 by Medvedev and was one of the few liberal governors. It was under his watch that the Kirovles case unfolded, in which Navalny (and two local business people) in mid-2013 received a five-year suspended sentence after a local court found him guilty of embezzlement. Kirovles became part of the forest-management company now cited in the case against Belykh. On 1 February 2018, a Moscow court sentenced Belykh to an eight-year jail term. Another prominent governor to face corruption charges is Aleksandr Khorashavin, the former head of Sakhalin Oblast who was detained in March 2015 and taken to Moscow. Searches of his various homes found millions in cash and expensive jewels.

In July 2016, Andrei Belyaninov, the head of the Federal Customs Service (FCS) since 2006, was unceremoniously sacked amid accusations of corruption. His dismissal and search of his house, in which a large sum of cash was found, was spearheaded by the FSB. In September 2016, Colonel Dmitry Zakharchenko was arrested and found to be in possession of $460 million and €300 million. Officially, he was only the deputy chief of the MVD's GUEBiPK but had clearly been in a position to extract rents on a massive scale. His family had also benefitted, with his father, mother, sister, four ex-wives and one daughter also found to have hundreds of millions of dollars and euros in foreign bank accounts and owned twelve luxury flats in Moscow. Zakharchenko had taken bribes in return for warning business people about probes into their affairs and for settling conflicts with the MVD. For example, Zakharchenko warned the owners of Nota-Bank that the government was planning to revoke its licence and helped them steal ₽26 billion from the commercial bank's accounts.[72] The only reason Zakharchenko was brought down now was because of a reorganisation in the Lubyanka and the loss of his powerful patronage in the FSB. More than that, the FSB's economic security service now attacked its rival MVD Main Directorate. As Alexei Shlyapuzhnikov of Transparency International Russia puts it, the case had 'nothing to do with fighting corruption or corrupt individuals, but the latest round in the ongoing confrontation between Russia's all-powerful secret services, which increasingly resembles a turf war between criminal groups'.[73]

This appears to apply to Sechin's robust business ethics and his implacable legal violence against opponents, earning him the moniker Darth Vader. In 2012, Sechin masterminded the TNK-BP deal and swap share between Rosneft and BP, and in the same year Rosneft signed an extensive exploration and production agreement with Rex Tillerson, the CEO of Exxon-Mobil. In the end, these plans were shelved because of the toughening sanctions regime. Sechin appears to have been behind the attack on Yevtushenkov, the head of the mighty Moscow-based business empire, AFK Sistema. Yevtushenkov is a classic case of a Yeltsin-era oligarch who adapted to the new conditions and kept out of politics, but this was not enough to save him once he fell foul of Sechin. He was placed under house arrest in September 2014 and was forced to hand ownership of the Bashneft oil company back to the state at a steep discount. The company had long been coveted by Sechin. Facing intense budgetary pressures in an era of sanctions and relatively low oil prices, in 2016 there were plans to privatise Bashneft and thus raise some much-needed cash. There were also plans, announced in July, to privatise 19 per cent of Rosneft. The privatisation programme had been launched by Medvedev on ideological grounds – to reduce the state's share of the economy – but now the priority was revenue generation. Sechin had other ideas and decided that Bashneft should become part of Rosneft, while in the end blunting the part-privatisation of Rosneft. Rather than selling the Rosneft stake in global markets, a deal was struck with a previously small trader, CEFC China Energy, based in Shanghai, which acquired a $9 billion stake in Rosneft.

The minister for economic development, Alexei Ulyukaev (a liberal who had occupied the post since 2013), opposed the takeover of Bashneft, arguing that the Rosneft offer would not bring significant funds into the treasury. From his technocratic perspective, the law on the privatisation of state and municipal property in any case forbade the participation of companies in which the state has a 25 per cent or greater share. Following a revised and more generous financial package worth $5.5 billion, in mid-2016, Ulyukaev approved Bashneft's takeover by Rosneft. All of this had been settled when Ulyukaev went to Rosneft's headquarters late in the evening of 15 November 2016. As he left, Ulyukaev was arrested. Ulyukaev asserts that he received two gifts, a basket of sausages made from the meat of animals hunted by Sechin and a locked bag that he thought contained fine wines to go with the meat. Instead of wine, it held $2 million in marked neatly bundled cash. This was the highest-ranking serving minister arrested since Stalin's death in 1953. On that day, Putin sacked him from his government post.[74] The whole case is strange, since on the face of it there seems little reason for Ulyukaev to go in person to Rosneft's headquarters to receive money for a deal that had clearly been approved by Putin. It would have been beyond reckless to extort a man with such a fearsome reputation. The incident smacks of a sting operation masterminded by Sechin personally. At the same time, Ulyukaev was a leading systemic liberal and, thus, the attack was taken as a sign that the *siloviki* were moving against Medvedev's government and the economic liberals in charge of macroeconomic policy.

The trial started in August 2017 in the Khamovnichesky District Court (where Khodorkovsky's second trial had been staged) and continued until December. It was now alleged that Ulyukaev had asked Sechin for a bribe on a trip they took together to Goa in October 2016. On 16 August, Sechin was personally named and blamed by Ulyukaev, and later the judge made the surprise decision to allow the transcript of Sechin's conversations to be written into the court record. It turned out that Ulyukaev had been wiretapped by Rosneft's security service, headed until August 2016 by the FSB general and Sechin's long-term associate, Feoktistov, whom we have met before. Sechin was heard complaining that it was easier to do business with the Japanese and the South Koreans than with China and India, two key Rosneft partners; he griped about paying more taxes than ExxonMobil and he criticised Putin's deal with OPEC to stabilise oil prices.[75] Sechin had always been a lone wolf, but now he was in danger of falling prey to the 'Beria syndrome', where the whole elite unites against the man they perceive to be a danger to them all. Even his management of Rosneft was criticised by a Sberbank equity report in 2017, which suggested that Rosneft was mismanaged and only kept growing because of discounted acquisitions. Sechin was requested four times to testify, but each time he refused on the grounds that he was too busy. Even Putin agreed: 'Sechin should have come to court, what is the problem anyway? He could show up and repeat what he said during the preliminary investigations and interrogations.'[76] On 15 December 2017, Ulyukaev received an eight-year sentence in a hard labour camp and a fine of $2.2 million, and had his property confiscated. The verdict was almost certainly agreed with the Moscow City Court but this was far harsher than most people had anticipated and the first time since 1953 that a federal minister had been jailed.

The manner in which the criminal case was constructed became public, and it did not in the least look convincing. Ulyukaev insisted that the whole affair was a 'monstrous provocation' and refused to admit his guilt. His sardonic comments on the case rang true, while Sechin's reputation was further damaged: 'He started out as the omnipotent mastermind but turned into an offended schoolboy, who gives rare and caustic comments and runs away from court appointments. … Ulyukaev is of course crushed, but the all-powerful Sechin does not look like a winner.' In his final speech, Ulyukaev spoke about the 'gladiator with a cardboard sword', noting that the bell 'could begin tolling for any of you' – a warning that not only liberals but also anyone who fell foul of the system was vulnerable.[77] Sechin appears to have opened the Pandora's box of unrestrained elite competition, leading potentially to the system's disintegration.[78] In the eyes of his enemies, Sechin had once again shown himself to be implacable, greedy and vindictive, and ready to use the law to achieve revenge and his personal ambitions. Even control of Bashneft was not enough for him. He launched successive lawsuits against AFK Sistema, a London-listed equity company, resulting in sharp falls in the value of shares in its highly successful Russian assets such as Mobile TeleSystems (MTS) and the children's store Detsky Mir. The Ulyukaev case further tarnished Russia's investment image and was hugely damaging for all concerned, and perhaps above all for the regime itself. Sechin appeared intent on crushing AFK Sistema, whatever the damage. Putin had always struggled to constrain intra-elite conflicts, but now it appeared that he was no longer interested in doing so. The elite appeared to be turning upon itself, with no one safe: 'Sechin broke the unspoken rule of the competition between the Russian elite groups: to keep conflicts between them out of the public eye.' Sechin humiliated a member of the group most antagonistic to him, namely the pragmatic and economically liberal circle around Medevedev, suggesting that 'Sechin's ultraconservative elite group has gained the upper hand in Putin's system and, thus, disrupted the balance within it'.[79] The case discouraged those who believed in intra-systemic change.

At the same time, the man who managed the operation against Ulyukaev, FSB general Feoktistov, was dismissed in March 2017 as head of Rosneft security (although he seems no longer to have worked in this capacity from August 2016), and no alternative post was found for him, even though he tried to claim the post of deputy head of the FSB's SEB.[80] There is speculation that the rising generation of 'young technocrats' were now claiming their share of top roles, forcing the old generation to give way.[81] The case of the arrest of Oleg Korshunov, the deputy director of Russia's Federal Penitentiary Service (FSIN) in September 2017 is no less intriguing. On the face of it, this was just another case in the Kremlin's struggle against corruption, but Korshunov was famous for his skills as a financial intermediary. In financial and bureaucratic circles, he was known as 'Pukhly' (Pudgy). Before gaining his post with the FSIN, he had been an adviser to the senator from Ryazan Oblast in the FC, a common cover for other activities. In this case, it appears that Korshunov was a 'financial operator', whose function was to convert resources, including budget funds, into cash. With Putin's 'de-offshorisation' campaign after 2012, it became harder for officials and politicians to open foreign bank accounts or to buy real estate abroad, and it was far too risky to deposit the money in a Russian bank account, while spouses or children could not always be trusted. Financial operators take the money and invest as they see fit but every month make interest payments in cash of some 2–3 per cent. Alexander Perepilichny, who died in London in November 2012, was allegedly one of these financial operatives, reportedly managing money on behalf of the top managers of the tax inspectorate. When his pyramid collapsed, Perepilichny fled to London in 2009, but someone with a grudge at their losses may have taken their revenge (although the inquest suggested that he died of natural causes). As for Korshunov, he predicted that he would soon be out on parole: 'The system, in other words, is still stronger than attempts to punish illegality.'[82]

The demonstrative arrest of the senator from Karachai-Cherkessia, Rauf Arashukov, on 30 January 2019 served as a further warning that the impunity of the elite could no longer be guaranteed. He was detained during a live session of the FC on suspicion of ordering two murders. His arrest came after the upper house voted to revoke his immunity from prosecution. At the same time, his father, Raul, a senior manager in Gazprom, was arrested on suspicion of embezzling $400 million of gas supplies. The case showed the growing confidence of the FSB – and, thus, of the *siloviki* as a whole. It also damaged the reputation of parliament by raising the obvious question about how such a man could have represented the North Caucasian republic since 2010. At the same time, figures such as Dmitry Peskov, Putin's long-time press secretary, became the subject of criticism from within the administration itself.[83] Competition within the regime could turn into an all-out intra-elite war, presaging the end of factional equilibrium, the overturning of the balance between the two wings of the dual state and the destruction of Putin's power *vertikal*. As high-ranking figures become uncertain of the future, the temptation to defect will grow. It also shrinks time horizons for officialdom, as intimations of the end of Putinite stability increased. This is why Surkov penned his rather strange article in February 2019 insisting on the long-term future of the Putin system, which he had done so much to create.

The arrest of fund manager Michael Calvey, a US citizen, on 14 February 2019 dealt another blow to Russia's already perilous investment climate. Calvey set up the private equity partnership Baring Vostok Capital Partners in 1994 and by the time of his arrest had $3.7 billion under management from foreign funds such as Calpers and the European Bank for Reconstruction and Development (EBRD). It had invested $2.8 billion into eighty companies, including such spectacular successes as Yandex, Vimpelcom, Tinkoff and Vkusville. Since 2016, the company had invested $900 million in the country, representing nearly half of total foreign direct investment (FDI) in 2018. Calvey and five colleagues were arrested as part of a commercial dispute with Vostochny Express Bank, in which Baring had invested. A minority shareholder now claimed to have been defrauded of $38 million. Calvey argued that the real motive was a dispute with Vostochny Bank's largest minority shareholder, Artem Avetisyan, who apparently has close links with the security services. Calvey was kept in pretrial detention, although this ran against numerous injunctions by Medvedev and Putin not to jail business people involved in commercial disputes. He was the first Western executive to face time in prison, at a time when over six thousand businessmen are held in pretrial detention over similar disputes.[84] Many of Russia's 4.5 million entrepreneurs became subject to pressure from law-enforcement agencies, often in cahoots with business rivals.[85] In his annual address to parliament on 20 February, as mentioned, Putin returned to the situation he had described in 2015, arguing that 'honest businesses should not face the risk of criminal or administrative prosecution', and he went on to note,

> Today, almost half of all cases (45 per cent) opened against entrepreneurs do not get to trial. What does this mean? This means that they were opened in a slipshod manner or under some unclear pretext. And what does this mean in practice? As a result, 130 jobs are lost on average every time a business closes down as result of an investigation. Let us think about this figure; this is becoming a major economic problem.[86]

Typical of the contradictions of Putin's rule, the man charged by the Kremlin to tackle the problem of unfair prosecutions was none other than Avetisyan. He is chair of the 'Leaders' Club', a Kremlin-sponsored group of entrepreneurs seeking to improve the business climate, as well as a leading member of the Agency for Strategic Initiatives, an organisation headed by Putin that sponsors investment projects.

On 26 March 2019, the former Open Government minister (2012–18) Mikhail Abyzov and five accomplices were charged with stealing some $60 million from energy companies in the Novosibirsk Oblast and hiding the money abroad. Abyzov was a close ally of Prime Minister Medvedev, suggesting that even he could be sacrificed if political necessity (such as a sharp fall in Putin's popularity) demanded a scapegoat. Medvedev had been the subject of national humiliation up to 2013, but when forced to choose between sacking and supporting him, Putin chose the latter. It was clear that high-level administrative protection (his *krysha*, or roof) had been withdrawn from Abyzov, leaving him to his fate. The perception that it was now open season for elite repression was reinforced by the detention by the FSB of Viktor Ishaev, who had been governor of Khabarovsk Krai in the Russian Far East (RFE) between 1991 and 2009, just days after Abyzov's arrest. In the September 2018 gubernatorial election, Ishaev had supported the eventual winner, the LDPR candidate Sergei Fungal, against the incumbent, Vyacheslav Shport, and he was now paying the price. The signal was sent that even the mighty were not immune. Only three high-ranking officials were prosecuted between 2001 and 2005, whereas in 2018, thirty-five senior members of the government and parliament were charged, with the investigations mostly led by the FSB.[87] The PGO reported that in 2018 1,303 officials were sacked for corruption offences, up from the 1,251 fired in 2017.[88] The elite pacts on which Putinite stability was based appeared to be breaking down. The various arrests threatened to destabilise factional equilibrium. The Putinite balancing act was weakening, allowing the ambitions of the most powerful groups (notably the *siloviki*) to radicalise, potentially threatening the stability of the whole system.

Intra-systemic factionalism not only debilitates effective governance but also damages the business environment and imbues the whole system with a permanent sense of crisis. This micro-factionalism operates at many levels and acts as a subterranean basement beneath visible politics. This is compounded by what can be called meso-factionalism, the various alignments of business groups. Two rival factional meso-groups were identified as shaping the 2018 presidential campaign, with far greater influence than the formal co-chairs of Putin's campaign Elena Shmeleva, Sergei Kogogin and Alexander Rumyantsev. The actual campaign was run by the head of the PA, Anton Vaino. Earlier, such campaigns had been run by the deputy head responsible for domestic politics, namely Surkov, until his abrupt dismissal in December 2011 (following the botched parliamentary campaign), and then by his successor Volodin (although formally the 2012 presidential campaign was headed by the film director Stanislav Govorukhin). Vaino's father, Eduard, has long been associated with the business lobby headed by Sergei Chemezov (the head of Rostec, formerly Rostekhnologii, the state holding company established in 2007). Chemezov became friends with Putin in Dresden, when they lived in the same building, and then followed Putin into the PA in the late 1990s and in the Putin years became one of the most influential figures.

Chemezov is reputed to have been behind the appointment of Denis Manturov, the minister of industry and trade, as well as of a new generation of 'young technocrats' to replace the older, more 'political', regional governors. These include the governor of Sevastopol, Dmitry Ovsyannikov (formerly Manturov's deputy), Anton Alikhanov in Kaliningrad, Gleb Nikitin (another of Manturov's deputies) in Nizhny Novgorod and Dmitry Azarov in Samara (the home of the giant Avtovaz car plant, where Eduard Vaino [Anton's father] is one of the deputy directors).[89] Kogogon, incidentally, is the director of the Kamaz truck plant, 49.9 per cent of whose shares belongs to Rostec. This is where Putin declared his candidacy on 6 December 2017, and the industrial working class is the foundation of Putin's social support. Chemezov is one of the most influential figures in Russia today, and his power base is growing. By early 2018, the state conglomerate Rostec encompassed more than seven hundred subsidiaries, ranging from arms manufacturers to motor plants, but its appetite had still not been sated. In February 2018, Chemezov conceded that with Trump's election, Russia was 'expecting normal relations to be re-established', which would have allowed, for example, the partnership with Boeing to deepen to cover aircraft sales not only in Russia but also in Asia and Africa. He stressed that while most of Rostec's work was in the defence sector, the plan was to raise the share of civilian production to 50 per cent.[90]

The Chemezov industrial lobby is balanced by the financial interests represented by the Kovalchuk brothers. Yuri and Mikhail were old friends of Putin's from his St Petersburg youth and since at least 2016 had been increasing their political influence. Yuri Kovalchuk, the chair and leading shareholder of Rossiya Bank, is often referred to as 'Putin's personal banker' and in that capacity has been placed on various US sanctions lists. The brothers are considered to have come into conflict with Volodin, who consequently after the September 2016 parliamentary election had been moved over to become Duma speaker. He was replaced by Sergei Kirienko, who is considered close to the group. Since 2005, Mikhail Kovalchuk has been head of the Kurchatov nuclear research institute, while Kirienko was appointed to head Rosatom in the same year and remained in this post until he became deputy head of the PA in October 2016. The Kovalchuks are reputed to influence the Russian media, with the head of the TASS news agency, Sergei Mikhailov, thought to be associated with them, and on the leading TV channels, which are run by the VGTRK state-holding company, including (through the National Media Group) the First Channel, REN TV and the Fifth Channel.[91] Factionalism works at many cross-cutting levels, demonstrating that the Putin phenomenon is a sophisticated mechanism to manage complex relationships, and one should be less surprised that it sometimes fails but that it works at all.

5 MANAGED CAPITALISM

Russia's post-communist economy has always been a political endeavour and, thus, mimics with reverse intention the Soviet project itself. While the Communist Party sought to extirpate market relations to create a planned economy, from the late 1980s, the aim was to restore market relations to make the economy more competitive, dynamic and 'modern'. In the absence of capitalists, this entailed the encouragement of a nascent class of 'bourgeois' entrepreneurs, who in the 1990s consolidated their hold over the economy in the form of a peculiar type of state-sponsored oligarch capitalism. The methods employed have been described as 'market Bolshevism', which undermined the foundations of democracy.[1] The 'bourgeoisie' that emerged was of a distinctive sort. In the Yeltsin years, this was 'political capitalism' in the raw, with proximity to power the vital ingredient in gaining property, accompanied by features of 'state capture' by the newly empowered 'oligarchs'. Putin threw the old-style oligarchs out of the Kremlin and in the famous roundtable between business and state representatives in July 2000 imposed a new balance in relations. This was accompanied by elements of 'business capture' by the state, in which businesses could conduct their affairs as long as they aligned their strategies with those of the state. Property rights remained weak, subject to predatory 'raids' by powerful interests in collusion with state officials, law enforcement officers and corrupt courts. Today in Russia, private property exists, but as Maksim Trudolyubov argues, 'the problem is just that property and freedom in Russia are entirely separate: they occupy parallel universes'.[2] In other words, unlike in the Lockean Anglo-American experience, private property so far has not become the foundation of a rights-defending middle class. Property holders in Russia remain dependent and vulnerable, and have not yet been able to exercise class power of the sort envisaged by Barrington Moore when he asserted, 'No bourgeois, no democracy'.[3]

State and market

Managed capitalism is nothing new in Russia. The Russian state from at least the time of Ivan the Terrible in the sixteenth century was handing out licences for salt mines in the Urals, as well as granting concessions and monopolies, such as in the fur trade. In the late tsarist years, the state devised an ambitious industrialisation and infrastructure-building programme. Between 1891 and 1916, the world's longest railway, the Trans-Siberian, was built linking Moscow with Vladivostok 9,289 km and eight time zones away in its recently acquired territories in the RFE. The Soviet planned economy emulated this, building the 4,324 km Baikal-Amur Mainline (BAM) from the 1970s. Post-communist Russia thus inherited not only an enduring historical model but also the vast apparatus of a state-managed economy, and to this day economic relations are shaped by this legacy. The structure of economic relations has drastically changed, but Russia today retains the characteristics of a developmental state. The instruments of economic management are no longer centralised ministries but state corporations, state-aligned energy companies and state-owned holding companies of various sorts, as well as private companies headed by Putin's associates.

Speaking fluent German and having lived in East Germany, Putin has been called 'the German in the Kremlin'.[4] In this context, Putin clearly appeals to the theory of ordoliberalism, devised in the 1930s and 1940s and then applied to underpin the German 'social market economy' in the 1950s. The German ordoliberals of the Freiburg School, notably Walter Eucken, learnt from the bitter experience of *laissez faire* capitalism of the 1920s to formulate a model of liberalism in which a strong state provides the framework for economic competition and market stability, accompanied by a social safety net (in Germany to counter the threat of socialism and in Russia to prevent a neo-communist resurgence). Ordoliberals consider themselves the true neo-liberals and view the Friedrich von Hayek school and his Mont Pèlerin society as 'paleoliberals', loyal to nineteenth-century ideas of self-correcting markets.[5] However, post-communist Russia is far from achieving the central precept of ordoliberalism, the independence of the law and an impartial regulatory state, and instead is prey to elements of 'crony capitalism' while the legal system is abused to abet raiders rather than to protect the rights of entrepreneurs and other economic actors. Nevertheless, the Putinite emphasis on the regulatory role of the state and the maintenance of a developed (although inadequately funded) welfare state lies in the mainstream of post-war European social democratic thinking. The absence of strong and independent trade unions and of a serious social democratic party (JR at one point sought to fill this niche) only reinforces the regime character of a top-down social contract, built not on political consensus but on depoliticised techniques of stability-focused regime management.

Russia is not exceptional in having a highly politicised economy, but the depth and intensity of the relationship between power and property is unusual. Despite some obvious distortions and the enduring effect of nominally non-economic agents in economic affairs (notably the security agencies of various stripes), Putin's economic policy has been remarkably consistent and well designed to achieve the regime's key goal of restoring state power and authority. Conservative fiscal and monetary policies provided economic stability and growth, but the prevalence of personalised economic relations and unpredictable interventions (in the form of raiding and by monopolistic economic actors) stifled investment and dampened growth.[6] Characteristic of a stability system, radical structural reform was postponed to avoid social dislocation and protest, but the price (or so orthodox economics would suggest) was relatively low GDP growth rates and low productivity. With declining growth rates, already by 2013 it was clear that energy rents were no longer acting as the locomotive of economic growth, and a new model was required.

There is a rich literature in the field of institutional economics on the way that varying arrangements can foster different types of economic and political behaviour. In their study, Douglass North and his colleagues contrasted extractive institutions (focused on deriving rents) with others that are inclusive and which promote development. What they call 'open-access orders' (contrasted with limited-access orders) allow the political and economic systems to develop and together constrain violence.[7] Similar points were later advanced by Acemoglu and Robinson, who argue that underdevelopment is a function not of geography but of political institutions, with more pluralist and open societies fostering education and initiative, whereas the focus on extraction by more closed systems stifles innovation and development.[8] In this context, the leading Russian economist Alexander Auzan makes the important point that

> it makes little sense for Russia to move full-steam ahead with institutional reform – even if backed by political capital, and even if this reform is multipronged – until we have a firmer understanding of, first, which type of institutions, extractive or inclusive, are at play in the country, and second, how these institutions relate to the sociocultural circumstances of the country, and therefore how they reproduce themselves with the help of informal practices.[9]

He argues that the character of Russia's transition has been misunderstood and that instead of creating a market economy and democratic society, it was directed towards overcoming the failings of the Soviet deficit-burdened economy and creating a consumer society, and, thus, the institutions of a consumer market were created, not those of a democratic society. In the fat years of the 2000s, when raw material profits poured in, living standards rose dramatically and a consumer society was created, but 'in essence, those institutions that contributed to the structure of the demand economy became extractive institutions, based on the extraction of rents – not only rents from natural resources but also monopoly and administrative rents'.[10]

Putin is acutely aware that without a dynamic economic foundation, his foreign policy ambitions and search for status in the world would prove illusory. Putin may not have read Paul Kennedy's study of how economic, military and technological balances determined the fate of the great powers in the twentieth century, but he intuitively understands the notion of 'imperial overstretch'.[11] Russia inherited a heavy institutional legacy from the Soviet system, including the prevalence of indirect bureaucratic controls, an extensive second economy with the related corruption networks, negative value added in many industries and a 'rent-management system' through which the state redistributed, via formal and informal channels, the value gained from energy exports.[12] By the mid-1990s, Russia appeared to have a 'virtual economy', which simulated a market economy while the state redistributed energy rents to loss-making industries.[13] The system evolved in later years, but it remains a rent-distribution system combining the not always compatible goals of social stability and economic development.

Putin modified the economic model he inherited, although in keeping with his evolutionary style he incorporated much of the oligarch system into a new state-centred model of managed capitalist development. The most egregiously political of the old oligarch class were forced into exile (notably Boris Berezovsky and Vladimir Gusinsky), while the rest adapted to work with the regime. The Yeltsin-era 'oligarchs' were tamed to become 'stoligarchs', and state capture was eliminated. The opposite process now took hold as the market state of the Yeltsin years gave way to the creation of a state market. Powerful business interests, often with personal ties to Putin, align with the regime to combine profit maximisation with rent-seeking. The combination opened the door to corruption and exposed businesses without adequate political support to 'raiding' by corrupt state officials (often from the security apparatus) working in collusion with the courts, administrative offices and law-enforcement agencies. Nevertheless, Putinite economic management cannot be reduced to any simplistic formula but instead has responded remarkably effectively to the challenges, and we can only speculate about the degree to which other responses would have been more effective.

The various reform plans issued in the Putin years are the functional equivalent of Soviet-era five-year plans. The first, *Strategy 2010*, was devised by German Gref in 2000, and many of the recommended tax and financial reforms were implemented. The liberal proposals for the economy included the introduction of a flat-rate (regressive) income tax of 13 per cent, which endures to this day. Mass tax evasion was ended and tax receipts grew, but so did inequality. There were similar improvements in the corporate sector, including from the energy companies as new laws after the end of Yukos in 2004 allowed a large part of the profits from oil and gas exports to enter the federal exchequer. The greatly enhanced rent-extraction model provided the regime with the financial resources to shape the new model of 'managed democracy' and developmental capitalism. In that context, it became less urgent to modernise the economy, and only about a third of the proposals in this area were implanted and no more than a fifth of the ideas to reshape the bureaucracy.

From the mid-2000s, the model once again changed when it became clear that the impasse in international affairs would not be soon overcome. Issues of state security became a priority, although in the relatively soft form of 'preparation' (*podgotovka*) for some putative future confrontation rather than 'mobilisation' for some specific and imminent conflict. A list was drawn up of security-sensitive industries and plants. This was not full-scale militarisation, but it did entail the 'securitisation' of parts of the economy, in particular though elements of import substitution to reduce reliance on strategic foreign items accompanied by the imposition of restrictions on foreign influence. A Putinite industrial strategy was formulated, drawing on some of the ideas he had formulated earlier in his academic thesis. Civilian aircraft manufacturers were consolidated into the United Aircraft Corporation (OAK), military jet manufacturers were rationalised into two major holding companies, shipbuilding companies were merged into the United Shipbuilding Corporation (OSK), while the two major sea-going shipping companies became one giant concern, Sovcomflot. The giant Rostec conglomerate works as a holding company for a vast array of manufacturing and engineering industries. By 2019, Russian internet companies accounted for about 4 per cent of the GDP, and their contribution was rising fast. In short, Putin's ambition was to ensure that Russia remained a full-service economy, repudiating former senator John McCain's rather nasty jibe that Russia was no more than a 'gas station masquerading as a country'.[14]

This was the strategy pursued by Labour administrations in the UK in the 1960s and 1970s, and had long been part of post-war French *dirigisme*. The post-war Japanese (*keiratsu*) and South Korean (*chaebols*) also provided directed development based on industrial strategies. The creation of 'national champions' in Russia undoubtedly prevented a number from going bankrupt, while insulating them from asset stripping and foreign acquisition (although foreign partnerships were welcomed). Thus, while the model is internally coherent and rational, and draws on the solid, although mixed, international experience, the Russian model, naturally, has its own specificities. Although corruption is far from unique to the Russian model, the weakness of the rule of law and the interpenetration of economic and political elites created a distinctive ruling class. The military dictatorships in Egypt and Pakistan had also fostered fused elites, as also in Indonesia earlier, but in the Russian case, a civilian elite structure makes it impossible to tell where politics ends and business begins.

The financial crisis from 2008 once again prompted the evolution of the Putinite economic model. The anti-crisis programme of March 2009 pumped trillions of roubles into the economy to prevent businesses from collapsing, and in return they maintained employment without wage reductions. Cheap government loans or subsidies ensured that production continued irrespective of competitiveness. From the very beginning, Putin had insisted on the 'social responsibility of business', but this was a new form of 'public-private partnership'. As one commentary on the period puts it, 'In giving up on economic logic, businesses and individuals start to follow a quasi-political logic.' This applies not just to corporations but also to the behaviour of social groups: 'Instead of defending their own economic interests, they start to compete over the amount of money and preferential treatment provided to them by the government.' This provided a loyalty base for the regime, which was mobilised against protestors in 2011–12 and then consolidated at the time of the patriotic mobilisation over Crimea in 2014. The new model introduced selective protectionism accompanied by the growth of government contracts, notably in the defence industries, accompanied in early 2013 by the ban on the sale of strategic Russian assets to foreigners. In other words, after 2008, the economy became increasingly 'governmentalised'.[15] This was not outright nationalisation, but it certainly impeded the implementation of the various plans for privatisation. This was a quasi-war economy, which anticipated confrontation with the West and allowed Russia to weather the sanctions from 2014.

In August 2012, nineteen years after its original application, Russia finally joined the World Trade Organisation (WTO), just at the time when domestic and international pressures were pushing the government away from the liberal integration model. However, Putin's policy in this area as in others is always a combination of often incompatible elements (the uncharitable would call them inconsistent, if not mendacious). Amid clear signs of economic slowdown, the Kremlin's *Strategy 2020* in 2012 outlined the priorities for Putin's third term. These included a new growth model based on improved labour productivity, technological innovation, reformed social policy, economic diversification and international integration. The *Strategy 2020* reform plan was devised by policy experts from several Moscow think tanks and called for a new model of economic growth based on the shift from a demand to a supply economy accompanied by a fundamental reorientation of social policy. A sluggish economy, shrinking workforce and an aging population required greater investment in the health and welfare system, but this in turn required accelerated economic growth and a stronger political voice for those on whom the burden of reforms would fall.[16] This was a grandiose, comprehensive and ambitious plan for reform, running to 864 pages, but in the event, investment slowed from 2013 as oil prices fell, and the crisis in international affairs and sanctions stymied reform.

Structural problems are compounded by the weakness of Russian financial institutions, which cannot effectively intermediate household savings (which in Russia are quite high) into productive investment. Much of the money goes abroad, or is hidden at home in the form of valuable goods or foreign currencies. Auzan had long identified Russia's fundamental problem as one of 'path dependency', a point elaborated by the economist Sergei Guriev. He noted that the growing gap between Russian and US GDP could only be overcome if Russian economic growth exceed America's by at least a factor of two over twenty-five years. The fundamental factors that shape long-term economic growth – human capital, economic and political institutions, geography and culture – change only slowly, and their interaction create 'development traps, in which Russia now found itself. Economic agents require confidence that the state would commit to long-term rules, and liberal democracy was a system designed to protect investors from expropriation and to restrain predatory behaviour.'[17]

Commonly quoted figures suggest that by 2017, the state's proportion of the economy had risen from some 35 per cent when Putin assumed power to 70 per cent, but this figure has been challenged. An alternative study suggests that consolidated state expenditure rose from 30 per cent of the GDP in 2000 to 36 per cent in 2016 (of which some 13 per cent comprises pension and other social payments), and as a proportion of the labour force, 30 per cent were employed in the state sector, including the federal and municipal levels and the twenty-five largest state corporations. Out of the six hundred largest corporations, only 41 per cent belong to the state, representing 45 per cent of total output in 2016. In sum, taking into account various statistical methodologies, the state sector comprises between 26 and 41 per cent of the total economy, a far cry from 70 per cent.[18] Other studies suggest that the state sector accounts for some 46 per cent of Russia's GDP. Whatever the precise figure, it is clear that state-owned enterprises (SOEs) do enjoy advantages, including preferential financial treatment and access to relevant figures in the government bureaucracy, which distorts the competitiveness of the economy. The regulatory burden remains high, despite numerous attempts to reduce sanitary, fire and other inspections. The small- and medium-enterprise (SME) sector is still underdeveloped, in part because of the high contributions that they have to make to social funds. Overall, the quality of corporate governance has greatly improved, helped by the introduction of a corporate governance code in 2015. Financial and ownership transparency, the defence of shareholder rights and the appointment of genuinely independent directors were all improved, in part spurred by earlier hopes that Moscow would become a major international financial centre. Even without those dreams, a stable polity and effective economic management allowed businesses to improve internal governance. This is not to suggest that everything is rosy, and the weakness of defensible property rights continues to hamper business development and investment.

This does not amount to the recreation of Soviet-style state capitalism, in which market forces are not only constrained (as they are in Russia today) but also effectively abolished in favour of administrative regulation and control. Rather, the Putinite system can be described as 'statist capitalism'. As in the political sphere, this is a dual economy in which market relations structure the normative framework but are tempered by state interventions. Many countries in the post-war period applied *dirigiste* strategies to protect and develop vulnerable industries, and Russia today is doing the same – although with a lag of fifty years, in which time the world has moved on and today frowns on ramified 'industrial strategies'. As so often, Russia appears to be trying to implement a model that has already become archaic. While there is something to this, it is misleading. Russia's perception of itself as a great power requires investment in military industries and the armed forces, and also prompts it to try to achieve full-spectrum development from shipbuilding, space exploration, aircraft manufacture, nuclear power, car and truck making, as well as electronics, avionics and the financial and services sectors. The goal is to decrease Russian vulnerability to external pressure in conditions of global confrontation and to increase 'resilience' – the ability of a system to return to its previous status after a period of stress.

The statist model is challenged by some of the liberal bloc, although there are also some statist liberals who accept an enhanced role for the state in the transition to a more sustainable economy. In Putin's first two terms, it became common practice to appoint officials to the boards of companies where the government had a stake. Medvedev sought to distance the state from direct management, including, as noted, the ban in 2011 on state officials serving on the boards of SOEs. When the ban was removed by Putin in 2014, an influx of bureaucrats joined the boards of state companies. The elite reproduced itself as the children of senior officials moved into top positions. For example, Petr Fradkov, the son of Mikhail Fradkov, a former prime minister and former head of the Foreign Intelligence Service (SVR), became first deputy chair of Vnesheconombank (VEB), the state-owned development bank. Sergei Ivanov's son, also called Sergei, became president of Alrosa, the state-owned diamond company, while Dmitry Patrushev, the son of Nikolai Patrushev (the secretary of the Security Council) became head of the supervisory board of the Russian Agricultural Bank, and in May 2018 Dmitry was appointed minister of agriculture, bringing the so-called 'golden youth' into governmental positions. Aleksei Rogozin, the son of the former deputy prime minister responsible for the defence industries (2011-18) and now head of Roscosmos, Dmitry Rogozin, became director general of the Ilyushin Aviation Complex. All this demonstrates the blurred line between the state and business, and between state officials and business people. A key commodity in Russia is access to policymakers, and there are many ways this is achieved. One of these is by business people becoming legislators, an issue that the State Duma has long recognised as reducing its legitimacy. Parties have imposed quotas on the number of business people who can join their lists. The phenomenon is replicated at the regional level where up to 40 per cent of legislators come directly from the business world, to great profit for themselves and their companies.[19] Russia has still not adopted a law on lobbying, legislation that could regulate and possibly limit the phenomenon.

The distribution of rents is exceptionally 'lumpy', with Russia becoming one of the most unequal countries in the world.[20] The richest 10 per cent own 87 per cent of the country's wealth, with some hundred billionaires at the summit, while some twenty million people (13.8 per cent of the population) still fall below the poverty line. One per cent of the Russian population holds 46 per cent of all the personal bank deposits in the country.[21] Because of the redistribution of energy rents, inequality has slightly decreased, and income inequality is roughly at the same level as the United States. The Gini coefficient measuring income inequality (where 0 means complete equality and 1 compete inequality) shows the United States at 0.39, Russia at 0.41 and China at 0.49.[22] In other words, Russian wealth stratification is one of the worst of any major economy in the world, and offshore wealth is about three times greater than Russia's official net foreign reserves. As incomes stagnate, the middle class has been eroded.[23] Inequality is compounded by gross differences between regions, with the Republics of Tyva and Altai on the bottom of most scales, while the big Russian cities and Tatarstan are on the top. Thus, nearly half the population in Tyva is below the poverty level, while in Tatarstan, it is only 7.4 per cent.[24] The most effective way to tackle income inequality is progressive taxation, but Putin has ruled out any change to the flat rate 13 per cent income tax introduced in his first year in power.

The challenges of the digital revolution have been recognised by the Russian government as the country enthusiastically embraced the new technologies. The tension between security and cyber freedom is as sharp here as elsewhere. The attempt by the government regulator, Roskomnadzor, in April 2018 to ban the messaging app Telegram, established in 2013, because of its refusal to hand over the encryption keys to the FSB provoked a vigorous reaction. At least twelve thousand people turned out to protest.[25] The 'Yarovaya' law, named after its main sponsor, the UR member of parliament Irina Yarovaya, came into force on 1 July 2018. It requires internet service providers (ISPs) to keep records of their clients' traffic and to hand them over to security officials on request. The law also requires communications companies to hand over encryption keys on request. Attempts to close down Russia's extraordinarily open internet culture threatened the core values of the more modernised part of Russian society. Already the government had blocked web networks, as in the case of LinkedIn, and there was even talk of shutting down Facebook, with its twenty-five million Russian users. Telegram, however, was a different case, with fourteen million users in Russia and two hundred million worldwide. Its founder, Pavel Durov, had already four years earlier been forced to relinquish control of his Facebook equivalent, VKontakte (VK), which was taken over by the Kremlin-friendly Alisher Usmanov. Roskomnadzor justified its actions by the struggle against extremism as well as the 2014 law that requires all internet services in Russia to store their data on servers that are physically located in the country. LinkedIn failed to comply, hence all of Russia's 4,500 ISPs were ordered to restrict access to the site. In July 2017, a law was adopted banning the use of virtual private network (VPN) services, which allows users to mask their identities. The law was ineffective, and following the ban on Telegram, VPN usage soared and Durov shifted to the cloud services of Amazon and Google.

Russia is learning from China how to build internet firewalls, but the political context is very different.[26] Russians are ready to defend global internet access, and as new laws to create a 'sovereign internet' were passed in April 2019, forcing internet providers to install devices to filter traffic, protests also gathered pace. The technical situation is also different, with only three operators effectively controlling all traffic in China, whereas in Russia there are thousands.[27] Above all, the government had 'no plans to shut anything down', when asked about social media networks in his Direct Line on 7 June 2018, although Putin noted his concern about terrorists using encrypted messaging systems but insisted that as a former security official he knew 'how easy it is to ban something, but it is more difficult to find civilised solutions'. He would encourage the security services to use 'modern investigation methods' to prevent terrorist attacks 'without limiting freedom, including on the internet'.[28] With ninety million users, Russia is Europe's largest internet market (it overtook Germany in 2011), and internet penetration exceeds 75 per cent of the country and is growing mainly due to the older generation increasingly using mobile devices to connect to the network. The internet in Russia has been largely free since its inception, yet the pressure of controls continues to mount. Ignoring street protests and the advice of the Kremlin's own Presidential Council for the Development of Civil Society and Human Rights, the Duma in March 2019 adopted the law against 'fake news', imposing large fines for publishing 'untrue' reports that threaten 'life, health, public order, security, infrastructure, and almost any public institution'; in other words, about almost everything. As if that was not enough, parliament adopted a second law allowing officials to shut down any content containing 'information expressed in indecent form which insults human dignity and public morality and shows obvious disrespect for society, the state, and official symbols of Russia, the Russian constitution, or other agencies that administer government power in Russia'.[29] The new legislation gave Roskomnadzor enormous discretionary powers, and they would no doubt be used selectively against critical voices.

Russia still faces the challenge of closing the long-term economic gap with its peers. Auzan talks of three paths. The development of *private capitalism* requires improvement in the administrative quality of the state, above all the strengthening of the rule of law, the enhanced protection of property rights and the fostering of competition (accompanied by less emphasis on 'national champions'). He warned that unless there is improvement if the quality of governance, the private capitalism route risks reverting to the situation of the 1990s, when regulators were captured by business, laws were not observed and competition worked towards negative selection – the most predatory survived. The *state capitalism* model requires a different emphasis, above all improved strategic planning and an active state engaged in public-private partnerships and state companies, all within the framework of a long-term economic strategy. The third model, and the one favoured by Auzan, is what he calls *popular capitalism*, in which the savings accumulated during the consumer society period are funnelled into a national investment strategy. This 'Hamiltonian' strategy (Alexander Hamilton had devised the 'American System' that played a large part in US development in the first half of the nineteenth century) requires a strengthened institutional investment sector, including pension funds, insurance companies and, of course, banks, to allow the direct entry of Russian citizens into the stock market and investment funds.[30] This sort of people's capitalism (reminiscent of Thatcherite rhetoric) requires improved institutional trust as well as high-quality human capital, and, above all, determined efforts to break path-dependent inertia. Elements of all three models are already being implemented, reinforcing the hybrid character of the Russian economy.

The independent Russian banking system was born in the 1990s, with many created to leverage money from enterprises to shareholders or to scoop up undervalued state enterprises rather than to intermediate finances into productive investment. Money laundering and cash conversion operations remain rife. The Central Bank of Russia (CBR) in the Putin years, against stiff resistance, sought to clean up the banking sector. Over two-thirds of over 3,000 banks lost their licences, with the number since 2012 falling from 937 to around 500 today. The cull included most of the small regional and personal banks as well as some of the major players such as Otkritie. However, administrative rather than market measures were used to manage the process, including the failure to introduce adequate investment risk for investors. The Deposit Insurance Agency still covers investor losses up to $25,000 when banks go bust.[31] One of Putin's main achievements has been to restore stability to the financial system and to heal the scars of the various bank defaults and repeated loss of people's savings in the 1990s. The question now is whether the stick has been bent too far the other way. The banking system is a good example of Hellman's 'partial reform equilibrium', the concept popularised in the late 1990s to explain the way that further economic reform is blocked by the early winners of the reform process.

Economic performance and plans

Even before the sanctions and fall in oil prices in 2014, it was clear that the Russian economy was stalling. Growth averaged 7 per cent in the golden years to 2008 but had slowed to 1.3 per cent in 2013 and 1.1 per cent in 2014, before falling by 2.2 per cent in 2015 and 0.2 per cent in 2016, with modest growth of 1.5 per cent returning in 2017 and 2.3 per cent in 2018. During the recession, inflation accelerated to over 15 per cent, the budget deficit rose to 3.5 per cent of the GDP, interest rates peaked at 17 per cent, there was a 40 per cent depreciation in the value of the rouble (compared to the dollar) and there were large capital outflows (much of which was used to pay off corporate debt). The government used its Reserve Fund and the Sovereign Wealth Fund, as well as the rent-management system as a whole, to cushion the social impact and shielded corporations and the financial sector from its effects. Despite many alarmist predictions, the various sovereign wealth funds, as in 2009, worked in a countercyclical manner to ward off a financial crisis, and although diminished, they were not depleted and in 2017 started accumulating again. In 2018, Russia enjoyed a current account surplus of $115 billion, but real incomes fell for the fifth year in a row. The federal budget recorded a surplus of 2.2 per cent, the first since 2012. By mid-2019, the country held $520 billion in reserves, while sovereign external debt was extraordinarily low at just 15 per cent of the GDP, compared to the Organisation for Economic Cooperation and Development (OECD) average of 78 per cent.

The sanctions imposed in response to the Ukraine crisis targeted individuals associated with the annexation of Crimea in March 2014 and then were extended to cover the export of dual-use and military technologies, the financial sector (making long-term borrowing abroad more difficult) and parts of the energy sector. The Atlantic system and its allies (such as Japan and Australia) joined forces to 'impose costs' on Russia for its actions, but some major industrial countries such as China, India, Brazil, Indonesia, Turkey, Iran and South Korea refused to participate, and made up for the shortfalls in financing, technology and manufactures. In this respect at least, the world has become multipolar. A European study showed that in 2014–15, the sanctions resulted in $114 billion in lost revenue, with the pain shared almost equally between Russia, which lost more than $65 billion, and the United States and the EU, which together lost more than $50 billion. Over 90 per cent of that was borne by the EU, with Germany alone shouldering 40 per cent of the West's losses.[32] By early 2019, 26 per cent of Russia's total imports came from China and only 7.8 per cent from Germany – a historic shift that was unlikely to be reversed. In one way or another, Russia has endured various forms of sanctions for a century as the West sought to undermine Soviet economic and military power and to modify its international behaviour. However, as Christopher Davis notes, 'Western economic warfare neither prevented the Soviet Union from becoming a superpower nor played a significant role in bringing about the collapse of the communist regimes in the late 1980s.'[33] Even before the Ukraine-related sanctions, the United States after 9/11 had banned the export of some high-technology military and dual-use goods. The USSR had a sophisticated system of counter-sanctions, and Russia now resumed these practices, above all through its *spetsinformatsiya* (technical information) system (otherwise known as industrial espionage).

Russia today is the world's sixth-largest economy in purchasing power parity (PPP) terms (after China, US, India, Japan and Germany), with a GDP of $4.1 trillion, increasing almost sixfold from $620 billion in 2000. In nominal terms (and this depends on a fluctuating exchange rate), Russia ranks a more modest eleventh, with a GDP according to the International Monetary Fund (IMF) of only $1.72 trillion, about the same as Australia's. GDP per capita in PPP terms rose from $9,889 to reach $27,900 by 2017, the highest among all the Brazil, Russia, India, China and South Africa (BRICS) members, with the next highest, China, at $16,624. Over the same period, nominal monthly wages grew almost elevenfold, from $61 to $652, and following a decline during the recession, real wages were now rising across all sectors. Unemployment fell from 13 per cent in 2000 to 4.7 per cent in May 2018, a record low for the post-communist period, while pensions increased over 1,000 per cent from $20 to $221, although in real times they are still very low. In 2000, inflation was running at 36.5 per cent, whereas today it has fallen to a post-communist low of 2.4 per cent. When Putin was elected, Russia had barely $12 billion in reserves and a public debt that ran to 92 per cent of the GDP, while reserves (having provided a financial lifeline in the 2009 crash and the recession of 2014–16) have been restored and are still rising, and public debt, as noted, has shrunk to 15 per cent of the GDP, the lowest among the G20 nations. The government's debt load of 33 per cent of the GDP is also extraordinarily low for an industrialised nation and is less than a third of America's 105 per cent in 2017. Putin, in fact, has something of an obsession with debt, and spent his early years paying off foreign state and private creditors (completing the repayment of the Soviet Union's $104.5 billion foreign debt early). He then built up reserves in sovereign wealth funds, a prudent countercyclical strategy that as we have seen saved Russia twice – in the 2008–9 global financial crisis and the 2014–16 recession. Even the budget deficit by 2017 had fallen to only 1.6 per cent of the GDP, an amount easily financed by the government, and with the rise in oil prices and export diversification, Russia once again enjoyed a budget surplus in 2018.

The CBR under Elvira Nabiullina pursued a conservative fiscal policy focused on inflation targeting through positive interest rates and a floating exchange rate (introduced in November 2014). This is accompanied by the Gaullist strategy of building up gold reserves to loosen the grip of the dollar. Gold reserves in the Putin period more than quadrupled to reach 1,828 tonnes (worth some $454 billion) in 2018, and Russia remains the world's largest purchaser of gold and the world's third largest producer.[34] Russia is one of many countries, including China, India and Turkey, who for obvious reasons have repatriated their bullion from the United States, and potentially the creation of a gold-backed cryptocurrency could topple the US dollar as the world's reserve currency. Digital acceleration and geopolitical rivalry combine to challenge US economic predominance.[35] At the same time, Russia in 2018 sharply reduced its exposure to US Treasury bills, falling by more than 85 per cent from $96.9 billion to $13.2 billion. In October 2017, China launched a 'payment versus payment' (PVP) system for transactions in yuan and roubles, eliminating the need for the dollar to intermediate transactions, most prominently in oil trades. Russia and China were not only insulating themselves from US extraterritorial pressure but also sought to reduce their exposure to the next global financial crisis. By May 2018, global debt reached $237 trillion, higher than it had been before the 2008 financial crisis, while just in the first quarter of 2018, the US Treasury borrowed a record $488 billion and annual deficits broke all records. In 1971, the United States had severed the final link between the dollar and gold, and since then it has been a purely fiat money system, meaning that the dollar's value is no longer based on an independently redeemable asset but faith in the US government.[36] As that faith erodes, the move away from the dollar is in danger of becoming a stampede.

Russia is in danger of catching the 'Japanese disease', long-term stagnation but at a lower developmental level. Any attempt to stimulate the economy through a fiscal stimulus would only increase inflation and corruption. This is why structural reform has been proposed to stimulate economic growth. The term denotes changing the regulations and structures in an economy to make it more competitive. The demographic changes facing the country add urgency to such plans. Up to 2012, the natural population (excluding migration) had inexorably decreased, but as a result in part of Putin's pro-natalist policies (first introduced in 2007), including generous maternity capital, between 2012 and 2015, births exceeded deaths, but this trend reversed in 2016. In 2017, the natural population declined by 135,000 and in 2018 by 86,700, largely as a result of the demographic crisis of the early 1990s, as the lower number of women born then had fewer children two decades later. A return to natural growth is anticipated in 2024, but in the meantime a new maternity capital programme launched on 1 January 2018 granted increased support to low-income families, accompanied by measures to increase life expectancy. According to the federal statistical agency Rosstat, the population (including Crimea) on 1 January 2019 was 146.8 million.

A number of interlocking structural reforms have been proposed. First, a return to the privatisation programme of the 1990s although now conducted in a less anarchic and distorted manner. In the Putin years, an increasing proportion of the economy came into state hands, although there was no concerted nationalisation plan. The expropriation of the Yukos and Sibneft oil companies in the mid-2000s was followed by the restoration of state control over key sectors such as shipping, shipbuilding and aircraft production. The idea was to create 'national champions' that could compete in global markets. In the recent period, some private banks have been taken over as part of the attempt to clean-up the sector. In the early 2000s, the mastermind of earlier privatisation, Anatoly Chubais, was put in charge of the marketisation of the giant electricity monopoly, RAO EES. He divided the system into production and distribution companies, and sold them off to the market. However, very soon, many of these companies fell back into the hands of state-owned companies. While perhaps rational at a certain stage of development, liberal ideology asserts that state-controlled companies tend to breed inefficiencies and, in Russian conditions, corruption and rent-seeking. Russia certainly needs more world-class private companies, but the experience of some botched privatisations (notably the railways and utilities) in countries such as the UK acts as a salutary warning that the state is still required not only to defend the national interest but above all to defend the public interest from short-term profit-seeking and the dysfunctions of semi-competitive markets.

A second issue is the need to 'de-securitise' the economy. In Putin's second term, the government designated over forty industries as 'critical for national security'. Reform here would expand access to these industries by foreign investors, which would reduce the privileges (often abused) by industry insiders and expand access to financial markets, cutting-edge technologies and competitive management methods. The downside would be increased exposure to market failure and the loss of the employment security still enjoyed by Russian workers. This brings us to the third issue, the question of political reform to resist the baleful influence of the 'third state' and its associated corruption and 'raiding'. Fourth and above all, structural reform is intended to unleash Russia's entrepreneurial potential to allow GDP growth rates to rise substantially, based not just on natural resources but also through the market mechanisms of a diversified economy. To achieve this, structural reform would entail the consistent application of the rule of law, freedom to act commercially and the equal treatment of all investors. There have been major achievements in all three areas, but substantial shortcomings remain.

The country has seen a succession of technocratic development plans. Less than 40 per cent of the Gref plan in the end was implemented, and its successor, *Strategy 2020*, was derailed by the recession. Some of Russia's best economists and reform-minded politicians have been involved in crafting these plans, and they attest to the importance with which specialists are endowed in Putin's Russia. However, the problem of partial implementation lies less in the quality of the plans than in their undefined goals. It is not so much that the strategies are embedded in a technocratic rationality (in an era when expertise is too often denigrated, respect for experts can only be commended) but that there has been a lack of political will in pushing through necessary reforms, and this lack of will itself is an outcome of the consensual model of politics practiced in the Putin years, as well as the power of horizontal structures which pushed back against reform (notably when it comes to privatisation) when vested interests are threatened. This applies not just to the endemic struggle between powerful corporate groups but also to social constituencies. Although trade unions still operate largely according to neo-Soviet logic, elements of the former Soviet social contract also apply. Workers are not sacked in a downturn, and a range of social benefits continue to be provided by the workplace. Only radical liberals have the appetite for a Thatcherite neo-liberal shake-out of the economy. Russia today, thus, looks rather like Britain of the 1970s, with all of its achievements and failings including not only a ramified social security system and welfare state but also inefficient monopolies and nationalised industries.

With the economy still mired in recession, in early 2016, Putin appointed the former minister of finance, Kudrin, co-chair of the Presidential Economic Council. In his speech to Putin and experts on 25 May 2016, Kudrin presented a report prepared by the CSR calling for fiscal consolidation, structural reform and greater incentives for investment. The plan, on which over 1,700 experts had toiled, outlined seven priorities: improving quality of life, doubling the number of entrepreneurs, increasing productivity, expanding the non-commodities sector of the economy, introducing new governance methods, accompanied by urban development and court and military reforms. Kudrin argued that without structural reform, it would be impossible to return to pre-crisis levels and annual growth would not exceed 2 per cent, with the economy trapped by institutional constraints. He noted that the structural growth rate – the part of the GDP based on growth in labour, capital and productivity – had steadily declined since the mid-2000s and was now less than 1 per cent a year.[37] Returning to the theme that had provoked his dismissal, Kudrin warned that Russia had to settle its disputes with the West if it wished to achieve the desired growth.[38] At that time, Russia's military spending was set to increase by $10 billion, when the same amendments to the budget envisaged $7 billion worth of cuts to welfare spending.[39] In 2017, the CSR once again stressed the need to cut defence and security spending as a share of the GDP (from 4.4 per cent of the GDP to 2.8 per cent), and increase investment in human capital (health and education) and other productive investments (such as transport and communication). Kudrin and his team were particularly concerned that with an aging population, Russia would be spending an ever-increasing share of its budget and national income on pensions and healthcare.[40]

Although Russia returned to cyclical growth in 2017, Kudrin and his team argued that without structural reform it would remain low. Kudrin's key proposals included continued macroeconomic restraint, reform of state administration (including greater public control over law-enforcement officials), raising the pension age, reducing the government stake in large companies through substantial privatisation and tightening revenue collection from the shadow economy. This was to be accompanied by some modest increased investment in healthcare and education to reinforce improvements in the business environment through judicial reform, designed to make the courts more independent. These reforms would all carry political and social costs, hence Putin's reluctance to take this path. Valery Fedorov, the head of the All-Russian Centre for the Study of Public Opinion (VTsIOM) polling agency, identified a battle between two political agendas. The first was the 'patriotic' programme, focusing on foreign policy and Russia's role in the world, while the second was the 'socio-economic' agenda, devoted to domestic issues and in particular the economic crisis.[41] Kudrin identified with the second, whereas the main protagonist of the former was Sergei Glazyev, Putin's advisor on regional integration between 2012 and

2019. Glazyev favoured fiscal expansion, a low refinancing rate for the CBR and increased protectionism.[42] From the neo-traditional statist perspective, 'structural reform' was little more than a synonym for surrender to the West. Putin, typically, tacked between the positions, although Kudrin's return to a public role signalled reinforcement of the liberal position.

The battle of the economic plans continued in the run-up to the 2018 presidential election. In early 2017, the government and two expert bodies delivered their reports to the Kremlin. One was devised by Kudrin's team at the CSR and the other by the business ombudsman Boris Titov, who was appointed to the post in 2012 to defend the rights of business owners, and his Stolypin Club. By contrast with the 'macroeconomic' restraint recommended by Kudrin, the Stolypin Club advocated a surge in spending to be financed by monetary emission and by easing limits on the budget deficit to allow it to grow to 3 per cent of the GDP. This in effect meant 'printing money' (a Russian version of quantitative easing) whose effects would be predictable: increased inflation and corruption.[43] The Ministry of Economic Development also had its plans, which tended to be conservative with moderate policies, including holding down wage growth to allow profits to grow, thus allowing for more investment.

Those opposed to more 'structural reform' argued that Russia had already achieved much. It had a floating exchange rate (as of late 2014), prices set by supply and demand, a relatively flexible labour market, a flat rate tax and private property rights (although threatened by raiders). Russia's positions in the World Bank's Ease of Doing Business rating had dramatically improved, rising from 120th in 2010 to 35th (out of 190 in the world) by 2018. The rights of minority shareholders had been flagrantly abused in the 1990s, but now Russia ranked 51st for their protection (higher than some major industrial countries like Germany and Japan), while it ranks 18th for enforcing contracts.[44] Weak points remain the poor quality of the financial market and banking, indefensible property rights, inadequate judicial independence and corruption. To raise the headline GDP growth rate, serious challenges would have to be addressed: tax optimisation, especially to reduce the tax burden on small businesses; demography, and in particular investment in human capital, at a time when the working-age population of the country is falling and the ratio of workers to pensioners is also falling – currently there are two social security contributors to one pensioner, which by 2035 would fall to one-and-a-half to every pensioner – increasing pressure to raise the retirement age (Kudrin suggested 63 for women and 65 for men); industrial technologies, including technical education; public administration (in other words, political reform); increasing productivity; and the thorny issue of privatisation. The overall goal was to improve the economic growth rate and reduce dependence on natural resources. The central question was whether this could be achieved without dismantling the 'rent-management system'.

On 13 May 2017, the *National Economic Security Strategy to 2030* was adopted, the first since 1996, identifying the main challenges and threats to Russia's economic security and outlining measures to combat them:

> The implementation of this Strategy should ensure the economic sovereignty of Russia and the resistance of the national economy to external and internal challenges and threats, strengthen sociopolitical stability, maintain sustainable socioeconomic development and enhance the standard of living and quality of life in the country.

The *Strategy* divided challenges into four groups. The first focused on natural and climatic changes, which could cause droughts, floods, food shortages and ultimately increased competition and conflicts. The second dealt with global economic processes including fluctuations in global financial and commodity markets, economic shifts, new types of regulations and changes in global energy demand, all of which could affect Russia. The third group covered challenges directed against the Russian economy, such as discriminatory provisions and sanctions, including restrictions on financial flows. It was against these threats that Russia advanced its version of 'resilience', trying to insulate the Russian economy from external threats by reducing reliance on foreign technology and services, especially in the energy and defence sectors. Russian technological and human capital resources were stimulated by this sort of economic pressure but effectively meant partial deglobalisation. The fourth group focused on internal economic dynamics, including inadequate development of competitive employment in advanced sectors of the economy and the underdevelopment of the service sector. Russia has few non-resource companies in the world's top rank, and enduring problems of underinvestment remain. The export-oriented commodities-based economy had natural limits, including the exhaustion of the resource base.[45] The document noted the long-term trends moving against Russia, including the depletion of energy fields, declining labour resources and the global competition for talent. Like so many of Russia's strategic documents, this one was torn between accepting the need for global integration, if Russia was to remain competitive, and the perceived imperatives of security.

Sanctions reshaped Russia's economic policy. In agriculture, Russia's response built on the lessons learned during the spike in food prices in 2007–8, which had shaped a food-security system that enhanced protectionist measures. On 6 August 2014, a package of counter-sanctions placed an embargo on food imports from the EU, the United States, Australia, Canada and Norway, measures which without the sanctions would have been very hard to reconcile with WTO membership. In June 2017, the counter-sanctions were applied to an expanded list of countries and products, and were repeatedly extended. The policy triad of counter-sanctions, food security and food self-sufficiency boosted output in a range of products, many of which had earlier been satisfied through imports. Every grain harvest between 2014 and 2018 exceeded 100 million tonnes, beating the Soviet record set in 1978. The record grain harvest in 2018 brought in 135 million tonnes, including nearly 80 million tonnes of wheat. Russia in 2015/16 overtook the United States to become the world's largest wheat exporter, increasing its share of the global wheat market from 4 to 16 per cent by 2017. Combined exports of agricultural products rose by 20 per cent alone in 2018 to $25.9 billion, worth almost double as much as exports of arms and weapons. The year 2018 also saw record harvests for maize (corn), sunflower, soy, vegetables and fruits, accompanied by a rapid increase in the output of dairy products. With farming benefitting from the protectionism afforded by the food embargo, the agricultural lobby became one of the strongest constituencies in favour of continued sanctions.[46] The sector's response to climate change was minimal, and the industrial agricultural model offered few opportunities for organics and more sustainable models of farming, leading to continued soil and environmental degradation.

The liberal model of economic reform was challenged by more statist approaches. A recent study notes that 'most successful reforms in Russia were initiated from the top down, and that conversely, the withdrawal of a unified and strong central authority from the country's life led to an intensification of inter-clan struggles for revenue, widespread theft by oligarchs, and the flight of many economic players in the subsistence economy'.[47] Russia was faced with two contrasting economic reform plans. Kudrin advocated investment into economic multipliers such as infrastructure, social services, education, health and, above all, increasing labour productivity, while the alternative programme advanced by Titov and the Stolypin Club called for massive borrowing and New Deal-style spending to boost economic growth. Titov's plan focused on the need for new economic stimuli but ignored corruption and the weak rule of law, which were the significant factors depressing economic growth. Putin, as usual, temporised. This was evident in his annual news conference on 14 December 2017, when he noted that his electoral programme would focus on 'infrastructure development, healthcare and education', as well as high technology and improving labour efficiency. In response to another question, he asserted that Russia's GDP had increased by 75 per cent, and industrial production by 60 per cent, since 2000, and although real wages had somewhat declined in the last three years, since the early 2000s, real incomes had risen by 250 per cent and real pensions by 260 per cent. Infant mortality had decreased 2.6-fold and maternal mortality by 75 per cent. He warned of the 'demographic pit' because of earlier periods of high mortality and low birth rates, even though life expectancy had now risen to 73 years (67.5 for men and 77.6 for women) because of the lower death rate. There had been some impressive achievements, but ultimately it was remarkable by how little the overall GDP had increased in nearly two decades of his leadership. More than that, real incomes were declining, with a 0.7 per cent fall in 2014, 3.2 per cent in 2015 and

5.9 per cent in 2016, at a time when two-thirds of the working population received below-average wages.[48] Putin announced that there had been almost weekly meetings of experts to identify growth drivers, but he gave no indication of what these were, although he stated that economic development would be increasingly driven by domestic demand.

Putin recognised the need to improve labour productivity but reiterated the importance of fulfilling his 'May Decrees' of 2012, which set goals on increasing the wages of teachers, doctors, kindergarten workers, a programme that placed enormous pressure on regional budgets. Most doctors, health workers, teachers and cultural workers in Russia are paid by the state, and their wages remain low by international and even domestic standards. When wages do go up, it is often at the expense of new equipment and facilities. In his press conference in December 2017, Putin claimed that 90 per cent of the targets of the May Decrees had been fulfilled, although there is some scepticism on this count. Poorer regions were pushed into debt, with eight of them having a debt-to-revenue ratio over 100 per cent (with Mordovia the worst at 194 per cent), but dozens of regions simply could not afford the costs associated with the goals.[49] Putin also temporised on raising the retirement age, which stood at the level set in 1932 (55 for women and 60 for men) when life expectancy was much lower. He conceded that even Russia's closest neighbours, Belarus and Kazakhstan, had raised the retirement age, and that if Russia did not follow suit, 'there will be more and more people ready to retire and less able to work', with a shrinking pot all round so pensions would have to be reduced. Nevertheless, with an election in view, Putin insisted 'a final decision has not been made'. He also promised that taxes would not be raised before the end of 2018. His overall position was that 'shock treatment of the kind we had in the 1990s is unacceptable'.[50]

Powering Putinism

Putin and energy are indissolubly linked. Although a lawyer by education, Putin in the second half of the 1990s wrote his doctoral (*kandidatskaya*) thesis on the use of natural resources for national development, arguing that the state needed to be able to control their development to ensure that they were used to best effect. Although there has been considerable diversification of the economy away from the old energy-based model, natural resources remain the foundation of Russian economic performance. Today, oil and gas exports account for 40 per cent of Russia's budget revenues, although energy as a proportion of total exports fell from 70 per cent in 2013 to 59 per cent in 2017. When combined with revenue from other commodities such as iron, steel, aluminium and copper, revenue from natural resources represents 75 per cent of Russia's total exports and together represents 60 per cent of gross GDP ($844.58 billion in value as of 2017).[51] The fatal dependency on energy prices remains, to which the Soviet Union had already succumbed when prices plunged in 1985 and which Russia suffered from in the 1990s. In 2008–9, the price of oil plummeted from over $140 to around $40, and GDP contracted by 7.8 per cent in 2009. Oil prices soon recovered, allowing the country to return to a growth of 4.5 per cent in 2010. By the time oil prices once again fell precipitously, from $100 to under $60 in 2014 and below $35 by late 2015, economic growth had already tailed off and now the country was plunged into recession, exacerbated by sanctions. Supply-cut coordination between Russia and Saudi Arabia from 2017 forced up the price of oil and, thus, increasing revenues, threatening to return Russia to the old pattern of oil dependency.

The policy now is to ensure that the rouble stops being a volatile petro-currency. This is why the 'fiscal rule' was introduced, stipulating that all revenues above a certain level (in early 2019, $42 a barrel) would be allocated to reserves rather than to spending. The idea is to break the link between energy prices and the budget, and with it the strength of the rouble. Although every additional $1 per barrel is worth $2.5 billion a year, with most going into the federal budget via taxes, oil dependency only increases vulnerability. Russia had occasionally run budget deficits even when oil was above $100 a barrel, but the fiscal rule weakens the correlation between the rouble exchange rate and the oil price, and ensures a more solid footing for public finances. It also avoids the recurrent danger of the Dutch disease, when a country becomes excessively dependent on a single resource, and when the value of that item goes up the currency strengthens, undermining the competitiveness of other sectors in international markets. With energy prices once again rising from 2017, the pressure for a fiscal stimulus increased, although it would be unlikely to prove effective: 'Given the Russian economy's "supply-side" demographic and investment constraints, expansionary monetary and fiscal policies would produce only inflation, real exchange-rate appreciation, and deteriorating external balances. A classic boom-bust overheating episode would be all too predictable.'[52]

The old economic model based on oil is no longer delivering growth. In addition, in the era of sanctions, the government cannot easily borrow on foreign financial markets and is thus forced to live within its means. The floating rouble exchange rate is accompanied by tight fiscal discipline. If in 2013 the budget needed $115 to balance, by 2018 it had fallen to $54. As oil prices once again rose in 2018, the budget again moved into surplus (for the first time since 2011). One way to sterilise the cash inflow is to buy gold, which Russia, as we have seen, did in great quantities. This makes the rouble effectively a gold-backed currency, unlike the American fiat system. Moscow also looked for ways to free itself of the dollar burden in oil trade to strengthen its economic sovereignty and resilience in the face of sanctions. At the same time, Moscow used the extra budget revenue to increase its foreign exchange reserves. All this at a time when the ratio of public sector debt to GDP is below the G20 average, the ratio of gross – including commercial – external debt to GDP is around 32 per cent (Putin was obsessive about paying off external debts), and the country has low inflation and is running a current account surplus of 2–3 per cent. Higher oil revenues would only generate instability, and, thus, Russia sought a stable oil price of around $70. In 2008, Russia needed an oil price of $115 per barrel to break even, but this has now fallen to $49. Saudi Arabia needs more than that to break even, while higher prices only encourages US shale oil producers, thus increasing long-term competition in energy markets, and accelerates the shift to non-carbon sources of energy.[53] Putin has a well-deserved reputation as a fiscal conservative. These are not the characteristics of a petro-state, let alone a 'kleptocracy'.

The energy issue is one of the most divisive in Russo-West relations. In the 1970s, the Soviet Union began to export gas to West Germany and later to the rest of Western Europe, as well as supplying its East European allies in the Soviet bloc. The Druzhba (Friendship) oil pipeline was built in the 1960s, against American opposition. The Bratstvo (Brotherhood) pipeline system from Urengoi through Ukraine was built from the 1980s to transport gas from the giant Western Siberian fields to the new markets, as well as funnelling gas from Turkmenistan to the West. Already in 1997 the Yamal–Europe gas pipeline was built through Belarus and Poland to Germany to increase capacity and to circumvent Ukraine, part of a strategy that long predates the current crisis.[54] Gazprom has a monopoly over Russia's gas pipelines to Europe, and the system is monitored on a giant screen at Gazprom's headquarters in Moscow, acting as the pulsing heart of Europe's energy networks. In 2013, Gazprom exported 234.4 billion cubic metres (bcm) of natural gas, 97 per cent of which (228 bcm) was delivered by pipeline to Turkey and the rest of Europe (Ukraine, Belarus, Moldova, the Balkans and the EU), with the EU alone taking 149.5 bcm (64 per cent). Of this, 86 bcm transited through Ukraine, accounting for some 30 per cent of Europe's total gas imports. Ukraine earned some $3 billion a year from transporting gas to Europe, although from 2016 it did not directly import Russian gas for domestic use. Even though political relations had broken down, in 2017, 94 bcm of Russian gas still transited Ukraine to the EU. The European Commission lobbied hard to maintain Ukraine as a gas transit state, otherwise it feared having to make up the loss of revenues. The present contract expired on 31 December 2019, and with new bypass pipelines being constructed, the fate of Ukraine as a transit state for Russian gas is at best uncertain.

In 2018, Gazprom exported a record 201.8 bcm, supplying 37 per cent of Europe's gas market. In 2017, Russia's gas exports to Europe alone rose over 8.1 per cent to a record level of 194 bcm and topped 200 bcm in 2018. Gazprom's total production rose by 12.4 per cent to reach 471 bcm.[55] Germany was by far the largest and fastest-growing market in 2015, importing 45.3 bcm, followed by Turkey with 27 bcm and Italy with 24.4 bcm; even distant UK was Russia's fourth-largest market in Europe, importing 11.1 bcm that year.[56] The share of Russian gas imports in Germany is 28 per cent; in Italy 37 per cent; in Slovenia, Greece and

Hungary between 41 and 45 per cent; while the Czech Republic, Slovakia, Finland, Estonia, Latvia and Lithuania are close to 100 per cent dependent on Russian gas.[57] Long before the Ukraine crisis, Moscow sought to diversify transport routes, and this is why the Yamal line was built. The two parallel lines of Nord Stream 1 run 759 miles (1,222 km) from Vyborg on the Gulf of Finland to Greifswald in Germany, with the second coming on stream a year after the first in October 2012. Nord Stream 2 enters the Baltic at Ust-Luga in Leningrad Oblast and enters Germany in the resort town of Lubmin. It doubled the existing Nord Stream line's capacity of 55 bcm when it came into operation in early 2020. Ukraine and Poland tried to block the new line, joined later by the United States (keen to sell its liquefied natural gas [LNG] to Europe). The German government insisted it was a purely commercial venture (built by a partnership of Gazprom with Germany's Wintershall and Uniper, Austria's OMV, France's Engie and the Anglo-Dutch Shell), thus allowing the scheme to go ahead. Given Russia's enormous reserves, the country 'will continue to provide the lowest-cost gas for export to Europe through the 2020s'.[58]

The EU devoted considerable effort to joining the gas pipelines from Europe, Asia and Africa into the Trans-Europe Network (TEN) to ensure security of supply to Europe, while Russia has diversified its exports markets to Asia and into LNG. The first shipment from the giant $27 billion Yamal LNG plant in December 2017 was originally thought to be destined for the UK but in fact (after trans-shipment at the Isle of Grain terminal) was delivered to the Everett gasification plant near Boston. The boom in LNG production means that natural gas, like oil, is becoming a global commodity increasingly freed from the physical constraints of pipelines. Nevertheless, pipelines are still the cheapest way of delivering large volumes of gas. In May 2014, at the height of the Ukraine crisis, Russia and China signed a thirty-year $400 billion deal to deliver 38 bcm of East Siberian gas from the Chayanda and Kovytka deposits via a specially built pipeline called Power of Siberia, passing through the eastern sector of the Russo-Chinese border. On 10 November 2014, after a decade of negotiations, the two sides signed a framework agreement for the long-awaited 'Western route' to channel West Siberian gas through Altai to China, but this did not mean that the pipeline would be finally built. Despite the enormity of the deals, the total planned capacity of the two routes is only 78 bcm, compared to the 146 bcm Russia sold to Europe and Turkey in 2014. The Power of Siberia pipeline came on line in late 2019.

At the same time, the Druzhba oil pipeline is the world's longest, running from Western Siberia to Western Europe through Belarus and Ukraine. It started supplying oil to what was then the fraternal socialist republic of Czechoslovakia in 1962 and since then has become a ramified network. With the construction of the Baltic Pipeline System 2, significant quantities will be exported through the recently completed Ust-Luga oil terminal, with a branch line to the Kirishi oil refinery. This renders Russia less dependent on transit countries, especially difficult ones like Poland and Ukraine, and opened up new markets to tanker trade. Russia's oil output by 2019 had risen for eleven consecutive years, despite the restrictions agreed with the Organisation of Petroleum Exporting Countries (OPEC) to limit production to force up prices. In 2017, Russian production reached 10.98 million barrels per day (bpd). Russian output under Putin has nearly doubled, rising from 6.1 million bpd in 1999, and output peaked at 11.23 million bpd in October 2016 before the OPEC cuts of 300,000 million bpd.[59] Russia has now become the largest supplier of crude oil to China, reducing supplies available for the European market. China receives the bulk of its Russian oil through newly built pipelines, with the capacity of the East Siberia–Pacific Ocean (ESPO) line doubling on 1 January 2018 to 30 million tons annually, or about 600,000 bpd. Some oil is still exported by tanker from the Russian ports of Kozmino, De-Kastri and Prigorodnoe. Overall, Russia supplied China with some 1.3 million bpd in 2017.[60]

Despite mutual interdependence, the Russian-European energy relations are characterised by distrust – and the persistence of this phenomenon reveals perhaps an underlying structural incompatibility between Russia and Europe, a view that is gladly endorsed by Eurasianists in Russia and Russophobes in the West. Ever since the Soviet Union established an energy relationship with Western Europe, there have been fears, fanned by Washington, that political autonomy would be compromised by dependence on Russian supplies. This attitude remained even after the Soviet Union disappeared, accompanied by persistent calls from the United States for Europe to reduce its energy dependence on Russia. In recent times, this has taken the form of the 'Putinisation of energy' thesis, advanced by Marin Katusa. He argues that at the end of the Cold War, Russia sought to control global oil and gas trades as part of the global struggle for energy markets between the United States, Saudi Arabia and other states.[61] The Ukraine crisis intensified calls for a common energy policy for the twenty-eight countries in the European Union. In February 2015, an energy union was announced to create an integrated energy market by building a network of connector pipelines to create an integrated European energy market, with states cooperating to increase their energy security and to decarbonise their economies. The term 'hybrid warfare' has become popular to describe the multiple forms of pressure one country can exert against another and reflects the intensified 'securitisation' of interstate relations. The term was used by Matthew Bryza, the former US ambassador to Azerbaijan, when he argued that 'energy is a weapon in Moscow's "hybrid" war against Ukraine, along with covert invasion, military advisors and mercenaries, and information warfare'.[62] The strategic purpose was clear when the idea of an energy union was first mooted in April 2014 by Donald Tusk, at the time Polish prime minister and later president of the European Council. He stressed the need to remove 'Russia's energy stranglehold' on Europe.[63]

The EU's so-called Third Energy Package (TEP) of September 2009 sought to create a more competitive gas and supply market in Europe by separating production from transport and ensuring third-party access to pipelines. The TEP is a series of legislative acts designed to reduce monopolies in the energy market, including a provision which prohibits gas producers from owning primary gas pipelines. As far as Russia was concerned, this was an 'anti-Gazprom' law, since it was directly affected by the legislation. Although Russian energy policy is often characterised as 'geopolitical' and the EU's as market-based, both indulge in the two. Russia responded to the TEP largely through legal and technocratic instruments typical of the market approach.[64] On 24 May 2018, the EU and Gazprom resolved a seven-year antitrust dispute. No fines were imposed on Gazprom, but instead the state-controlled gas company agreed to change the way it operates in Central and Eastern Europe (CEE), removing restrictions on how its customers in the region can use gas, removing the ban on exports to other countries and ensuring a competitive price for gas, with Gazprom committed to take active steps to integrate gas markets in the region. The countries now have the right to demand a price review to bring their rates in line with those rates at which Gazprom sold gas to Germany and the Netherlands.[65]

While the EU perceives itself to be at market risk, Russia has long been worried by transit risks. This in particular concerned Ukraine, through which half of Russian gas deliveries to Europe passed. Since the 1990s, there had been endless controversies over deliveries across the country and to the Ukrainian market. Shutdowns in 2006 and 2009 caused irreparable reputational damage to Russia, irrespective of the specific rights or wrongs of its case. Understandably, Russia intensified efforts to bypass Ukraine as a transit country. In addition to Nord Stream, by early 2014, Russia had just about everything in place to build South Stream, the 2,386 km-long pipeline under the Black Sea to Bulgaria and then up through the Balkans to Hungary and the Austrian hub at Baumgarten. The project had been introduced in 2007 as an alternative to the EU's Nabucco pipeline intended to bring Azerbaijani gas to Europe via Turkey and when running at full capacity would have supplied Europe with up to 65 bcm of natural gas annually. Following pressure from the United States and the EU, Bulgaria in June 2014 pulled out of the project, forcing Putin to cancel the whole scheme in December 2014. Instead, he announced what came to be known as Turkish Stream. Instead of tracking west, the pipes go south to Turkey, and then ultimately arrive at a new gas hub on the Turkey–Greece border, delivering the same amount of gas but through this alternative route. Distribution is then a matter for the EU to sort out. This is the sort of démarche that we have come to expect from Putin. Making the announcement, Putin noted, 'If Europe does not want to carry out the project, then it will not be carried out.' Putin stressed, 'We will re-concentrate our energy resources on other regions of the world', and he added for good measure, 'We think this is against Europe's best economic interests and is causing damage to our co-operation.'[66] He reiterated the point in his press conference of 17 December 2015, arguing that Bulgaria abandoned the South Stream project because the leading EU institutions, notably the European Parliament and the European Commission, had pressured Sofia to renege on its agreements to build the pipeline across its territory.[67] The struggle over energy pipelines is yet another indication of the enduring confrontation that has returned to Europe.

Sanctions and their effect

The new era of sanctions began with the December 2012 Magnitsky Act, which imposed penalties on Russians allegedly involved in the death of the auditor Sergei Magnitsky, and the list thereafter was periodically extended. Punitive sanctions were first introduced in 2014 in response to the Ukraine crisis and since then have been gradually ratcheted up. Their immediate effect was to amplify the impact of the fall in the price of oil with which they coincided. The EU and the United States repeatedly renewed the sanctions regime, and unless there is some sort of breakthrough in the European security order, they will remain for the foreseeable future. However, when used by the Trump administration to favour US energy companies (above all, shale gas producers for the LNG market) by trying to block the construction of Nord Stream 2, Germany and Austria objected. In the 1980s, European banks and companies (supported by their governments) resisted US attempts to block the construction of West Siberian gas pipelines to Europe, and the sanctions regime today provokes similar resentment in European businesses. Above all, the sanctions regime indicates that a long-term adversarial relationship has become established between the Atlantic powers and Russia.

On 25 July 2017, the House of Representatives voted 419–3 in support, and on 28 July, the US Senate voted 98–2 to adopt new sanctions, officially called 'HR 3364 Countering America's Adversaries through Sanctions Act' or CAATSA. The CAATSA sanctions limit the president's ability to ease or lift the existing ones. The earlier measures imposed by President Barack Obama through executive orders were now given legislative force and, thus, could not be rescinded by the president.[68] Given the huge majorities, a reluctant Trump had no choice but to sign it into law on 2 August. This was a monster of a law, effectively 'expropriating' the management of foreign policy from the White House, and establishing a mechanism that could poison relations between Russia and the US for generations to come. Although the early Trump White House is typically portrayed as incompetent, in passing this legislation, Congress clearly feared that Trump would be too effective and would be able to weaken or even remove the existing Obama-era hostile legislation against Russia, and, thus, to defend its institutional prerogatives, and closed ranks in a bipartisan manner against the president.[69] The adoption of CAATSA undoubtedly marks a watershed in Russo-US relations.[70]

The CAATSA measure stipulated twelve sanctions measures against Russia. Section 241 called for the Treasury Department in consultation with others to submit within 180 days a detailed report identifying 'the most significant senior political figures and oligarchs' in Russia, as determined by their closeness to the Russian regime and their net worth. This prompted Putin in a meeting with business people on 21 December to approve the idea of creating new mechanisms for the return of capital to Russia, including external government bonds denominated in foreign currency. The law extended sanctions to countries outside Russia (extraterritoriality) where US corporations or persons provided goods, services and technology for certain projects 'in which a Russian firm is involved', raising the concerns of European leaders and companies (especially those involved in building Nord Stream 2).[71] The package allows the president in consultation with US allies to sanction any entity that provides technology, services, investment or other support valued at $1 million or more to Russian export pipeline projects. They were condemned by Germany for meddling in Europe's energy supplies. The US ambition clearly was that US LNG exports to Europe could fill the gap if the Russian project was blocked. However, LNG is at least 20 per cent more expensive than pipeline gas and, thus, stands little chance of pushing Russia out of the European gas market. Nord Steam 2 representatives, moreover, insisted that with plenty of global LNG capacity, no single supplier was in a position to use gas supplies as a political instrument in Europe.[72]

The Trump administration was as resolute as its predecessors in seeking to block energy interdependence between Russia and Europe. For the first time since the end of the Cold War, US sanctions were not coordinated with Europeans and indeed appeared directly to challenge their economic interests. American LNG exports were now slated to replace Russian gas, even though it was more expensive. Other American corporate interests appeared no less concerned than European ones, and a number started lobbying against sanctions, including ExxonMobil, General Electric, Boeing and many others. However, their efforts could at most lead to a mitigation of the rules in individual sectors and were unlikely to lead to the lifting of sanctions in their entirety.

The 'Kremlin list' as stipulated by Section 241 was issued on the very last day allowed, 29 January 2018, and proved a disappointment to those who anticipated a harsh line. It appears that a list drawn up by experts in the hawkish Atlantic Council was jettisoned; instead, 114 names of top officials was drawn from the English-language part of the Kremlin website and the 96 oligarchs came from the list of Russian billionaires of Forbes Russia. No immediate sanctions were placed on the 210 (except for the 22 who were already on previous sanctions lists), drawing an angry response from the likes of Senator Ben Cardin, the ranking member of the US Senate Foreign Relations Committee, who wrote to Secretary of State Rex Tillerson stating that the failure to impose new sanctions was 'unacceptable'.[73] He did not have long to wait (although by then Tillerson had been dismissed as secretary of state). In response to the poisoning of Sergei and Yulia Skripal in Salisbury on 4 March 2018, 153 Russian diplomats were expelled in a concerted moved by the UK and its allies, and the Russian consulate in Seattle was closed. In response, Russia expelled a commensurate number of Western diplomats from Russia and closed the British consulate and British Council offices in St Petersburg.

Amid a worsening diplomatic atmosphere, on 6 April 2018, Trump imposed the most devastating sanctions yet seen, in part in response to the Skripal affair and the alleged use of chemical weapons in Douma on the outskirts of Damascus. They targeted what the United States said were individuals and companies that aided or benefited from what were considered the Kremlin's 'malign activities' around the world, including the alleged interference in the 2016 US presidential election, supplying weapons to President Bashir al-Assad in Syria and subverting Western democracies. The US Treasury Department imposed sanctions on seven so-called Russian oligarchs, twelve companies they either owned or controlled, and seventeen senior Kremlin officials. The sanctions made it difficult for those on the list to do business in the United States or gain access to financial markets. In particular, Oleg Deripaska, the head of one of the world's largest aluminium companies Rusal, was targeted 'for having acted or purported to act for or on behalf of, directly or indirectly, a senior official of the Government of the Russian Federation'. He had been a former business partner of Paul Manafort, Trump's one-time campaign chairman and subsequently indicted by the Mueller investigation.[74] The disruption of the aluminium market forced a partial reversal in December 2018 once Deripaska had divested himself of his interest in Rusal.

These sanctions came out of the blue and were intended to 'impose costs' on Russia's generally insubordinate behaviour. While Trump and his associates declared that they were no longer in the regime-change game, the militants in Congress still hoped to use coercive measures to shape Russian policy or even to provoke elite discontent leading to Putin's overthrow. Instead, American pressure tended only to reinforce solidarity around the Kremlin and even advanced Putin's goal of getting Russian capital (and even leading business people who had gone abroad for various reasons) to return. The goal of the American sanctions was not clear, but the overall intent appeared to be to provoke some sort of coup against Putin's administration, either through creating splits in the elite or by stimulating a grass-roots movement in support of regime change. In fact, the vague and all-embracing charges against Russia only rallied the country behind Putin.

Medvedev condemned the April 2018 sanctions as 'outrageous and obnoxious' but stressed that they forced Russia to rethink its place in the world. In his view, the policy of containing Russia was part of the West's enduring strategy: 'Our international partners will continue to pursue it regardless of how our country may be called. They did this with regard to the Russian Empire, and they did this many times with regard to the Soviet Union and Russia.' Russia would adapt and respond through import substitution and improvements to its own social institutions. The assumption was that 'sanctions will remain in place for a long time'.[75] This was view shared by the Russian public, with 43 per cent at that time believing that they would not be lifted in the next few years.[76] Putin himself noted, 'We are not surprised by any restrictions or sanctions: this does not frighten us and will never force us to abandon our independent, sovereign path of development.' And he went on to declare: 'I believe that either Russia will be sovereign, or it will not exist at all.'[77] The sanctions, in the early stages at least, strengthened Putin and weakened the liberal agenda, reinforcing conservative narratives of self-reliance and independence.

The summit between Putin and Trump in Helsinki on 16 July 2018 proved a disaster, with Trump apparently acquiescing with Putin's view that Russia had not 'meddled' in the 2016 US presidential election. A new Congressional bill was introduced among others by senators Bob Menendez and Lindsey Graham, with the latter arguing that the legislation's goal was to impose 'crushing sanctions'. The measures included the 'nuclear option' of sanctioning Russian sovereign debt and state banks, which would devastate Russian and global financial markets. The draft bill, called 'Defending American Security from Kremlin Aggression Act' (DASKAA), included four key provisions.[78] The first proposed banning Russia's banks, including Sberbank, VTB Bank, Gazprombank, Rosselkhozbank, Promsvyazbank and Vneshekonmbank, from operating in the United States, which would effectively block them from dollar settlements and ban US citizens buying Russian sovereign debt. Second, in the energy sector, a ban on investments in any government or government-affiliated companies outside Russia worth more than $250 million. There would also be penalties for any involvement, including providing equipment or technology, on new oil projects inside Russia worth more than $1 million. Third, within sixty days of the law's adoption, the White House would have to provide a new list of Russians suspected of cyberattacks against the United States; the Treasury Department would have 180 days to update its 'Kremlin List' of Russian state officials and 'oligarchs'; the Director of National Intelligence would investigate the 'personal net worth' of Putin and his family; and the State Department would have ninety days to determine whether Russia should be designated a state sponsor of terrorism. Fourth, there would be a new Sanctions Office to reinforce CAATSA, and an 'Office of Sanctions Coordination' in the State Department to coordinate work with the Treasury.[79] The overall effect would be to cut Russia off from US financial markets to a degree not seen since the US freeze on Japanese assets and a prohibition on trading its debt in 1941, effectively putting an end to all bilateral business. The result of that policy is well known.

There was a pause in sanctions activity as politics focused on the November 2018 midterms. The Defending Elections from Threats by Establishing Redlines Act (DETER) was on hold, and the absence of any significant Russian activity lowered the pressure for action. The House of Representatives was retaken by the Democrats, but this made little difference since sanctions activity had been conducted on a largely bipartisan basis. In February 2019, the US Senate returned to the DASKAA bill, with Russia's 'malign influence' in Syria now cited as one of the reasons for reintroducing the legislation. The bill prohibited US nationals from 'engaging in transactions with, providing financing for, or otherwise dealing in Russia's state debt', as well as imposing restrictive measures on Russia's shipbuilding sector along with twenty-four senior officers in the FSB. This was in connection with the detention of twenty-four Ukrainian sailors after a confrontation in the Kerch Strait on 25 November the previous year, when three Ukrainian naval vessels were accused of violating the rules of passage from the Black Sea to the Sea of Azov. Investment in Russian export LNG energy projects located outside Russia would also be banned. Freezing measures against the operations and assets of state-run financial institutions such as Sberbank and VTB had been removed from the earlier version. The Director of National Intelligence was to submit a detailed report on the personal net worth and assets of the Russian president no later than 180 days after the bill's enactment.[80] The sanctions were getting personal.

They were also getting more general. The new version of DASKAA was non-specific and was effectively a way of waging the Cold War against Russia rather than tied to any specific policy goal. The sanctions regime looks set to endure for years, if not decades, as part of the neo-containment policy against Russia. The Russian response was correspondingly broad and can be summed up as follows. First, a range of counter-sanctions were imposed, including those of August 2014 (and later extended) on food imports from sanctioning countries. In June 2018, Putin signed a legislation allowing 'counter-measures against unfriendly actions' by the United States and other foreign countries, effectively an upgrade of a December 2006 law providing for 'special economic measures'. The new law was defensive and tempered some of the earlier ideas mooted by impassioned deputies in parliament, most of which would have caused more damage to Russia than the sanctions themselves.[81] Second, the country's political economy was reoriented to ensure greater resilience and autonomy. The state's role in the economy was enhanced, import substitution strategies intensified and self-reliance became the guiding principle. This did not entail a return to autarchy, but there were elements of deglobalisation and the intensification of deleterious facets of the Russian economy, above all, intensified state control.[82] Stability-oriented economic policies were strengthened, reducing long-term prospect for economic growth. Third, in international affairs the sanctions acted as a form of ersatz war, entrenching the growing hostility between Russia and the West and intensifying the 'Second Cold War'. On both sides, there was a reluctance to engage in a full-frontal assault, although the military posture of both sides adjusted as the other was increasingly perceived as a potential military adversary. Doors were kept open for engagement, but structured dialogue was limited. Fourth, the Atlantic system became even more concerned with maintaining its unity and preventing Russia from driving a 'wedge' between its two wings. This is a strategy that since the foundation of NATO in 1949 has become a synonym for blocking innovative ideas about restructuring European security.

Fifth, Russia devoted considerable efforts to the 'heartland' policy of making Eurasia a centre in its own right rather than a periphery to Europe and Asia, above all, through accelerating Eurasian integration accompanied by the intensified modernisation of Siberia and the RFE. Sixth, Russia accelerated its long-term rebalancing towards the East, with China in the vanguard but with improved trading and political engagement with India, Japan and the Association of South-East Asian Nations (ASEAN) bloc as a whole. Seventh, Russia actively encouraged the development of post-Western associations, ranging from the Shanghai Cooperation Organisation (SCO), the BRICS group and a whole set of anti-hegemonic actors as well as the G20. These were not anti-Western but represented a framework for an anti-hegemonic alignment to structure what the Russia's call a polycentric (multipolar) world. Eighth, all of this represented a long-term shift in global politics. The scholar and commentator Sergei Karaganov calls this an 'end to the Petrine period in Russian history', in which Russia looked to Europe for innovation and development. Russia would maintain good-neighbourly relations with Europe, but its horizons and model of the future would no longer be located there.[83] In other words, the West's sanctions regime, and the abuse of the open-trading regime and the rules-based order that it claimed to represent, was perceived in Moscow as only accelerating the West's own marginalisation. The rest of the world had more positive agendas to pursue.

Sanctions remain the cure-all first resort of American policy but increasingly failed to build in mechanisms for their withdrawal and, thus, became a blunt instrument of foreign policy. They were used to punish any country that the United States did not like, but by limiting access to American financial markets, they undermined the primacy of the dollar and US financial institutions. Sanctions make life more uncomfortable for Russians and depress economic growth by at least an annual half percentage point, but neither Russian behaviour nor strategy will change. Sanctions stimulate anti-Americanism and encourage import substitution and resilience strategies. It is America that has become more isolated than Russia. It is now clear that Russia will have to live under a US sanctions regime 'for a long time and seriously' (*nadolgo i vserëz*), as Lenin described the introduction of the New Economic Policy in 1921. Lenin also added 'but not forever' (*no ne na vsegda*), although Russians who recalled that the Jackson–Vanik amendment endured for thirty-eight years until in December 2012 it was immediately replaced by the Magnitsky Act could be forgiven for thinking otherwise.

6 FROM PARTNER TO ADVERSARY: RUSSIA AND THE WEST

Domestic and foreign policy in post-communist Russia interact to shape the polity. Russia emerged from the Soviet system with a protean state and an unformed foreign policy, and these interrelated identities were mutually reconstituted in the post-communist years. The representation of Russia as a 'great power' was paramount, drawing on the legacies of the Muscovite, Imperial and Soviet periods, while at home, the idea of a strong state gradually reasserted itself under Yeltsin and became foundational under Putin.[1] As Putin put it in his annual address to the Federal Assembly on 20 February 2019, 'Russia has been and always will be a sovereign and independent state. This is a given. It will either be that, or will simply cease to exist. We must clearly understand this. Without sovereignty, Russia cannot be a state. Some countries can do this, but not Russia.'[2] This is why unmediated membership of an enlarging Atlantic community, unlike for most of its neighbours, would have entailed status demotion. Russia's relations with the West has veered between cooperation and conflict because of the tension between adaptation to the expanding West and the striving for foreign policy autonomy. In the end, relations settled into a pattern of enduring confrontation, the Second Cold War. Putin stamped his personality on Russian foreign policy statecraft, but he operated in the context where enduring structural patterns reasserted themselves. Russian foreign policy is not directly derived from its domestic order, although, of course, there is a dynamic interaction between the two. On coming to power, Putin argued that Russian foreign policy should serve domestic economic development, but at the same time he insisted that Russia was to be taken seriously as a major international power, goals that turned out to be incompatible.[3]

The clash of post-Cold War world orders

The end of the Cold War was accompanied by a startling claim by the Soviet Union and then by Russia: that by remaking itself with Russian membership, the West would revive and save itself, and overall would become a stronger and more enduring presence in international affairs. In other words, by transforming itself, Russia effectively demanded that the historical West should also change. This ambitious demand – seen as arrogant and unnecessary in the West, but as benign and essential in Russia – is the source of much misinterpretation. The Soviet and Russian leaderships insisted that the end of the Cold War was a common achievement, and hence the historic West could become a greater West with the addition of Russia, a more pluralist order with a diversity of systems, although with all committed to a new peace order. However, the Atlantic system was constituted not just as a military alliance but also as a community of values, and hence the pressure from the East to transform itself was perceived in Western capitals as a way of dissolving the alliance and dividing the European and American wings. In short, the roots of the new era of confrontation derive not from any fundamental ideological divide but from deep-rooted ideational differences about the character of the post-Cold War era and the level of institutional change required to ensure European security.[4]

The origins of the Second Cold War lie in the way that the first ended. Gorbachev believed that the end of the Cold War represented the common transcendence of the increasingly archaic but no less dangerous confrontation across the heart of Europe and globally. Russia was committed to a democratic transformation, but given its heavy legacy of authoritarianism, repeated attempts to modernise in a dangerous security environment, the Gorbachevian logic – taken up later by Russian leaders – was that it would be better for the historical West to include the rough but receptive Russia and allow the transformation to take place within the framework of what would now become a greater West. The initial Gorbachev position was that the reformed Soviet Union would co-exist alongside the historical West but that their relationship would no longer be conflictual, since with the end of the Cold War and the USSR's shift towards democracy, there was no reason for security competition to continue. Russia's early post-communist leaders built on this but with the important modification that instead of a pluralist and cooperative international system with multiple centres of power, Russia sought to internalise pluralism within a transformed West itself. Liberal Atlanticists like the foreign minister, Andrei Kozyrev, wanted Russia to join the historical West and thereby to make it a greater West. Other factions sought a more pluralistic international order, described as multipolarity, yet in the early days, most accepted the need for Russia to join a transformed European security community.

The tension remained between those who wanted Russia to be in the West and those who considered that Russia should be alongside the West. On the Western side, there was an understandable reluctance for Russia, with all of its enormous problems and unresolved conflicts, to be taken in prematurely and on its own terms. As in a business merger, there was a struggle between two companies retaining their own identity after coming together or one effectively taking over the other. The Gorbachevian line came to be a dialogical third option: that both sides would change their identity to create something entirely new. The West was naturally reluctant to change its identity, since it had come out on top at the end of the Cold War. In military, economic and ideological terms, it appeared the victor. Russia was a much reduced power, so what need was there to undertake institutional change (for example, by dissolving NATO and creating common security bodies in which Russia would enjoy veto powers)? There was also the danger of normative dilution, since Russia by any standard has a poor record of respect for human rights and for resolving conflicts by legal means. Although the West supported Yeltsin's forceful crushing of the parliamentary *fronde* in the autumn of 1993, it only intensified concerns about a 'premature partnership' with Russia.[5] These concerns were greatly intensified by the start of the brutal first Chechen war in December 1994.

Despite the manifest inadequacies, the West took a benign view of Yeltsin's Russia and even helped devise the manipulative strategies that ensured his re-election in 1996. There was no transformation of the historical West, and instead Russia and the West stood face to face. Russia, too, feared to undertake an internal transformation that would deny the elements of its own identity that made it a separate actor in world politics. Russian independence was accompanied by the explicit attempt to join the world as a liberal democracy but one shaped by its own traditions and able to assert its views in international affairs. Russia's internal transformation was considered its choice and not part of any Western 'democracy promotion' strategy. Russia embraced democracy as an ideal that was its own and not an import from abroad, and its transformation was considered a function of internal developments and not a manifestation of any alleged Western victory. As a result, post-communist Russia refused to dissolve itself into the existing Atlantic community. It was not a defeated power like post-war Germany or Japan or an ex-imperial power like France and Britain ready to accept its reduced status and power by associating its fortunes with the dominant power of the age. France compensated by taking the lead in developing what is now known as the EU, which has the potential of becoming an independent power centre, and Russia likewise in one way or another would remain the dominant power in Eurasia, rendering any putative dissolution into the Atlantic system even less likely.

These strategic questions are entwined with normative issues. The debate over the international implications of democratic development continues to this day. As far as the Russian elite were concerned, democracy may now represent the only universally acceptable and legitimate form of government, but it does not resolve fundamental questions of political economy and geopolitics. Democracy in the abstract does not come with ready-made answers about problems of national identity, state coherence, security or the balance to be drawn between traditionalism and what used to be called modernisation. Neither does it resolve the structural problems of international order. Russia's status as a great power was not something that could be gifted or withdrawn by external actors but was part of Russia's character and destiny, as Putin repeatedly stressed. When this status is not recognised, it generates feelings of *ressentiment* and encourages intensified social competition.[6] The Atlantic system certainly wanted Russia to be part of its community, and thus exclusion was by no means a defined strategy. The problem was a structural one – an incompatible understanding of what the end of the Cold War meant and the character of the international system and Russia's part in it. Russia could join the historical West, but as a subaltern; whereas Russia wanted to join a greater West, transformed and, in Russia's view, rejuvenated by Russia's membership.

Instead of the transformation desired by Moscow, the country faced enlargement of an already functioning system, into which it was invited but inevitably as a subaltern. This gave birth to the cold peace between 1989 and 2014, in which none of the fundamental questions of European security and post-Cold War international order were resolved. Faced with the implacable logic of enlargement, a process encouraged by the former Soviet bloc and Washington, exclusionary practices came to predominate. Enlargement was complemented by a globalist ideology in which the values of the expanding system were taken as universal. As far as Moscow was concerned, this was an asymmetrical peace in which Russia's role in overcoming the Cold War was not adequately acknowledged. There was an astonishing lack of institutional innovation, and in time, this inertia reproduced the ideological stereotypes of the past. Various ideas to create new bodies, such as a European security council under the Conference on Security and Cooperation in Europe (CSCE), were not developed. Instead, Western bodies expanded to fill the available space. The Atlantic community's emphasis on international law and a rule-based order, as defined by that community, prevented a structural transformation of that community to encompass Russia. Ambitions for a fundamental transformation to create a greater West were abandoned, but insistence on Russia's special status remained. Anything less would represent the conclusive dissolution of Russian self-identity as a great power and as a separate civilisation, and a continuation of its disintegration as an actor in post-Soviet Eurasia and in world politics. The costs of taking this route appeared too high, but what was the alternative? The reassertion of geopolitical ambitions and a sphere of influence alarmed Russia's neighbours and revived archaic patterns of international politics. Russia had nowhere to go. The normative space was covered by the apparent triumph of liberal democracy as exemplified by the Atlantic powers and the EU, and Putin was certainly not going to revive the communist ideological challenge. Russia was stymied at all turns in geopolitical space, since any attempt to reassert even 'privileged' relations in post-Soviet Eurasia met with resistance from the new states reinforced by condemnation by the Atlantic community.

Post-communist Russia has been a permanently dissatisfied power. There was not much it could do about it in the 1990s, even though there were permanent growls of dissatisfaction. Already in 1992, foreign minister Kozyrev talked about the onset of a period of 'cold peace'. This was the term used by Yeltsin in December 1994. It was clear that Russia from the beginning was uncomfortable with the structure of post-Cold War international power. The growls became stronger when Evgeny Primakov took over as foreign minister in January 1996. He shifted policy away from Kozyrev's Atlanticism towards a greater emphasis on Russia's great power status, closer links with other 'rising powers' such as China and India, and advanced 'multipolarity' as the desired model of the international system. The growls turned into roars when the NATO powers, ostensibly to halt genocide in Kosovo, bombed Serbia from 24 March 1999 for seventy-eight days without UNSC authorisation. The offensive demonstrated to Moscow that it had failed to achieve the social status that it desired, as an equal partner in the management of European security. Strobe Talbott, Clinton's advisor on Russia, records Kozyrev commenting, 'You know, it's bad enough having you people tell us what you're going to do whether we like it or not. Don't add insult to injury by also telling us that it's *in our interests* to obey your orders!' (italics in original).[7] Although relations were re-established soon after, the long-term effect of the Kosovo crisis can hardly be underestimated, contributing to the loss of mutual trust.[8]

In the 1990s, the structural tensions were masked by a strong personal relationship between Yeltsin and Bill Clinton. Russia became embedded into European international society, signing the PCA with the EU in 1994 (because of the Chechen war, it only came into effect in December 1997) and joining the Council of Europe (CoE) in 1996. Despite domestic criticism, Art. 15.4 of Russia's 1993 constitution, granting priority of international law over domestic norms, remains in force, although tempered by an amendment of December 2015 granting the Russian Constitutional Court the right to adjudicate whether rulings of the ECtHR are compatible with Russian law. In other words, Russia remains committed at the vertical level to the governance bodies of international society, above all the UN but also the WTO and all the other bodies of international legal, economic, financial and environmental governance and their European manifestations. However, what Russia would never accept is the claim by any power or set of powers at the horizontal level to 'own' the international governance institutions, as part of some 'US-led liberal international order'. Moscow insisted on the autonomy of these institutions and Russia's right to interact with them directly and not mediated through any other order. This conservative internationalist view of the international system is shared by Beijing and other partners in BRICS, SCO and the Non-Aligned Movement (NAM).

When Primakov took over as foreign minister in January 1996, he changed the business model of unification with the West. The emphasis now was on both retaining their identity. His call for multipolarity and critique of uncritical adaptation to Western norms represented an enduring aspiration for ideational and geopolitical pluralism that continues to shape Russian foreign policy, and this is why Primakov is one of the few post-communist leaders who is respected across the factional spectrum, with the exception of radical liberals. However, the common identity model did not disappear, and in his early years Putin envisaged Russia joining NATO, driven by the continuing belief that it would be in the interests of all to transform the historical into the greater West. Despite the later sharp deterioration in relations and the emergence of an anti-hegemonic alignment with China, the two models of Russo-Western relations – one based on common identity and the other on separate but merged identities – still interact in surprising ways. In the event, and not through conscious choice, a third model – demerger and competition – came to predominate. All the evidence suggests that this was not the Kremlin's preferred option, and neither was it the policy option desired by most of the historical West's leaders.

However, it did enjoy significant support in what can be called the 'new West', the former communist countries of Eastern Europe. Some countries were more virulent than others in viewing Russia as the once and future enemy. With the support of those in Washington who share their concerns (some of whom were East European émigrés), a powerful alliance was formed that helped shape a policy towards Russia that ultimately provoked a rift and conflict. In other words, instead of creating a greater West (with Russia inside), or even a wider West (with Russia a 'strategic partner' substantiated by some sort of institutional and ideational underpinnings with the EU), the traditional anti-Russian animus of the historical West, forged during the Cold War, was not dismantled but was radicalised through enlargement. As NATO and the Atlantic system as a whole expanded, its appetite grew, and Russia's concerns were dismissed more forcefully. The enemy earlier had been the Soviet Union, with its programme to advance a world revolution to displace the capitalist ruling classes of the West, but it now became Russia, with its stubborn insistence on autonomy in international affairs and its claims to be a great power and thus an equal with the United States in managing global affairs. The radicalisation of the West meant that the denunciations of Russian behaviour and identity became more extreme. In the Cold War years, there had always been an implicit assumption that the object of attack was Soviet communism and the associated power complex, which held the 'captive nations' in thrall, but now Russia as an independent subject of international affairs and even as a country became the subject of condemnation. What began as a relatively narrow strand of East European 'Russophobia' became a flood after the Orange Revolution in

Ukraine in the autumn of 2004, the gas disputes of 2006 and 2009, the 'Maidan' revolution of 2013–14 and Russia's intervention in Syria in 2015, although the antagonism had deep historical roots.[9]

A parallel process was underway in Russia. There had always been powerful strands critical of a merger with the West on any terms, notably among the neo-traditionalists and Eurasianists, while the security bloc was wary for obvious reasons. The shift was in part prompted by structural factors, above all the contradiction between liberal aspirations and great power ambitions. In the Putin years, this became the defining feature of his rule. This does not mean that Russia cannot be a great power and a democracy at the same time, but this requires a transformation of the international environment. Even France under Charles de Gaulle faced problems of adaptation after the loss of its empire, provoking tension with the Atlantic community of which it was a founding member. The challenges for Russia were incommensurately compounded by cultural and historical traditions that questioned Russia's European credentials. On the other side, the Atlantic community was buoyed by the myth of victory in the Cold War and by the new challenges of terrorism and global insurgency, and could see no reason to embrace fundamental change, let alone dissolution. Russian critiques of the US-led liberal world order were condemned as typically Soviet attempts to drive a wedge between the two wings of the Atlantic alliance. These fears were greatly enhanced by the accession of the East European states, who considered the Atlantic community the guarantee of their security and development.

Putin's frustrations spilled over in an angry and recriminatory speech at the Munich Security Conference on 10 February 2007. He condemned the 'unipolar' aspirations of a' world in which there is one master, one sovereign' and argued that 'at the end of the day this is pernicious not only for those within the system, but also for the sovereign itself because it destroys itself from within':

> Today we are witnessing an almost uncontained hyper use of force – military force – in international relations, force that is plunging the world into an abyss of permanent conflicts. ... We are seeing a greater and greater disdain for the basic principles of international law. ... One state and, of course, first and foremost the United States, has overstepped its national borders in every way.[10]

This is how the new era of confrontation began. In Europe and the West, there was no strategic space for the reassertion of Russian power and status to develop. The only path that remained was adaptation to the norms and institutions of the Atlantic community, a path that Putin did not reject as long as it was accompanied by flexibility in the management of the historical West. One way he tried to achieve this was by returning to Gorbachev's idea of a common European home, now 'rebranded' as the project for a 'greater Europe'. This reprises the old Gaullist idea of pan-European integration, advanced by Charles de Gaulle in his famous speech in Strasbourg on 23 November 1959: 'Yes, it is Europe, from the Atlantic to the Urals, it is Europe, it is the whole of Europe, that will decide the fate of the world.'[11] This was stymied in the years of the cold peace by structural factors (the predominance of Atlanticism and American hegemony) and systemic issues – the alleged incommensurability between Russian and EU ideas of democracy and human rights prompted by governance problems in Russia. Instead of greater Europe, the EU advanced its own wider Europe agenda to draw its neighbours into the EU's orbit of good governance and democracy. By contrast with the pluralism of greater Europe, the wider Europe project is based on a series of concentric rings emanating from Brussels, weakening at the edges but nevertheless focused on a single centre. Russia's concern about the monist character of wider Europe were intensified by the development of the Eastern Partnership (EaP), formally launched in May 2009 in Prague. The result was a new division of Europe. Despite the aspirations voiced in the Charter of Paris in November 1990 for a 'Europe whole and free', new dividing lines were established.

The logic of Russian foreign policy

There is a high degree of consensus on Russia's foreign policy strategy, but there are plenty of debates over priorities and tactics. Russian governance is centralised in the hands of the president, but the Kremlin coordinates policy with a wide range of institutional actors while ensuring that it remains broadly in line with public sentiment. The Kremlin itself is the site of differing views, captured in the phrase 'the Kremlin has many towers'. There is agreement that Russian power and influence abroad should be increased, but how this should be achieved and the forms in which 'power' should be exercised is the subject of considerable disagreement.[12]

A number of enduring themes shape Russian foreign policy. The first is the refusal to accept any external hegemonic authority. The 'Mongol yoke' was formally repudiated in 1480 and the Poles were defeated in 1612, and thereafter Russia entered the European state system as a great power. This precipitated the Great Northern War, leading to the crushing defeat of the Swedes at Poltava in June 1709, and continued through Russia's decisive intervention in the Seven Years' War and then numerous wars with the Ottoman Turks and the 'great game' with Britain. In the Soviet period, resistance gained the ideological mantle of world revolution and, after 1945, the refusal to accept the Atlantic model of world order. Russian policy today is torn between accepting the indubitable fact of American predominance while resisting elements of US primacy. Primacy in the Clinton to the Obama years took the format of 'leadership' and was later formulated by Donald J. Trump as 'greatness'. However defined, Russia resisted the un-negotiated enlargement of the US-led Atlantic system, culminating in wars in Georgia and

Ukraine, and what was perceived as irresponsible American dominance in the Middle East, prompting Russia's military intervention in Syria in September 2015. Putin noted that up to 2,500 fighters of Russian origin and another 4,500 from Central Asia had gone to Syria, and warned that 'the collapse of the Syrian state could potentially result in the creation of a massive terrorist hotspot that would last for a very long time, for many decades. And having a second Afghanistan here, right next to us is not the best of pleasures.'[13]

The second theme is the striving to be recognised as a great power. Despite some early talk of *velikoderzhavnost'* (great powerness) when Putin first came to power, the term was barely mentioned in later years and after 2006 has never been used in the main foreign and security policy documents. The negative reaction to the idea of Russia becoming an 'energy superpower', a phrase Putin used in December 2005, warned him that the term was provocative and counterproductive.[14] The focus up to 2012 was on domestic economic and social development, and given the lack of military resources and the weakness of the economy, Russia sought little more than to maintain its position as a regional power. The discursive shift was more than a PR exercise and reflected Putin's understanding that excessive international ambition threatened domestic stability and development, as he had learned from the Soviet experience. This does not mean that he was indifferent to Russia's status, but in his earlier years these were given an 'economistic' twist. It is all the more paradoxical that in his third term Putin found himself locked in the classic Soviet trap, where foreign policy activism undermined domestic development. From the Kremlin's perspective, if the international environment had been more benign, Russia's reduced ambitions would have allowed the country to focus on domestic development.[15] However, Atlantic enlargement, as the Georgian and Ukrainian crises demonstrated, forced Russia to act. Frustration at the strategic impasse burst out in a more active foreign policy.

The third theme in the Putin years was the enhancement of Russia's military potential. According to SIPRI databases, Russian defence spending stood at $31.3 billion in 1995, $28.8 in 2000, $43 billion in 2005, $60.9 billion in 2010, $84.8 billion in 2013 and peaked at $91 billion in 2015 (in constant 2014 dollars). The share of defence as a proportion of the GDP rose from 3.6 per cent in 2000 to 4.2 per cent in 2015 before falling back a little. In real terms, expenditure increased nearly threefold and in PPP terms is equivalent to some $200 billion. This is how Russia has been able substantially to modernise its equipment and combat readiness.[16] Over the same period, the armed forces were reduced from 1,004,100 to 850,000 personnel: 250,000 conscripts, 354,000 contract soldiers (*kontraktniki*), 220,000 officers and 30,000 military school cadets. Russia is one of the few European countries to maintain the draft, despite much discussion of moving towards an entirely volunteer force. Difficulties in recruiting and retaining *kontrakniki*, despite greatly improved conditions of service, stalled plans for the phased abolition of conscription. This was accompanied by a modernisation programme based on the

Leninist principle of 'better fewer, but better'. The hard-won victory over Georgia in August 2008 precipitated a long-delayed reform from autumn of that year that transformed the force structure and military capacity of the Russian armed forces.

It is in this context that we can identify four phases in Russia's post-communist foreign policy. The *liberal internationalist* period lasted to the mid-1990s, when all sides believed that a new post-communist community could be established, although it soon became clear that the West and Russia had very different ideas of how this would be constituted. In the context of its apparent victory in the Cold War and Russian weakness and chaos, the historic West was unwilling to share leadership with Russia, and thus the problems that would later divide the continent were already evident. At the same time, Russia's struggle for foreign policy autonomy was not based on anything approaching neo-Soviet notions of Russia as the core of an alternative geopolitical or ideological bloc. In the early years, Russia was highly cooperative, and even when there were differences of views, as over Bosnia in 1995, Russia continued to work with its Western partners. In the second phase, the era of *competitive coexistence*, Primakov shifted Russian policy from what traditionalists condemned as uncritical Atlanticism towards an ill-defined multipolarity and strategic competition with the West. What remained of the cooperative stance was tested in 1999 with the NATO bombing of Serbia.

Nevertheless, soon after Putin tried to reboot Russia's engagement with the West through the *new realism* strategy, the third phase that endured in various forms from 2000 to 2012. The strategy was realist not only because it accepted the fundamental premises of the realist paradigm in international relations but also because of its pragmatic orientation; and it was new because Putin tried to forge a novel synthesis of cooperative engagement while maintaining Russia's independent stance and great power concerns. He believed that Primakov's model of competitive coexistence was too close to Nikita Khrushchev's policy of peaceful coexistence of the 1950s, predicated on inherent competition between the USSR and the West but not necessarily leading to war. Putin believed that a democratising post-communist Russia could do better than that. He tried to move beyond neo-Soviet representations of inherent confrontation. However, following the American abrogation of the 1972 Anti-Ballistic Missile (ABM) treaty in June 2002, the perceived lack of support for Russia's 'anti-terrorist' second Chechen war, the US invasion of Iraq in 2003, turmoil in Ukraine and much more, this, too, ran into the sands. By 2007, the disillusionment was complete, as reflected in his Munich speech, yet the new realist strategy continued through the reset and Medvedev's leadership, which sought to find new forms of accommodation. In the event, no viable formula was found to place Russia's relations with its Atlantic partners on a sustainable long-term basis.

Putin's return to the presidency in 2012, accompanied by protests against electoral fraud that were perceived by Moscow to have been part of Western attempts to destabilise the system, signalled the onset of a new spiral in the deterioration of relations. Russian foreign policy entered a new phase of *neo-revisionism* and resistance. Neo-revisionism in this context means a defence of the international system, including the institutions of global governance at the top (the UN, WTO, and other instruments of legal, environmental and financial governance), but resistance to the practices of the US-led hegemonic powers.[17] This was accompanied by the conservative consolidation of the regime accompanied by a shrill rhetoric of defiance and attempts to develop an ideology of resistance. Much of this was ill-considered, and in many cases counterproductive, yet it reflected the deep sense of strategic suffocation. The failure to establish an order in which Russia could thrive resulted in the internalisation of external tensions and the externalisation of domestic contradictions. In the end, everything was in place for a resumption of confrontation.

These changes were reflected in Russia's official documents. Each built on previous iterations, but together they sum up Russia's view of itself and its place in the world. Drawing on earlier versions of April 2000 and February 2010, a new *Military Doctrine* was adopted on 25 December 2014.[18] A year later, on 31 December 2015, drawing on the earlier versions of January 2000 and May 2009, the new *Security Strategy* was signed by Putin.[19] Then, developing the earlier versions of July 2008 and February 2013, on 30 November 2016, a new *Foreign Policy Concept* was adopted.[20] The doctrines, strategies and concepts dealt with different issues, but together they convey the main foreign policy concerns of the contemporary Russian state. Some traditional themes were repeated. First, Russia's status as a leading world power whose sovereignty was to be defended and respected, pursuing an independent policy in world affairs. Russia was to be recognised as a great power, as one of the two major nuclear powers and a permanent member of the UNSC, and has a special responsibility to manage global issues. Second, the documents converge on a view of the world as increasingly chaotic and unmanageable, marked by intensified competition for resources and influence between the major powers. Even the Arctic was becoming a source of vulnerability. Third, to ensure that the post-Soviet space remains a sphere in which Russia's influence could be maintained, although this is studiously not couched in the language of a 'sphere of influence'. Russia should remain influential both in bilateral relations and through the multilateral institutions such as the Commonwealth of Independent States (CIS), the EEU and the Collective Security Treaty Organisation (CSTO). The development of integration processes in the post-Soviet space is an enduring theme.

The *National Security Strategy* of 31 December 2015 revealed Moscow's heightened sense of insecurity. The document starkly warned about the threat:

> Expanding the force potential of NATO and endowing it with global functions that are implemented in violation of international legal norms, the bloc's heightened military activity, its continued expansion and the approach of

its military infrastructure to Russia's borders, all create a threat to national security.[21]

The *Strategy* portrayed Russia as a global player with legitimate concerns in its region and noted the containment strategy deployed against it. Despite the paradigm shift in global affairs towards conflict, the *Strategy* remained remarkably consistent with previous iterations. Confrontation with the West was now defined as a threat, accompanied by warnings of the 'hybrid' wars allegedly conducted against Russia. The country's self-reliance and self-sufficiency was stressed, but there was no substantive shift towards the 'securitisation' of new policy areas. Securitisation is not the same as militarisation and indicates the way that 'normal' politics gives way to the priority of national security discourses, which then shape policy.[22] After 2014, NATO shifted from the language of 'strategic partnership' towards militarisation, and a whole series of policy areas underwent a creeping securitisation (including the monitoring of the media to counter 'Russian propaganda' and 'fake news'), although the process was uneven and divisions remained between the allies.[23] While most European countries were reluctant to engage in the wholesale securitisation of relations with Russia, the United States went the furthest. Already its *National Security Strategy 2015* warned that the United States 'will continue to impose significant costs on Russia through sanctions' and would 'deter Russian aggression'.[24] Trump's proclaimed intention of improving relations with Russia provoked a storm of hostility in which Republican neoconservatives and Democrat liberal internationalists united to stymie moves in that direction.

However, typical of the Putinite moderation of extremes, the new *Foreign Policy Concept* issued on 30 November 2016 reflected no imputed condition of 'war' between Russia and the Atlantic community. The revised *Concept* stressed Russia's desire for good relations with all of its 'partners', the continued commitment to multilateral organisations and international economic integration, the supremacy of international law, the central role of the UN, the importance of democracy and Russia's contribution to peace and security in Europe. The general stance remained the same: 'The contemporary world is going through a period of profound changes, the essence of which is the formation of a polycentric international system.' The West's attempt to impede this natural shift generated instability in international relations. Russia would 'resist the attempts of individual states or groups of states to revise the generally recognised principles of international order', for instance, using the principle of Responsibility to Protect (R2P) to intervene in the internal affairs of other countries. At the heart of the document was a defence of Russia's status as an independent player in international affairs, a reluctance to be drawn into any alliances or putative blocs and the attempt to strengthen the ability of news media 'to convey the Russian viewpoint to broad circles of the world community'. Even though at the time Russia was embroiled in the Syrian conflict, the Middle

East was still ranked behind the post-Soviet space, Europe, the United States and the Asia-Pacific in its regional priorities.

Rather than enunciating an alternative ideological project or the creation of some sort of Eurasian civilisation, the *Concept* reiterated Russia's support for 'universal democratic values'. Regional integration would be in conformity with WTO rules, and there was no suggestion that Russia would turn its back on globalisation. Instead, the document stressed Russia's ambition to establish 'constructive, stable and predictable cooperation with the countries of the EU'. Despite the tensions, the greater Europe ambition was retained in the form of Russia's wish 'to create a common economic and humanitarian space from the Atlantic to the Pacific Ocean on the basis of the harmonisation of the processes of European and Eurasian integration'. Even NATO was spared some of the harshest criticism, although it registered 'a negative attitude towards NATO's expansion and the alliance's military structure approaching Russia's borders'. Instead, Russia sought 'an equal partnership' while establishing 'mutually beneficial relation with the United States'. The *Concept* accused the United States and its allies of undermining 'global stability' by trying to 'contain' Russia and reserved the right to 'react harshly to any unfriendly' moves. Cooperation was only possible on the basis of 'equality, mutual respect of interests, and non-interference in one another's internal affairs'. Russia's goal was good relations with all states based on 'mutual respect', and there was no enunciation of an anti-hegemonic strategy, although 'polycentrism' was defended and 'full-scale' partnership and cooperation with China was stressed. The tone overall was defensive, although enunciated in a confident manner that suggested a belief that the tide of history – what in Soviet parlance had been called the 'correlation of forces' – was running in Moscow's favour. The document stressed Russia's enduring commitment to universal principles, as long as these were not abused to justify interference in the internal affairs of states.[25]

The confident style was reflected in Putin annual address to the Federal Assembly on 1 December 2016. The focus was on reform in domestic policy, although there were no substantive ideas on how to tackle economic stagnation, and the foreign policy passages were conciliatory in tone. He noted, 'Unlike some of our colleagues abroad, who consider Russia an adversary, we do not seek and never have sought enemies. We need friends. But we will not allow our interests to be infringed upon or ignored. We want to and will decide our destiny ourselves and build our present and future without others' unasked for advice and prompting.'[26] The conciliatory tone indicated that Moscow hoped to repair relations with the United States in the framework of a multipolar world order and recognition of Russia as a great power. Inevitably, the sticking point would be the tension between a 'values-based foreign policy', which in the historical West was a code for American leadership of the hegemonic liberal world order in which there was no room for 'spheres of interest' (in other words, for spheres in which the West did not dominate), or a more interest-driven recognition of a pluralist international system in which great powers could have divergent concerns, and to avoid conflict, some sort of diplomatic process was required.

Some new themes emerge in recent documents and speeches. First, as Russia strengthens and pursues an independent foreign policy, it encounters increased opposition if not outright hostility. This provokes the revival of traditional containment (*sderzhivanie*) strategies against Russia, applying the whole gamut of military, economic and informational instruments. Second, interstate relations are becoming more competitive but deceptive because of the mobilisation of 'hybrid warfare' through financial and cyber instruments. Third, the dominant position of the West was being eroded by the rise of new powers, which prompts the historic West to defend its declining positions more assertively, above all through the containment of challenger powers. Fourth, the documents shift between asserting that a multipolar world is in the making to the view that it is an established fact.[27] All these points reinforce Russia's enduring critique of the Western-led international order and reflect Russia's perceived structural exclusion from that order as equal and constituent member.

A new era of confrontation

Putin came to power a committed Europeanist. A native of St Petersburg, a city built precisely as a 'window to the West', Putin was immersed in European culture. Although he grew up in Soviet times, his education drew on the classical repertoire of European culture. He lived for five years in Dresden, a city that in so many ways epitomised the peaks and troughs of European civilisation. At the time when Putin worked there for the KGB in the late 1980s, the result of the bombing of February 1945 was still evident. The ruins of the Frauenkirche, one of the finest examples of Protestant baroque architecture of the eighteenth century, had been left as a war memorial by the East German authorities, and rebuilding only started in 1994. Why, then, did Putin the European become so alienated from the West?

Putin sought a new relationship with the EU, building on the PCA to develop the four Common European Economic Spaces, launched at the St Petersburg Russia–EU summit in May 2003. The Moscow summit in May 2005 outlined a series of 'road maps' for their implementation. However, as Igor Ivanov, foreign minister between 1998 and 2004, argues, 'The roadmaps that were supposed to have developed into cooperation in several areas never turned into full-fledged detailed documents. The Russia-Europe summits held twice a year gradually became pompous and insignificant events. And a full-fledged security dialogue was never developed because of NATO's reluctance to accept the new realities in Europe and the world.'[28] The exhaustion in mutual relations is reflected in the desultory negotiations to devise a new framework to supersede the PCA after its ten-year expiration, with very little achieved by the time negotiations were suspended in 2014. This also applies to the Partnership for Modernisation, agreed by the Rostov summit in July 2010, which sought to revive the stalled common spaces programme. Again, not much had been achieved by the time the EU imposed targeted sanctions in July 2014 restricting access to capital markets, defence, dual-use goods and sensitive technologies (including in the energy sector).

Declassified documents released in December 2017 showed that Western leaders had repeatedly promised their Soviet counterparts that NATO would not expand into Eastern Europe. Secretary of State James Baker's famous assurance in his meeting with Gorbachev on 9 February 1990 that NATO would not move 'one inch eastward' was only one of a plethora of Western assurances throughout the period of German unification in 1990 and into 1991.[29] This sense of betrayal and Western lack of trustworthiness informs Putin's neo-revisionism. It reflects the Russian belief that the alliance's enlargement left Europe in a security limbo. In its review of 2014, the Russian Ministry of Foreign Affairs (MFA) noted that the year was 'marked by a build-up of elements of instability and an increase in outbreaks of crisis in international relations, which are currently transitioning to a new multi-polar world order'. The review noted the increasing competition in all areas, including over developmental models and moral values, accompanied by a series of 'full-blown regional conflicts'. The Ukrainian crisis was the worst of these. According to the MFA analysis,

> It reflected major system-wide problems in the Euro-Atlantic area associated with the policy of Western countries, pursued during the last 25 years, aimed at strengthening their own security without taking into account Russia's interests, and at ongoing eastward expansion of the geopolitical space under their control, which showed in successive waves of NATO enlargement contrary to the assurances issued at the highest level. The historic opportunity to form a system of equal and indivisible security was squandered.[30]

A stark division emerged between those within the enlarged alliance and those outside, above all Russia, and what had become zero-sum struggles over the countries in between.[31]

It was over Ukraine that all parties stumbled, and 'everyone lost'.[32] Two fundamentally different principles of state-building came into conflict, the monist and the pluralist.[33] A domestic conflict over identity and the shape of Ukraine state-building became internationalised.[34] Putin's speech on 18 March 2014 justifying the takeover of Crimea stressed a number of themes. First, he held the Western powers responsible for the breakdown of the European system, to which Russian actions were considered a response. He excoriated them for ignoring international law in their various interventions, arguing that it was the height of hypocrisy and 'double standards' to accuse Russia of actions that were no more than a replication of Western behaviour. On this occasion and later, he referred to the UN International Court of Justice judgement of 22 July 2010 on Kosovo, which stated, 'General international law contains no prohibition on declarations of independence.' Second, Putin justified the annexation by the need to defend the 'Russian world' (*Russkii mir*). The term is vague with unclear boundaries, but it appeals to the sense that the Russian nation is broader than the Russian state of today, encompassing a community of *sootechvenniki* (compatriots). The concept was applied by the insurgents in the Donbas who claimed a cultural affiliation with Russia.[35] In Crimea, it was reflected in the overwhelming vote in support of reunification with Russia in the referendum of 16 March. Although the term became popular at this time, and has been used to describe an eponymous cultural organisation since June 2007, Putin soon stopped using the phrase. Characteristically, Putin has an instinctive aversion to a concept that could constrain his freedom of action.

Third, Putin generalised the crisis as an indication of the broader breakdown of global order:

> Like a mirror, the situation in Ukraine reflects what is going on and what has been happening in the world over the past several decades. After the dissolution of bipolarity on the planet, we no longer have stability. Key international institutions are not getting any stronger; on the contrary, in many cases, they are sadly degrading.

In particular, he stressed that NATO enlargement 'meant that NATO's navy would be right there in this city of Russia's military glory [Sevastopol], and this would create not an illusory but a perfectly real threat to the whole of southern Russia'. Fourth, Putin insisted that he was a friend to Ukraine: 'I also want to address the people of Ukraine. I sincerely want you to understand us: we do not want to harm you in any way, or to hurt your national feelings. We have always respected the territorial integrity of the Ukrainian state, incidentally, unlike those who sacrificed Ukraine's unity for their political ambitions.'[36] On this and other occasions, he insisted that Ukrainians and Russians were one people, although this does not mean that he thought that they should be part of the same state. Ukraine remains the rock impeding the normalisation of relations between Russia and the West.

All this looks like a Cold War, defined as a struggle which is deeply entrenched and with the potential to become an outright military conflict but in which neither side is actively preparing for immediate war. The original Cold War represented entrenched ideological conflict waged on a global scale both within and between states. Robert Legvold is right to argue that this is not a repetition of *the* original Cold War but represents *a* new Cold War.[37] Andrew Monaghan notes that the idea of a new Cold War is anachronistic and misplaced, looking back to the previous conflict rather than examining the dynamics of the present one.[38] However, the renewed confrontation is part of a broader reconfiguration of international order and is taking on systemic forms. In European and US-Russian relations, elements of a new Cold War have been restored, and although relatively localised in spatial terms, they are accruing some of the ideological quality of the earlier conflict. The renewed confrontation has global aspects, and the rhetoric at times is quite vicious, with the epicentre once again a battle between competing visions of Europe. Ideational conflict is no longer driven by the left-right division of the First Cold War but a struggle between self-defined democracies and authoritarian systems. The conflict is generated by unresolved issues at the end of the Cold War, notably a stable and inclusive security order for Europe, as well as by the radicalisation of positions, in part generated by contestation over the new West in the borderlands of Europe.

Russo-EU relations became hostage to the Ukrainian crisis. The emphasis on unity over Ukraine overshadowed the potential for new policies rooted in an understanding that the crisis had multiple dimensions for which all sides bore responsibility. Instead, alternatives to 'maintaining a strong and united Russian policy' were condemned as 'doomsday scenarios', including the most awful in which Trump and Putin achieve a 'grand power bargain', which 'allows Russia to bring Ukraine into its sphere of influence'.[39] A 'grand bargain' would not necessarily entail the latter outcome but would in fact represent a move towards averting the real 'doomsday scenario', the potential for nuclear conflict between the great powers. The appropriation of this language to prevent a negotiated solution to the Ukrainian impasse indicates the depth of the crisis. Putin remains a committed European, but he became increasingly sceptical about the EU. Earlier acceptance that 'Europeanisation', defined as the normative incorporation of EU practices and standards into domestic legislation, gave way to resistance. From the beginning, Russia rejected the fundamental premise of 'conditionality' of the EU policy of granting certain privileges in return for normative subordination to the EU. The EU's promotion of itself as the promoter of a certain historically defined model of virtue (values and normative standards) undermined Russia's status as a great power and thereby eroded its identity. In the main, it is not the values themselves that are rejected but the way that they are promoted within the framework of an enlarging Atlantic system. Normative rhetoric is not free-standing and floating in some sort of disembodied 'normasphere' but is deeply embedded in a power system that operates according to the logic of enlargement that riled Russia from the first post-Cold War days. If these same normative standards had been less representative of an enlarging Atlantic system, but part of a growing and deepening common endeavour of a greater Europe, then some of the contradictions and tensions may have been avoided.

The return of geopolitics represented the defeat of the aspirations for a 'common European home' or for a 'Europe whole and free' in the post-Cold War era. It is not clear how the impasse can be resolved. The solutions to earlier problems of post-Cold War order now became the problems to be resolved. The stalemate in relations between these two representations of the post-Cold War world order took physical form in the new jagged frontline across Eastern Europe, and psychological forms in the new propaganda war waged across various platforms, from think tanks to new social media and traditional print media. This geopolitical and hermeneutic impasse provoked a range of alternatives. In Europe, these are usually termed 'populist', and this is true in the sense that many reject the old elite politics, which provide a stunted and limited vision of the future. It is no accident that much of the left and right populism unite in condemnation of traditional Atlanticism and looks for an improvement of relations with Russia. The extent of Russian support and sponsorship has been greatly exaggerated. Moscow no doubt encourages any movement that could potentially break the impasse and allow Russia to escape neo-containment, but these movements are generated by domestic processes and international contradictions. Although Moscow's bony hand was sought behind Britain's vote to leave the EU in June 2016, no substantive evidence has been found of Russian 'interference'. Equally, it is not accidental that liberal globalists and neoconservatives in the United States combine to use Russia as a stick to beat Trump's assertion of conservative neo-isolationism and neo-mercantilism.

Trump came to power with very few consistent positions, but one of them was that it made sense 'to get on with Russia'. However, any initiative once again to 'reset' relations with Russia were stymied by the claims of Russian 'collusion' in getting Trump elected, accompanied by charges of 'hacking' and the use of social media to sow discord and undermine American democracy. Together, these charges became known as 'Russiagate'. Although the evidence for these charges is thin to non-existent, the affair had enormous consequences and prevented any moves towards a rapprochement between the two countries. In fact, Trump's appointments to defence, security and foreign policy posts were mostly hard-line critics of Russia. By contrast, Russia sought to end its diplomatic isolation and to that end in March 2017 sent an ambitious proposal to Washington to normalise relations across the board. The offer was rejected, and Russia in July then offered a more modest non-interference agreement, which was also turned down. Instead, relations took a sharp turn for the worse, resulting in the Congressional initiative to impose the CAATSA sanctions. This provoked an escalating cycle of expulsions of diplomatic staff and the closure of facilities.

Putin's frustrations boiled over in his speech at the annual conference of the Valdai Discussion Club on 19 October 2017. He condemned the one-sided character of US-Russian interactions in the sphere of nuclear security, holding the United States responsible for not reciprocating Russia's unilateral granting of access to its nuclear weapons facilities in the 1990s. Putin charged the United States of having taken advantage of Russia's weakness at the time. He recalled the Megatons to Megawatts programme, which ran between 1993 and 2013, whereby Russia down-blended its enriched uranium from the equivalent of about twenty thousand nuclear warheads into low-enriched uranium to be used as fuel in US power stations. As part of the deal, 'US officials made 170 visits to top secret Russian facilities' and 'set up permanent workplaces in them adorned with American flags'. He noted that 'from the Russian side unprecedented openness and trust was demonstrated', but this was not reciprocated: 'What we got in return is well-known – a complete disregard for our national interests, support for separatism in the Caucasus, a circumvention of the UNSC, the bombing of Yugoslavia, the invasion of Iraq, and so on. The US must have seen the state of our nuclear weapons and economy and decided to do away with international law.' Putin identified America's unilateral abrogation of the 1972 ABM treaty in 2002 as the key turning point in disrupting strategic stability. Washington's hostility was 'returning the relationship between the two countries to the 1950s', although he noted that during the Cold War, 'there was at least more mutual respect' between the two superpowers.

He noted that the previous month Russia had finally disposed of all its chemical weapons stockpiles, whereas the United States had persistently postponed its own destruction schedule and now planned to complete the process in 2023 at the earliest. He also criticised the Intermediate-range Nuclear Forces (INF) Treaty, signed on 8 December 1987 that banned deployed and non-deployed missiles of intermediate range (1,000 and 5,500 km) and shorter range (500–1,000 km). As a result, some 2,692 American and Russian ground-based missiles were destroyed (the treaty did not apply to sea- or air-launched missiles). Putin complained that not banning air-based and naval launchers advantaged NATO states, and it represented 'another case of Russia making unilateral concessions'. On Ukraine, Putin harshly condemned the West for having provoked the conflict and for the stalemate in implementing the Minsk 2 peace accords.[40]

This was reminiscent of his Munich speech in 2007, reciting a litany of complaints about Western behaviour. Since then, Putin's list of grievances had become even longer, including the recognition of Kosovo's independence, intervention in Libya and the war in Syria, with Putin accusing the West of practicing 'double standards' throughout. Putin argued that many of the achievements of the West, above all the creation of the welfare state, had been a response to the Soviet challenge. The big picture is the one that Putin, and before him Yeltsin and Gorbachev, had identified: the failure 'to open a truly new chapter in history' after the Soviet Union ceased to exist. Instead, 'after dividing up the geopolitical heritage of the Soviet Union, our western partners became convinced of the justness of their cause and declared themselves the victors of the Cold War', and then interfered 'in the affairs of sovereign states, and exporting democracy just like the Soviet leadership had tried to export the socialist revolution to the rest of the world'. These strictures were no doubt justified when seen from Moscow's perspective, but they did not offer a way out of the impasse. The ball as far as Putin was concerned was decidedly in the West's court, but this reduced Russia to a reactive stance. Putin's speech simply reaffirmed the strategic impasse in which Russia was trapped.

Russiagate damaged relations at a time when both Russia and the United States faced a number of common challenges, ranging from the war in Syria, the Islamic State insurgency in Iraq and Syria, the continuing war in Afghanistan, the development of North Korea's and Iran's strategic potential, as well as strategic arms control between Russia and the United States. Intervention in Syria was in large part determined by Russia's experience of radical Islamic insurgency in the North Caucasus and the fear that if entrenched in the neighbourhood (and for Russia, the Middle East is part of its neighbourhood), then Russia would once again come under threat. Putin worked to ensure that Islam in Russia, encompassing some twenty million people, remained within traditional channels. Enormous efforts were devoted to training imams in Russia, insulating the country from Saudi-style salafi fundamentalism (Wahhabism) and even more from the revived caliphate.[41] Despite the strained relations, a communication channel was established at the level of deputy foreign ministers (between Sergei Ryabkov and Thomas Shannon).[42] The potential for a dangerous drift towards military conflict has rarely been higher as the various Cold War mechanisms to constrain and manage confrontation and deterrence have been dismantled.

The US *National Security Strategy* unveiled on 18 December 2017 warned against the 'revisionist powers of China and Russia', ranked alongside the 'rogue powers of Iran and North Korea' and the 'transnational threat organisations, particularly jihadist groups'.[43] The theme was developed in the *National Defence Strategy*, a summary of which was issued on 19 January 2018, which argued that the United States was emerging from a period of 'strategic atrophy' and needed to face 'increased global disorder' in which 'inter-state strategic competition, not terrorism, is now the primary concern in US national security'. Top of the list of challengers was China, which was characterised as 'a strategic competitor using predatory economics to intimidate its neighbours while militarizing features in the South China Sea'. As for Russia, 'it has violated the borders of nearby nations and pursues veto power over the economic, diplomatic, and security decisions of its neighbours'.[44] The two states, as in the *National Security Strategy*, were labelled 'revisionist powers'. The *Nuclear Posture Review* revealed on 27 January 2018 once again lamented that in some way, the United States had 'continued to reduce the number and salience of nuclear weapons', while others, 'including Russia and China, have moved in the opposite direction'.[45] The document outlined an ambitious programme for the modernisation of US nuclear forces (something that Obama had begun) that could not but ramp up nuclear confrontation. On 20 October 2018, Trump announced that the United States would leave the INF Treaty, and on 1 February 2019, Mike Pompeo, the US secretary of state, gave Russia sixty days to come into compliance. On 4 March 2019, Moscow officially announced that it was withdrawing from the INF Treaty. Moscow had long chafed at its restrictions, and its abandonment now deprived the United States of its status as the guarantor of security in Europe. The collapse of the old arms-control regime also affected the 2011 New Strategic Arms Reduction Treaty (START), due to expire in February 2021. Paradoxically, the treaty came into full effect just at this time, on 5 February, with both sides having met the limit of 1,500 deployable weapons. The *Nuclear Posture Review* showed no enthusiasm for its renewal. As the Russian foreign ministry commented on 3 February, 'the document is focused on confrontation and is anti-Russia'.[46]

Putin's annual address to the Federal Assembly on 1 March 2018 both confirmed the start of a new arms race and denied it – as far as he was concerned, since 2002 Russia had devised a range of powerful weapons, and therefore there would be no need to match the United States weapon for weapon. The latter third of the two-hour speech introduced an awesome range of strategic and nuclear-capable armaments that Russia had or was developing. Putin lamented US withdrawal from the ABM treaty in 2002, the foundation of the arms-control regime, followed by the development of a ballistic missile defence (BMD) shield, including the deployment of interceptor missiles in Poland and Romania, against Russia's strenuous objections. Putin noted the many proposals Russia had offered to work together on BMD issues, but 'all our proposals, absolutely all of them, were rejected'. As Putin put it, 'We tried to talk to our partners. Russia is a major nuclear power. They kept ignoring us. No one was talking to us. So listen to us now.' The new weapons included the Avangard system (a winged glider with speeds of up to Mach 20 on a flat trajectory in the atmosphere, avoiding traditional ballistic missile launch threats), the Sarmat super-heavy intercontinental missile, the Peresvet laser system and the aviation systems equipped with Kinzhal hypersonic ballistic missiles (to be carried on MiG-31 interceptors), the Burevestnik nuclear-powered cruise missiles of unlimited range and the Poseidon unmanned underwater vehicle, also of unlimited range. Putin insisted that Russia would not be the aggressor and that the military build-up had been forced on Russia. Moreover, always the legalist, Putin insisted that the new nuclear technology were compliant with arms-control agreements and Russia's security commitments, including limiting the use of nuclear weapons in retaliation to a first strike by an enemy if Russia or its allies faced an existential threat.[47]

Putin took up the theme again in his 20 February 2019 address. He stressed that 'building relations with Russia means working together to find solutions to the most complex matters instead of trying to impose solutions', and noted that US withdrawal from the INF Treaty was 'the most urgent and discussed issue'. He would have preferred that the United States had behaved as 'openly and honestly' as they did when they walked away from the ABM Treaty in 2002. Instead, 'they violate everything, then they look for excuses and appoint a guilty party', as well as 'mobilising their satellites' (a rather contemptuous reference to the United States' NATO allies). He warned that 'Russia will have to develop and deploy weapons that can be used not only against areas from which a direct threat will come but also against territories where decision-making centres are located'. Despite the US violation of the INF Treaty by building the installation in Romania and Poland that Moscow alleged could be used to launch adapted Tomahawk cruise missiles, Putin stressed that 'Russia does not intend – this is very important, I am repeating this on purpose – Russia does not intend to deploy such missiles in Europe'. To have done so would have risked repeating the confrontation of the 1980s. He gave an update on the development of the weapons mentioned the previous year and added a new one, the Tsirkon (Zircon) 'hypersonic [cruise] missile that can reach speeds of Mach 9 and strike a target more than 1,000 km way both under water and on the ground'. He stressed that it 'can be launched from water, surface vessels and from submarines'. In other words, the oceans were no longer the US fortress but the launch site for Russian missiles from vessels stationed off US shores. Putin was quick to add that 'Russia wants to have sound, equal, friendly relations with the USA. Russia is not threatening anyone, and all we do in terms of security is simply a response, which means that our actions are defensive.'[48] As in any arms race, the response to an adversary building up their military is to enhance one's own capabilities, thus provoking a cycle that may lead to war, financial overstretch or state failure, or all three.

7 RECREATING THE HEARTLAND: EURASIAN PARTNERSHIPS

The centrepiece of Putin's third presidential term was the deepening of Eurasian integration. In September 2013, he argued that 'Eurasian integration is a chance for the entire post-Soviet space to become an independent centre for global development', while insisting that its members would retain 'their political independence'.[1] The creation of the EEU on 1 January 2015 represented the culmination of this endeavour, but even this soon became part of even more ambitious schemes. From 2016, Putin talked of a 'Greater Eurasian Partnership' (GEP), although he was vague on what institutional form such a macro-regional bloc would take. Its geographical limits were also unclear, and in some versions it included just post-Soviet Eurasia and China, while in others it encompassed all of Western Europe and the whole ASEAN region. However, in all variants, one aspect was clear: for Russia and its allies to retain autonomy in the new construct and not be swallowed up by the Chinese giant on the one side or the historical West on the other. This could only be achieved by enhancing the collective weight of post-Soviet Eurasia. This is what can be called Putin's heartland strategy. Halford Mackinder, the founder of modern geopolitical thinking, in his 1904 article submitted to the Royal Geographical Society, 'The Geographical Pivot of History', introduced the argument that he formulated in 1919 as 'who rules East Europe commands the Heartland; who rules the Heartland commands the World-Island; who rules the World-Island commands the world'. The pivot area in this conception covers most of Eastern Europe and northern Russia. In the event, with the development of air and sea power, it did not quite work out as Mackinder anticipated. Today, this area is in danger of becoming not only peripheral but also an extended zone of contestation between external powers. Zbigniew Brzezinski spoke of Eurasia 'as the globe's central arena' and devoted himself to ensuring that it was not dominated by Russia. By contrast, Putin sought to construct a Eurasian regional order that would remain an independent actor in the new geopolitical environment. However, the Ukrainian crisis and the annexation of Crimea dealt Eurasian ambitions a deadly blow, as Russia's neighbours wondered if they would be next to face Russia's wrath.

Eurasian integration in perspective

The concept of Eurasia as a distinct political community is relatively new, dating back to the late nineteenth century.[2] Eurasianists are now one of the four great blocs defining Russian modernity, but their ideas are far from homogenous. Putin at most is a pragmatic Eurasianist, although the project to make Eurasia a new centre of political integration is overlain with various ideological concerns. The core of Putin's strategy is to overcome peripherality and make Eurasia a centre of development and political influence. This represents not only a developmental project but also a civilisational challenge in which 'to become modern is no longer equivalent to becoming Western'.[3] Neither is it to become Chinese. The Belt and Road Initiative (BRI) has the potential to reorder geopolitical and modernisation perspectives. Also known as One Belt, One Road (OBOR), the plan draws on memories of the various ancient Silk Roads that ran from China to Europe to establish a land-based Silk Road Economic Belt (SREB) and a maritime counterpart, the Maritime Silk Route, to connect China with its trading partners. Fears that Eurasian integration would impede convergence with the EU became irrelevant as ties with China and Asia as a whole increased. Even East European EU member states established direct contact with Beijing (the 16+1 initiative established in April 2012, with some Balkan countries), indicating the potentially declining relevance of Brussels, while for the post-Soviet Eurasian states, BRI opened up new horizons. The failure at the end of the Cold War to create a greater Europe, bringing together Russia, the EU and all the states 'in between' ceded the geo-economic initiative to greater Eurasia.[4]

The core of this strategy was the development of the EEU. When initially outlined in his landmark article of October 2011, the putative Eurasian Union was envisaged as a full union on the EU model.[5] However, when formally established in 2015, it focused on a customs union and the single market, and the more ambitious elements of supranational political integration were relegated to some indeterminate future. The goal was certainly not to recreate something akin to the old Soviet Union, as notoriously suggested by Hillary Clinton. Instead, the aim was rather more complex and had three aspects. The first falls within the ambit of classical economic regionalism, where countries come together to reduce tariffs and other obstacles to encourage economic activity and interconnectedness. This functionalist angle is especially pertinent in a region that had once been a single economic unit and where cultural and social ties are intense. However, these traditional ties also proved to be an obstacle, provoking fears that the Soviet Union or Russian Empire was being recreated in the form of a new greater Russia. The second goal was to create a substantive partner for the EU and, thus, to provide a broader platform for a potential greater Europe. For this reason, the EEU has developed in a manner complementary to that of the EU, operating within the functionality and regulatory regime of the WTO. However, in the short term, the planned EEU only exacerbated tensions over the lands in between, provoking the crisis over Ukraine from late 2013. The third factor is the attempt to provide more substance to the Eurasian heartland in the face of the expansion of Chinese capital into the post-Soviet Eurasian region.

A customs union came into effect in 2011, and the EEU formally came into existence as an economic union on 1 January 2015 with three founding members: Belarus, Kazakhstan and Russia, with Armenia joining the next day and Kyrgyzstan later that year. The combined population of the bloc in 2016 was 183.2 million (see Table 7.1). The EEU shares the goals of other regional economic associations: to enhance intra-regional ties, to modernise economies and to improve international competitiveness. The EEU has an ambitious agenda to create a single market. To advance this goal, the Eurasian Development Bank (EDB) was established in 2006 and now encompasses all EEU members plus Tajikistan. By 2017, the customs union and a common customs tariff had been introduced; the creation of a common labour market was underway; the old Soviet standards framework (GOST) was being replaced by new technical regulations, most of which were compatible with those of the EU, potentially facilitating a free trade area (FTA) 'from Lisbon to Vladivostok', if ever the historic opportunity returns; and the institutional framework for integration was developing, including the EEU Court and the Eurasian Fund for Stabilisation and Development. The Board of the Supreme Eurasian Economic Council (SEEC) consists of two representatives from each country. The inaugural chair for a four-year term was the former prime minister of Armenia, Tigran Sarkisyan, and he was to be succeeded by a Belarusian in 2020 in keeping with the principle of alphabetical rotation. While the EEU explicitly took the EU as its model, it significantly lagged behind the EU in developing the autonomy of its legal order and in the effective functioning of its organisation.[6] The member states jealously guard their sovereignty, especially Russia, and as a result, the development of supranationalism is greatly overshadowed by intergovernmental instruments.

With low oil prices, sanctions and economic recession, the EEU was launched in inauspicious circumstances. Trade volumes decreased across the board in the early period, although intra-bloc trade volumes fell at a lower rate than external trade and thus acted as a type of 'shock absorber'. However, Table 7.1 demonstrates the extraordinarily low level of intra-bloc trade, with only Belarus approaching half. While in political terms the EEU has disappointed those who

Table 7.1 The EEU in figures

	Armenia	Belarus	Kazakhstan	Kyrgyzstan	Russia	Total
Population (million)	3	9.5	17.9	6	146.8	183.2
GDP ($billion)	10.8	48.1	128.1	5.8	1,267.8	1460.5
Foreign trade ($billion)	3.6	24.4	48.4	3.5	430.0	509.9
Mutual trade ($billion)	0.4	11.3	3.9	0.4	26.6	42.6
GDP growth (% year-on-year)	+0.2	−2.6	+1.0	+3.8	−0.2	−0.1
GDP nominal ($billion)	10.8	48.1	128.1	5.8	1,267.8	1,460.5
PPP-based GDP ($billion)	26.6	165.4	460.7	21.0	3,745.1	4,418.7
PPP-based per capita, $	8,881.0	17,496.5	25,669.2	3,467.3	26,109.1	21,288.3
Unemployment rate (%)	18.1	5.6	4.9	8	5.3	–

Source: Eurasian Development Bank: Centre for Integration Studies, *Eurasian Economic Integration 2017*, Report 43 (St Petersburg: Eurasian Development Bank, 2017), pp. 8, 9, 28, 70.

Notes: All data for 2016, based on current prices

hoped for more political integration, in functional terms, there has been steady although slow progress. Non-tariff barriers were gradually removed, with 81 out of 450 obstacles removed by late 2016.[7] Equally, only slow progress was made towards harmonisation of the medical drugs and medical products market. There was member state convergence to Russia, with four of the countries closing the development gap, although the poorest, Kyrgyzstan, showed little sign of convergence. The common labour market is one of the successes. Remittances from Russia traditionally made up some 30 per cent of GDP in Kyrgyzstan, although this declined during the recession of 2014–16. As the economies recovered, so did the scale of labour migration and volume of remittances. In 2016, 2.35 million EEU member state citizens were registered as migrants in Russia. In that year alone, 362,000 people arrived to work from Kyrgyzstan, 210,000 from Armenia, 98,000 from Belarus and 72,000 from Kazakhstan.[8] At the same time, the EEU has an ambitious programme to establish FTAs with third countries. The first was with Vietnam and came into force in October 2016, and others are being negotiated including a non-preferential one with China. The enduring problem remains the top-down character of many of the integration efforts, promoted by the Eurasian Economic Commission, the equivalent of the EU's European Commission. Plans to encourage horizontal links between businesses across borders were only slowly realised.

All states are wary of Russian preponderance and, despite commitment to integration, seek to the maximum extent to preserve their sovereignty. Russia's failure to consult its EEU partners over policies that affected them deepened concern. Russia took the fundamental decision to annex Crimea without consulting the EEU, and the dealings of the bloc with BRI are largely bilateral. The decision to impose counter-sanctions on the import of foodstuffs from sanctioning countries was taken unilaterally, a problem that was exacerbated when Russia treated the re-export of goods by Belarus and Kazakhstan, which they had the perfect right to do, as hostile conduct and imposed sanctions on the former. The transfer of Crimea broke the post-Soviet moratorium on border changes (similar to the established consensus in postcolonial Africa), alarming all of Russia's neighbours, above all those with significant Russian minorities such as Belarus and Kazakhstan. Russia responded to Belarus's introduction in January 2017 of a five-day visa-free travel through Minsk airport by establishing a security zone with border controls along the Belarus-Russian border and moved flights to Belarus from domestic to international terminals. Surprisingly, although the two have been part of a putative Union State from April 1996 (whose founding treaty was formally signed on 22 December 1999), there is no common visa regime. Russia now suggested the establishment of a Schengen-style single-visa area, but Minsk has been reluctant to reduce its sovereignty in this sphere.[9] The developmental goals of the EEU too often ran aground on the flaws in Russia's domestic governance system. This was most sharply in evidence in the appointment in October 2017 of Belyaninov to head the

EDB. As we have seen, Belyaninov was dismissed as head of the customs service in July 2016 amid serious corruption allegations and the seizure of valuables at his home, although he was not charged with a criminal offence. Under his leadership, the FCS became notorious for its arbitrariness and punitive methods of revenue extractions, favouring some companies at the expense of others. His appointment threatened to undermine the integrity of the EDB and reduced the credibility of the EEU as a whole in the eyes of potential partners, notably the EU and China.

As with the EU on which in some ways it is modelled, the EEU suffers from the tension between supranationalism and national interests. The struggle to preserve national sovereignty means that intergovernmentalism became the main form of interaction, and the Supreme Eurasian Commission remained relatively weak, although like all such bodies it seeks to extend its prerogatives. The principle of unanimity for decisions slows matters, with delegated officials often more loyal to their national governments than to Eurasian integration. Above all, Russia's interest in Eurasian integration was susceptible to change, since its economic gains from integration were negligible. The EEU accounts for just 6–7 per cent of Russia's foreign trade. As with so many issues, there is no consensus in Russian public or elite opinion in favour of integration, and even the Eurasianist faction is divided since most condemn the liberal model that is being applied, while liberals condemn the protectionist (and authoritarian) features of Eurasian integration, fearing that it impedes Russia's necessary modernisation. The internal market does not function well, with frequent trade disputes, sanctions, border closures and exceptions to common tariffs. These problems could well be overcome over time, and the EEU is by far the most ramified attempt at integration in the region since the disintegration of the USSR, bringing together countries that share a common history and sociology, as well as geographical proximity. The ultimate challenge is to achieve the 'integration of integrations', including the harmonisation of trade policies and technical standards with the EU while finding a place for the EEU in the context of BRI.

China's 21st Century Maritime SREB was outlined by Chinese president Xi Jinping at the Nazarbayev University during his visit to Kazakhstan on 7 September 2013, and in October, on a visit to Jakarta, he outlined how SREB would develop regional infrastructure and trade with ASEAN. This bloc has traditionally defended the sovereignty of its member states, although in recent years there have been moves towards greater intergovernmental solidarity. On 28 March 2015, China officially announced the OBOR strategy, a grandiose plan to link Asia, Eurasia and Africa with transport and infrastructure. This was the background to Xi's visit to Moscow to celebrate the seventieth anniversary of the end of the Second World War in Europe on 9 May 2015, an event boycotted by most Western leaders (but not, appropriately, by Germany's chancellor Angela Merkel). Xi and first lady Peng Liyuan were given pride of place at the Red Square victory parade. The previous day, Putin and Xi agreed to coordinate the work of the EEU and OBOR. This became known as 'conjugation' (*sopryazhenie*) and meant that the two initiatives would cooperate while retaining their separate identities. At that time, thirty-two agreements were signed, including two framework declarations related to the economy. Russian companies gained access to Chinese finance, including credit lines in yuan. At that time, about 7 per cent of mutual trade was conducted in their respective currencies, reflecting the mutual desire to reduce dependency on dollars and euros for payments. The joint declaration committed the two sides to engage in 'dialogue' and signalled the beginning of a transformative process based on what was termed 'mutual benefit'. The two countries pledged to cooperate over the two partially competing projects, Russia's EEU and China's SREB. The ultimate, though remote, goal according to the declaration was the establishment of a 'common economic space'. As if to confirm the centrality of the EEU in Xi's plans, he visited the two other founder members of the EEU, Belarus and Kazakhstan. Although not yet proclaimed, a greater Asia was in the making.

BRI is part of a grand strategy to focus resources on what Xi calls the 'China dream of the great rejuvenation of the nation'. BRI is a long-term developmental strategy intended to come to fruition by the hundredth anniversary of the founding of the PRC in 2049. By December 2018, over one hundred countries and international organisations had signed cooperation agreements within its framework. The partnerships could ultimately provide a new model of global leadership. Power redistribution does not necessarily entail frontal confrontation but could evolve through the gradual erosion of American primacy, at a time when the very notion of primacy is contested. China furthermore developed its own multilateral institutions such as the Asian Infrastructure Investment Bank (AIIB), which has already become the world's second biggest multilateral development agency with more members than the Japan-sponsored Asian Development Bank. There are also pan-Asian alternatives, notably the Regional Comprehensive Economic Partnership (RCEP), working in partnership with the BRICS New Development Bank (NDB) and the SCO. Economic development policies and programmes like BRI have important geopolitical implications. This was evident at the first Belt and Road Forum held in Beijing on 14–15 May 2017, where Putin's developed his thoughts on GEP. In particular, he announced that at the heart of GEP would be a Eurasian Trade Facilitation Agreement. This decentralised approach was reminiscent of BRI itself. For Russia, a China-centric system would undoubtedly be more benign than the neo-containment policies predominant in the West.

BRI represents a foundational shift in global affairs, with China working without Western partners to advance joint projects in Eurasia. BRI is a core element of China's grand strategy for the twenty-first century. Although prompted by a slowdown in the growth of the Chinese economy, the US pivot to Asia and the deterioration in relations with its neighbours, it is a defensive response while trying to gain 'strategic space' for the rising China.[10] It is proclaimed open to all nations and reflects a positive-sum dynamic to create what the Chinese call a 'community of common destiny'. It is in keeping with the anti-hegemonic thinking of the two countries. Nevertheless, there are some important unresolved issues. Just as Russia had been concerned about the knock-on effects of Ukraine joining the EU free-trade zone, so China was concerned that the creation of the customs union would create barriers for Chinese goods entering what would become the EEU. In the event, the demand for Chinese goods in Russia and Kazakhstan remains insatiable. The main entry point is Kyrgyzstan, and it remains an enormous 'back door' for cheap Chinese imports into Central Asia. The EEU forced the imposition of an external tariff barrier, much to the dissatisfaction of Beijing. The removal of customs posts between Kyrgyzstan and Kazakhstan rendered this route increasingly attractive, and vast new trading complexes (including the dry port on the Chinese border at Khorgas) are being established with Kazakhstan.

With Eurasia becoming the centre of various global geostrategic collisions, it is hardly surprising that Central Asia once again became the focus of some sort of new great power contest, although not a reprise of the nineteenth-century 'great game' between Russia and Great Britain.[11] Today, there are at least four powers involved, although with different degrees of intensity, with Turkey and Japan asserting a regional presence. The EU at various points announced its intention to engage more actively in the region, but in the end, it lacked the resources and commitment to become a major player. The focus of the United States in the 1990s was on energy politics, but after 9/11, Russia endorsed a more active military presence to facilitate the campaign in Afghanistan. The Americans leased a short-term base in Kyrgyzstan, and Russian pressure prevented this becoming permanent. Ultimately, the two main players remain Russia and China. Despite increasingly close ties at the global level, the two jostle for influence and position in Central Asia, although each is careful not to damage the interests of the other. As distinct from the original great game, the five republics – Kazakhstan, Kyrgyzstan, Tajikistan, Turkmenistan and Uzbekistan – are now active agents, playing off the various external powers while struggling for regional hegemony and status among themselves.

The EEU's place in the broader context of European politics remains contested. Member states seek the maximum room for manoeuvre with minimum commitment while gaining maximum benefit. There will always be tension between member states and supranational bodies, but the balance between gains in exchange for the loss of sovereignty is far from clear. Britain's withdrawal from the EU (Brexit) sharpened the fundamental question about the necessity of Eurasian integration. The global trend towards regional integration appears to have reversed. This relates to the broader question of whether Eurasian integration can be seen as a progressive project. Moscow proclaims its commitment to the negative norm of non-interference in the internal affairs of other states, and its definition of a great power is based on a type of order enshrining sovereignty, non-interventionism and a pluralism of regime types.[12] Thus, Eurasian integration is nested in normative criteria that undermine integration, a contradiction that will sooner or later have to be resolved.

The post-Atlantic world

Putin's leadership from 2012 was characterised by alienation from the historical West, accompanied by a 'pivot to Asia'. In one of his election papers in early 2012, Putin argued that China's economic growth represented 'a chance to catch the Chinese wind in the sails of our economy'.[13] Russia hosted the 2012 Asia-Pacific Economic Cooperation (APEC) summit in Vladivostok, a grandiose (and expensive) affair acting as Russia's declaration of intent to become an Eastern power. The burgeoning Russo-Chinese alignment was given an additional impetus by the Ukraine crisis from early 2014, accompanied by further estrangement from the West. Instead of the failed 'greater Europe' idea, Putin devised no less ambitious ideas for a greater Eurasia, encompassing at its maximum not only Russia and China and much of Asia but also the EU. The ambitions are boundless, but their physical and political limits are unclear. Russia's vision of the future now extends beyond the customary aspiration to become European to encompass a more comprehensive global dimension, accompanied by a complex process of reimagining territories, boundaries, political communities and citizenship across the vast Eurasian space. Achievement necessarily falls far short of ambition, but the long-term direction of travel has been set.

Putin first mooted the idea of GEP in his annual address to parliament on 3 December 2015 when he called for discussions to establish an economic partnership between the EEU, ASEAN and the SCO. His speech drew on the ideas outlined in a Valdai Club report of June 2015 on how to link the EEU and SREB within a larger Eurasian framework. The aim was to maintain stability in Central Asia and to avoid Russo-Chinese rivalry.[14] The project was then mentioned on several occasions in 2016. At the St Petersburg International Economic Forum (SPIEF) on 17 June 2016, Putin outlined grandiose plans for 'greater Eurasia'. The details were vague, but the basic thrust was clear: Russia would encourage the 'integration of integrations' across a range of institutions encompassing all of Eurasia. Instead of the much-vaunted but stillborn greater Europe, Putin announced, 'As early as June we, along with our Chinese colleagues, are planning to start official talks on the formation of comprehensive trade and economic partnership in Eurasia with the participation of the European Union states and China. I expect that this will be one of the first steps towards the formation of a major Eurasian partnership.' He was at pains to stress that this did not mean rejecting Europe: 'Despite all the well-known problems in our relations', the EU remained Russia's 'key trade and economic partner'. He thus invited Europeans to join the project for the Eurasian partnership and welcomed the initiative by Nazarbayev to hold consultations between the EEU and the EU.[15] Contrary to those who argue that Putin seeks to weaken the EU and to exacerbate its internal divisions, the ambitious plan for a trading bloc from the Atlantic to the Pacific sought to make the EU a full partner, with the support of the Chinese leadership. Russia refused to choose between Europe and Asia, and instead the greater Eurasia idea tries to unite the two.

Russia was marginalised in the Atlantic system, but by repositioning itself as a Eurasian power, it seeks to regain centrality. The GEP is more than a way of compensating for failures in the West but represents what many in Moscow consider is a long-delayed rebalancing of policy. Russia emerged as the main proponent of the creation of a parallel set of global institutions, and this helps explain the ferocity of the onslaught against the country. Russia, like China and other partners in 'post-Western' ventures, fear exclusion from the privileges and benefits of the historical West and its assertion of extraterritorial power through sanctions and other measures.

The latter concern encouraged the emergence of a parallel set of regional and global governance institutions. The SCO is one of the major bodies at the heart of the anti-hegemonic alignment. First established as a coordination body for five powers in 1996, it was transformed into an organisation in 2001 with the addition of Uzbekistan. The 2009 SCO summit in Ekaterinburg created a new category, 'dialogue partner', and granted that status to Sri Lanka and Belarus, with Turkey joining the group in June 2012. Pakistan was the first to apply for membership in 2006, while Iran lodged its application the following year, with India following suit in 2010. Russia advocated SCO enlargement on the grounds that it would create a more balanced and powerful organisation. Understandably, China and some Central Asian states were hesitant. Russia argued that if Pakistan were to join, so should India, a view that in the end was accepted by China. Following the admission of India and Pakistan in 2017, the eight-member SCO accounts for a quarter of global GDP, 43 per cent of the world's population and 23 per cent of the planet's territory. It is also the most rapidly developing part of the world.

Although encompassing countries at very different levels of development, disparate geographies and populations, various types of political regimes and with different economic challenges, in purely quantitative terms, the BRICS bloc matters, comprising 44 per cent of the world's population and 25 per cent of the global economy, and with all the countries enjoying enormous growth potential. BRICS created an independent financial system to finance their development. The BRICS NDB was launched in 2015 with an initial capital of $100bn, and its Contingent Reserve Arrangement (CRA) also became operational in that year with a $100 billion fund. There is also a BRICS currency reserve fund with $100 billion. The BRICS financial institution, together with China's AIIB, provides the financial infrastructure to advance its international economic agenda. A Chinese plan to make the yuan the reserve currency of BRICS was rebuffed by the other members, and this reflected some of the internal tensions in the bloc.[16] The group's seventh summit in Ufa on 8–9 July 2015 agreed to develop and strengthen its international status. Putin noted that there was a moratorium on enlarging the group until adequate structures were developed.[17] The ninth BRICS summit took place on 3–5 September 2017 in Xiamen, China, accompanied by the usual debates whether the grouping represented an alternative to the established players allied in the G7 grouping. At the Xiamen summit, Xi promised $4 billion to support the NDB's business development operations.

The BRICS alignment was established to enhance the influence of emerging economies in global governance, and it has had some influence in that respect. More profoundly, the bloc represents a broadening of the anti-hegemonic ambitions of its two core members, Russia and China. They do not challenge the post-war US-led liberal international order as such, since all the BRICS members in one way or another are beneficiaries of that system, but they do challenge the power system embedded in the liberal order and instead demand a more pluralistic world order. This is not simply the demand for multipolarity but represents a broader attempt to create an alternative world order within an international system regulated by more representative versions of the post-war institutions of global governance. The Russian deputy foreign minister Sergei Ryabkov stresses that 'BRICS is in fact an already established new centre of the multi-polar world and a new and more democratic system of international relations'. In a pointed rebuke to the US-led Atlantic community, he noted that 'BRICS is a phenomenon of the 21st century and this is different from military and political unions that come from another epoch and alliances of states built under a principle of hierarchism'.[18] He argued that 'there is hardly any other international entity more dynamic and rapidly strengthening its positions than the BRICS interstate association', and insisted that 'against the background of the aggravation of the international situation there is the growing need for coordination of the BRICS countries' positions on resolving the crisis situations in various parts of the world'.[19]

The Russian foreign minister Sergei Lavrov insists that 'Russia views strengthening of ties with the BRICS states as its foreign policy priority'.[20] The official Russian long-term objective is 'the gradual transformation of BRICS from a dialogue forum and a tool for coordinating positions on a limited range of issues into a full-scale mechanism for strategic and day-to-day cooperation on key issues of world politics and the global economy'.[21] Georgy Toloraya, the executive director of the National Committee on BRICS Research, notes that 'Western countries had from the very beginning regarded BRICS as an undesirable and dangerous rival and wanted to bring pressure to bear on the association, trying to prove its unviability and emphasizing contradictions between its member states'.[22] Some of the criticism is justified, but both the SCO and BRICS promote dialogue even between traditional contesting countries.

The EEU has a dual rationality – as a functional integration project for post-Soviet Eurasia and as an instrument to provide a platform for macro-regionalism. The latter aspect was clear at the joint May 2015 Ufa summit of BRICS, the EEU and the SCO, where Putin and Xi discussed concrete plans for the conjugation of the EEU and SREB. As for the SCO, the Ufa meeting stressed its growing role in improving cooperation in the financial sphere and providing project financing, accompanied by plans for an SCO development bank and a special drawing account. Putin expressed the wish that Chinese companies would develop Siberia and the Russian Far East.[23] The scholar Alexander Lukin argues that the SCO initiative was given momentum by the behaviour of the West:

> Thus, while the US was celebrating its victory in the Cold War and Francis Fukuyama was announcing the 'end of history', China, India, Brazil and many other states in Asia, Africa and Latin America were eyeing the situation with concern. Had the US shown more restraint, developments would have taken a different turn. But Bill Clinton and especially George W. Bush chose to consolidate American successes and seek total US dominance in the world. Europe was unwilling to navigate an independent course and followed in Washington's wake.

For Lukin, 'The united West increasingly took on the role of the world's policeman, substituting its ad hoc decisions for international law.'[24] Although the organisations were not directed against the West, with its participants in one way or another part of the Western system, its members 'coordinated their responses to aspects of the new incarnation of the system that didn't suit them', prompting the creation of associations without western involvement.[25]

The SCO summit in Tashkent in June 2016 took the coordination programme a step further, especially when it came to the construction of regional transport infrastructure. The meeting agreed that India and Pakistan would join the SCO in 2017. There would now be four of the world's nine nuclear powers in the SCO, changing the balance of power in the organisation. Afghanistan, Iran and Mongolia remain prospective members. At the forum's seventeenth meeting in Astana on 8–9 June 2017, India and Pakistan were formally admitted to join the existing members Russia, China, Kazakhstan, Kyrgyzstan, Tajikistan and Uzbekistan. The observer states at that time included Afghanistan, Belarus, Mongolia and Iran, and there were a number of dialogue partners. The final press release restated the SCO's key goals:

> The heads of state noted the importance of the Organisation's further consolidation as an effective full-fledged regional platform aimed at active participation in building a more equitable, polycentric model of world order that meets the interests of each and every state, promoting the process of

democratisation of international relations, creating an effective global and regional architecture of security and cooperation, and forming a human community linked by a common destiny.[26]

The group agreed to intensify cooperation to combat the 'three evils' of terrorism, extremism and separatism. On the sidelines of the summit, Xi met with the Indian prime minister Narendra Modi, and the two pledged to enhance mutual trust, deepen practical cooperation, align development strategies and cooperate on major international and regional issues. They would have a lot of work to do to achieve these goals. In addition to long-standing border issues, the China-Pakistan Economic Corridor (CPEC) as part of BRI exacerbated tensions since the railway from Xinjiang enters Pakistan through the part of Kashmir occupied by that country. This was one reason why India did not send a delegation to the BRI Forum in Beijing in May 2017, reinforcing scepticism whether BRI would be of benefit to India.

Within BRICS, the Russo-Chinese 'authoritarian modernisation' axis is countered by the more conventional democracies of Brazil, India and South Africa. They also have divergent international orientations, with India more aligned with the United States, while China has traditionally supported Pakistan. The border dispute between India and China reflected a deeper geopolitical antagonism between the two countries. When it comes to reform of the UN, and in particular widening permanent membership of the UNSC, Russia and China wish to maintain their existing status, whereas Brazil and India have long sought to become members. China has the additional concern that its traditional rival, Japan, could also be the beneficiary of any substantive reform of the UN system. The BRICS countries meet as a group on the sidelines of G20 summits, but agreed positions on fundamental questions do not always emerge. At the same time, the BRICS Plus format has brought in a number of other countries. Mexico, Egypt, Thailand, Kenya and Tajikistan were invited to the Xiamen summit, while Indonesia and Turkey have been considered for full membership of the bloc. In fact, so many countries have been considered candidate countries – in addition to those listed above, Vietnam, Nigeria, Pakistan, Egypt, Iran and the Philippines have been mentioned – that the moratorium on enlargement is probably a sensible strategy for the present.

The ambitious schemes for pan-Asian integration encompassing Russia, China, India, South Korea and many other countries represent variations of the Silk Road idea. The intensity and scope of these plans for spatial integration vary greatly, yet all are groping to find a formula for states to combine in various integrative endeavours. The degree to which a substantive degree of sovereignty will be ceded to the institutions of integration remains contested. Nevertheless, together they suggest an alternative architecture and offer some substance to the idea of Eurasia and Asia aligning along a different axis to that of the West. The surge in continental regionalism reflects the attempt to find mediating institutions in a world lacking the stable bipolarity of the Cold War and aspirations to overcome the subsequent asymmetries in the international system.

Russia assiduously works to create a greater Eurasian community, encompassing its partners in the EEU as well as China, India, Iran and ASEAN in an attempt to create 'a major Euro-Asian political and economic arc, one which spans from Belarus all the way to the border with Australia'.[27] The goal was not to repudiate globalisation or the institutions of international society but to render them less West-centric. In that aim, Russia found many willing allies in Asia and, indeed, within many Western countries. The anti-hegemonic strategy was not anti-Western but a complex attempt to introduce pluralism into the international system and to render international society more autonomous of what was perceived to be the double standards and opportunism of the American-led international liberal order. The development of substantive multipolarity has profound geopolitical ramifications. Oliver Stuenkel argues that the Ufa Declaration and associated documents signalled an important step towards the creation of a post-western world.[28] Western sanctions forced Russia to redouble its efforts to engage with greater Asia, while China sees Eurasia as an essential part not only of its economic but also of its political future. With 'Sino-Russian relations ... closer than they have been at any time in the past fifty years, giving them the chance to reshape the global order to their liking', Kissinger's worst nightmare is coming to pass.[29] The creation of systemic alternatives is not intended to be anti-Western but to act as models for a more inclusive and plural international system. Non-Western alternatives exist and are taking increasingly structured forms.

Putin's Asian gambit: Escape from confrontation?

Karaganov, one of the earliest advocates of a turn to the East, argues, 'The concept of Greater Eurasia can also help to solve European security problems created by the expansion of Western alliances and Russia's natural reaction to that, and unsolvable within the old framework.' He argues that along with Russia taking firm action 'to deter the most dangerous manifestations of American policy, it is necessary to build a constructive alternative to the ruined bipolar world order and the crumbling unipolar one. A partnership or community of Greater Eurasia can and should become one of the key elements of this new world order.'[30] The sentiment was shared by Lavrov on the eve of APEC's Lima summit in November 2016, when he noted, 'The Russian initiative on the Greater Eurasian Partnership ... is intended to harmonize the emerging Eurasian multilevel system of integration structures and to combine the potential of the interested Asian countries and, in the future, of Europe as well.'[31] The GEP in his view did not mean that Russia was turning its back on Europe. By December 2016, Lavrov listed the countries with which the EEU was negotiating FTAs, including China, Israel and Egypt. He stressed that these were part of the broader plan to develop greater Eurasia, where the EEU, SCO and ASEAN countries 'can participate based on different forms of cooperation'.[32] The secretariats of the three organisations met on the sidelines of the Russia-ASEAN summit in Sochi in May 2016, which confirmed the interest of the South-East Asian countries in cooperation.

In this context, the intensifying engagement between Russia and China represents far more than a banal 'pivot to Asia' or a response to Russia's alienation from the West.[33] The path to rapprochement has been long and difficult. China has not forgotten the 1.5 million square kilometres of Siberia seized by tsarist Russia under what it calls the 'unequal treaties' dating back to 1689. In 1969, this provoked armed clashes over disputed islands along the Ussuri River. By 1971, the USSR had forty-four divisions stationed along the border. It was in this context that Henry Kissinger travelled to Beijing in 1971 to arrange the epochal visit of Richard Nixon the following year. Fear of the Sino-American axis prompted the Soviet Union to engage in détente and the Four-Power agreement on Berlin. It took a major effort by post-communist Russia to normalise relations with China. The Treaty on Good-Neighbourliness, Friendship and Cooperation was signed on 16 July 2001, outlining the main principles and features of bilateral cooperation. Finally, Putin visited Beijing in October 2004 to finalise the border agreement and sign deals on energy cooperation. A resurgent Russia and modernising China began to align and presented a potential counterweight to American hegemony. On the fundamental issues in world politics, their positions are remarkably similar.

Russia and China had long been dissatisfied with the structures of international governance, considering that they had not been treated as equals in that system.[34] Russian leaders from Gorbachev to Putin argued that Russia had voluntarily ended the Cold War and transformed the domestic order, and considered that the country by right deserved to be integrated as an equal in the top table of international leadership, irrespective of its economic and military weight. China's route to neo-revisionism was rather more convoluted, although also based on the view that its equality was merited by its history and size. Both sought to adapt the Western developmental model to modernise their societies, although China's use of the opportunities offered by engagement in the international division of labour more adroitly avoided alienating its Western interlocutors. Neither was ready to repudiate the horizontal ties with the West, but both had come to the conclusion that it would be mutually beneficial to strengthen their links in the context of the vertical commitment to international society. The deepening institutionalisation of non-Western regional and global associations meant that Russia achieved more in a decade with China than in a quarter century with the EU and the historical West.

In practical terms, this meant intensifying interactions between the anti-hegemonic states. Russia's trade with China rebounded strongly after the recession, expanding by 31 per cent in 2017 to reach $87 billion and exceeding the target of $100 billion in 2018. Russia became the largest supplier of energy to the Chinese market, supplying 50 million tons of oil in 2017, and with the completion of the Eastern Route pipeline in 2019, Russia became China's top supplier of gas. China became Russia's top trade partner, representing 15 per cent of its total foreign turnover. The structure of bilateral trade also improved, with an increasing share of engineering and high-tech goods. China's direct capital investment had also increased to reach $4.5 billion in mid-2018, with seventy-three projects approved and eleven projects worth $11 billion already implemented. China held a 29.9 per cent stake in the giant Yamal-LNG project, along with France's Total (20 per cent), and the two countries were cooperating to build a large-body long-haul airliner, a heavy helicopter, and were implementing a joint space programme for 2018–22.[35] The sanctions regime against Russia had a dampening effect, with Chinese financial institutions reluctant to lend to Russia for fear of falling foul of US sanctions. Nevertheless, China became Russia's single largest trading partner, taking 17 per cent of Russia's international trade in 2018, accompanied by a rising trend for mutual payments in yuan and roubles as both countries worked to render themselves sanctions-proof by de-dollarising. On 17 May 2018, the EEU and China signed an agreement on economic cooperation that left the tariff regime unchanged but covered trade policy, technical regulations and phytosanitary control. To avoid the various bottlenecks in the sea lanes to Europe, China was particularly interested in exploiting the new opportunities of the increasingly ice-free Northern Sea Route.

All of this is based on the deep personal relationship between Putin and Xi. Following Xi's visit to Moscow for the 9 May 2015 anniversary, in September, Putin stood next to Xi in Beijing in the military parade to celebrate the seventieth anniversary of China's victory in the Second World War. China was allied with the Soviet Union in the war against Japan and also suffered catastrophically in a conflict which in various forms had started with the Japanese invasion of Manchuria in 1931. These forms of solidarity between the two countries may be largely symbolic, but they generate a deepening climate of trust. In June 2016, Putin completed his fifteenth visit to China, where the two sides agreed to develop the mentioned wide-bodied long-haul plane, a heavy helicopter, and to coordinate their space programmes. There is constant close interaction between the Russian and Chinese leaderships on the whole gamut of developmental and international issues. Critics call this an alliance of autocrats, but this underplays the degree of normative convergence between the two countries on the basis of anti-hegemonism, multipolarity and distinctive models not of autarkic but of autochthonous development. Speaking with journalists following the fifteenth Direct Line on 15 June 2017, Putin stressed the complementarity between the EEU and BRI outlined at the BRI Forum the previous month, and stressed that the initiative was the achievement of 'our great friend, and my personal friend, Xi Jinping'.[36]

By the time of his state visit to China in June 2018, Putin could argue that the two countries had 'built a relationship that probably cannot be compared with anything in the world. It is truly built on consideration of each other's interests.' In 2017 alone, the two leaders met five times, and the close personal relationship meant that 'President Xi Jinping is probably the only world leader I have celebrated one of my birthdays with'.[37] In stark contrast to the evident disarray at the G7 summit held in La Malbaie in Canada in June 2018, at the SCO's Qingdao summit in China at that time, a spirit of constructive cooperation prevailed. Xi for the first time described the relationship with Russia as 'strategic': 'President Putin and I both think that the China-Russia strategic partnership is mature, firm and stable'; and for good measure he added about Putin: 'He is my best, most intimate friend.' The meeting pushed ahead with the ambitious China-Mongolia-Russia Economic Corridor, a key item in BRI, and advanced plans for interconnectivity between BRI and the EEU. By that time, China had invested some $84 billion in SCO countries. Iran attended as an observer, and Russia reiterated its support for the country's full membership. The SCO-Afghanistan contact group behind closed doors discussed plans on how finally to resolve the Afghan conflict without Western 'interference'.[38] In his concluding press conference, Putin stressed that the combined SCO had a greater GDP than the G7 in PPP terms, and he showed no great interest in Russia returning to the G7, stressing the importance of the G20.[39] At this time, Karaganov urged Russia to 'stop being afraid, let alone feel ashamed, of its Asianism', and he called on 'the whole of Russia' to 'realise that it is no longer an oriental periphery of Europe'.[40]

By 2024, the Communist Party of China (CPC) will have been in power longer than the 74-year lifespan of Soviet Russia. As memory of the October 1917 revolution fades, the Maoist developmental model that came to power in October 1949, with all of its vicissitudes and modifications, appears to be more enduring. Putin's neo-revisionism saw China's growing power as less of a threat than a massive opportunity. Reform communism in Russia had proved a disaster, and Putin could only look on with envy at the success of post-Mao 'communism of reform'. However, both countries faced the difficult transition from mechanical to organic stability, although in Russia that path should be much easier. It has spent three decades creating the foundations for genuine constitutionalism, and theoretically, as the manual manipulations of the regime system erode, the institutions of the constitutional state are ready to assume the burden of governance. However, historical experience demonstrates that Russia has the unique ability to snatch defeat from the jaws of victory, so it is impossible to predict what comes after the Putinite stability system.

Bobo Lo notes that 'the Kremlin seeks to build an alternative ideational and political legitimacy that challenges Western notions of global governance and moral universalism'.[41] This is not quite accurate, since the challenge is to the perceived inadequacies of the existing system of global governance, a dissatisfaction that is shared by a number of countries and prompted the creation of alternative structures. Equally, the challenge is not to the practices of moral universalism, since Russia has no intention of repudiating such foundational acts as the UN Charter and the Universal Declaration of Human Rights, and remains a member of CoE (although its voting rights in the Parliamentary Assembly of the Council of Europe (PACE) were suspended between 2014 and 2019). Russia and its allies considered that the values-based policies of the post-Cold War years had been applied instrumentally and selectively to advance the hegemonic power of the West rather than genuinely to advance the realm of justice. From Moscow's perspective, it simply made no sense to condemn Russia's failings while giving Saudi Arabia a free pass, where the abuse of human and civic rights is far more egregious. Moscow's critique had some substance and, as far as Saudi Arabia is concerned, was even acknowledged by Obama in an interview in *The Atlantic*.[42] This fails to recognise that the historical West's commitment to the principles as outlined in the Atlantic Charter are genuinely foundational, however flawed in implementation. Equally, the West tends to underplay the hegemonic and commercial distortions in the application of its value-based policies.

The critique of 'an imposed model that presents itself as universal' provoked a 'demand for alternatives'.[43] From our neo-revisionist perspective, this does not fully capture the ambiguities of Russia's policy. It seeks to temper the practical application of moral universalism in what are perceived to be arbitrary and punitive ways while ensuring that the instruments of global governance reflect global concerns. The goal is not simply the reproduction of polarity in a single world order but the creation of an alternative world order whose very existence would ensure geopolitical and ideational pluralism. Talk of an alternative globalisation does not mean the reproduction of what was increasingly seen as Western monism. As the Valdai discussion paper put it,

> The Atlantic community is a unique example of value unification. By contrast, non-western states are together in stressing the importance of diversity, insisting that no uniform emblems of a 'modern state and society' are either desirable or possible. This is an approach more in tune with the conditions of a multipolar world.[44]

Even the Valdai paper failed to recognise the potential radicalism of the anti-hegemonic perspective. Western sanctions accelerated the trend to find alternatives to the dollar, such as pricing oil in gold and other currencies, but this did not entail withdrawal from global economic integration. China helped Russia withstand the sanctions, while the BRICS countries began to create an alternative to Atlantic-dominated international institutions. This is a non-West that remains part of the global economy but seeks to ensure that universal rules became impartial and less embedded in a particular power system. In other words, a pluralistic multi-order world would remain based on the UN system and the internationalisation of economies but would move away from the narrow perspectives of the historical West. If Russia could not join a new West, then it would become a founding member of a post-Atlantic international community.

Global Russia

In 2014, Obama claimed that 'Russia is a regional power that is threatening some of its immediate neighbours, not out of strength but out of weakness'.[45] In a paradoxical way, Obama was right. If Russia had been able to assert its positions over the previous quarter century to create what it considered a more equitable European security system, if it had been able to block NATO enlargement to the point that the issue was off the table, if it had been able to avert the showdown over Ukraine and prevent what it considered to be the illegal overthrow of the legitimate Ukrainian government, and if it had other ways of preventing the ultimate nightmare of American forces occupying the Sevastopol naval base, then it would not have felt the need to undertake such a risky venture as returning Crimea to Russian sovereignty. This was patently a repudiation of the norms of international conduct established in Europe after the end of the Second World War, but it was also no less obviously a defensive reaction to what was perceived to be the reckless advance of a potentially hostile Atlantic system. The expansive Atlantic order in Moscow's view had become a revisionist force that threatened not only to undermine Russian security but also openly posed the question of regime change in Moscow itself. Soon after, Obama asserted that Russia 'stands alone' in the world, and he worked hard with his European partners that this would remain the case.[46] A range of neo-containment measures were imposed, including sanctions, the beefing up of NATO forces along the border with Russia, exclusion from the G8 and treatment as a diplomatic pariah.

None of this changed Putin's thinking or behaviour in the slightest, and it only stiffened Moscow's resolve. The hostile actions by the Atlantic system and its allies only confirmed the Kremlin in its diagnosis that it was impossible to work with the West on equal terms and that there would be no negotiated settlement to the impasse in European and global affairs. Russia now abandoned its last cold peace inhibitions and understood that it could act as a global player without reference to what at one point were called 'strategic partners'. Instead, in a series of striking initiatives, Putin sought to assert Russia as an indispensable actor on the world stage. Moscow had always maintained a strong diplomatic presence in the world affairs, but this was now reinforced by some bold moves. On 30 September 2015, Russia intervened in the Syrian conflict, and within a little more than a year, it had not only stabilised the Damascus regime but had also effectively paved the way to the defeat of the insurgency across the country. With the fall of Islamic State's headquarters in Raqqa in October 2017 and the establishment of 'deconfliction' zones in the areas still contested by insurgents, the Syrian civil war entered its endgame. In a whirlwind visit to the Middle East, Putin on 11 December 2017 declared victory at the Khmeimim air base and ordered (not for the first time) a scaling down of the country's forces in Syria. In Egypt, he signed a multibillion-dollar contract for a nuclear reactor on the country's Mediterranean coast and restored historic links, including arms sales. In Turkey, Putin and Erdoğan condemned Trump's recognition of Jerusalem as Israel's capital. Putin brokered deals with a range of leaders, many antithetical to each other. Putin was intent on restoring Russia as a global power, and this was achieved through adroit and supple diplomacy.

The Syrian intervention involved no more than a few dozen jets and several thousand support troops. By comparison, although Obama avoided military engagement, he ended up in conflict with most US allies, including Israel and Saudi Arabia, while Trump's incoherent policies only exacerbated conflicts, even between former allies such as Saudi Arabia and Qatar, while his decision on 6 December 2017 to move the US embassy from Tel Aviv to Jerusalem ran counter to numerous UN resolutions and the conventional model for resolution of the Israeli-Palestine conflict, and was met with universal condemnation. Putin prevented Syria becoming a new Afghanistan and instead saved the Assad regime from collapse and achieved a type of peace that promised to preserve the integrity of the country, even though this will inevitably require a high degree of devolution to Kurds and other peoples. The Russian military displayed its enormous improvement since the Russo-Georgian war in 2008, where there had been no modern communications and weapons. Now the forces showed discipline and professionalism, armed with precision weapons and furnished with expertly trained pilots. The cruise missiles launched from the Caspian Sea demonstrated Russian ability to project power over long distances. The danger of conflict with Ankara had been averted, and despite the shooting down of a Russian plane in the autumn of 2015, amicable relations were soon restored. Moscow cooperated with Iran in Syria, while recognising Israel's security concerns.

The Israeli prime minister, Benjamin Netanyahu, acknowledged the warm relations with Putin when visiting Russia on Holocaust Memorial Day and the anniversary of the lifting of the siege of Leningrad on 29 January 2018:

> My friend, Mr President, I would like to thank you for the invitation to visit this impressive Jewish Museum and Tolerance Centre. I must add that I know this museum would not have been established without your assistance. I was very excited to see the description of the history of our nation in Russia, including the current period when Jewish life in Russia is thriving, largely owing to the support of the authorities and your personal support.[47]

The impressive Jewish Museum and Tolerance Centre in Moscow is one of the world's largest of its kind and is part of the Jewish renaissance in the country, with many newly built synagogues. Although some two million Russians qualify for an Israeli passport because of their Jewish ancestry, there is no exodus currently underway, despite the sanctions and sluggish economy. Russia appears to have witnessed a sharp decline in anti-Semitism in recent years, and Jewish businesses are thriving.[48] Even relations with Saudi Arabia, a staunch backer of the opposition in Syria and a Russian antagonist since Cold War days, had warmed, resulting in a grandiose visit to Moscow by King Salman and a huge retinue in October 2017. Russia needed money for domestic investment and to fund its economic projects abroad, while both countries were interested in high oil prices.[49] They disagreed over Syria, where Russia pledged to stay. The refuelling base in Tartus is projected to become a full-scale naval port capable of simultaneously hosting up to eleven ships. The 49-year lease agreement also grants the Russian Navy access to the territorial waters and other ports of the Syrian Arab Republic. At the same time, Egypt, formerly a major Soviet ally, allowed Russia airplanes to use bases there.

Russia's claim as a great power to conduct an independent foreign policy included the ability to shape exceptions to the rules. In the first two post-communist decades, Russia was in no position to assert this model of great power prerogatives and largely limited itself to attempts to influence decisions from the sidelines while criticising Western policy. Only with Putin's return to the presidency in 2012 was criticism turned into a more assertive strategy. Russia no longer aspired to become part of the Euro-Atlantic liberal order, and instead it advanced a basket of nested regionalisms, including the idea of a greater Europe, a greater Eurasia and a greater Asia (in partnership with China), as well as a type of new globalism with its BRICS and other partners. Although the policy was crafted by Putin, it represented an important shift that in the view of Karaganov and others had been long delayed. It was required to ensure the development of RFE regions, to rectify what was considered to have been the dangerous over-reliance on relations with a hostile West. The modernisation of the RFE would allow Russia to become part of the world's most economically dynamic region, one where Russian values of sovereign independence, non-interference in the internal affairs of other states and conservative mores were reciprocated.

Russia refused to enter the historical West as a subaltern player, and it was now recognised not only as a global actor but also as one of the main challenger powers. Of the three great powers, Russia is by far the weakest economically, hence the contest would be deeply asymmetrical. Putin stressed that Russia would not overextend itself or be drawn into conflicts which it could not hope to win. Putin's strategy is to avoid a major escalation, to avert major incidents, to regulate the situation in Ukraine and above all to stabilise the new normality of enduring confrontation. Putin also seeks to strengthen Russia's economy and domestic resources through technological modernisation and strategic industrial development. This does not mean, however, that Putin will renounce his politics of resistance. Russia looks for a way to break out of the strategic impasse in which it felt it had been trapped for a quarter century, and for that, a new model of world order was sought. This reflected the deeper impasse in which Russia found itself, with its historical space for development constrained by the closed character of the Atlantic system. Only in the East were there opportunities for political development and where the traditional niceties of diplomacy and restraint from interfering in the internal affairs of states were retained.

All this should be kept in perspective. Russia clearly lacks the economic muscle to reproduce anything like the former Soviet Union's global stance. Russia is a great power but with patent limits. Through skilful diplomacy, Putin was able to multiply Russia's power, but this is not a structural resource and will wane as Putin's leadership ends. Russian policy is forced to be defensive and reactive, but this is now nested in the broader neo-revisionist strategy and growing partnerships in the East. Putin accepts that Russia is stymied when it comes to establishing balanced relations with the United States and now believes that there can be no 'strategic partnership' with the EU. However, as Britain was to discover as it tried to negotiate its exit from the EU, the world is not waiting to embrace outcasts from the existing world order. Russia is in a rather different position, because after the end of the Cold War, it tried to enter the Atlantic system, but in the end, the terms for both sides were unsatisfactory. Russia sought to transform the community it was trying to join, which its existing members, for understandable if ultimately short-sighted reasons, could not accept, and instead demanded that Russia adapt to the existing rules and power hierarchy, which Russia equally found unacceptable. The costs of failure for both were high: the Atlantic community reverted to a Cold War stance, diverting resources to enhanced military preparedness, accompanied by the political vilification of its new antagonist. Russia also hunkered down and revived Cold War anti-Westernism accompanied by the cultural condemnation of its protagonist. This impasse is set to endure for at least a generation, unless some major event resets the calculations of all the parties concerned.

8 THE WINDS OF CHANGE

Putin's aversion to competitive elections is a sentiment no doubt shared by many democratic politicians but ultimately recognised by them as the price to pay for a healthy pluralism and a legitimate political system. Instead, Putin approached elections as a general does a battle, with bureaucratic mobilisation, the concentration of maximum force and the unloosing of the massed ranks of media cannons. Elections in this model are not seen as an expression of democratic contestation but as a deadly battle against foes seen and unseen. The struggle is against both the physical opponents, who are typically subjected to savage criticism by regime-allied media, and against the more intangible enemies who allegedly work to undermine Russia and who support attempts to stage a 'colour revolution'. In 2012, this was perceived to be the 'white ribbon' movement, which after the election morphed into an intense period of contentious politics. The main driver was revulsion at sham elections and crude falsification, as well as calls for change. The fundamental demand was for equal and universal citizenship with competitive elections where the vote is counted accurately and where the outcome is respected. This fundamental norm of a democratic polity is rooted in the principles of the constitutional state, but in a system where the administrative regime predominates and its technocratic rationality seeks to manage political processes, the quality of democracy is inevitably undermined.

Towards Putin's fourth term

The protests of 2011–12 depressed Putin's popularity to 60 per cent, the lowest since 1999, but after the reunification of Crimea, his public approval rating soared to 86 per cent, the level around which it remained until his re-election in 2018.[1] Public sentiment felt that a historical injustice had been righted. However, the view that the Ukrainian events changed the character of Putin's leadership, shifting it from electoral to war leader legitimacy, is exaggerated.[2] Putin certainly enjoyed the accolade that came from putting himself at the head of a patriotic upsurge, but he soon pushed back against militant Russian nationalism. The Putin style of leadership fears political autonomy more than anything else, even if it is supportive, aware that independent movements are volatile and demand commitment from the leader, something Putin was never willing to grant. Putin refused to be captured by nationalist mobilisation, just as earlier he had fought oligarch and regional constraints on his leadership. Putin values his political autonomy above all else. His alliances are far from contingent, but they can never be absolute.

The Kremlin defeated the nascent opposition through a mix of coercion and concessions. The coercive measures included the trial of some thirty Bolotnaya activists (and simple participants), and over twenty were sentenced to prison or served time in pretrial detention.[3] The repressive measures included tightening the rules on rallies in June and the 'foreign agents law' of July 2012, followed by the June 2013 'anti-gay propaganda law' and a law against 'anti-religious extremism' to defend the feelings of believers. This was balanced by the 'regime reset' (see Chapter 4), a gradual political decompression intended to start from below and work its way upwards. As we have seen, the regime reset allowed some independent and opposition figures to become mayors and to enter regional legislative assemblies. It was in this spirit that the mayoral elections were fought in Moscow in September 2013, with Sobyanin allowing Navalny to make his impressive run. The regime stabilised the political situation while conducting an assertive foreign policy. As the presidential election of March 2018 approached, the economy and living standards were pulling out of recession, and Putin continued to enjoy astronomical popularity rates.

However, popular sentiment was shifting. If earlier the desire for stability predominated, there was now a growing demand for change, in particular among the younger generation. For the first time since 2003, those in favour of stability were in a minority. Some 51 per cent believed that the country needed 'significant reform', the first time that 'reform' won out over 'stability' since 2003. Younger people were most in favour of reform (62 per cent), dropping to 51 per cent for those aged between 31 and 40, while those above were evenly split, with pensioners most in favour of stability. The greatest demand was for social equality and fighting corruption, reducing dependence on hydrocarbons, followed by the reform of science, education and health. Stability was now associated with stagnating economic conditions and social crises, so there was increased demand for improved living standards and a more stable social situation, with political concerns relatively low down the list.[4] Other studies stressed that in Moscow there was higher than average support for substantial reform, above all, for improvements in the social sphere accompanied by judicial reform and government support for business. Overall, views were evenly split, with 42 per cent of Russians in August 2017 calling for decisive large-scale change, while 41 per cent favoured small-scale incremental change, but only 11 per cent wanted no change at all.[5]

This was the public face of politics. However, developments in the 'basement' were more decisive. The Crimean crisis strengthened the hand of the *siloviki* over the liberals, and although Putin remained the decider, his policies reflected the changing factional balance. As he aged, he appeared to have become more conservative, although without repudiating his fundamental principles, which as we have seen are a mix of Soviet and post-communist sentiments. Putin's managerial approach failed to enunciate an inspiring vision of Russia's future, but the Crimean events for the first time in post-communist Russia gave vent to ideological enthusiasm, in this case grounded on patriotic and even nationalist views. While the regime soon brought independent nationalist mobilisation to heel and the patriotic enthusiasm evaporated, the strengthened position of the 'guardians' endured. In other words, while popular sentiment was demanding real change, elite structures were going the other way and dug in to defend Putinite stability. This, sooner or later, was the recipe for a political crisis.

As the 2018 presidential election approached, elements of the 'regime reset' returned, although this did not add up to any substantive 'thaw'. At most, this was a technocratic response to the political challenge of presenting the regime in the best light. The activist Ildar Daldin was released, and the sentence on Evgeniya Chudnovet, a teacher jailed for sharing an abuse video, was reconsidered. This was accompanied by a tempering of the patriotic rhetoric and a shift in media policy to allow a more diverse range of voices to be heard. There was less of the militant rhetoric condemning the liberal 'fifth column'. In parliament, deputies such as Natalya Poklonskaya, the former prosecutor general of Crimea and 'hero' of unification and an ardent monarchist, were forced to temper their militancy after she had called for Alexei Uchitel's film *Mathilda* (about the affair between Nicholas II and the Polish-Russian ballerina Mathilda Kschessinskaya) to be banned. As in the late Soviet period, even unsanctioned activity in support of the regime threatened the stability of the system, especially when it took potentially destabilising radical conservative forms. In the event, in August 2017, the film was approved for general release. In other words, the 'guardianship' role of the regime was tempered. In the Duma, Volodin limited the scope of legislative initiative to prevent the seventh convocation once again becoming the 'crazy printer', spewing out repressive and declaratory laws characteristic of the previous session. As Tatyana Stanovaya notes, the regime sought to constrain the 'lateral competition that they have themselves engendered'.[6]

On 28 March 2016, the long-time hard-line head of the Central Election Commission (CEC), Vladimir Churov, was replaced by the respected human rights activist Ella Pamfilova. She was appointed too late to change the legislation concerning the September 2016 State Duma election but fought against electoral malpractices. Despite her stated intentions, the election was attended by some credible charges of ballot stuffing and vote fixing, in particular, to depress the Yabloko vote in its St Petersburg heartland.[7] Overall, the regime-reset strategy was successful to the extent that there was no repetition of the earlier protest mobilisation. Pamfilova spoke of her intent to ensure that the 2018 presidential and regional elections would be fair, above all, through increased public monitoring of polls by political parties and NGOs to increase transparency.[8] She warned the governor of Kemerovo Oblast, Aman Tuleev, not to use 'administrative resources'.[9] Her efforts were greeted with scepticism. The problem, critics argued, was that erstwhile liberals (such as Igor Artemyev, the former Yabloko members Elena Mizulina and Irina Yarovaya, human rights officials Vladimir Lukin and Mikhail Fedotov, and Pamfilova herself) once in office were 'digested' by the administration and became 'court democrats': with some becoming 'fierce guardians of the regime, others turning into quiet task managers'.[10] The principles of inclusion and exclusion remained arbitrary and selective, with the Yabloko leader, Yavlinsky, calling the signature requirement 'a means of political corruption'.[11] Pamfilova called for reform of the municipal filter system, possibly to lower the threshold or to allow local lawmakers to support more than one candidate, although she agreed that the filter was required to prevent 'scoundrels and fake parties' to stand.[12]

In December 2016, Navalny announced his intention to run for the presidency, and by mid-2017, he had established a network of 130,000 dedicated campaign volunteers in over 63 regional offices, supported by tens of thousands of sympathisers and more than 1.7 million subscribers to his online video channels. Dissatisfaction with corruption and stagnation was brilliantly exploited by Navalny. His organisation Rospil chronicled the abuses and excesses of the elite. In early 2017, Navalny issued a very professional and slick fifty-minute film, with English subtitles, called *He is not Dimon to You* (*On vam ne Dimon*) about Medvedev's properties and assets, including a Tuscan vineyard and villa, whose ownership was hidden behind a number of front companies.[13] Another notable exposé a year earlier discovered the alleged links in the chain hiding the assets of the prosecutor general Yuri Chaika. Navalny's polished and powerful videos gained millions of viewers, with the one on Medvedev viewed over ten million times on YouTube in the first month of its release. Navalny's exposure of venal corruption, the acquisition of properties and assets in Russia and abroad, provided a damning indictment of the meta-corruption associated with the rule of the Putin elite. Tens of thousands of people rallied against corruption. However, the regime still enjoyed widespread poplar support, and a popular revolution was unlikely.

Navalny's presidential bid was dogged by uncertainty because of his criminal conviction. Russian legislation forbids a convicted felon from running for public office, a rule introduced in 2012 to prevent any potential electoral gambit by Khodorkovsky. Navalny's alleged crime dates back to the Kirovles scandal when he served on a voluntary basis as an advisor to the liberal governor of Kirov Oblast, Nikita Belykh, in 2009. In July 2013, Navalny was sentenced to five years in jail, but it was subsequently suspended, allowing him to participate in the September 2013 Moscow mayoral election. His impressive 27 per cent vote made him the unofficial leader of the democratic opposition. In a second case, in December 2014, Navalny and his brother Oleg were convicted of embezzling over $500,000 from the cosmetic company Yves Rocher. The brothers had apparently established an intermediary transport company which won a contract from Yves Rocher to use its services, even though in practice the work was done by subcontractors, with the brothers allegedly pocketing the difference. The scheme continued for four years, during which time Yves Rocher paid some ₽55 million ($1.6 million), with over ₽20 million going to the brothers. Alexei received a suspended three-and-a-half-year sentence, while Oleg (who at the same time worked as a manager in state-owned Russian Post and whose involvement was crucial for the alleged scheme) received three-and-a-half years in prison, and each was fined ₽500,000 and had to pay ₽4.4 million to a company whose interests were allegedly damaged.

The ECtHR judgement on the Kirovles embezzlement case in February 2016 declared that Navalny's right to a fair trial had been violated, that Navalny and his business partner Pyotr Ofitserov had been convicted as a result of the arbitrary application of criminal law and that their actions were part of ordinary commercial activities. In November 2016, the Supreme Court overturned the sentence against Navalny in the Kirovles case and sent it to retrial. On 8 February 2017, the Leninsky District Court in Kirov once again found Navalny guilty of the theft of 10,000 cubic metres of timber products owned by Kirovles, and Ofitserov was found guilty of having abetted this crime. The pair were given five-year and four-year suspended sentences, respectively, and fined. The ECtHR on 17 October 2017 also announced its adjudication in the Yves Rocher case, refusing to accept that the embezzlement charges were politically motivated but finding that the Russian court and investigators violated the Navalny brothers right to a fair trial, as well as the right to lawful punishment, and ordered the Russian government to pay the brothers €10,000 each in compensation as well as €62,800 in combined court fees. On 25 December 2017, the CEC ruled that his criminal record meant that Navalny could not be registered as a presidential candidate. Thus, one of the main opposition leaders was judged ineligible, casting a shadow over the fairness of the election.

As the election approached, there was an accelerated turnover of regional governors. The last time such mass dismissals had taken place was in the late 2000s, when Medvedev changed over thirty governors in the first two years of his presidency. A number of long-standing governors with the traditional 'Soviet manager' profile were replaced by 'young technocrats', often with no links to the region they were expected to govern. At least four governors were in jail, awaiting either a trial or a court verdict on corruption charges, including Belykh. Most of the new appointments were in their thirties or forties, with the exception of the 68-year-old former policeman Vladimir Vasiliev who took over from the veteran Ramazan Abdullatipov in Dagestan. Vasiliev was the first non-Avar or non-Dargin leader of Dagestan since 1948, a region in which the proportion of ethnic Russians had fallen from 9.7 per cent in 1989 to 3.6 per cent in 2010. The appointment was clearly intended to break the hold on regional resources by local strongmen.[14] The Kremlin no longer feared elections, and its nominations were almost invariably elected. Governors, moreover, were now more circumscribed in taking decisions independently, and even if they fulfilled the main criteria – that there were no major protests, that federal elections produced the appropriate results and that the Kremlin's orders were obeyed – it was not enough to ensure the survival of some of the veterans. Even the delivery of economic development did not seem to be the key criteria. The Kremlin applied various 'key performance indicators' as neo-liberal governmentality reinforced traditional patterns of authoritarian management. The result was the further erosion of Russian federalism.[15]

Although Putin is uncomfortable talking about his 'legacy' and how he will be remembered, he is clearly concerned about how he will be viewed in historical perspective, and he certainly believed that there was still unfinished business to be completed in a fourth term. The election was a political and strategic test for the system. Kremlin-aligned think tanks, scholars and polling agencies were assigned to devise 'an image of the future' that Putin could use in the campaign. In the end, no consensus emerged despite several changes of the 'curator' responsible for the project – prompting the anecdote that Putin did not have a future. The initial triad of 'justice, respect and trust' was considered as the main slogan.[16] The focus of social demands had also changed. In 2011–12, the emphasis was on civic dignity and political inclusion, but following the economic recession, social justice became the main concern. The problem for the regime was how to reconcile recognition of the legitimacy of the demands without undermining its own record. Even though Putin surrounded himself with billionaires, he never forgot that his popularity was founded on forcing employers to pay wages and for the state to fulfil, at least minimally, its constitutional obligations for social welfare. It is easy enough to attack instances of venal corruption, but any assault on meta-corruption would undermine the foundations of the regime itself.

The cultural turn in Russian politics after 2012 advanced 'traditional values', 'spiritual values' and 'sacred lands', and reflected the intensification of confrontation with the West. However, as he faced re-election, his team understood that an appeal to transcendent values at the time of growing economic hardship and stagnant living standards was liable to backfire. Russians had been forced to cut expenditure on transport and mobile phones, while the proportion expecting the government to initiate reforms had grown from 30 per cent to 44 per cent in the previous two years, indicating a demand for change.[17] Equally, an exaggerated emphasis on Putin personally also required a more substantive grounding in a practical programme of renewal and development. It would not be enough to parrot Volodin's infamous declaration of 'no Putin, no Russia'. The emphasis was to ensure legality – for the election to pass off without major incidents of fraud while achieving the desired result – to ensure that Putin's re-election was considered legitimate. The problem with this rather minimalist definition of legitimacy is that it did not take into account the larger issues, including the quality of governance and regime performance in delivering stability, equality and rising standards of living, as well as the enduring problem of creating a more dynamic, innovative and competitive economy.

The return of politics

Navalny exploited the liminal character of Putinism by exploring the tension between its regime and constitutional character. A state of exception, even if for a long period it becomes the norm, presupposes a base normality. In post-communist Russia, this is precisely the constitutional state, and this is what provides the dual state with its dynamism, generated by the inherent tension between the normality represented by the legalism of the normative state and the exceptionalism represented by the administrative regime. Above all, the contradiction between political reality and constitutional normativity opened up a fertile terrain for resistance and opposition.

By August 2017, Navalny had registered 570,671 signatures ready to support his candidacy.[18] His programme mobilised some powerful slogans, predicated on the belief that rooting out corruption would release enormous funds for increased health, education and welfare spending. He proposed a one-off 'oligarch tax', to be levied on the beneficiaries of the 1996 loans-for-shares privatisations, on the lines of New Labour's windfall tax of 1997, and a ₽25,000 (about $415) minimum monthly tax threshold and subsidised loans to allow people to buy their own homes. Later, Navalny outlined a bold programme of political reform, including greater powers for local government, federalisation, the reduction of presidential powers, parliamentary and judicial reform, amendment of the Criminal Code, reform of the FSIN and reform of the media's regulatory framework. The economic programme was less coherent, including the contradictory promise that state property would be transferred to the Pension Fund and that it would be sold. The platform attacked various groups in favour of some mythical 'people', a classic populist strategy.[19]

Social and political protests increased. Social protests covered such issues as the violation of social rights, falling living standards, job losses, defrauded investors, increases in utility charges, dangerous landfills and the non-payment of wages.[20] One of the largest protest movements involved truckers incensed by the Platon system of road tolls introduced in November 2015, managed by Rostec and the Rotenberg brothers. As for political protests, the most notable were organised by Navalny and his supporters. In 2017, Navalny initiated nationwide protest rallies on 26 March and 12 June, reflecting dissatisfaction with falling living standards, economic inequality, corruption and political stagnation. Most alarming for the authorities was the youthfulness of the protesters. The initiative shifted from the older generation of middle-aged 'angry urbanites' to a new generation of disaffected youth. Navalny's call for a monthly minimum wage of ₽25,000 was accused of being populist, and in a time of budget deficits, it meant that the middle class would be squeezed to provide the funds.

Navalny is part of a larger wave of revived political competitiveness. The opportunities opened up by the regime reset were exploited by the United Democrats coalition forged by Dmitry Gudkov and Maxim Katz in Moscow for the municipal elections on 10 September 2017. Five years earlier, the protests against national electoral fraud had prompted activists to contest the 4 March 2012 Moscow municipal elections. They ran for seats on Moscow's 146 district councils, each composed of between 8 and 12 deputies elected for five years. Of the two hundred independents who entered the ballot, seventy won seats. In 2017, Yabloko joined the United Democrats, despite its long-term refusal to enter coalitions. This time, 1,046 non-regime candidates balloted, running either as independents or as party candidates. The outcome demonstrated that Moscow deserved its reputation as a liberal city, with the United Democrats winning 267 seats, joined by a number of independents and over 70 members of the systemic opposition.[21] Yabloko increased its representation tenfold by winning 176 seats, making it the second-largest party in the city.[22] UR won 1,152 of the 1,502 seats, but the authorities lost control of 38 municipal councils. In eight, including the district where Putin lives and votes, not a single UR deputy was elected. The innovative electoral strategies of the opposition paid off.[23] However, even in districts where the opposition won a plurality of seats, such as Filëvsky Park, they were prevented from taking the chair because of the rule that the incumbent remains in post after an election unless two-thirds of the councillors vote for a change. The law does not explain what should be done where no group can muster such a majority.[24] A similar situation held in the Konkovo municipal district council. Elsewhere, democratic activists such as Ilya Yashin, now the head of Krasnoselsky municipal district, demonstrated that they could govern in a new manner.[25]

The victory of a new generation of talented young activists demonstrated that there are plenty of people capable of building democratic institutions in Russia. Although their powers are limited, district councils can shape how a locality is run. They also provide a safe haven for meetings and demonstration, which tend not to be allowed in UR-run areas. As noted, reforms enacted in 2012 stipulate a 'municipal filter' whereby between 5 and 10 per cent of deputies have to nominate a candidate, which in Moscow means that candidates have to gather signatures from at least 110 municipal deputies to register their candidacy. Navalny's run in 2013 had only been possible with the help of UR deputies lending him their support. The opposition in Moscow now sought to nominate a regime opponent to run in the 9 September 2018 mayoral contest. The opposition united to form the Party of Changes, including Ksenia Sobchak and Dmitry Gudkov, although Ilya Yashin and Yabloko refused unified primaries. With deputies in only 62 districts, the opposition failed to unite to meet the threshold of nominations from 110 districts. Navalny played a destructive role by refusing to endorse any opposition group, and no democratic oppositionist was registered.[26] The incumbent, Sobyanin, won with 70 per cent of the votes, with the Communist candidate coming a distant second with 11.4 per cent.

Navalny became the charismatic face to the opposition to Putin's rule. He was one of the few politicians in Russia with an independent network of regional volunteers able to mobilise at short notice. Navalny advanced classic liberal postulates on the rule of law, transparent government and constitutionalism, but he also embraces ideas drawn from the more conservative repertoire of nationalist ideas. In a well-publicised debate on 20 July 2017 with Igor Strelkov (Girkin), the militant nationalist and virulent monarchist who took his forces from Crimea to foment rebellion in the Donbas in March 2014, both came out as losers. Strelkov appeared to lose interest in the discussion, while Navalny failed to advance any coherent world view. The debate was important primarily because it took place at all and without official interference, indicating the return of elements of free public political debate. More disturbing, the discussion showed that Strelkov had strong and consistent nationalist views, combining a distinctive understanding of the global economy and various conspiracy theories, while Navalny was unable to advance a coherent response.[27] For Navalny, the main enemy was domestic crony capitalism, and he vowed to clean up the vast procurement system, which accounts for 37 per cent of the economy. By contrast, the enemy for Girkin was the West, which in his view carved up the USSR according to borders drawn by the Bolsheviks and destroyed Russia's industrial base.[28] Strelkov advanced the classic conspiracy idea of Russia as a 'besieged fortress'.[29] Strelkov noted that in 2014, he believed that Putin was ready to stage a 'revolution from above' in Ukraine, but by 2015 when the 'revolution' did not come, he lost faith in Putin. He also criticised the official line on Chechnya. The debate once again demonstrated that the greatest threat to Putinite stability comes not from the liberals but from nationalists.

This is perhaps why Navalny became subject to sharp attack from Western-oriented liberals, who condemned him for his refusal to accept that Crimea should be returned to Ukraine, for his attack on migration from Central Asia and for his erstwhile slogan of 'stop feeding the Caucasus'. In the context of the alleged contemptuous dismissal by liberal globalists of the wave of populist resistance to globalisation, Gordon Hahn notes that 'the Russian liberals' assault on Navalny suggests the persistence of an equally disturbing pattern: the Russian liberal intelligentsia's mimicking the Western liberal-leftist elite and ignoring conservative and libertarian strains in Western democratic political thought and culture'. In his detailed study of the liberal critique of Navalny, there is one persistent theme: the danger that Navalny could become a second Putin. For example, the journalist Oleg Kashin attacked Navalny in the *New York Times*, calling him an authoritarian leader in the mould of Boris Yeltsin, while Vladislav Inozemtsev, a theorist of so-called post-industrial society, argued that Navalny lacked a 'vision for the future'.[30] The political culture of the Russian democratic movement shared the authoritarian traits of the Putinite system. Too often its participants were divisive, intolerant, uncompromising and dismissive of the concerns of others.[31]

Nevertheless, Navalny articulated popular demands applying not only nationalist themes but also edging towards class politics, of the sort that had appeared to be delegitimated by the Soviet experience, although he remained firmly pro-market. He condemned Putin for having created a system of predatory capitalism which profited only the top 0.1 per cent. Although Navalny was accused of Trump-like irresponsibility and populism, unlike Trump, he had no intention of skewing the tax system further towards the rich. As the election approached, Navalny's ability to mobilise a protest movement appeared to be on the wane. In response to his call for a 'voters' strike' on 28 January 2018, barely a thousand turned up in Moscow, although protests took place in a hundred towns across the country. Navalny himself was briefly detained and then released, a pattern that was repeated many times. The authorities sought not to inflame the situation and to avoid the mistakes of 2011. Navalny tried to broaden his appeal from the rather narrow liberal segment of Russian society to the national democrats, those who support the strengthening of democratic institutions while not renouncing Russia's national interests in international politics accompanied by a strong role for the state in economic development. Russian national democracy had been the driving force in the destruction of the Soviet Union during perestroika and became the foundation for Putin's 'centrism', the core electorate that Navalny now sought to win over. Navalny tempered some of his more extreme nationalist sentiments and focused on his anti-corruption campaign and on building a national movement. His Party of Progress established branches across the country but failed to be officially registered. Despite his prominence and high name recognition, his polling support remained in the single digits. Putin's unassailable lead was untouched by Navalny's strictures, and rather than banning him from participating in the presidential election, it would have probably been wiser for the regime to let him run. But that would have entailed accepting a rather different legitimation strategy for the regime – one based on a genuine democratic mandate – rather than one based on the plebiscitary approval of Putin's leadership.

The 2018 presidential election

In January 2018, Putin became the longest-serving Russian leader (as president and prime minister) since Stalin, exceeding Brezhnev's record of eighteen years and one month. Putin ran as an independent candidate, highlighting his position above the existing institutions and party system, and accentuating UR's marginalisation. Although UR won a constitutional majority in the September 2016 elections, its 'brand' was tainted and it was never able to shake off Navalny's epithet as 'the party of crooks and thieves', a term he first used in a radio interview on 2 February 2011.[32] Putin's independent run emphasised his distance from the ruling elites and his historical role as the arbiter of Russia's future.

As part of the 'regime reset' since 2012, there had been major changes to electoral legislation concerning presidential elections and the personnel managing the process. The redoubtable Churov was no longer at the head of the CEC, and, instead, Pamfilova changed its membership. There were at least fifteen changes to presidential election legislation between 2012 and 2017, with fifty-nine out of the law's eighty-seven articles and all four appendices amended. Two changes were crucial. The first lowered the number of signatures required to register. Candidates running as independents have to gather 300,000 signatures, with no region accounting for more than 7,500, while those backed by non-parliamentary parties have to submit 100,000 signatures. Those running as representatives of parliamentary parties, as before, do not need any signatures. A second change bars candidates with a criminal record from running for office for fifteen years, a stipulation that kept Navalny off the ballot box.[33] In addition, amendments to the law on political parties that came into effect on 1 January 2018 tightened the rules on sources of party funding, in conformity with recommendations from the CoE's Group of States against Corruption (GRECO).

The 'systemic' opposition parties were still led by the veterans of the late Soviet period: Zyuganov and Zhirinovsky were in their seventies, while Yavlinsky had been leader of Yabloko since its foundation in 1993. Some activist members of parliament (MPs) from JR had been involved in the 2011–12 protests, including Ilya Ponamarev and father and son Gennady and Dmitry Gudkov, but they had been purged from the Duma. The staid and uninspiring Sergei Mironov reasserted his authority, and JR soon declined into irrelevance and did not bother to stand a presidential candidate. The party had been established by Surkov in the mid-2000s to provide a left-centre balance to UR, but it failed to develop as an autonomous social democratic party. As the presidential election approached, plans resurfaced once again to create a two-party system. Mironov would be replaced by a more authoritative leader, and the party boosted to provide credible balance to UR. This would be difficult, since the CPRF already absorbed the protest vote, while the LDPR filled the populist niche, even though in practice it was little more than the radical branch of UR.[34]

Of the sixty-four declared candidates, in the end seven were registered, including some well-known names. Top of the list, of course, was Putin. He declared his candidacy in a Soviet-style meeting with workers at the Gorky Automobile Plant (GAZ) in Nizhny Novgorod on 6 December 2017. When asked an apparently spontaneous question about his plans, Putin answered, 'Yes, I will run for … president of the Russian Federation.' By announcing his candidacy in a working people's collective, Putin rallied his blue-collar voter base. While polls showed a consistently high level of support, the problem would be to get the vote out on polling day. If victory was a foregone conclusion, then what was the point of making the effort? A Levada Centre poll at that time found that only 58 per cent of Russians planned to vote, a significant fall from the 65.3 per cent who turned out for the 2012 presidential election.[35]

As for his opponents, the old guard represented by Zhirinovsky and Zyuganov was hardly likely to set the electoral pulse racing. In the event, instead of the veteran 73-year-old Zyuganov, the CPRF nominated Pavel Grudinin, the 57-year-old head of the Lenin State Farm (*sovkhoz*) on the outskirts of Moscow. He had been a member of UR until 2010 and did not join the CPRF, but his record made him a strong candidate. He saved his *sovkhoz* from privatisation and break-up in the 1990s and turned it into a model socialist collective, producing top-quality fresh fruit and vegetables for the city. He paid his workers about $1,370 a month, over double the Russian average. Grudinin was a fresh face and appealed to those tired of Putin after eighteen years. Like Putin, he appealed to Russians who regretted the Soviet collapse (58 per cent according to a poll in late 2017), and like Navalny, he spoke out against economic migrants from Central Asia. He ran on a populist platform, criticising corruption and inequality, and sought to restore elements of the former Soviet economy. As with the oligarch Mikhail Prokhorov's presidential bid in 2012, it was not clear whether Grudinin really sought to replace Putin or simply to boost the turnout and gain the share of the vote allotted to the opposition to give the election an air of legitimacy and competitiveness.[36] The onslaught against him from the official media suggested that the authorities recognised that the communists retained a powerful voter base and that in the right circumstances and with the right leader, the orthodox left could pose a serious challenge. The CPRF appealed to the disaffected working class and the mass of the bureaucracy, as well as the older generation, but the 'red-brown' alliance of neo-traditionalist communists and nationalists was looking increasingly tired and failed to address the concerns of workers or even to defend trade union rights.[37]

Candidates included the 39-year-old Maxim Suraikin, who was nominated by the Communists of Russia, a party registered in 2012 as part of the regime reset. The CPRF considered it to be little more than a spoiler organisation, designed by the authorities to confuse voters and to draw voters away from itself. In 2014, Suraikin had run for the governorship of Nizhny Novgorod Oblast and won about two per cent of the vote. The list naturally also included the 71-year-old Zhirinovsky, the emotional ultranationalist at the head of the LDPR who was now running for the presidency for the sixth time, having won 6 per cent of the vote in 2012. The list also included the 59-year-old Sergei Baburin, the veteran nationalist who had been one of the leaders of the parliamentary rebellion against Yeltsin in 1993 and a State Duma MP until 2007. He then served as a rector of Moscow State University. He now sought to return to national politics as the nominee of a small nationalist party, the Russian All-People's Union. The liberal-conservative Party of Growth nominated their 57-year-old leader, the business ombudsman Boris Titov. He was a successful entrepreneur himself, a co-owner of the Russian sparkling wine brand Abrau-Durso and the head of the Russian Winemaker's Union. He gathered the requisite one hundred thousand signatures and was registered as a candidate. As noted, he advanced a moderate programme of reform, accepting that 'Russian society, dominated by civil servants and millions of poor, is not ready for democratic change'.[38]

As the representative of the Yabloko party with no Duma MPs, the 65-year-old Grigory Yavlinsky successfully collected the required signatures. Yavlinsky is known as the 'perennial candidate', having fought two earlier presidential elections. In the first, in 1996, he came fourth with 7.35 per cent of the vote, but in 2000, as the self-declared democratic candidate, he came third behind Putin and Zyuganov, with 5.8 per cent of the vote. In 2012, his candidacy was not registered on the grounds that over 20 per cent of the signatures were invalid, and his registration this time indicated the Kremlin's concern for the election to be seen as more legitimate. Yavlinsky's programme included his long-term themes, including the struggle against corruption, democratic renewal and a balanced economic policy that eschewed the excesses of radical liberalism and neo-Soviet statism. The party had long campaigned for the return of elected mayors, arguing that 'mayors in 1,555 out of 2,044 of our country's towns and cities are getting appointed and displaced without any regard to the opinion of those who live in these cities and towns'.[39] His eye-catching promise this time was to grant every Russian citizen a free one-acre plot of land on which to build a home. Yavlinsky represented the old guard of the anti-communist revolution, the 'lone knight of democracy and the market economy with a human face', who 'continues stoically to defend the ideals that had filled the hearts of millions of our citizens in the years of perestroika and the early 1990s'.[40]

The 36-year-old Ksenia Sobchak stands out among the candidates. She is the daughter of Putin's former mentor and sponsor, Anatoly Sobchak, the mayor of St Petersburg in the first half of the 1990s, and was even rumoured to be Putin's god-daughter. She entered politics during the protest wave of 2011–12 and became one of the most recognised opposition leaders. She then hosted a talk show, *Sobchak Live*, on TV Rain (*Dozhd*), one of the few remaining independent networks in Russia. Following months of speculation, she declared herself a candidate in October 2017. She denied accusations that she had been put up to it by the Kremlin to boost turnout. In fact, she asserts that when she told Putin (at a meeting devoted to making a film about her father) in the autumn of 2017 that she planned to run, he was not pleased.[41] Sobchak was nominated by the Civic Initiative Party and successfully collected the requisite one hundred thousand signatures. Her goal was to 'create a new majority', although her campaign focused on mobilising the radical liberal minority. Sobchak hoped to use the campaign as a springboard for a political career. She argued that Russia broke international law in taking over Crimea, but Yavlinsky was the only candidate who called for international mediation to help resolve the issue.[42] Nevertheless, she adopted a generally sympathetic approach towards Putin, arguing that he was a 'patriot', determined to hold Russia together and avoid a slide into 'a sort of a military-junta situation'. Sobchak was even considered a possible successor to Putin, since she would guarantee his security and immunity from prosecution, just as Putin had done for her father (and for Yeltsin). She believes that Putin would be prepared to leave office if his personal security and wealth could be guaranteed.[43]

Sobchak declared that she would give up her candidacy if Navalny somehow managed to get on the ballot paper. Even though not a candidate, he dominated the campaign through his call for voters to spurn the election. The boycott strategy was dismissed by Sobchak as 'pointless'.[44] The veteran opposition politician, Vladimir Ryzhkov (now the leader of the Choice of Russia movement), who became a co-chair of Yavlinsky's campaign staff, also condemned Navalny's call: 'The boycott of the election is the demobilisation of our supporters. I mean the people who want change', a group he estimated to comprise 25–30 per cent of the population, 'who share democratic values.'[45] Navalny acted as if he was campaigning, issuing a programme that was subjected to withering criticism, even by liberals. Its incoherent left-wing populist economic proposals combined with the right-wing nationalist idea to issue work visas for migrant workers from Central Asia, together with the unsustainable promise to double the minimum wage.[46] Typically, he launched a blistering attack on Yavlinsky, Sobchak and other candidates, condemning them for falsifying signatures. He accused Yavlinsky of forging 60 per cent of his signatures and the others of up to 99 per cent. The grounds for the charge were unclear, but his attack on the establishment liberals damaged his standing. It appeared that Navalny was trying to discredit not only the election but also the candidates, a strategy that only accentuated his isolation from mainstream politics. In the event, he and his chief of staff, Leonid Volkov, were arrested on 22 February 2018 and held for thirty days for repeated public-meeting rule violations, taking him out of circulation for the rest of the election.

In his annual press conference on 14 December 2017, Putin was guarded about what his presidential programme would look like, although he stressed that 'Russia must be spearheaded into the future. It must become a modern country with a flexible political system, its economy must be based on high technology, and labour efficiency must increase manifold.' He announced that he would run as an independent candidate, but 'I count on support of political forces who share my views on the development of the country'. In response to a question from Sobchak, who had announced that she would be running on a platform 'against all', Putin asked, 'What are your proposals for solving today's existing problems?' He argued that 'the character mentioned by Sobchak' (continuing his tradition of refusing to use Navalny's name in public) was no more than a local version of the former

Georgian president Mikheil Saakashvili, who would 'destabilise the situation in the country'.[47]

Putin's campaigning was hard to distinguish from his usual presidential activities, although there were now more meetings with voters. Visiting the Tver Carriage Works in mid-January, Putin reinforced the point that his interventionist industrial strategy had twice saved the plant from bankruptcy. During the economic crisis of 2009, Putin diverted millions of dollars from state funds to pay for orders, and once again in 2017 when he introduced major long-term tax breaks on the purchase of long-distance rolling stock, prompting hundreds more orders for railway carriages.[48] The visit reinforced Putin's base among the industrial working class, which he had protected from job losses while ensuring the regular payment of wages and stable expectations for the future – a far cry from when he had come to power in 2000. Despite the talk about youth dissatisfaction, Putin's core electorate – workers, bureaucrats, pensioners and small-town residents – held fast to the belief that Putin represented the best option in the given historical situation. Not surprisingly, Putin's confidence rating among ordinary Russians reached a 2017 record high of 57.7 per cent in December, with his approval rating remaining unchanged at 84 per cent.[49]

The campaign lacked a clear focus. In 2008, it had been 'modernisation', and in 2012, 'regaining sovereignty', but in 2018, the ideas of modernisation and reform were notably absent. The opposition remained vague on how their aspirations would be implemented, whereas Putin's campaign focused on himself: 'A strong president is a strong Russia.' His engagement was lacklustre, reinforcing his long-held dislike of the electoral process. Unlike in earlier campaigns, notably in 2011–12 when he had issued a range of position papers in the media on fundamental policy issues, he limited himself to set-piece presentations. The most significant was the postponed annual address to the Federal Assembly on 1 March 2018. The latter part of the speech, as noted, presented a range of strategic super weapons, but the oration was less about guns than butter. The address outlined ambitious plans to boost GDP growth above the global average and to raise the country's GDP per capita by 1.5 times by 2025 by increasing labour productivity, intensifying capital investment, expanding non-hydrocarbon exports and developing the small- and medium-business sector. Spending on healthcare was to double to 4 per cent of the GDP, while some ₽11 trillion ($190 billion) was to be invested in infrastructure by 2024. Over the same period, the poverty rate was to be halved, while raising household incomes was identified as a 'key task' of the next decade. Some 29 per cent of the population had been living in poverty when he assumed office in 2000, but this had fallen to 10 per cent by 2012, but as noted, the recession pushed some 20 million (13 per cent) under the poverty line. In a significant theoretical shift, Putin noted, 'Stability forms the foundation, but it is not enough to ensure further development.' The stability system was to give way to a new developmental model based on the technological revolution as well as reindustrialisation.[50] Despite the militant talk about new weapons, the speech represented a victory for liberal economists like Kudrin, who had resigned in protest over increased defence spending in 2011.

It would be hard to match the 65 per cent turnout of 2012 when Putin had won with 63.6 per cent of the vote, even though the Kremlin set the unofficial goal of 70/70 – whereby Putin would receive 70 per cent of the votes from a 70 per cent turnout. The historically low turnout of 47.8 per cent in the September 2016 parliamentary elections served as a warning, especially when the total was even lower in major cities such as Moscow and St Petersburg, with barely 30 per cent of voters turning out. To broaden his appeal, Kudrin oversaw the preparation of Putin's election manifesto.

Putin won a triumphant endorsement for a fourth term, winning 76.69 per cent of the vote on a 67.5 per cent turnout (see Table 8.1). He was supported by over half (51.76 per cent) of the total population with the right to vote, receiving 56.42 million of the 73.58 million ballots cast, his biggest win ever. Compared to 2012, turnout rose by 2.4 per cent and Putin's vote rose by 13 per cent over the 46.6 million votes he received that year. Grudinin took second place with only 11.77 per cent (8.7 million votes) and Zhirinovsky came a distant third with only 5.65 per cent (4.1 million votes). Pamfilova insisted that the election had been 'transparent, competitive and in line with the law', although Western commentary was harshly critical. The Organisation for Security and Cooperation in Europe (OSCE) report found the whole operation wanting, although well run. The group's election observation mission concluded, 'Overall, the campaign was marked by a lack of genuine competition among contestants.'[51] The full report issued in June came to the same conclusion, eliciting a furious attack by the Russian foreign ministry on the OSCE's Office for Democratic Elections and Human Rights (ODIHR), based in Warsaw, which it condemned as 'once again being politically engaged', and called on it to change its election monitoring practices.[52] Although a few videos of ballot stuffing appeared, Pamfilova achieved her goal of running one of the cleanest elections in the post-communist period. The new system of 'absentee voting' did allow some multiple ballots to be cast, but the habitual 'electoral sultanates' (to use Dmitry Oreshkin's term) curbed their enthusiasm, and in Chechnya, instead of the customary 110 per cent of the vote on a 99 per cent turnout, Putin received a more modest 91.5 per cent of the vote. Even the veteran election-fraud analyst Sergei Shpilkin noted that falsifications were a record low, although in his view it still affected some 8.5 million votes.[53] New forms of administrative mobilisation appeared to have been at work.[54] All agreed that electoral malpractice this time round were lower than previously, although estimates range from some six million votes subject to some form of fraud to almost none. Whatever the precise figure, any fraud and managerial manipulation of turnout is too much.

Despite being advised against, Trump telephoned to congratulate Putin, as did German chancellor Merkel, French president Macron and EU Commission

Table 8.1 Presidential election of 18 March 2018

Candidate	Vote (million)	Percentage
Putin, Vladimir (independent)	56,430,712	76.69
Grudinin, Pavel (CPRF)	8,659,206	11.77
Zhirinovsky, Vladimir (LDPR)	4,154,985	5.65
Sobchak, Ksenia (Civil Initiative Party)	1,238,031	1.68
Yavlinsky, Grigory (Yabloko)	769,644	1.05
Titov, Boris (Party of Growth)	556,801	0.76
Suraikin, Maxim (Communists of Russia)	499,342	0.68
Baburin, Sergei (Russian People's Union)	479,013	0.68
Electorate	109,008,428	
Number of ballot papers issued	73,578,992 (1.08% invalid or blank)	
Turnout	67.54%	

Source: Central Electoral Commission, 'Rezultaty Vybororov Prezidenta Rossiiskoi Federatsii', http://old.cikrf.ru/analog/prezidentskiye-vybory-2018/itogi-golosovaniya/.

president Jean-Claude Juncker. The election was certainly not a 'fraud' or a 'sham', although clearly it had a plebiscitary element. The Kremlin enjoys a monopoly on 'administrative resources' and dominates the mass media, but all candidates were given plenty of airtime in the televised debates. Navalny was not allowed to run, but Sobchak and Yavlinsky were serious candidates. However, the liberals in total received less than 3 per cent of the vote, fewer than the 4 per cent received in the September 2016 Duma election. Communists and nationalists remain the centre of gravity of opposition, who together garnered some 19 per cent. Pastukhov argues that this represented a 'political defeat' by the Russian liberals that could not be simply ascribed to administrative or other resources ranged against them. Putin's political course enjoyed, in his view, real support among the electorate, and even if all candidates and parties were allowed to participate and if the media was opened wide, even then Putin would have won, and in all probability so would a successor with a similar programme. Thus, the view that the 'post-Putin' period would automatically improve the chances of the liberal opposition represented 'one more utopia of the intelligentsia'.[55]

The election reflected the broader duality of the system, combining authoritarian and democratic elements. If the election is considered a barometer of the mood of society, then it was clear that Putin enjoyed enormous popularity, and the vote provided him with a solid endorsement for his fourth and presumably final term in office. There was a palpable desire for change, but change within the system and not from outside. The ideology of stability had prevailed, and although Putin no longer required electoral legitimacy to the same degree as before – after Crimea and so many years in office he had become a type of national leader – the election confirmed him as the president who promised to deliver both stability and change.[56]

Challenges of Putin's fourth term

Putin's inauguration on 7 May 2018 was less macabre than the similar event six years earlier. Once again there were protests but not as violent as on the earlier occasion. In Moscow, Navalny moved the date and site of an official meeting to coincide with the inauguration, and across the country, demonstrators, whose youth was noticeable, chanted Navalny's slogan: 'Not Our Tsar'. The heavy-handed attempt to close down the messaging app Telegram provoked a strong reaction in society. There remain profound social and political blocks on reform, including the lack of agreement on the need for structural reform at all. The term 'stagnation plus' was used to describe a system that was growing but at anaemic rates and in which some fundamental underlying questions were unresolved.

In his inauguration speech, Putin insisted, 'Russia must be a modern and vibrant society ready to take up the challenges of the time and respond to them with all its energy in order to consistently build up its leadership in areas where our positions have been traditionally strong.' He argued, 'We need breakthroughs in all areas of life. I strongly believe that only a free society that is open to all new and cutting-edge advances, while rejecting injustice, ignorance, obscurantist conservatism [*dremuchee okhranitel'stvo*, which can also be translated as 'backward-looking guardianship'] and bureaucratic red tape, is capable of achieving these breakthroughs.'[57] Returning to the Kremlin from which he had not departed, Putin faced a number of fundamental challenges: the need to boost the economy through structural reform of social and political relations, the related question of how to temper the hostility of the West and how to manage elite relations in the context of the likelihood that this would be his final term in office. The race to shape the succession had begun.

According to the constitution, following a presidential election, the government has to resign, and the Kremlin then has two weeks to nominate a candidate to parliament for approval as prime minister. Medvedev had occupied the post since the fateful *rokirovka* in 2012, and there was considerable speculation whether he would be replaced. Suggested alternatives included the CBR governor Nabiullina, Moscow mayor Sobyanin, industry minister Denis Manturov and even Kudrin, who had fallen out with Medvedev over military spending in September 2011. The decision would shape economic and social policy in Putin's fourth term while preparing for the anticipated succession. The prime minister takes over when the incumbent president leaves office early and is, thus, in pole position for the succession. Putin's dislike of disruptive personnel changes is well known, and in the end, he plumped for continuity. Medvedev was nominated and overwhelmingly approved by parliament to continue as prime minister. The choice disappointed those who looked for an end to liberal dominance in economic and social policy. Medvedev occupies a centrist position, and although he clearly favours the relaxation of state control and more liberalisation, he remains within the Putin consensus. Medvedev's loyalty, hard work and lack of independent political ambition served Putin well at a time of heightened speculation over a possible successor.

In the ensuing cabinet reshuffle, the existing political balance was retained. Eight ministers were replaced, and a new minister added through the division of the ministry of science and education. The security and foreign policy bloc remained virtually the same, with the exception of the emergency situations ministry, but there were significant changes in the economic and defence portfolios. Medvedev's long-term ally Konstantin Chuichenko became the government's chief of staff, while Dmitry Rogozin, responsible for the defence and space industries, was replaced by deputy defence minister Yuri Borisov. There was disappointed anticipation that Kudrin would be given some sort of advisory role to manage economic reform and to rebuild relations with the West. Kudrin was not given a top ministerial or advisory post, but his allies dominated the cabinet, notably the finance minister, Anton Siluanov, and the former head of the Audit Chamber, Tatyana Golikova. Kudrin had long urged structural reform and argued that democratisation of the political system would help alleviate tensions with the West.[58] His plans for structural reform, issued by the CSR and dubbed 'Plan K', included slashing the number of bureaucrats by 30 per cent in six years, a resumption of the 'administrative reform' launched by Putin when he first came to power, which would see expenditure on the state apparatus falling from the current 2.5 per cent of the GDP to 1.74 per cent. He called for significant increases in spending on education, healthcare and infrastructure, noting that Russia devoted 11 per cent of its GDP to this, whereas the average in the West was some 14 per cent. In short, Kudrin sought a 'transition from a band-aid approach to development'.[59]

In the event, it was impossible for Kudrin to join the cabinet as a deputy prime minister because of his strained personal relations with Medvedev. Instead, Kudrin was appointed head of the Audit Chamber, disappointing those who looked for radical reform. Kudrin set himself four goals in his new post: curbing corruption, linking Russia's strategic goals to the actual budget, enhancing budgetary control and informing the public on progress in fulfilling national development goals.[60] The Audit Chamber's regulatory powers over regional expenditures were expanded through amendments to the Budget Code on 30 May, and later it was given a broader mandate to fight corruption and greater oversight powers over government expenditure. In that context, 'Plan K' stood a good chance of being implemented, accompanied by continued budgetary conservatism and macroeconomic stability. It also meant the possible launching of unpopular reforms with potentially catastrophic social and political consequences. These included the dismissal of up to a third of all Russia government officials as part of attempts to slim the bureaucracy as governance became increasingly digitised. It could also mean the closure of some inefficient factories, including those in the three hundred so-called company towns (monotowns, or *monogoroda*), in which a single industry or employer dominates the local economy, with devastating results for the fourteen million people living in them. It would also mean serious moves to dilute the centralisation of power and resources. In 2019, Moscow and St Petersburg together produced 32 per cent of Russia's output, compared to 25 per cent fifteen years earlier. Kudrin's call for some other urban centres, such as Ekaterinburg, Nizhny Novgorod, Novosibirsk and Vladivostok, to become locomotives for growth was reflected in the government's 'Spatial Development Strategy until 2025', adopted in February 2019.[61] Above all, discussions over raising the pension age took place against the background of the long-term decline of pensions as a proportion of working-age incomes. Various studies projected that raising the pension age would have a considerable effect on boosting GDP growth.[62] Overall, in his post at the Audit Chamber, Kudrin was set to influence economic policy and maintain macroeconomic discipline.

Putin's Federal Assembly address of 1 March was given force through a new set of 'May Decrees' issued on the evening of his inauguration, 7 May 2018, outlining his plans for the next six years. With military modernisation considered complete, attention now returned to social and economic development. The ambitious goals included accelerating productivity growth to 5 per cent (the average since 2009 had been 1 per cent), doubling the share of SMEs in the GDP from 20 per cent to 40 per cent and increasing the number of people employed by SMEs from nineteen million to twenty-five million. The number of people living below the poverty line, at the time some twenty million people or 13.8 per cent of the population, was to be halved. The focus was to be on domestic development, accompanied by cuts to the defence budget. There would be a surge in spending on roads, education and healthcare accompanied by increases in real incomes, raising pensions and cutting poverty, as well as investment in high-tech, export-oriented industries and the creation of 'transport corridors' to improve Russia's road, rail and sea connections with the outside world. This was to achieve the goal of creating at least $250 billion in non-resource, non-energy exports annually, part of Russia's long-term diversification strategy. Russia was to join the group of the world's five largest economies by 2024 by raising its growth rate above the global average while maintaining macroeconomic stability (a warning shot against the mobilisation school of national development), with inflation not to rise above 4 per cent.

The detailed implementation plan drawn up later imposed detailed key performance indicators for twelve national projects. These ranged from demography, healthcare, education, housing, ecology, motorways, labour productivity, science, culture and SMEs to international cooperation and support for exporters. Life expectancy (currently averaging 72 years: 77 for women and only 66 for men) was to be increased to 78 years (80 years by 2030), and the 'unacceptable' poverty rate was to be halved. Development of the digital economy was a priority, including a large and secure information and communication technology (ICT) infrastructure for high-speed broadband, accompanied by a shift to the use of home-produced software. Information security was to be achieved by using domestic technologies.[63] These were all worthy goals, but as critics like Kudrin pointed out, they avoided addressing the crucial issue of reform of the justice system and tackling corruption. As one commentator noted, Putin had governed Russia as a rich country, spending on extravagant showcase projects and military modernisation, whereas governing Russia as a poor country would focus on tackling poverty, inequality, energy efficiency, education and health.[64]

The national projects were estimated to cost some ₽8 trillion ($126 billion), with the funds in part coming from cuts in the defence budget. Military spending had grown by around 10 per cent annually for much of the Putin era to reach 6.6 per cent of the GDP in 2016, but by 2018, this had fallen to 3.9 percent and was projected to fall further. The shift in priorities from guns to butter reflected what the Levada Centre had identified as a growing 'war weariness' in the population. Although half of Russians appreciated the country's restoration of great power status, 45 per cent faulted Putin for having failed to ensure a more equitable income distribution. Meanwhile, VTsIOM found that although Putin's personal approval rating remained astronomically high, at 82 per cent, almost 90 per cent said that the country needed reform, while only 2 per cent considered no change necessary.[65] If Western sanctions were designed to alienate the Russian people from Putin, then they had spectacularly failed.

With the election out of the way, the government on 14 June 2018 announced a rise in value-added tax (VAT) from 18 to 20 per cent from 2019. Even more portentously, Medvedev on the same day, the opening of the World Cup, introduced legislation to increase the retirement age for men from 60 to 65 years by 2028 and from 55 to 63 years for women by 2034. The forty-four million pensioners comprised a third of the country's population, although twelve million continued to work and twelve million had disabilities. Russia's working-age population was decreasing as a proportion of the total population, having fallen from 62 per cent in 2010 to 58 per cent in 2018. The proportion of pensioners was anticipated to rise sharply over the next decade, at a time when the Russian Pension Fund (RPF) is already running a deficit of $53 billion, with the shortfall made up by transfers from the general budget. Pension spending was approaching 9 per cent of the GDP. It was estimated that the reform will save the government some $27 billion a year while allowing pensions to be increased.

Even though the change would not affect current pensioners, the move provoked a wave of protests. Given Russia's enormous natural wealth, it was not clear why the National Welfare Fund was worth just 5 per cent of the GDP. Similarly, why not increase taxes on the rich, decrease spending on 'vanity' projects and foreign wars (Ukraine, Syria), reduce corruption, and divert more energy revenues directly into the RPF. The pension reform appeared to break the fundamental premise of the Putinite social contract: the continuation of Soviet-era benefits in return for Soviet-style political quiescence. Navalny intiated some twenty demonstrations on 1 July, but more significantly the trade unions organised protest meetings across the country. A Levada Centre poll found that 89 per cent viewed the pension reform negatively, reinforcing popular alienation from the state.[66] The Supreme Court announced an easing of the harsh rules governing street rallies, imposed in June 2012 in the wake of the Bolotnaya protests, limiting the right of municipal authorities to ban meetings. After a long period of silence on the issue, on 29 August, Putin offered concessions, reducing the pension age for women to 60 years, guaranteeing pre-pensioners the right to work in the five years before the retirement age set by the new law and some other measures.[67] Putin undoubtedly remembered how plans to monetise Soviet-era social benefits in 2005 provoked the largest mass protests over social issues of his presidency.

A Levada poll in July 2018 found that only 16 per cent of the population supported Putin's foreign policy, down from 22 per cent two years earlier, reinforcing the need to focus on domestic issues.[68] At the same time, it was clear that Putin was looking for a way to mend fences with the West, and, thus, despite the cascade of sanctions he kept the door open for a summit with Trump. Kudrin had long argued that the restoration of economic growth required an easing of sanctions and access to Western finance and technology. Instead, it appeared that the virtual state of war with the West had become the new normal. However, Putin tried to avoid being driven into a 'fortress Russia' corner, and this is why his fourth term began with such ambitious developmental plans. There was nothing here about self-isolation, although a robust response to what were considered Western provocations would continue. The overall strategy was 'Russia first', with the emphasis on spending on roads, education and healthcare. There were ambitious growth targets, but macroeconomic stability was not to be sacrificed. It was in this context that Putin met Trump for their first summit in Helsinki on 16 July 2018.

Expectations for the meeting were deliberately kept low, and in the event, even less was achieved because of the catastrophic fallout of the Russiagate allegations.

As for the succession, no sooner was he elected than the question was posed. On the evening of his victory, Putin was asked whether he planned to change the constitution, to which he replied that he had none in mind 'yet'. When asked to clarify whether this allowed the possibility of him becoming president again in 2030 if he did not change the constitution, Putin replied, 'Listen to me … Let us count. Am I supposed to be president until I am 100 years old? No.'[69] On 25 May 2018, on the sidelines of SPIEF, Putin confirmed his intention to abide by the constitutional limit of two consecutive terms. In a news conference, Putin answered, 'I have always abided strictly and will abide by Russia's constitution.' He went on to note, 'Now I am serving the second consecutive term. … As you remember, I was president twice before and then stepped down from office since the Constitution does not allow to be elected for the third term. That's all. I am going to comply with the rule in future.'[70] He conducted a minor reshuffle of his administration. Vaino remained chief of staff, but his first deputy, Kirienko, gained two additional briefs: managing the affairs of the State Council (there are persistent rumours that this could be a vehicle for Putin to retain power after 2024) and responsibility for information technologies and e-democracy, allowing him to fight attempts by the security services to clamp down on internet freedom.

The regional elections in September 2018 revealed powerful protest sentiments, with the CPRF winning regional legislatures in three regions and UR forced into run-off gubernatorial elections in another four, while the opposition won the mayoral election in Yakutsk. In Primorsky Krai, the CPRF candidate, Andrei Ishchenko, was heading for victory when a late surge of votes allowed the UR candidate to win. This was obviously fraud, and Pamfilova insisted on a rerun. It was not clear why there was such 'manual intervention' in the vote, since Irkutsk Oblast had long been run by opposition parties and the sky had not fallen in. In the new vote, the winner (with 62 per cent of the vote), Oleg Kozhemyako, ran as an independent, confirming the trend towards governors losing party affiliation as the UR 'brand' became increasingly toxic. The Primorsky case shows how the fight for mechanical stability had become such a deeply ingrained reflex that it came to undermine stability. Pension reform and the rise in VAT alienated voters, and it was only to be expected that this would be reflected in the ballot box.[71] It was also reflected in the sharp fall in Putin's personal ratings. By early 2019, trust in Putin had fallen to a thirteen-year low, slipping down to 33.4 per cent in January, the lowest since January 2006. His approval rating remained high at 62.1 per cent, still above the historic low of 59 per cent in August 2013. Nevertheless, this represented a sharp fall from the historic highs of an over 80 per cent approval which had been maintained since the Crimea crisis.[72] The Crimea boost was clearly over. These data confirm the pent-up demand for change, accompanied by a desire for greater equality, to be delivered by the traditional paternalistic distributive mechanisms.[73]

The catastrophic consequences of the last bout of major reform in the late 1980s – the dissolution of the political system and the disintegration of the country – still casts a long shadow. The concept of 'reform' has negative connotations. Nevertheless, Russia appears to move in thirty-year cycles, and there is a pent-up demand for change, although different parts of society understand the term differently. Up to 80 per cent of respondents in one survey wanted change, with those who had gained least from earlier reforms – people over 55, poor and without higher education living in towns with fewer than a hundred thousand inhabitants – the keenest for radical change. There was a large bloc of gradualists, many of whom supported Putin, who wished for judicial reform, free elections and media freedoms – a very large constituency which could be found in Moscow and the big cities. Contrary to popular views, young people were not the only drivers of change, although the generation who had grown up with Putin knew no alternative and feared losing the stability given by his system. There was a general consensus across all social groups that the government's priority should be the people's welfare, including higher living standards and greater justice, and, thus, less of a focus on foreign affairs. There is a strong awareness that reforms come at a cost, and over three-quarters oppose changes in social benefits. Russia was caught in a bind: change was recognised as necessary, but people were reluctant to countenance changes that would affect their immediate personal welfare.[74] This is the dilemma at the heart of the Putin phenomenon.

Putin's presidential address to Federal Assembly on 20 February 2019 recognised these issues in a speech that was largely devoted to domestic affairs and socio-economic development. He described the resources devoted to the national projects, in particular to deal with the demographic challenge. He outlined an impressive list of promises to deal with poverty, schools without heating or running water, waste problems, access to medical care, high-speed internet, nurseries, mortgage lending, ways of dealing with economic crimes and much more.[75] All this was highly ambitious but reflected Putin's view that with military modernisation largely completed and Russia defended by the various advanced missile and other systems (he devoted a fifth of the speech to this issue), he could return to the agenda outlined when he first took office – to concentrate on domestic development. Putin's renewed focus on development and social issues reflected concern that the whole edifice of Putinite stability was fragile and could collapse under the pressure of external sanctions and the pent-up demand for change at home. The systemic and non-systemic opposition was weak and divided, yet street fighters like Navalny could, in a crisis, mobilise the masses.[76] The extensive protests in the summer of 2019 against the exclusion of independent non-systemic candidates from the Moscow City Duma elections of 8 September acted as a warning of what could be to come. The heavy-handed response, with mass arrests and brutal beatings, served only to swell the number of participants. These protests were largely leaderless and demonstrated the mobilising power of social media. The fundamental question is the degree to which the roots of organic solidarity had sunk through the carpet of mechanical stability into the society below, and the extent to which the institutions of the constitutional state could assume the burden of governance if regime mechanisms retreated or were destroyed. In other words, could Putinite stability endure without Putin?

9 THE PUTIN PHENOMENON

We are now in a position to reflect on the Putin phenomenon more broadly, including an assessment of his character and reception abroad. We can ask whether there is such a thing as 'Putinism', and if so, what its main characteristics are. Equally, it is appropriate to examine whether some 'grand strategy' underpins Russian policy in the Putin era and, in particular, in foreign policy. A grand strategy is defined as some deep structure to domestic and foreign policy that transcends individual leaders and which has some overarching purpose. A grand strategy identifies a nation's core interests, what external forces pose a threat and who are the country's friends, and how the country's leadership can respond. By contrast, one of the main criticisms levelled against Putin is that he is brilliant at tactics, above all, in factional manoeuvring, but lacks an overarching vision of where Russia should go. There is some truth in this, and certainly Putin avoids any grand statement of his 'certain idea of Russia' (to paraphrase Charles de Gaulle's 'All my life, I have had a certain idea of France'), but Putin has never been reticent about talking about the problems and challenges facing Russia, from his *Millennium Manifesto* onwards. He was unequivocal in stating that foreign policy should serve domestic development, but from the Russian perspective (and this is the consensus view of the Russian elite at least since Primakov), the failure to devise an adequate post-Cold War peace order forced Russia into a more assertive foreign policy stance. Russian domestic development is inextricably entwined with foreign policy issues, although neither can be simply reduced to the other, but it is out of this dynamic interplay that the Putin phenomenon has been shaped.

Putin's people and power

Putin is one of the most traduced political leaders of our era. Matt Taibbi calls this 'Putin derangement syndrome', the exaggerated and fact-free assertion of supernatural and typically demonic powers to the man. Putin emerged as some sort of universal demiurge in the 2016 US presidential election, and in the following period Russia was the stick used to beat Trump and to weaken his authority. Much of the Russiagate scandal was a fact-free zone in which political fantasies and conspiracy theories played out. Russia was involved in the election, through the social media activities of the St Petersburg-based Internet Research Agency, as well as possibly the exfiltration of material from the servers of the Democratic National Committee and others associated with the Democratic Party campaign, but the scale and effect of this activity still remains to be assessed. Russia's 'hacking' of American democracy allowed the worst prejudices against Russia to be given free rein, accompanied by vindictive sanctions. Liberal globalists and neoconservatives united in their condemnation, and only orthodox conservatives (like Patrick Buchanan) and elements of the traditional left challenged the consensus.

Brian Taylor argues that the phenomenon can be defined by what he calls 'the code of Putinism', a certain worldview of Putin and his associates combined with a set of beliefs about the strong state, conservative values, anti-Westernism and hyper-masculinity. The Putin system in his view is more than Putin's personal preferences but represents a certain mentality and social construct based on 'clans' and 'networks'. The system in his view is also dysfunctional, making Russia 'an underperforming country at the domestic level and an overambitious one at the international level'.[1] The 'code of Putinism' explains the 'move from a frail but functional semidemocratic system in 2000 to the authoritarian hyperpresidentialism we see today'.[2] Matters are rather more complicated than that. The roots of post-communist authoritarianism reach back to the anti-communist revolution and the 1990s, the power system remains fragmented although superficially concentrated and the alleged 'hyperpresidentialism' of the 'power vertical' is challenged by powerful horizontal forces.

The pressures unleashed by Putin's style of governance impelled one of his bravest and most perceptive critics to flee the country. Yulia Latynina has a column in the investigative *Novaya Gazeta* newspaper and a weekly programme on the politically independent *Ekho Moskvy* radio station. After an escalating series of provocations, including the release of some sort of gas into her home and her car being burnt, she left Russia in September 2017, although she continued her journalistic work. In her valedictory letter she notes,

> My departure from Russia comes as a surprise – even to me. I always laughed at those who, seven or eight years ago, said Russia was a dangerous country and that Putin was worse than Stalin. Because this was not the case. When Anna Politkovskaya was murdered in 2006 we journalists understood this to be an exception – she had been investigating Chechnya. There were cases where people were poisoned, like Alexander Litvinenko, but we understood that he was a former KGB agent and Putin regarded him as a traitor. ... Now the situation has changed drastically. A tidal wave of violence has been unleashed,

with the attacks around the film 'Mathilde' being just one example. It's not that Putin or the Kremlin are directly instigating these kinds of attacks. ... They're empowering 'local talent', and those people are given a free pass ... to become great in the eyes of Putin. This doesn't absolve the Kremlin from responsibility. It makes it worse.

She went on to make the case for the classical Weberian state: 'The state should have a monopoly over violence. And by withdrawing the direct connection between the people who perpetrate violence and the Kremlin – which sanctions it, but does not order it – it is renouncing control.' She is right to note that the

> watershed moment was the murder of Boris Nemtsov [on 27 February 2015]. Putin was furious. He saw the murder as an encroachment on his power and it was. Under the guise of serving Putin, the man who gave commands to the Chechen killers showed that he, and not Putin, is all-powerful, because for him real power is the power to kill anybody.[3]

I have quoted Latynina at length because she accurately diagnosed the failure to impose the monopoly on violence and, indeed, to uphold the law when it came to business raiding and the emergence of regime-affiliated business and other interests that the regime could challenge only at the peril of its own existence. Equally, the pact with the Chechen leadership provided short-term benefits but in the long run undermined the integrity of the state and potentially even unleashed forces that could challenge the power of the regime. Despite all of this, Latynina promised, 'I will be back. Once things sort themselves out.' We look forward to her return; and, with her, so many who have been forced to leave their homeland not because of Putin's presidentialism but because of the culture of power that he fostered and because of his pusillanimity when it came to challenging horizontally entrenched societal forces and interests. He did in the end take on the *vory v zakone* but not the entrenched interests closer to home.

The perception of systemic disruption intensified as Putin entered his fourth term. Sechin exerts enormous informal power at the head of Rosneft, but in destroying Ulyukaev he may well have wished to consolidate his political status as an untouchable political actor.[4] His heavy-handed assertion of what he took to be Rosneft's interests created enemies while alienating allies. The attack on Ulyukaev warned the whole elite that no one was safe.[5] At the same time, long-dormant institutions were coming back to life. Following the September 2016 parliamentary elections, Volodin revamped the Duma's organisational apparatus, changed legislative procedures and tried to impose greater discipline on the voting behaviour of deputies. The Duma no longer churned out ill-considered laws, although by all means not all were wise. Almost half of the Duma's members changed in the elections of September 2016, while in 2017 alone, one-fifth of the country's eighty-five regional governors were replaced. In mid-2017, the leadership of UR changed. Although Medvedev remained the nominal leader, Andrei Turchak took over at the head of the party's General Council. He moved quickly to revive the party's governing structures and tried to make UR a more 'constructive' actor in the making of policy and management of political affairs. Above all, he sought to reduce UR's dependence on the executive. As one perceptive commentary puts it,

> Turchak's stance is an indication of how there are now different autonomous forces in Russian domestic politics, whose leaders have their own personal access to the main stakeholder, Vladimir Putin. Each structure has its own bargaining power and can form coalitions with others under the umbrella of a 'Domestic Policy Corporation'. … Meanwhile, the subsidiaries will continue to break away from the grip of a once-unified domestic policy holding and try to take over their counterparts.[6]

Amid the signs of elite turbulence, there were indications of rising centrifugal trends. Elements of resistance in the regions suggested that the power of 'horizontalism' remains as strong as ever. In January 2017, for example, the governor of Belgorod Oblast since 1993, Yevgeny Savchenko, ignored pressure from the Kremlin to resign and announced that he would run for re-election, and in due course he was voted back into office. Belgorod in the 1990s had been part of the so-called 'red belt' of communist regions but since then had flourished within the framework of a distinctive model of regional developmentalism. Tatarstan has long defended its privileges, and although in summer 2017 Moscow refused to renew the federal treaty, the republic continues to resist centralising pressures. Attempts to remove Tatar language courses as a compulsory part of the school curriculum were stymied, although the struggle continues. There was also a battle over budget revenues, with Sakhalin managing to retain 50 per cent of its oil production revenues, when Moscow tried to take 75 per cent.[7] Overall, despite attempts at renewal and technocratic reformulation, the Putin system is based on extreme elite stability. A Reuters study in late 2017 compared the profiles of 784 current regional governors, members of the Federal Assembly, the government, the Security Council and the presidential administration to the 768 who were in power in May 2012. It found little sign of renewal. Of the 784 positions, 314 had changed hands in the previous two years, fewer than in May 2012 when that figure was 368. Typically, when an official loses their job, they are found another post. The average age of all officials rose from 52.6 in 2012 to 55.5 in 2017.[8]

The shift into a neo-revisionist stance after 2012 was accompanied by attempts to 'nationalise' the elites. The ultimate goal was to reduce the threat of splits and betrayal, but the immediate goal was to render Russia less susceptible to foreign pressure by ensuring that political and business leaders kept their wealth and property at home. Harsh registration requirements were imposed on foreign holdings, and certain categories of politicians were totally prohibited from owning foreign property or bank accounts. As in the economy, a long-term import substitution strategy was applied to insulate the country from foreign threats. Putin treated the country in the way that he managed his leadership: maximum autonomy and minimum dependency. The repatriation of funds and property had the incidental benefit, from the regime point of view, of rendering the elite more vulnerable to domestic constraints.

The former Kremlin adviser, Gleb Pavlovsky, has long talked about a 'collective Putin' – suggesting that he is the aggregator of the consensus views of the Russian elite and that his role has become 'more formal and less decisive'.[9] The independent behaviour of such business leaders as Alisher Usmanov and, above all, Sechin reinforces the argument that the elite could comfortably survive without him. In the 2018 election, Pavlovsky went further to argue that 'it is now possible to talk about a system that operates without Putin', with Putin less inclined to intervene in the power struggles within the elite, and as an apolitical president, one who 'never been interested in classical "politics", seeing it as an empty term', allowing decisions to be taken in his name. Russia was developing, in his view, into a 'collective regency', with Putin's inner circle and the presidential administration as a whole becoming independent players in their own right. The accelerated appointment of 'technocrats' was the first step of the 'transition into the post-Putin Russia'. Thus, 2018 was not about getting to a post-Putin Russia but about planning the transition.[10] There is something to be said for this, but Putin's independent agency should never be underestimated.

The Minchenko analytical company has long been tracking changes in the elite through the use of the 'Politburo 2.0' metaphor, rejecting the 'collective Putin' model in favour of the old Soviet Politburo archetype of delegated power. The term was coined in a report published in 2012 arguing that the Russian power system comprised a network of delegated authority reminiscent of the Soviet Politburo.[11] The new representation of the Politburo is not a formal institution, and unlike its predecessor it does not meet regularly in the Kremlin's Walnut Room, and neither does it have any formal procedures. The new model includes the most influential figures in contemporary Russian politics, including the top government officials and business interests that are aligned with the Kremlin. The focus is on the so-called 'power vertical', but the Politburo model once again reinforces the argument that the 'power horizontal' is no less important. In a later report, the Minchenko group argued that the Russian governance model had changed from a binary or 'bipolar model', in which two micro-factions broadly balanced each other, towards a sectoral approach in which Putin's power rested on his ability to adjudicate the allocation of resources to key sectors, including the defence industrial complex, the energy sector (notably Sechin), industrialists and manufacturers (Chemezov), the financial sector and the security apparatus.[12]

The authority of the government officials is derived both from their formal offices as well as their closeness to Putin. This group includes Medvedev, the minister of defence Sergei Shoigu, as well as the mayor of Moscow, Sobyanin. The other major group comprises business people who are part of Putin's inner court: Arkady Rotenberg, Gennady Timchenko and Yuri Kovalchuk. Some figures bridge the two constituencies, notably Sechin, who in certain respects became a law unto himself. The Politburo analogy is complemented by the 'court' model, comprising various individuals with no formal government authority or business interests but who nevertheless are influential. These include Tikhon Shevkunov, the Orthodox bishop formerly at the Sretensky Monastery and now Metropolitan of Pskov and Porkhov, who is considered Putin's confessor. Individuals who began their careers as part of Putin's court later moved to occupy official positions, notably Putin's protocol officer Anton Vaino who became head of the PA, Alexei Dyumin, Putin's former chief security guard and advisor before becoming governor of Tula Oblast in February 2016, and Yevgeny Zinichev, a former bodyguard who before being appointed minister for emergency situations in May 2018 was acting governor of Kaliningrad region.[13] The old generation was not leaving but there was a gradual transition to new leaders. The existing system tried to renew itself to avert transitioning to a new order.

Is Putin an ism?

Is there such a thing as Putinism? Can his name be associated with a distinctive political practice and ideology to merit the addition of the 'ism' suffix? Or is Putin just another transactional rather than transformational leader?[14] Despite his longevity in office, is Putin simply part of the long tradition of Russian authoritarian leaders whose top-down methods fail to achieve Russia's genuine modernisation?[15] Perhaps ultimately the whole Putin phenomenon is little more than a Russian version of postmodern populism or nativist illiberalism? Putin undoubtedly has an inimitable style, but that in itself does not add up to an original combination of ideas and practices. Or by contrast, did Putin reshape politics to the degree that he set Russia on a trajectory that will shape the country's future?

Putinism certainly exists in the limited sense that it is a distinctive response to specific problems of Russian development and governance. Although it represents a certain style of governance and type of statecraft, it has much in common with the one devised by Yeltsin within the framework of the dual state but made to work much better. This model of regime-society relations delivers certain public goods, but it is profligate and stunts talent and the entrepreneurial spirit, although it does not stifle them entirely. Above all, the system of managed democracy undermines the transformation of the consumer and bourgeois into a *citoyen*, someone aware of their political and social rights in a constitutional state and ready to defend them. There has been no attempt to restore even a basic level of Soviet-style equality, and instead Russia remains one of the most unequal countries in the world. Putinism is a distinctive synthesis of authoritarian managerial practices and democratic proceduralism, neo-liberal social policies and neo-Soviet paternalism, partial decommunisation and hesitant destalinisation, and a combination of adaptation and resistance to the US-led liberal international order. But is it an enduring historical or international phenomenon, even if elements are replicated elsewhere and will no doubt be repeated in Russia? From this perspective, the moniker 'Putinism' is inappropriate. Putinism is not a movement with an enduring structure that will outlast the rule of its founder. It not an original programme for the transformation of economy and society, and its foreign policy is in line with that pursued by Russia for decades if not centuries. It is not an ideology in which adherents can have faith, providing coherent answers to the mysteries of national fate and destiny. The defence of national sovereignty and cultural traditions does have resonance elsewhere, but it is far from unique to Russia. Putinism is a rational (although not necessarily the optimal) response to immediate challenges, and to that extent gains support if not adherents, but it lacks a transcendent quality that offers a better vision of the future or which could be substantively appealing to other countries.

Considered in its time and place and within the framework of a pragmatic lens, Putin provided answers to many of the questions facing post-communist Russia. Putinism may not have been the ideal solution, but in the harsh conditions of a country trying to reconstitute itself from the debris of a collapsed social order and in which the dominant external powers, generously but misguidedly, tried not only to turn Russia into a new version of themselves but also to render it a toothless international power, Putin's solutions were cogent and logical. Ultimately, Putin did not repudiate the principles on which post-communist Russia is founded and thus remains heir to the aspirations of the anti-communist democratic revolution. Equally, Putin remained loyal to the vision of a proud and independent Russia initially enshrined in the Declaration of State Sovereignty of 12 June 1990. No less important, the country's political economy remains market capitalism, although with a state corporatist neo-patrimonial twist. In all three respects Putin is transactional, believing that what works in a given situation is best. Putin tamed the extremes of leftist restorationism and right-wing revanchism, and drew on the power of the four main ideo-interest currents to preside over an unprecedented era of political consensus and even of concord. But this has been achieved in a bureaucratic manner and in a technocratic style to achieve mechanical solidarity. Will the stability generated by that consensus be maintained without Putin's skilled and pragmatic leadership? The historical situation remains open, and the tension between the two wings of the dual state represents divergent options for Russia's future development. In his absence, will the institutions of the constitutional state come into their own and sustain a more competitive and accountable democracy, or will the incumbent elites rally round to consolidate the authoritarianism of the regime state? Can there be a smooth transition to genuine constitutionalism, or will the country once again descend into a war of all against all?

We have described the anti-revolutionary ethos underlying the transactional and pragmatic Putin phenomenon. Russian history since 1991 represents some sort of 'restoration', as after the English Revolution in 1660 and Napoleonic France in 1815. In both cases, the achievements of the earlier period were incorporated into the new system, although shorn of their radicalism. There is no attempt to reverse the results of the revolution, but the principles on which the revolution was conducted are repudiated. In the Russian case, Putin not only incorporated much of the welfare benefits of the Soviet system into his social policy and reproduced a Soviet-style social contract of stability and progress in return for political passivity but at the same time also accepted the results of liberal revolution of the 1990s. Putin came under pressure from both the communists and liberals like Navalny to challenge the 'loans-for-shares' privatisations of the mid-1990s, but apart from the appropriation of the Yukos oil company (for a specific set of reasons), the property settlement of the 1990s remains largely in place. In fact, Putin accelerated the creation of the legal framework for a market economy, and although in rhetorical terms he condemned the excesses of the period, he accepted that he was a legatee of its achievements. He understood that even in the late Yeltsin period under the management of Chubais, Nemtsov, Kirienko and others, and above all Primakov when he was prime minister from September 1998 to May 1999, the oligarchs were already on the retreat, the public finances were better managed and from late 1999 the economy had already returned to growth.[16]

Putin's restoration, in other words, has been a very moderate one, and it certainly did not represent a counter-revolution. The corollary of Putin's anti-revolutionism is the profound moderation of Russian politics after more than a century of excess. The second half of the nineteenth century saw the increasing radicalisation of the Russian intelligentsia, with a part assuming a revolutionary strategy and others adopting more militantly conservative, even reactionary, positions. This culminated in one of the most radical events of the twentieth century, the Bolshevik revolution. The extreme wing of the revolutionary socialist movement then imposed perhaps the world's most ambitious attempt to eradicate market relations, although tempered by numerous tactical retreats. In the end, the success of the project proved its greatest failing. The refusal even in the post-Stalin years to integrate market mechanisms into the planned economy (the Chinese-style 'communism of reform' gambit) ultimately fostered inefficiency, declining growth rates, shortage of consumer goods and services, and ultimately the collapse of the system. Once again, as in 1917, rather than an evolutionary transformation, 1991 saw systemic collapse and the disintegration of the country. And once again, a radical faction of the intelligentsia drove forward a plan for the transformation of the country in a form of anti-communist neo-Bolshevism.[17] In comparison to his predecessors, Putin is the great moderator. This is the fundamental source of his popularity. He represents a period of stabilisation after the revolutionary and counter-revolutionary storms that have racked the country for over a century.

A moderate is someone who tracks a path between extremes, and this is the essence of Putinism. While drawing on certain neoliberal ideas, Putin is far from a neoliberal, and the same applies to neo-traditionalism. His conservatism does not embrace such positions as banning abortions, although the percentage of Russians who consider the practice unacceptable has tripled over the last twenty years, from 12 to 35 per cent.[18] The centre, as these data show, is never static but moves with the currents of political passion and interests; but Putin has moderated the political consequences of the shifts. There is a normative core to moderation, as well as a sociological and historical foundation. Just as Charles II after the Restoration in 1660 sought to draw the passion out of politics, and thus tempered the radicalism that had provoked the English Civil War, so the Putinite restoration focuses on pragmatic and technocratic consolidation and conservative modernisation. Equally, after the great transformative storm unleashed by the French Revolution in 1789, the Directory and then Napoleon Bonaparte sought to incorporate the positive without the radicalism of the revolutionary period, although it would take another half-century after his final defeat in 1815 before France entered a proto-Putinite period of consolidation under Napoleon III (see below).

Moderation is not abstract but has fundamental policy consequences. Putin's resistance to the practices of Western hegemony resulted in his demonization, but he remains a moderate in foreign and domestic policy. In systemic terms, the Ukraine crisis was provoked by the radicalisation of all parties – Russia's politics of resistance and neo-revisionism, the unmediated expansion of the Atlantic security system though NATO enlargement or bilateral US links, and the EU's un-negotiated attempt to enlarge its sphere of influence to the East – but within that framework Putin's response could have been far more extreme. Intervention in Crimea certainly represented the repudiation of the rules-based system as formulated after 1945, but from the Kremlin's perspective, these rules had long been infringed by the Western powers when it suited them (the Israeli annexation of the Golan Heights is often mentioned in this context, as well as recognition of Kosovan independence), including the 'coup' that overthrew the legitimately elected leader of Ukraine. Zhirininovsky was pressing for Moscow to occupy the whole of Ukraine to liberate it from 'fascist occupation' and to restore a legitimate government in Kiev, while the CPRF also sought to free Ukraine from the alleged fascist yoke. A similar argument can be made about the Middle East, when 'Putin was the moderate who saved Syria from destruction'.[19]

Putin is in the Bonapartist tradition in seeking to fuse the left and the right, offering a combination of stability and reform. A Bonapartist situation is one where social forces are equally balanced (in our case, between the bureaucracy and nascent political representations of the middle class), allowing the regime to act with autonomy. Promoted as the ideology of reconciliation (comparable to *trasformismo* in late-nineteenth-century Italy, discussed below), the inconclusive nature of the system takes the form of a dual state, with all of its inherent contradictions and accompanying stalemate. This is accompanied by the rejection of class politics, although when under pressure (as in 2012), Putin took advantage of his support among blue-collar and industrial workers to threaten the insurgent 'angry urbanites', the nascent middle class demanding equal political inclusion and free and fair elections. At the same time, although political conformity is necessary for career progression, the Putin system does not demand internalised loyalty. It is not an ideological regime, and instead passivity or formal conformity is enough; even criticism is welcomed as long as it remains within the discursive bounds established by the regime. This provides a recipe for social peace and the pacification of political extremes, but it can hardly inspire. While China still retains a belief in 'the Marxist vision of a purposeful, ever-forward-moving, scientifically progressive history, one where the future is always better than the past',[20] post-communist Russia is devoid of such historical optimism.

Following the 1848 revolution and the overthrow of the 'bourgeois' rule of Louis Philippe, Louis Bonaparte, the nephew of Napoleon I, was elected president in December of that year and then, in a 'self-coup' on 2 December 1851, dissolved the National Assembly and thereafter ruled as Napoleon III, with the 'Second Empire' declared in November 1852. The events are powerfully described by Karl Marx in his *The 18th Brumaire of Louis Napoleon*, and his comments on the restoration of empire have relevance to Russia today: 'Instead of *society* having conquered a new content for itself, it seems that the *state* only returned to its oldest form, to the shamelessly simple domination of the sabre and the cowl.'[21] Napoleon III appealed to French 'greatness', modernisation and a cross-class agenda of authoritative leadership cutting across the divisions of modernity. This is Putin's agenda, drawing on the four main constituencies in contemporary Russia but entirely beholden to none. However, in both cases fundamental political issues remained unresolved: in France, the ideals of the French revolution, and in particular the principle of popular sovereignty, came into contradiction with renewed imperial rule, while in Russia the normative ideals expressed in the 1993 constitution come into contradiction with the leadership and guardianship role arrogated by the administrative regime. Putin is rather less bombastic in foreign policy, although some would argue that Bonapartist adventurism in Mexico has its analogies in Putin's actions in Ukraine and Syria. Napoleon III ruled until the Franco-Prussian War of 1870, which led to the catastrophic defeat of the Second Empire and his exile in England.

Bonapartism, as described by Marx, argues that the class stalemate (between the bourgeoisie and the working class) allowed Napoleon III to stand above all classes. The stability of the twenty years of the Second Empire saw the massive development of the railway network, the reconstruction of Paris and other cities, access of women to higher education and belated industrialisation, but the political system in Marxist terms 'lagged behind' the economic base. This could be argued to be the case today in Russia, with a political regime managing society and political affairs but not organically tied to the social structure. There is the interpenetration of economic and political elite structures, notably in the corruption and inter-elite conflicts of the third state, but the lack of transparency and political accountability derives from the administrative regime trying to insulate itself from capture by social interests (as in the 1990s) or by the passions of the extremes, notably a mixed bag of neo-communists on the left and various nationalists and populists on the right. As Marx noted of the Second Empire, 'Only under the second Bonaparte does the state seem to have made itself completely independent. As against civil society, the state machine has consolidated its position.'[22] To overcome the contradiction and to keep the public gaze on himself, Napoleon III needed to 'spring constant surprises, that is to say, under the necessity of executing a *coup d'état en miniature* every day'.[23] This describes Putin's state of exception outlined earlier, although the surprises have been few. There is force to the criticism that the Putinite system is an adequate response to the challenges of the mid-nineteenth century (and even that is questionable, as the fate of the Second Empire demonstrated) but not to those of the twenty-first century. That is to deny the specific features of post-communism in Russia, which in a paradoxical way reproduces the dilemmas of the earlier era. The Russian revolution put time out of joint, and Putin and his cohort insisted that the political temporality of Russia, as a modernising great power, could not be determined elsewhere.

Putin has forged not so much a 'historic bloc' as a mechanical politics of consensus. This is the combination of interests and ideas to create what is taken to be 'common sense', an appreciation of what is normal and appropriate for the times. This can be summed up in Russia today by the idea of 'conservative modernisation', in which the two elements, just like the broader political system, are combined in a relatively stable equilibrium. The system is conservative rather than reactionary, appealing to traditional conservative values such as social stability, a historical version of the family structure and its perceived social values, the repudiation of radical change, the appeal to patriarchal paternalism accompanied by a neo-Soviet commitment to social security, state paternalism and social emancipation, above all, for women. In other words, to be a conservative in post-communist conditions is different than being a conservative in a mature democracy (the radicalisation represented by neo-conservatism in these countries is another issue). In Russia, conservatism is still genuinely conservative, in the Burkean sense; it does not exclude ameliorative change and sensible reform, but it eschews a vision of transformation based on an ideological programme.[24]

Although Putin has an almost visceral fear of being constrained by any label or ideology, his leadership led a modernisation project. He did not allow himself to be trapped by the label (unlike Medvedev in his four-year term), but Putin is a cautious moderniser. His industrial policy is reminiscent of the post-war development strategies in Japan and South Korea, tempered by the *dirigisme* of post-war France and the social-democratic developmentalism of 'old Labour' in Britain. Rostec hoovered up whole industries and sectors, yet provided space for them to modernise and become competitive. The next stage in classical economic theory would be the privatisation of these now successful companies (such as the Kamaz lorry plant in Tatarstan or GAZ in Nizhny Novgorod), but this was a step that Putin's brand of conservative modernisation only hesitantly embraced, and even then largely for budgetary rather than ideological reasons. His was a conservatism that was statist in orientation and paternalist in social policy, rather than the Thatcherite version focused on hyper-individualism and rampant market forces. At the same time, Putin did not swerve to the opposite extreme, and there is little hint of proto-fascist, or even Orthodox, organicist ideas. Putin's conservatism is liberal rather than collectivist.

Putin forged a 'Putinite consensus' rather than an enduring 'historic bloc'. Just as in the factional model, the forces advancing the conservative modernisation project – the industrial managers, the working class, the bureaucracy, the organic intellectuals (Gramsci's term for the intelligentsia serving the needs of a given hegemonic order) and even elements of the progressive statist intelligentsia concerned about Russia's place in the world – all bought in to the Putinite model, while none were entirely satisfied. All have a stake but none can predominate; so in class terms, Putin speaks for the industrial working class, blue-collar workers and the vast state apparatus, while fostering the development of a consumer middle class while constraining their class power. Even intellectuals have bought into his vision of an independent and sovereign Russia conducting its independent foreign policy, while endorsing the limitations on oligarch power at home and the redevelopment of the country's industrial and technological base. Of course, traditional intellectuals chafe at the restrictions while the middle class strives to become a 'bourgeoisie', where their representations of common sense become hegemonic. Instead, the Putin system spawned a vast army of 'organic' intellectuals, serving the needs of the regime itself. No class could pursue a hegemonic strategy, while each received a degree of satisfaction from the system.

In ideological terms, Putin revived the hallowed Italian tradition of *trasformismo*, a flexible centrist system of government prevalent from the mid-1880s after Italian unification. Putin's reliance on the four major epistemic blocs structuring the Russian intellectual-interest community means that he pursues some liberal policies, but his administration is not liberal; and the same goes for the conservative-preservative tradition (the *okhraniteli*), the neo-traditionalists and the Eurasianists. The Soviet one-party system prevented the development of a classic West European-type party system, and conditions in post-communist Russia were not conducive to the belated construction of a classic left-right party system of the sort that in any case has been eroding in Europe. As a result, Putin reproduced an archaic method of political management (highly reminiscent of Napoleon III's), but one which was also becoming 'postmodern' in post-industrial societies. This is a result of the mimetic character of much of Putinism. To satisfy the neo-traditionalists, he went through the motions of restoring elements of the Soviet system; to please the *siloviki*, he restored their status and privileges; and his pragmatic turn to the East allowed Eurasianists of various stripes to support his leadership. However, the problem of drawing on the forms and not the substance of the various factions was at its most acute when it came to the liberals. Here the mimetic quality was not so easy to square with the need to create genuine institutions that would sustain economic competitiveness, entrepreneurialism and civic dignity. While mimetic practices drew the sting from reactionary forces, it also enervated the constitutional foundations of the state which Putin proclaimed to be building.

Putin is hardly alone in his rejection of revolution as a form of political change, but his aversion to spontaneous change from below is constitutive of his political identity and a core element of anything that might be called Putinism. This is one of the fundamental reasons why the contradictions with the Atlantic system gained such explosive force. The Kremlin leadership became convinced it was the West that had become revisionist and sought to achieve 'regime change' to put in place new leaderships in the post-Soviet space (and the Middle East) more amenable to Western interests. So-called 'colour-revolutions' from this perspective sought to align the character of regimes with the West's security interests, the process of 'transdemocracy': the combination of democracy promotion (sometimes taking forceful forms) and security as a way of creating the conditions for 'democratic peace'.[25] Putin is a legitimist – the belief that legally constituted regimes should be defended, whatever type of system they espoused, and hence the West's surprising adoption of strategies for revolutionary regime change was so disturbing for him (and for the Chinese leadership).

Putin's ideological aversion to revolution, reinforced by the anti-revolutionary current in late Soviet thinking, resulted in his typically pragmatic consequential approach. The disastrous results of Western interventions and most of the Arab Spring revolts only reinforced critiques of forced regime change, which in the post-Soviet space takes the form of support for anti-Russian forces. Legitimism is a reasonable position for a Kremlin leader but becomes dysfunctional when not accompanied by recognition that oppressed peoples have the right to demand change, that corrupt and self-serving elites are hardly likely to give up power without pressure from below, and that legitimacy is not derived only from that the way that a regime is constituted but also from its conformity with the norms of international, constitutional and natural law. Putin was right to criticise the instrumental and selective mobilisation of these principles by the Atlantic powers, but this does not mean that they could not be applied at all. The rejection of double standards does not mean the repudiation of the standards themselves.

Putin does not promise a substantive future and is very modest in his ambitions. There is a crisis of utopian thinking and action, accompanied by the longing for the mythic era of stability and order of the late Soviet years. The very modesty marks an explicit break with the exaggerated utopianism of the Soviet period and also with the unrealistic expectations generated in the transition from communism. This is in keeping with his persistent attempt to deradicalise Russian politics by removing 'the political' from politics. Putinism appears to lack a long-term perspective for the development of society and a people. Russia had been part of the Soviet future (although its national identity in that project had been diluted), and it was now intent on recovering its past to forge its own future. Putin is resolutely a pragmatic and transactional leader, and rejects any transformative agenda in day-to-day politics. He is the effective political manager *par excellence*, focused on incremental gains and the resolution of immediate problems. He rejected the grand schemes advanced by three of the four epistemic blocs, forcing him closer to the conservative-guardianship perspective. For much of the post-Soviet generation, utopian schemes for the betterment of humanity represent a dangerous illusion with potentially disastrous consequences for the societies on which these 'experiments' are conducted. Anti-utopianism generates a sceptical stance towards the socialist tradition, which is predicated on the possibility of the substantive amelioration of society, but it also deprives Putinism of a substantive core. By repudiating a long-term programme that could transcend the narrow horizons of the present, the Putin system became trapped in time: the continuing present began to look like stagnation.[26]

'Putinism' comprises many disparate elements, but there is no single synthesis. It is far from the single-minded ruthlessness of the great ideological projects of the twentieth century. There is no coherent and consistent theory underpinning Putin's politics, but there is a persistent set of principles. In economic policy, Putin is ready to privatise or effectively nationalise industries when appropriate, and he pursued an industrial strategy to develop priority sectors. This does not add up to a grand vision based on the anti-communitarian and individualistic logic of economic freedom and competiveness. Putin's political practice is an eclectic mix of unreconciled facets that together do not add up to a coherent philosophy of development or of the public good. Putin does not believe that socialism can integrate Russia's many traditions, while his conservatism draws on the late-Soviet stability system rather than on any philosophical text. His conservatism has tones of authoritarian neo-liberalism, although it appeals to ordoliberal ideas of a regulated social market economy. He does not believe that unbridled capitalism is the key to human happiness, hence market forces are constrained. Putin combines social conservatism with statist capitalism, a synthesis that appears to be a peculiarly Russian response to the problems of post-communist and late capitalist development. This distinctive recombination reinforces Russia's civilisational distinctiveness, but what it lacks in utopianism is balanced by a hint of traditional Russian messianism.

Putin's grand strategy

American grand strategy since 1945 has consisted of two mutually reinforcing principles: the development of a liberal world order, based on open markets, the rule of law and secure property rights; and the maintenance of US primacy (or what offensive realists call regional hegemony), ensuring that US power would not be challenged in its hemisphere while creating a global alliance system that in the first instance was directed towards the containment of the USSR but which after 1991 was intended to ensure US 'leadership' in global affairs. Chinese grand strategy asserts that the country has answers to some of the world's major challenges, and in particular for the Belt and Road Initiative (BRI) to facilitate China's geopolitical and economic insertion into world affairs, accompanied by a 'new type of great power relationship' with the United States.[27] Russian grand strategy develops in the shadow of the overwhelming primacy of the United States and its allies, and the re-emergence of China as a major power. Although Russian foreign policy has evolved in line with changing perceptions of the challenges facing the country and evaluation of Russian capacities, there remains a remarkable continuity in the country's three main principles: that Russia is a great power; that Russia is a constitutive member of the international community, subordinate to none and co-responsible for the management of international affairs; and that foreign policy should serve domestic developmental goals – a principle that was eroded in conditions of confrontation with the West.

But does Russia's leadership in the Putin years have a 'grand strategy' – defined as a coherent plan and vision for Russia's future reinforced by a detailed programme to implement the plans and the greater vision? Monaghan puts the question well: 'What does President Putin have in mind? Is he, indeed, a strategic genius – or is he making it up day-to-day?'[28] All leaders are constantly beset by immediate concerns, but the best have some sort of grander vision that would leave their country more prosperous and happier than when they assumed power. This is the definition of a 'good leader', but as a recent study has suggested, the recent period has been characterised by poor leadership and bad governance.[29] Archie Brown develops the theme to argue that it ill behoves a country to rely on the 'great leader' to solve its problems, and, instead, the development of sound institutions and good practices serves a people better.[30]

Monaghan cites contrasting views, ranging from the assertion that Putin fundamentally lacks a grand strategy and thus stumbles from crisis to crisis, that he is good at making early moves and then fails to follow through consistently, all the way to suggestions that Putin is 'a *bad* strategist, since he does not understand the relationship between military violence and political objectives, and is pursuing a self-defeating strategy that is reducing Russian power and leaving it isolated, all but ruining his ambition to return Russia to the ranks of the great powers'.[31] Such categorical views tend to miss the essential feature of Putin's leadership, namely its protean and changing quality. The challenges and crises are magnified by the country's size, diversity and accumulation of problems, compounded by the legacy of previous attempts to deal with them. Putin came to power with clear strategic objectives, many of them enunciated in his remarkable *Millennium Manifesto* of December 1999. There are few world leaders who have outlined in such detail their vision of the world and their country's place in it, as well as the strategic objectives facing their nation and ideas on how they can be achieved. Putin argued that the overriding goal was the country's economic and democratic development, and for that Soviet-style ideology, which had driven the country into a dead end, should be abandoned and instead global integration should be pursued. However, Putin insisted that Russia could not become a simple copy of the advanced capitalist democracies but that Russia should forge its own path, based on a reformulated statism, a reinvigorated patriotism and a new model of the greatness of Russia.[32]

In his early years, Putin pursued a *remedial* strategy designed to overcome the problems inherited from the Soviet Union and what were now defined as the excesses of the 1990s. The direct political influence of the powerful business magnates (oligarchs) was reduced, and the autonomy of regional governors curbed. However, the accompanying *developmental* strategy, devised in the early period by German Gref, and some others, including in the legal and municipal government spheres by Dmitry Kozak, were derailed by deterioration of relations with the West. The reforming drive was also blunted by the munificence showered on the country by the sharp rise in the price of raw materials, above all hydrocarbons, that filled Russia's exchequer and until 2008 drove annual rises in GDP of some 8 per cent. In Putin's second term, a security-driven statist model of development was adopted, based on national champions and restrictions on the scope of international capital. This won Putin many friends in the *silovik*, neo-traditionalist and Eurasianist camps but alarmed the liberals. Putin, typically, did not entirely abandon the latter and pursued an orthodox macroeconomic policy while heeding the advice of the minister of finances, Kudrin, and salted away enough of the bounty in sovereign wealth funds to save the country during periodic downturns.

The earlier tempo of economic growth was not restored following the global financial crisis in 2009, indicating structural economic problems. The slew of strategic economic plans in the latter period of Putin's premiership and then in his third term sought to address these issues.[33] However, while they identified the problems and set worthy goals, they appear to have entered a neo-Gorbachevite cycle of great ambition but inadequate and incoherent implementation. Monaghan notes, 'Strategy is *not* a plan, nor is it a set of goals or objectives. Instead, strategy is the combination of the formulation of plans in theory *and their implementation in practice*'. Thus, a strategy is 'a "bridge" between plans and action.'[34] Despite the deterioration of relations with the West and the onset of a new era of confrontation, the developmental model was not full-scale mobilisation, let alone military-style mobilisation, but the plans did seek to ensure that Russia would survive the intensification of sanctions, even a blockade, through domestic sourcing and the creation of financial and other substitutes. Self-reliance and self-sufficiency became the watchwords, although not full-scale autarchy. Putin and leading officials and commentators argued that the world was in crisis and becoming increasingly unmanageable and unpredictable, hence the country needed to insulate itself as far as possible from the spreading turmoil. As Putin noted in his landmark speech to the Valdai Club in October 2014, 'Today we are seeing new efforts to fragment the world, draw new dividing lines ... and steps of this kind inevitably provoke confrontation and counter-measures.'[35] The West appeared intent on achieving regime change in Russia, and hence resources needed to be mobilised to counter the threat.

At the micro level, many observers identify the almost permanent sense of chaos and incoherence in the day-to-day running of public affairs. Zygar stresses the absence of an overall plan and the predominance of tactical manoeuvres.[36] The incoherence is generated by the problematic intersection of the vertical and horizontal dimensions of Russian power. The vertical of power is based not on the due processes of the constitutional state but on the manual manipulations of the administrative regime, although legitimated and given force by the authority of the constitutional state. The economic groups, the departmental bureaucracies and the accompanying venal concerns operate according to a very different logic, exploiting positional advantage and individual and corporate benefit. The ability of the administrative regime to achieve basic governance goals is undermined by the second logic, undermining the coherence of the polity as a whole. Thus, there is a double contradiction: the endemic tension between the two branches of the state – its administrative and constitutional wings – and the broader contradiction between the vertical (although opposing) logics of administration and the horizontal set of informal practices rooted in the sociological character of power and the anthropological networks that have since the Soviet period devised informal network-style practices to survive and thrive in such a weakly ordered polity – what Ledeneva (among others) calls the *sistema*. The informal practices of the *sistema* subvert not only the authority of the institutions of the constitutional state but also the efficacy of the administrative regime.

The deleterious consequences of such a hybrid and multivalent system are clear. By the time of Putin's re-election for a fourth term, Freedom House issued its annual report *Freedom in the World 2018*, with the subtitle *Democracy in Crisis*.[37] Russia had long been considered 'not free', and it now scored 6.5 on a scale of 1 to 7, where 1 is best and 7 is worst, although as late as 2013 it still scored 5.5. Its aggregate score was a miserable 20 out of 100. Although the report identified some genuine problems, mitigating and complicating factors (such as the continued relative freedom of the internet and some major newspapers) were ignored. Anatoly Karlin, who has long satirised the remarkable coincidence in Freedom

House scores between states opposed to US policy and low ratings, noted that this meant that Russia was now considered as unfree as Azerbaijan, Bahrain, Burundi, Chad, China, the Democratic Republic of Congo, Cuba, Ethiopia, Laos, Libya, Swaziland, Tajikistan, United Arab Emirates and Yemen, and that it was considered less free than Qatar, Iran, Belarus and Egypt.[38] Any scale that puts Libya, a country suffering state collapse and civil war, and Russia at the same level must be suspect. This point was reiterated in another study, which questioned the World Press Freedom Index of November 2017, published by the Paris-based Reporters Sans Frontières, which ranked Russia at 148, well below not only Western countries but also below Arab states not known for their press freedom such as Kuwait (104) and the United Arab Emirates (119). As the study noted, 'Contrary to popular belief that Putin's rise to power in 1999 somehow triggered the gulf of assassinations of journalists, these assassinations have sharply dropped since 2000.'[39] Nevertheless, reports such as this have shaped foreign views of Russia in general and Putin's leadership in particular.

The Kremlin considered the Western intervention in Libya illegal and disastrous, and hardened Putin's view that the post-Cold War West was out of control and bound by none of the norms of international law and common sense that it proclaimed. This stiffened his neo-revisionist resolve to assert an independent Russia in international affairs while insulating the country from the Western pressure and vulnerability. This placed Russia on the direct path of confrontation with the historical West, to the detriment of both. The quality of political discourse was coarsened, and mutual vituperation took the place of reasoned analysis. This culminated in claims of Russian interference in Western elections and the onset of a new era of confrontation marked by sanctions, counter-sanctions and elements of a new arms race. The lack of restraint and the loss of old methods of managing conflict means that this confrontation is as dangerous, if not more so, than the original Cold War. It had taken the Cuban missile crisis in October 1962 to establish channels of communication and other forms of conflict management, but it is not clear that humanity would survive another such crisis.

10 PARADOXES OF PUTINISM

A paradox indicates something that at first sight does not ring true and thus reflects a duality of meaning. In his 'What Is Enlightenment', Immanuel Kant suggested that the whole modern world is paradoxical,[1] and in that sense Putin takes the paradoxality of modernity to new levels; or perhaps, he takes the inherent paradoxality to a point where it turns in on itself. Putin's statecraft exploits the paradoxes of modernity to the point that we begin to question the character of modernity itself. The Putin phenomenon is paradoxical in its very essence. Its politics are developmental and conservative, rational and romantic, secular and religious, patriotic and internationalist. The fundamental paradox is that a modernising project to overcome the apparent 'false modernity' of the Soviet developmental project (itself one of the notable paradoxes of our time) assumed certain archaic practices that mimicked the Soviet experience. However, and most paradoxically, it may be the archaic forms of statecraft and rule that endows the system with coherence and vitality that would otherwise be lacking. This dual modernity complements my dual state model. The earlier clash between the two modernising agents, the state and big business, after the Yukos affair from 2003 gave way to the pre-eminence of the state; but the way that this conflict played out confirmed the pre-eminence of the regime vis-à-vis the state. This ensured rule through, and not by, institutions; or put otherwise, rule *by* law and not the rule *of* law. The dynamic tension remains between the normativity of the constitutional state, with its concern for positive law, the rights and liberties enshrined in a liberal democratic polity, as well as the attempt to introduce elements of accountability through elections, parties and representative bodies, and the arbitrariness, opacity and formal rationality of the administrative regime. The two logics of statecraft are inextricably entwined and, in conditions of Putinite rule, dependent on each other. However, both are threatened by the corruption and criminality of the third state.

When success means failure

To the degree that there is such a thing as 'Putinism', its concerns have changed over time. In his first term, the focus was on the emergency restoration of governmental authority, the remedial strategy. He tackled the assumed prerogatives of the 'oligarchs' and regional governors, guided by the need to stop the country's descent into anarchy, criminality and global marginality. The second term shifted towards greater developmentalism accompanied by the rise of securitisation, the implementation of the strategy of conservative modernisation, with the creation of state corporations and 'national champions' in the form of Rosneft and Rostec, and the diversification of Gazprom into oil production. Medvedev's presidency saw Putin working as prime minister, where the focus rapidly turned to anti-crisis measures to deal with the consequences of the global financial crisis. Putin's third term sought to establish Russia as an independent pole in world politics through the policy of neo-revisionism, with Putin having lost not only any residual belief that the historical West could be transformed into a greater West but also that there could be any substantively fruitful relationship with the West at all. Hence, the emphasis was on advancing Eurasian integration and the development of Russia's Asian vector of development. However, as Putin entered his fourth term, he seemed to have run out of ideas. He appeared less interested in managing intra-elite conflicts and was clearly frustrated by endless manoeuvring between the four meta-factions while apparently unable or unwilling to manage the escalating micro-factionalism. The impasse in international affairs and mounting tensions with the Atlantic security system was pregnant with the possibility of open conflict. Nikolas Gvozdev notes, 'No one – not even the most liberal, pro-Western candidates running [in the 2018 election] – would advocate for Russian subordination in a US unipolar system.'[2] This was indeed the case, but some way had to be found out of the impasse.

Although the Putin era by definition remains open-ended in terms of its teleology and eclectic in its social base and orientations, can we nevertheless identify some fundamental principles underlying the system? Liberal critics argue that it is motivated by nothing more than avarice and corruption, but this argument is too reductionist – reducing a complex system to just one aspect. While kleptocracy is a feature of the system, it is not a kleptocratic system – if it was, the sovereign wealth funds would not exist but the money would have soon found its way into Swiss bank accounts. Equally, another set of critics, which in large part overlaps with the first, argue that power retention and maximisation is the guiding principle of the Putin system. Again, this is undoubtedly one of the fundamental aspects of Putinite rule.[3] However, in the context of the dual state model, this sort of rational-choice power maximisation thinking is just another form of reductionism. If power (and greed) was the only thing motivating the

Putinite elite, then a very different type of governance dynamic would be at work. Why bother with strict macroeconomic rigidity and tight fiscal discipline when the bounty could be showered on a grateful people? Why bother to force oligarchs to invest in public goods, if that money could be better stashed in the Cayman Islands? Why create corporations to develop aerospace, shipping, railways and the like, when the time could be more enjoyably spent in Mayfair? Above all, why even pay lip service to the constitutionalism that is so often breached in practice, when outright authoritarianism could deliver the venal goals with less fuss and bother?

One response would be that the Putin system is too clever to expose its real essence, understanding that thereby it would render itself vulnerable to popular hostility. That is why such a complex rent management system has been devised, to provide enough for the people to feel that they have a stake in the system's maintenance. Equally, capitulation to the banditry of the third state would undermine the tenuous balance between the four main elite factions and destabilise the system as a whole. These are substantive arguments but do not capture the paradoxes of a system in which the constitution guarantees great scope for economic and political freedom but in which regime management creates obstacles to its fulfilment.

This book has tried to outline a non-reductionist dynamic model of Russian politics. The system cannot be reduced to one single factor – greed, regime perpetuation or even Putin's love of power. Equally, no single term can capture the multiple dimension of the Russian governance system and culture of power, but each term contributes to our understanding of how the system works and what motivates it as a whole. Thus, Russia has elements of electoral authoritarianism, but this does not capture other features of the system. Certainly, Russia is characterised by patronal politics, but there are also features that distinguish it from other post-Soviet states with a similar character. Above all, there is a clear developmental strategy at work. There may have been more effective ways of achieving economic development, but there were also far more dysfunctional approaches to managing the economy. Instead of linear models, a dynamic approach is required that does more than describe features of how politics is conducted; the belief that by pinning some sort of label the system is thereby defined. Political scientists spend much time arguing over the correct terms to apply, but many of them remain stuck in linear models based on some assumed trajectory towards or away from democracy. Instead, a dynamic model seeks to understand the system in its own terms. It understands that democracy operates on a spectrum, and while it is desirable to have more, it is very easy to have less. This does not mean that normative judgements are inappropriate but that these need to be located within an understanding of the rationale of the system itself. Otherwise, judgement becomes little more than orientalist imposition of an externally generated set of values.

In this context, we can begin to understand the way that domestic and foreign policies interact. First, the maintenance of Russia as a great power is the core of its strategy. This means ensuring that the country retains its sovereignty, autonomy and independence in the international system. Second, Russia is a constitutive member of the international community and therefore has an inherent responsibility to be part of the management of global affairs. Anything else is considered a repudiation of Russia's history and an abnegation of the country's responsibility. Third, foreign policy should serve Russia's internal developmental goals. This element was introduced by Peter the Great and thereafter in one way or another remains a constant. Even in the Soviet period, when the communist regime opposed market economies, the capitalist states were used for technology and later as energy markets. In the post-communist era, these three elements recombined, but all remain operative. Putin from the beginning stressed that Russia's foreign policy should serve Russian developmental goals, but this later was tempered by the first two strands. What is definitely not part of Russia's grand strategy is a new 'gathering of the lands', of the sort that Russia had pursued since at least the sixteenth century. In 2014, it looked as if Russia's virtual empire, a zone of 'privileged interests', would become a real empire, but this turned out to be no more than a fleeting glimpse of a potentially dangerous path of development. Those who believe that Putin's departure would allow harmonious relations with the West to emerge fail to understand that Putin is the expression of Russian concerns rather than their instigator. A change of leadership provides an opportunity for relations to be reset, but fundamental interests and contradictions remain.

Towards the succession

Russian history is littered with cases when the long rule of powerful leader comes to an end and the struggle for the succession destabilises the painfully built structures of governance. By 2024, Putin will have been leader, both as president and prime minister, for over twenty-four years. The end of the reign of a 'long tsar' usually signals a period of turbulence, if not disintegration. When Putin confirmed that he would run for a fourth term, he also fired the starting gun for the battle for the succession.[4] Putin's fourth term became an extended preparation for Putin's envisaged withdrawal from direct management of political life. In conditions where conflict with the West has become part of the structure of domestic politics, the change of leader could offer the opportunity for a reset in relations, but it is important to stress that Putin's foreign policy reflects the consensus view of the Russian elite. Tony Wood emphasizes that Putin is the product of systemic factors, which will endure after his leadership ends.[5] This is indeed the case, but leadership matters, especially so in Russia.

There are seven basic models for the 2024 transition. First, the Central Asian option in which constitutional term limits are abolished, allowing Putin to run again in 2024 and as long as he wished thereafter. Putin did not take this option in 2008, and it is unlikely that he would do so now. The second scenario is a re-run of the Yeltsin model of a hand-picked successor, from which Putin benefitted in 1999. This model was applied in Kazakhstan when on 19 March 2019, Nazarbaev, after three decades in office and at the age of 78, handed over the presidency to his trusted associate Kassym-Jomart Tokaev, the speaker of parliament, while Nazarbaev took over as head of the Security Council for life while remaining Leader of the Nation and head of the ruling Nur Otan party. This was the Deng Xiaoping option, exercised by the Chinese leader in the 1990s as he withdraw from direct rule, and it was also applied by Lee Kuan Yew in Singapore. The third option is a variant of this, in which a placeholder is selected (as in 2008) until Putin is allowed to run again, which would mean another six years of tandem leadership, accompanied by policy paralysis. The fourth option is constitutional change to limit presidential powers and to strengthen those of parliament, in which the government would be headed by a more powerful prime minister resting on the primacy of their party in the Duma. Khodorkovsky has been one of the most consistent advocates of turning Russia into a parliamentary democracy, in the belief that presidentialism in Russia facilitates authoritarianism. When a version of this was tried in Armenia in the spring of 2018, it provoked a revolution and the elimination of the ruling party in the subsequent election. A variant of this is for Putin to remain as symbolic president, with executive powers transferred to a new cabinet government. The fifth version is for a single party to be proclaimed hegemonic and for its leader to become head of a strengthened executive. This is unlikely and the one-party model is unlikely to succeed – of the fifteen one-party systems in existence today, fourteen were established before or during the Cold War.[6] The sixth option is to create a presidency for the Union State of Russia and Belarus, rather like the rump Yugoslavia in the 1990s. The seventh option is to change the constitution to create a post that would keep Putin at the pinnacle of a new power structure, possibly as some sort of 'national leader'. This could involve granting the State Council, an advisory body made up of regional leaders, enhanced powers and an expanded membership – to make it something like the Soviet-era Politburo. Other options include a military coup, which is unlikely. There is, of course, an eighth option: that Putin leaves office as constitutionally mandated in 2024, and a successor is elected in a free and fair election. This would be Putin's culminating achievement; to leave office in a manner very different from the way he entered. The end of Putinism would, paradoxically, be its most triumphant vindication.

This does not mean that his successor will be a liberal in the Medvedev mould. More likely, a representative of the *siloviki* with a strong professional background in the security services would be entrusted to bear the standard against Russia's perceived opponents. By contrast, if Medvedev leads a successful economic reform programme in Putin's fourth term and living standards once again rise sharply and the economy enjoys sustained growth, then Medvedev would be in a strong position to return to the highest office. This will only be possible if the intensity of confrontation with the Atlantic system abates. What is clear is that China will shift from being a regional to a global player, there will be continued stresses in US domestic and global leadership, and Moscow's alignment with Beijing will remain, accompanied by deepening quasi-alliance relations with Turkey, Iran and some other countries. There will also probably be a degree of domestic institutional rearrangement, with UR possibly being reformed and merged. A government of national unity may even be formed, drawing on representatives of the CPRF, JR and even the LDPR to fill some cabinet portfolios.

Sooner or later the Putin era will come to an end, and the question then becomes – what will happen then? Can 'Putinism' survive without Putin? Elements of what we identify as the dual state model of governance were established before Putin, continued when Medvedev was president, and there is no reason to doubt that they will endure in some form afterwards. Putin, after all, is not a great institutional innovator, and although he created some para-constitutional bodies, he worked within the framework created by Yeltsin, in both its formal and informal aspects. Nevertheless, the dual state model suggests that the system remains in a permanent state of dynamic equilibrium: the strengthening of state institutions is followed by the reinforcement of the regime, and when the negative effects once again become apparent, there is a new campaign to strengthen state institutions. Without Putin to act as the supreme balancer, the system could develop in at least four plausible and interconnected ways: (1) a move towards the strengthening of the constitutional state, with greater autonomy for institutions and the gradual consolidation of a competitive liberal democracy; (2) by contrast, the consolidation of an autonomous regime ruling through more overtly authoritarian instruments and the open flouting (or management) of constitutional principles and legal conventions, backed up by overt coercion; (3) a continuation of the present unstable balance which is typically characterised as electoral authoritarianism, although probably managed with less of Putin's customary adroitness; and (4) the reinforcement of the corruption and economic claims of the third state, creating an openly predatory and kleptocratic ruling elite.

The power grab by the propertied elite could well prompt mass dissatisfaction and protest, opening the door to a forceful change of regime amid talk of democracy, before the attendant chaos and perceived capitulation leads to the reconstitution of a new authoritarian system. The cycle of reform, chaos and consolidation would be repeated. The lessons of Egypt's experiment with democracy are much discussed in Moscow. After twenty-nine years in power, President Hosni Mubarak was overthrown in a popular revolution (part of the Arab Spring) in February 2011, but following a period of turmoil, a new strongman military leader, Abdel Fattah al-Sisi, seized power in July 2013 in a violent coup. In Russia, intra-elite contestation rather than popular mobilisation is more likely, although a combination of the two is possible in which the various factions appeal to the people. Ultimately, popular mobilisation in such a case would be a function of elite rivalries. Only if the popular movement is strong enough to shape policy would such a model of events lead to greater democracy. Popular mobilisation in 1988–93 did not become an independent and enduring force. In contemporary Russia, this could be achieved if the systemic political parties, working with parties outside the Duma, become independent political actors. After nearly three decades, these parties have established regional networks and gained administrative experience, and thus the situation differs greatly from the late Soviet years. However, as in the earlier period, there is a vast security apparatus, with the FSB, the National Guard and much more, and any political breakthrough would depend on how these organisations behaved.

The various options outlined here are predicated on the view that there is nothing in Russia's political culture or attitudes to prevent the establishment of a competitive and accountable constitutional democracy, but the key variable is the route to that outcome. Within-system evolution and reform is the most likely path towards the creation of the stable institutions that are the essential foundation for a functioning democracy, whereas another revolutionary rupture and breakdown would only reproduce Russia's cycle of radical ambition and eternal disappointment. Thus, paradoxically, the consolidation of the Putinite dual state offers the possibility of an evolutionary path out of authoritarianism and societal disruption; at the same time, however, there is nothing inevitable about such an outcome. The sanctions regime imposed on Russia since 2012 is predicated on the view that the fourth model has already come to pass, with the consolidation of the power of 'Putin's cronies', and that the system has already become a 'kleptocracy'. Some genuine governance problems in contemporary Russia are identified in this model, but it is targeting a 'third state' that so far is not able autonomously to defend its privileges and is instead part of a far more complex dynamic of political relations. The sanctions, if anything, lead precisely to the consolidation of the third state as the regime closes ranks against its enemies.

No major transformation of the system is currently envisaged, but change can come in unanticipated ways. In his study of 201 cases of democratisation between 1800 and 2015, Daniel Treisman found that self-democratisation, where a regime curtailed its own powers, occurred in only 4 per cent of cases; in 16–19 per cent of cases, it took place as a result of some sort of elite pact, while in 64–67 per cent of cases, change took place as a result of what Treisman calls 'democracy by mistake'. These mistakes included attempts by regimes to increase their authority but in fact weakened it, when they underestimated the strength of the opposition and failed to apply the right mix of concessions and coercion and thus lost power (13–17 per cent of cases), or used too much repression, fuelling protests that provoked the overthrow of the regime (12–15 per cent), or scheduled elections or referendums that they unexpectedly lost, thus forfeiting power (6–9 per cent). A common scenario was the Gorbachevian one, where there are plans to reform the system but the process runs out of control, provoking dissolution and disintegration. Treisman notes that there are few cases of intentional democratisation after 1927.[7]

Pavlovsky put his finger on the issue when he noted that 'Putin is an uncontrollable natural phenomenon', his retention of power has nothing 'all-powerful' about it but represents the maintenance of the power of three 'classes', each in part feeding on each other, on which his power rested: the *siloviki*, the higher state bureaucrats (*chinovniki*) in the government and presidential administration, and the president's friends. This is a variation of my general model of the Putin system resting on a range of different factions. The key point is Pavlovsky's conclusion:

> Liberalisation is not the key to Russia's political future. Even though liberalisation of rules is essential for certain sectors – the world of entrepreneurs, culture and education, penitentiary policy, and network initiatives. But in general a Russia that becomes too rapidly politicised requires only a more open politics. Too often politicisation reaches an unbearable intensity, and its participants have to establish new rules of the game. What has Putin got to do with this? He is just one of the prizes to be won.[8]

A gap was opening up between Putin the man and the so-called 'collective Putin', the network made up of his closest associates. The system, for Pavlovsky, began to operate without Putin. The Putin system appeared to enter its terminal phase, however long-drawn-out that may be. If Putin completes the full six years, by 2024 he will be 71. It is unlikely that he will amend the constitution to allow a third consecutive term (something he had refused to do in 2008) or return to the 'castling' model employed at that time, which saw him become prime minister while Medvedev took over the presidency. The dying days of Yeltsin's presidency in 1999 were marked by intense elite conflict, upheaval in the party system, as well as by regional turbulence, the still-unexplained apartment bombings in Moscow and renewed conflict in Chechnya. When Putin's two mandated terms came to an end in 2007–8, rivalries in the security services descended into all out conflict, what was known as the '*silovik* war'. There were already signs towards the end of Putin's third presidency that elite and security service factionalism could once again spin out of control. There were intense intra- and interservice rivalries in the security agencies, and the imprisonment of Ulyukaev served as a warning of what could be in store as Putin's grip relaxed. As Putin entered the 'lame duck' period of his leadership, there would be intense struggles for power and property.

The shadow forces in the 'third state' were in danger of coming into their own. Konstantin Gaaze puts it nicely when he distinguishes between Russia's ruling regime as working 'a day shift and a night shift'. The day shift sees Putin running the government and international affairs, and there are only occasional glimpses of the night shift at work, as in Sechin's legal incarceration of Ulyukaev. Gaaze sums up the dilemma:

As Putin gets ready to serve a fourth presidential term from next March, the main question facing Russia is whether these shadowy night-time rulers will obey the orders of a leader whose time in office is beginning to expire, or whether they will act as freelancers, ignoring the man who created the authoritarian system that they will make use of.

Gaaze is basically describing the dynamics of the dual state. Every attempt to strengthen the power of the state bureaucracy allows it to 'emerge as a competitor to the ruling regime in the Kremlin. The regime would then embark on a course correction, dismantling any state structure that challenged illegitimate decisions. By utilizing its power – either through violence or intimidation – the regime could never allow state institutions to develop and mature.'[9] The administrative regime is forced to keep the institutions of the constitutional state in a permanent condition of underdevelopment and subordination. In 2002, according to Gaaze, this led to a purge of regional elites and in 2005 the nationalisation of several sectors of the economy (notably Yukos in the oil industry). This was a cyclical dynamic that entailed the constant reinvention of the state, followed by its disruption: 'By artificially rotating power between the institutions of the state and the personalized regime, Putin was able to maintain credibility at large while still ensuring that power remained concentrated in his hands.'[10] A similar argument is advanced by the Moscow political analyst Yekaterina Schulman, who argues (as reported by Pavlovsky) that we are now dealing with 'a frozen constitutional state: all the institutions exist but they simply do not work. Why don't they work?' Pavlovsky continues, 'Because around a president who can't be replaced is a narrow elite that benefits from his not being replaced.'[11]

This was the greatest challenge for Putin in his fourth term. His survival as a real, rather than nominal, leader may well require a confrontation with meta-corruption of the third state and the managerialism of the regime. In other words, to stay in power, Putin would have to destroy his system. This would require a strengthening of the modernising and developmental aspects of state power, possibly by the nomination of a respected reformist as prime minister. It could also require the strengthening of the independence of the institutions of the constitutional state – the courts, parliament and the governmental apparatus – drafted as allies against the appropriative behaviour of the third state, and perhaps above all it would require popular mobilisation. This would open the path to greater democratisation, with movements from above joining movements from below. This would entail its own costs as manageability would be reduced, and there would be greater scope for the excess demands warned against by Huntington and the nationalist populism that is characteristic of democratic polities today. Matters could swing the other way, with the relative autonomy of the state extinguished by an overtly authoritarian consolidation, and kleptocracy would become the governing principle. Putin would no doubt prefer to be remembered as the leader who finally brought Russia to democracy, however circuitous the path, rather than as the man who allowed the country to return to the chaos against which he had so long struggled.

Russia without Putin

As Putin eased into his fourth presidential term, Surkov warned that Russia faced 'one hundred years of solitude'. This did not 'mean complete isolation', but Russia's choices would be constrained. Russia's 'mixed breed' culture combined the East and the West: 'He is everyone's relative, but nobody's family'. Russia had to decide whether to become 'a loner in a backwater', or 'an alpha nation that has surged into a big lead' over other countries.[12] In early 2019, Surkov was dismissive of the idea of choice and instead argued, in an article called 'The long-lasting state of Putin', that Putinism was a programme of the Russian government for the next one hundred years.[13] In this system, there would be no power-sharing with oligarchs, social classes, parliament or parties or even with the Russian Orthodox Church, and instead the supreme leader would communicate directly with the people. Surkov argued, 'There is no deep state in Russia (all of it is on display); but there is a deep nation.' All institutions would be subordinated to the main task of communicating and interacting with the supreme ruler. 'Putinism is the ideology of the future', Surkov declared, and will continue to be 'a new type of state' for Russia. The historical precedent he drew on was not the pantheon which Putin himself used (above all Peter the Great), or even Catherine the Great or Stalin, but Lenin – a man whom Putin detested, as well as Kemal Ataturk and Charles de Gaulle. Surkov argued that just as Marx was no Marxist, 'the real Putin is hardly a Putinist'. This would be autocracy without Orthodoxy. The article predictably provoked a storm of criticism. Surkov was portrayed as a Putin sycophant and his article as typical of the low level of intellectual life in Russia. The criticism was apt, since the article sought to recreate a past that never existed.

One of the more thoughtful responses came from Alexander Dugin, the archexponent of new Eurasianism. Surkov's analysis reminded him of the old Soviet slogan about the 'inevitable victory of socialism', and he warned that in Russia a system was typically designated as 'eternal' just before its end. He understood Surkov's purpose as an attempt by the Putinite elite to perpetuate their rule. Their 'solipsism' could not replace 'history and political logic', and therefore Surkov's analysis of Russian politics was 'entirely and completely false in its very foundations'. Putin could dominate Russia's present but could not influence the future immediately after him. So it had been with Gorbachev and Yeltsin (and, it may be added, Stalin), and it would be with Putin. Putin had saved Russia and 'returned it to history', but none of his achievements had become irreversible. Putin's political regime, Dugin rightly noted, was built on compromises 'between all poles and the forces of the state and society'. Putin maintained stability, because he himself was a compromise

> between patriotism and liberalism in the economy, between Eurasianism and Europeanism in international politics, between conservatism and progressism in the sphere of ideas and values, between people and elites, between sovereignty and globalisation, between the 1990s and the non-1990s (that is, 'something else'). But this compromise works only while Putin is there. It is intuitive and authoritarian, based on manual control and constant adjustment of the course by Putin himself. It is not reflected in either the strategy or a project, and does not rely on society as a whole or on the elites.

Putin left the main elements of the 1990s in place despite his criticism of the period, and although he changed the formula by adding patriotism, he retained liberalism in the economy and the entire constitutional framework of the earlier period. Despite its successes, the Putin system had 'no clearly defined vector to the historical future', which meant 'the modern Russian regime has no future'.[14]

Sooner or later Putin's rule will come to an end, and although his system reflected the character of the country, the relationship between man and system is far from deterministic.[15] The fundamental question is whether Putinism can survive without Putin. Equally, can the system achieve an evolutionary path to something else, or will it repeat the traditional Russian pattern of collapse, chaos and reconstitution? Following the reign of Ivan the Terrible, Russia entered the Time of Troubles (*smuta*), and under Catherine the Great, popular discontent exploded in the form of the massive Pugachev rebellion. In 1917, the Tsarist system was swept away by the February revolution, and the short-lived Provisional Government in turn was destroyed by the Bolsheviks. Again, in 1991, the seventy-four-year Soviet system collapsed amid the ruins of the country. Is Russia on the eve of another upheaval on the historical pattern?

Six main paradoxes can be identified. The first is the way that power entraps its holder. There is no evidence that Putin loves power for its own sake but sees it as a means to an end, although Putin clearly appreciates the authority and responsibility that comes with high office. Putin's personal lifestyle is rather modest. He inhabits great palaces and offices, and none grander than the Kremlin itself, but he does not own them; and on relinquishing office, these accoutrements of power will also be renounced. Through intermediaries, Putin has allegedly amassed an offshore retirement pension plan, but despite much speculation there is no public indication of the size or location of Putin's alleged wealth. At the same time, Putin does not talk in grand utopian terms, but this does not mean that he lacks a sense of purpose, even of destiny, as the man chosen by fate to lead the country at a difficult time and to ensure that it ended up more prosperous and more respected in the world. This is the essence of successful statecraft. Many leaders have managed to stay in power for longer than Putin, so sheer longevity in office is a poor measure of the quality of statesmanship.

Putin appears trapped by the system of his own making. He cannot leave, as demonstrated when he kept hold of many of the reins of power during the tandem period, and allegedly he had been reluctant to return to the presidency in 2012. His return had always been the most likely variant, but it was not the only option. In the end, Putin could not leave, fearing the consequences for himself personally, for foreign policy, for the elite that had prospered under him and for the system of rule that he had created. Above all, the system needed his skills to keep it going and would not let him go. A credible version has it that Sechin warned Putin against allowing Medvedev a second term, and if Putin nevertheless had given Medvedev the go-ahead, some sort of elite revolt may have been on the cards. Not surprisingly, in his third term, Putin began by focusing on 'nationalising the elites' by limiting access to foreign bank accounts and property. This was part of the 'de-offshoring' strategy, which meant that elites became dependent on domestic power resources and in turbulent times would find it hard to escape abroad. Putin remained the guarantor of power and privilege, but by the same token his power and privileges require the constant monitoring of the balance between the elites and the factions. The guards were now guarding the guardian.

Second, Putin is very good at balancing hegemonic projects, but he has not been able fully to articulate a hegemonic project of his own. He draws on the power of others, but he never became the centre of a 'Putinite' movement. There is no equivalent in Russia to Peronism, of the sort practiced in Argentina, let alone a fascist movement led by a charismatic leader such as Benito Mussolini in Italy. Putin is a charismatic leader, but it is a paradoxical form of charisma that precisely accentuates its limitations and non-charismatic characteristics. Of course, the regime practices the usual deceptions that typically justify a system's conception of freedom, but it does so by claiming a normality that is abnormal because of its constrained quality. On most developmental parameters, Russia is a normal country, facing the typical challenges of a late developmental state.[16] However, this is an exceptional form of normality, since not only does the regime claim extended prerogatives over political life and exercises the politics of exceptionalism, but in post-communist conditions the ontological foundations of political normality have been absent. It would take a long period of social recuperation for non-exceptional practices to prevail over regime arbitrariness. By stressing its non-charismatic features, Putin's leadership, like the regime as a whole, seeks to normalise itself and shroud its exceptional character in routine, and this could well have provided the space for political normalisation in the long term.

Third, the dual state not only contours politics but also shapes developmental strategies. On the one side, talented engineers are encouraged to apply their skills to developmental projects, as in the impressive modernisation of Rosneft's Tuapse oil refinery (although the engineer responsible was later forced to flee the country), but this is accompanied by a darker side of factional conflict and outright asset-grabbing, as in Rosneft's seizure of Bashneft. In a system in which the normative and developmental states operate according to sanctioned principles of legal and economic rationality, but in which the 'prerogative state' exercises power arbitrarily and without constraints, at any given time it cannot be predicted which order will predominate. Unscrupulous operators take advantage of the tension between normative and prerogative features to achieve their goals. The goals can be positive, as in the struggle against organised crime, but the methods employed often subvert the rule of law. This is the core of the 'paradox' at the heart of Putin's statecraft: progressive policies are applied in a regressive manner.

Fourth, in international politics, Putin condemned American claims to exceptionalism, yet the underlying rationale of his foreign policy is a different form of exceptionalism – notably in the initial claim that Russia was a constituent part of the putative greater West because of its exceptional military (above all, nuclear) weight, diplomatic history and historic status. In other words, Russia sought to become a normal member of the Atlantic community on the grounds that it was an exceptional power. This paradox then has a number of subsidiary aspects. Above all, Russia calls for pluralism in the international system, defined as a polycentrism (multipolarity) in which there would be multiple great powers relating to each other not necessarily through a balance of power politics, since Russia is also rather keen on the 'concert' idea (leading to calls for a new Yalta) in which the rules of the game are established to allow the great powers to cooperate. However, while calling for pluralism externally, a monist political system (as this book has described) took hold at home. Although there remains a tension between the two wings of the dual state, and the various factions imbue the system with a deep level of sociopolitical pluralism, the articulation of interests at the political level takes parapolitical rather than overtly competitively political forms. The deeper paradox is that Russia's ability to make demands in international affairs may well be predicated precisely on the regime's dominance in domestic affairs. The contrast between the demand for pluralism abroad and the monist political system may in the end not be a contradiction but the condition for foreign policy autonomy. If foreign policy became subject to the same factional and institutional constraints as domestic policy, then policy paralysis would in all probability be reproduced. This in turn could generate the further paradox that if Russia had fully adapted to and aligned with the Atlantic power system, this could well have forced it into confrontation with China – an outcome that would in the long run be no less deleterious than confrontation with the West. In short, in foreign policy there are no easy options for Russia, and there is no 'natural', let alone indisputably 'rational', path to adopt.

Fifth, the Putin system devised a complex machinery to maintain power and to insulate itself from social forces, while ensuring that it retained discretion to respond to social and political pressures as it saw fit. But as so often in history, the institutions devised to maintain power can take control over the purposes they are meant to serve. The apparatus of regime power, attended by exceptions to the rule of law, genuine constitutionalism and independent competitive elections, came to trap its incumbents in a cycle of mutual dependencies that reduced the autonomy of each of the actors.

The sixth paradox, and perhaps the one with the most devastating implications, is that the Putin phenomenon, with all of its achievements, drawbacks and contradictions, may well be the system with greatest viability in prevailing conditions. At home, there is no hegemonic historic bloc ready to take power, and with class forces stalemated, the regime-state filled the void. Abroad, stalemate also prevails as competing models of world order rage against each other in a situation pregnant with renewed great power and ideational conflict. This is perhaps intuitively understood by the Russian people and establishment, hence the enduring high levels of popular support for Putin and continued elite loyalty. The support and loyalty are carefully managed, yet undoubtedly reflect genuine sentiments. Putin is not the dictatorial monster portrayed in much of the Western media but finds himself at the helm of a complex governance system that ultimately reflects Russia itself. But the phenomenon will not endure forever, and in the ultimate paradox, the system contains within itself the potential for its own transcendence. The regime rules within the constraints of the constitutional order, and thus it is far from an arbitrary dictatorship but reserves for itself the right to decide on the exception (the Schmittian definition of sovereignty).

In this system, the constitutional state acts as a fundamental resource for the ruling group to maintain itself in power, and there are therefore limits even to what can be defined as the exceptional. Therefore, the constitutional order contains within itself the potential to push back against the arbitrariness of the regime, gradually reduce the scope of the exceptional and ultimately to reduce the discretionary scope of regime power to the parameters that are found in any modern democratic order. The dual state, in which there is a permanent tension between two logics of rule, the legal and the discretionary, contains the potential to reduce the arbitrary elements by strengthening genuine constitutionalism. The ultimate paradox may well be that the revolutionary overthrow of the system of arbitrary power would in all likelihood only intensify arbitrary power as the new revolutionary authorities consolidate their position, purge the old elite, reform institutions and create a new logic of the exception. From this perspective, ultimately the most revolutionary act in contemporary Russia would be to eschew revolution in favour of an evolutionary politics that reinforces the legal order against the arbitrary regime within the system itself. The greatest revolution in Russia would be not to have one. The Putin paradox would thus end with the greatest paradox of all.

NOTES

1 PUTIN AND HIS TIMES

1. For the facets of his character, see Fiona Hill and Clifford Gaddy, *Mr. Putin: Operative in the Kremlin*, new and expanded edition (Washington, DC: Brookings Institution Press, 2015).
2. Personal notes and '"No Putin, No Russia", Says Kremlin Deputy Chief of Staff', *Moscow Times*, 23 October 2014, https://themoscowtimes.com/articles/no-putin-no-russia-says-kremlin-deputy-chief-of-staff-40702.
3. Patrick Lawrence, 'Discerning Vladimir Putin', *Raritan*, Vol. 38, No. 1, Summer 2018, pp. 1–15.
4. For more biographical details, see Richard Sakwa, *Putin: Russia's Choice*, 2nd edn (London: Routledge, 2008), on which this account draws.
5. 'Putin', directed by Andrei Kondrashov, part 2, published online 15 March 2018, https://www.youtube.com/watch?v=YI43tQx4hos.
6. Mark Urban, *The Skripal Files: The Life and Near Death of a Russian Spy* (London: Macmillan, 2018), p. 179.
7. Vladimir Putin, *First Person: An Astonishingly Frank Self-Portrait by Russia's President Vladimir Putin*, with Nataliya Gevorkyan, Natalya Timakova, and Andrei Kolesnikov, translated by Catherine A. Fitzpatrick (London: Hutchinson, 2000), p. 69.
8. Putin, *First Person*, p. 79.
9. Oliver Stone, *The Putin Interviews*. The four-part series was originally broadcast in the US on Showtime between 12 and 15 June 2017, and on BBC2 shortly afterwards. Part 1, https://www.youtube.com/watch?v=QvlKSbYkTXI.
10. Putin, *First Person*, p. 77.
11. Putin, *First Person*, p. 93.
12. Putin, *First Person*, p. 96.
13. The story is exhaustively detailed by Masha Gessen, *The Man without a Face: The Unlikely Rise of Vladimir Putin* (New York: Riverhead Books, 2012).
14. 'Doklad Mariny Sal'e i Yuriya Gladkova o deyatel'nosti V. V. Putina na postu glavy komiteta po vneshnim svyazyam merii Sankt-Peterburga', copyright 'Okalman', 28 November 2007, http://www.compromat.ru/main/putin/saliedokl.htm.
15. Putin, *First Person*, p. 113.

16 Harley Balzer, 'Vladimir Putin on Russian Energy Policy', n.d., *The National Interest*, http://nationalinterest.org/article/vladimir-putin-on-russian-energy-policy-600.

17 Michael Charakopos and Athanasios Dagoumas, 'State Capitalism in Time: Russian Natural Gas at the Service of Foreign Policy', *Europe-Asia Studies*, Vol. 70, No. 3, April 2018, pp. 441–61.

18 Hill and Gaddy, *Mr. Putin*.

19 For a good overview, see Steven Lee Myers, *The New Tsar: The Rise and Reign of Vladimir Putin* (London: Simon & Schuster, 2015). See also Angus Roxburgh, *The Strongman: Vladimir Putin and the Struggle for Russia* (London: I.B. Tauris, 2011).

20 The Russian 'krupneishei geopoliticheskoi katastrofoi veka' should be translated as 'a very great geopolitical catastrophe of the century', as one among other such disasters.

21 Vladimir Putin, 'Annual Address to the Federal Assembly of the Russian Federation', 25 April 2005, http://en.kremlin.ru/events/president/transcripts/22931.

22 Vladimir Putin, 'Russia at the Turn of the Millennium', in Putin, *First Person*, p. 212. The text was originally published as Vladimir Putin, 'Rossiya na rubezhe tysyacheletiya', *Rossiiskaya gazeta*, 31 December 1999.

23 On this, see Larissa Pautova, 'In Stability We Trust? A Brief Sketch of Everyday Semantics', *Russia in Global Affairs*, 6 June 2017, http://eng.globalaffairs.ru/number/In-Stability-We-Trust-18762.

24 Michael McFaul, *From Cold War to Hot Peace: The Inside Story of Russia and America* (London: Allen Lane, 2018).

25 Nicolai N. Petro, 'Are We Reading Russia Right?', *The Fletcher Forum of World Affairs*, Vol. 42, No. 2, Summer 2018, pp. 1–24.

26 Andrey Pertsev, 'President and Patriarch: What Putin Wants from the Orthodox Church', *Carnegie Moscow Centre*, 19 December 2017, http://carnegie.ru/commentary/75058.

27 For an extended version of this argument, see Richard Sakwa, *Russia against the Rest: the Post-Cold War Crisis of World Order* (Cambridge: Cambridge University Press, 2017).

28 Gordon M. Hahn, *Russia's Revolution from above, 1985–2000: Reform, Transition, and Revolution in the Fall of the Soviet Communist Regime* (New Brunswick, NJ: Transaction Publishers, 2002); Michael McFaul, *Russia's Unfinished Revolution: Political Change from Gorbachev to Putin* (Ithaca, NY: Cornell University Press, 2001).

29 For a discussion and references, see Sakwa, *Russia against the Rest*, pp. 121–40.

30 'Founding Act on Mutual Relations, Cooperation and Security between NATO and the Russian Federation', 27 May 1997, http://www.nato.int/cps/en/natohq/official_texts_25468.htm.

31 This is the description on NATO's website describing the NRC, http://www.nato.int/nrc-website/en/about/index.html.

32 'Nato-Russia Council, Rome Declaration, 28 May 2002', http://www.nato.int/nrc-website/media/59487/2002.05.28_nrc_rome_declaration.pdf.

33 'Russland hat Putin zerstört', *Sp iegel Online*, https://magazin.spiegel.de/SP/2017/30/152270478/. Summarised by Paul Goble, 'Putin Hasn't Destroyed Russia

but Rather Russia Has Destroyed Him, Konchalovsky Says', *Window on Eurasia: New Series*, 3 August 2017, http://windowoneurasia2.blogspot.co.uk/2017/08/putin-hasnt-destroyed-russia-but-rather.html.

34 E.g., Ellen Carnaghan, *Out of Order: Russian Political Values in an Imperfect World* (University Park: Pennsylvania State University Press, 2007).

35 For a recent commentary and interesting detail, see Hélène Richard, ' "Be Partisan and Bet it all on Red": When the US Swung a Russian Election', *Le Monde Diplomatique*, March 2019, https://mondediplo.com/2019/03/04russia.

36 Simon Shuster, 'Rewriting Russian History: Did Boris Yeltsin Steal the 1996 Presidential Election?', *Time*, 24 February 2012, http://content.time.com/time/world/article/0,8599,2107565,00.html.

37 Samuel Huntington, *Political Order in Changing Societies* (New Haven, CT: Yale University Press, 1968).

38 Sean P. Roberts, *Putin's United Russia Party* (London: Routledge, 2012).

39 Vladimir Pastukhov, 'O Naval'nom, Strelkove, liberal'noi auditoria i Otkrytou Rossii bez kavychek', *Republic.ru*, 31 July 2017.

40 Aleksei Yu. Zudin, 'Rezhim V. Putina: Kontury novoi politicheskoi sistemy', *Obshchestvennye nauki i sovremennost'*, No. 2 (2003): 67–83.

41 Putin, 'Russia at the Turn of the Millennium', p. 213.

42 Vladislav Surkov, 'Suverenitet – eto politicheskii sinonim konkurentosposobnosti', speech of 7 February 2006, *Politicheskii klass*, 31 March 2006, pp. 15–21.

43 Vladimir Putin, 'Presidential Address to the Federal Assembly', 12 December 2013, http://eng.kremlin.ru/news/6402.

2 STATE, SOCIETY AND REGIME

1 Shaun Walker, *The Long Hangover: Putin's New Russia and the Ghosts of the Past* (New York: Oxford University Press, 2018).

2 The point is also made by Tony Wood, *Russia without Putin: Money, Power and the Myths of the New Cold War* (London: Verso, 2018).

3 Grigory Yavlinsky, *The Putin System: An Opposing View* (New York: Columbia University Press, 2019), p. 19.

4 Yavlinsky, *The Putin System*, p. 45.

5 Yavlinsky, *The Putin System*, p. 66.

6 Convincingly analysed by Josephine T. Andrews, *When Majorities Fail: The Russian Parliament, 1990–1993* (Cambridge: Cambridge University Press, 2002).

7 The disastrous situation is vividly described by Yegor Gaidar, *Days of Defeat and Victory*, translated by Jane Miller (Seattle: University of Washington Press, 1999).

8 Quoted in Maxim Trudolyubov, 'The Hidden, Self-Reliant Russia', Kennan Institute, 16 August 2018, https://www.wilsoncenter.org/blog-post/the-hidden-self-reliant-russia.

9 Michael Urban, *Cultures of Power in Post-Communist Russia: An Analysis of Elite Political Discourse* (New York: Cambridge University Press, 2010).

10 David Frum, *Trumpocracy: The Corruption of the American Republic* (New York: Harper, 2018), p. 53.

11 This is the estimate given by Mikhail Khodorkovsky, in discussion with the author, London, 27 July 2017.

12 Owen Jones, *The Establishment: And How They Get Away with It* (London: Penguin, 2015).

13 For definitions, see Richard Sakwa, *The Crisis of Russian Democracy: The Dual State, Factionalism and the Medvedev Succession* (Cambridge: Cambridge University Press, 2011), pp. 85–130.

14 Marlene Laruelle, 'The Kremlin's Ideological Ecosystems: Equilibrium and Competition', Ponars Eurasia Policy Memo No. 493, November 2017, http://www.ponarseurasia.org/sites/default/files/policy-memos-pdf/Pepm493_Laruelle_Memo_Nov2017_0.pdf.

15 This meta-factional analysis is examined in my Richard Sakwa, *Putin Redux: Power and Contradiction in Contemporary Russia* (London: Routledge, 2014).

16 Henry E. Hale, 'Why Not Parties? Electoral Markets, Party Substitutes, and Stalled Democratization in Russia', *Comparative Politics*, Vol. 37, No. 2, 2005, pp. 147–66; Henry E. Hale, *Why Not Parties in Russia? Democracy, Federalism and the State* (Cambridge: Cambridge University Press, 2006).

17 Vadim Kononenko and Arkady Moshes (eds), *Russia as a Network State: What Works in Russia When Institutions Do Not?* (Basingstoke: Palgrave Macmillan, 2010).

18 For an overview, see Elena Chebankova, 'Contemporary Russian Liberalism', *Post-Soviet Affairs*, Vol. 30, No. 5, 2014, pp. 341–69.

19 Andrei Medushevskii, *Politicheskaya istoriya russkoi revolyutsii: Normy, instituty, formy sotsial'noi mobilizatsii v XX veke* (Moscow: Tsentr gumanitarnykh initsiativov, 2017).

20 INSOR, *Demokratiya: Razvitie rossiiskoi modeli* (Moscow: Ekon-Inform 2008).

21 INSOR, *Rossiya XXI veka: Obraz zhelaemogo zavtra* (Moscow: Ekon-Inform, 2010).

22 INSOR, *Attaining the Future: Strategy 2012* (Moscow: Ekon-Inform, 2011), p. 5.

23 This comes out in all of his main writings. See e.g. Mikhail Khodorkovskii, *Stat'i, dialogi, intervyu* (Moscow: Eksmo, 2010), and his 'memoir', Mikhail Khodorkovskii and Nataliya Gevorkyan, *Tyur'ma i volya* (Moscow: Howard Roark, 2012).

24 Mikhail Khodorkovsky, in discussion with the author, London, 27 July 2017.

25 E.g. Liliya Shevtsova, 'Beremennye revolyutsiei', *Radio Svoboda*, 17 October 2017, https://www.svoboda.org/a/28791261.html.

26 David White, *The Russian Democratic Party Yabloko* (Aldershot: Ashgate, 2006).

27 Dmitry Travin, 'Ordinary Russians Have No One to Tell Them How Miserable Their Lives Are Becoming', *Moscow Times*, 10–16 November 2016, p. 5.

28 Garry Kasparov with Mig Greengard, *Winter Is Coming: Why Vladimir Putin and the Enemies of the Free World Must Be Stopped* (London: Atlantic Books, 2015), pp. xix, xxiv, 9, 263.

29 Kasparov, *Winter Is Coming*, p. 29.

30 On the latter, see Kimberly Martin, 'The "KGB State" and Russian Political and Foreign Policy Culture', *Journal of Slavic Military Studies*, Vol. 30, No. 2, 2017, pp. 131–51.

31. Viktor Cherkesov, 'Nevedomstvennye razmishleniya o professii: Moda na KGB?', *Komsomolskaya Pravda*, 29 December 2004, p. 6; and the postscript is 'Vmesto poslesloviya: Chekistov byvshikh ne byvaet', *Komsomolskaya Pravda*, 29 December 2004, p. 7.

32. Jack Farchy, 'Putin Creates New National Guard to Seal his Authority', *Financial Times*, 6 April 2016, https://www.ft.com/content/3f906d98-fc14-11e5-b3f6-11d5706b613b.

33. Ivan Egorov, 'Kto upravlyaet khaosom', *Rossiiskaya Gazeta*, 11 February 2015, p. 1.

34. Ellen Barry, 'Rally Defying Putin's Party Draws Tens of Thousands', *New York Times*, 10 December 2011, https://www.nytimes.com/2011/12/11/world/europe/thousands-protest-in-moscow-russia-in-defiance-of-putin.html. See also Steve Rosenberg, 'Russia PM Vladimir Putin Accuses US over Poll Protests', *BBC News*, 8 December 2011, https://www.bbc.com/news/world-europe-16084743.

35. Egorov, 'Kto upravlyaet khaosom'.

36. Howard Amos, 'Vladimir Putin's Man in the Balkans', *Politico*, 21 June 2017, http://www.politico.eu/article/vladimir-putin-balkans-point-man-nikolai-patrushev/.

37. Alexander Bortnikov, 'FSB rasstavlyaet aktsenty', *Rossiiskaya gazeta*, 19 December 2017, https://www.rg.ru/2017/12/19/aleksandr-bortnikov-fsb-rossii-svobodna-ot-politicheskogo-vliianiia.html.

38. 'Putin Signs Bill Banning Web Anonymizers in Russia', *RT.com*, 31 July 2017, https://www.rt.com/politics/398087-putin-signs-into-law-bill/.

39. For a recent assessment, see David W. Rivera and Sharon Werning Rivera, 'The Militarization of the Russian Elite under Putin', *Problems of Post-Communism*, Vol. 65, No. 4, 2018, pp. 221–32.

40. Pål Kolstø and Helge Blakkisrud (eds), *The New Russian Nationalism: Imperialism, Ethnicity and Authoritarianism 2000–2015* (Edinburgh: Edinburgh University Press, 2017).

41. Thomas Parland, *The Rejection in Russia of Totalitarian Socialism and Liberal Democracy: A Study of the Russian New Right* (Helsinki: University of Helsinki Societas Scientiarum Fennica, 1993).

42. For a detailed study, see Edwin Bacon, 'Policy Change and the Narratives of Russia's Think Tanks', *Palgrave Communications*, 7 August 2018, https://www.nature.com/articles/s41599-018-0148-y.

43. Marlene Laruelle, 'The Izborsky Club, or the New Conservative Avant-Garde in Russia', *Russian Review*, Vol. 75, No. 4, 2016, pp. 626–44.

44. The website is https://izborsk-club.ru/. The interview is Mikhail Delyagin, 'Liberal'naya verkhushka unichtozhaet Rossiyu v ugodu zapada', 9 January 2018.

45. Charles Clover, *Black Wind, White Snow: The Rise of Russia's New Nationalism* (London: Yale University Press, 2016). The focus of the book is on classical and neo-Eurasianism and has little to say on Russia's 'new nationalism', which is more ethnocentric and inward-looking, and thus opposed to many of the postulates of classical Eurasianism.

46. Analysed by Andrei P. Tsygankov, 'In the Shadow of Nikolai Danilevskii: Universalism, Particularism, and Russian Geopolitical Theory', *Europe-Asia Studies*, Vol. 69, No. 4, 2017, pp. 571–93.

47 Marlene Laruelle (ed.), *Eurasianism and the European Far Right: Reshaping the Europe-Russia Relationship* (Lanham, MD: Lexington Books, 2015).

48 Anton Shekhovtsov, *Russia and the Western Far Right: Tango Noir* (London: Routledge, 2017).

49 The categorisation draws on Richard Sakwa, 'The Age of Eurasia?', in *The Politics of Eurasianism: Identity, Culture and Russia's Foreign Policy*, edited by Mark Bassin and Gonzalo Pozo (Lanham, MD: Rowman & Littlefield, 2016), pp. 205–24.

50 Mark Bassin, *The Gumilev Mystique: Biopolitics, Eurasianism, and the Construction of Community in Modern Russia* (Ithaca, NY: Cornell University Press, 2016).

51 Lev Gumilev, *Ethnogenesis and the Biosphere* (Moscow: Progress Publishers, 1990).

52 Aleksandr Kubyshkin and Aleksandr Sergunin, 'The Problem of the "Special Path" in Russian Foreign Policy', *Russian Politics and Law*, Vol. 50, No. 6, November–December 2012, pp. 7–18.

53 Dugin's thinking is usually described as Neo-Eurasianism, as opposed to the generic neo-Eurasianism described earlier in this paper. The thinking of Dugin and his acolytes is accorded a special section since it is representative of a far more consistent rejection of western liberalism and civilisation than most neo-Eurasianists. To avoid confusion, I term Dugin a New Eurasianist.

54 This point is made by Andrey Tolstoy and Edmund McCaffrey, 'Mind Games: Alexander Dugin and Russia's War of Ideas', *World Affairs Journal*, March 2015, http://www.worldaffairsjournal.org/93030.

55 Anton Barbashin and Hannah Thorburn, 'Putin's Brain: Alexander Dugin and the Philosophy Behind Putin's Invasion of Crimea', *Foreign Affairs*, 31 March 2014, https://www.foreignaffairs.com/articles/russia-fsu/2014-03-31/putins-brain.

56 On the sacralisation of territory, see Aleksandar Pavković, 'Sacralisation of Contested Territory in Nationalist Discourse: A Study of Milošević's and Putin's Public Speeches', *Critical Discourse Studies*, Vol. 14, No. 5, 2017, pp. 497–513.

57 Andreas Umland, 'Why Aleksandr Dugin's "Neo-Eurasianism" is not Eurasianist', *The Politicon*, 1 June 2018, http://thepoliticon.net/essays/546-why-aleksandr-dugins-neo-eurasianism-is-not-eurasianist.html.

58 Cf. Iver B. Neumann, *Russia and the Idea of Europe* (London: Routledge, 1996).

59 Elena Chebankova, 'Ideas, Ideology and Intellectuals in Search of Russia's Political Future', *Daedalus*, Vol. 146, No. 2, Spring 2017, pp. 76–88.

60 Mikhail Zygar, *All the Kremlin's Men: Inside the Court of Vladimir Putin* (New York: Public Affairs, 2016).

61 Serhii Plokhy, *Lost Kingdom: A History of Russian Nationalism from Ivan the Great to Vladimir Putin* (London: Allen Lane, 2017).

62 Zygar, *All the Kremlin's Men*, pp. 243–5.

63 Paolo Flores D'Arcais, 'Anatomy of Berlusconismo', *New Left Review*, No. 68, 2011, p. 139.

64 Antonio Gramsci, 'Notes on Italian History', in *Selections From the Prison Notebooks of Antonio Gramsci*, edited and translated by Quintin Hoare and Geoffrey Nowell Smith (London: Lawrence & Wishart, 1971), pp. 104–20; see also Robert W. Cox, 'Civil Society at the Turn of the Millennium: Prospects for an Alternative World Order', *Review of International Studies*, Vol. 25, No. 1, January 1999, pp. 3–28.

65 My model draws on, although differs in some crucial respects, Ernst Fraenkel, *The Dual State: A Contribution to the Theory of Dictatorship*, translated from the German by E.A. Shils, in collaboration with Edith Lowenstein and Klaus Knorr (New York: Oxford University Press, 1941; reprinted by The Lawbook Exchange, Ltd, 2006).

66 See Neil Robinson, *The Political Economy of Russia* (Lanham, MD: Rowman & Littlefield, 2012).

67 For a powerful application of the model to US politics today, in which he sees the 'Trumanite' security apparatus as an enduring constraint on 'Madisonian institutions', see Michael J. Glennon, *National Security and Double Government* (Oxford: Oxford University Press, 2016).

68 Richard Sakwa, 'The Dual State in Russia', *Post-Soviet Affairs*, Vol. 26, No. 3, July–September 2010, pp. 185–206; Sakwa, *The Crisis of Russian Democracy*.

69 Henry E. Hale, *Patronal Politics: Eurasian Regime Dynamics in Comparative Perspective* (New York: Cambridge University Press, 2015).

70 Henry Hale, 'The Continuing Evolution of Russia's Political System', in *Developments in Russian Politics 9*, edited by Richard Sakwa, Henry Hale and Stephen White (London: Palgrave Macmillan, 2018), pp. 205–16.

71 Irvin Studin, 'Introduction: Ten Theses on Russia in the Twenty-First Century', in *Russia: Strategy, Policy and Administration*, edited by Irvin Studin (London: Palgrave Macmillan, 2018), p. 1.

72 Richard Sakwa, *Putin and the Oligarch: The Khodorkovsky – Yukos Affair* (London: I.B. Tauris, 2014); Richard Sakwa, 'The Trials of Khodorkovsky in Russia', in *Political Trials in Theory and History*, edited by Jens Meierhenrich and Devin O. Pendas (Cambridge: Cambridge University Press, 2016), pp. 369–93.

73 Andrew Wilson, *Virtual Politics: Faking Democracy in the Post-Soviet World* (New Haven, CT: Yale University Press, 2005).

74 This section draws on Richard Sakwa, 'From the Dual to the Triple State?', in *The Challenges for Russia's Politicized Economic System*, edited by Susanne Oxenstierna (London: Routledge, 2015), pp. 128–44.

75 The term is from Jeremy Bransten, 'Public Chamber Criticized as "Smokescreen"', *RFE/RL Russian Political Weekly*, Vol. 5, No. 13, 1 April 2005.

76 James Richter, 'The Ministry of Civil Society? The Public Chambers in the Regions', *Problems of Post-Communism*, Vol. 56, No. 6, November–December 2009, pp. 7–20.

77 'Vstrecha s chlenami Obshchestvennoi palaty', 20 June 2017, http://kremlin.ru/events/president/news/54831.

78 Robert Horvath, 'Putin's "Preventive Counter-Revolution": Post-Soviet Authoritarianism and the Spectre of Velvet Revolution', *Europe-Asia Studies*, Vol. 63, No. 1, January 2011, pp. 1–25; Robert Horvath, *Putin's 'Preventative Counter-Revolution': Post-Soviet Authoritarianism and the Spectre of Velvet Revolution* (London: Routledge, 2013). On Nashi, see Maya Atwal and Edwin Bacon, 'The Youth Movement Nashi: Contentious Politics, Civil Society, and Party Politics', *East European Politics*, Vol. 28, No. 3, 2012, pp. 256–66.

79 Valerii Smirnov, *Front Putina: Protiv kogo?* (Moscow: Algoritm, 2011).

80 'Vladimir Putin Addressed Russian Popular Front Action Forum', 19 December 2017, http://en.kremlin.ru/events/president/news/56410.

81 Daniel Treisman (ed.), *The New Autocracy: Information, Politics, and Policy in Putin's Russia* (Washington, DC: Brookings, 2017).

82 Ellen Mickiewicz, *No Illusions: The Voices of Russia's Future Leaders* (New York: Oxford University Press, 2014).

83 Neil Robinson, 'Russian Neo-Patrimonialism and Putin's "Cultural Turn"', *Europe-Asia Studies*, Vol. 69, No. 2, 2017, p. 353.

84 These are analysed in greater depth in Sakwa, *Putin Redux*.

85 Edwin Bacon, *Inside Russian Politics* (London: Biteback Publishing, 2017), p. 3.

86 Moshe Lewin, *The Gorbachev Phenomenon: A Historical Interpretation* (Berkeley: University of California Press, 1988).

87 For a sophisticated analysis, see Jean L. Cohen, *Civil Society and Political Theory* (Boston, MA: MIT Press, 1994).

88 Stephen Kotkin, *Uncivil Society: 1989 and the Implosion of the Communist Establishment* (New York: Random House, 2009).

89 Robert Putnam, *Making Democracy Work* (Princeton, NJ: Princeton University Press, 1993).

90 Edward C. Banfield, *The Moral Basis of a Backward Society* (New York: Free Press, 1958).

91 See Harry Eckstein, Frederic J. Fleron Jr., Erik P. Hoffmann, and William M. Reissinger, *Can Democracy Take Root in Post-Soviet Russia? Explorations in State-Society Relations* (Lanham, MD: Rowman & Littlefield, 1998).

92 A concise outline of the argument can be found in Yurii S. Pivovarov and A. I. Fursov, 'Russkaya sistema i reformy', *Pro i Contra*, Vol. 4, No. 4, Autumn 1999, pp. 176–97. Pivovarov has published extensively on the issue. See his *Russkaya politika v ee istoricheskom i kul'turnom otnosheniyakh* (Moscow: Rosspen, 2006); 'Russkaya vlast' i publichnaya politika: Zametki istorika o prichinakh neudachi demokraticheskogo tranzita', *Polis*, No. 1, 2006, pp. 12–32; 'Mezhdu kazachestvom i knutom: K stoletiyu russkoi konstitutsii i russkogo parlamenta', *Polis*, No. 2, 2006, pp. 5–26; and *Russkoe nastoyashchee i sovetskoe proshloe* (Moscow: Tsentr gumanitarnykh initsiativ, 2017).

93 Stefan Hedlund, *Russian Path Dependence* (London: Routledge, 2005).

94 Alexander Yanov, *The Russian Challenge and the Year 2000* (Oxford: Blackwell, 1987).

95 David S. Foglesong, 'Putin: From Soulmate to Archenemy', *Raritan*, Vol. 38, No. 1, Summer 2018, pp. 18–41.

96 Elena Chebankova, 'The Evolution of Russia's Civil Society under Vladimir Putin: A Cause for Concern or Grounds for Optimism?', *Perspectives on European Politics and Society*, Vol. 10, No. 3, September 2009, pp. 394–416; Elena Chebankova, *Civil Society in Putin's Russia* (London: Routledge, 2013). Similar arguments are made in Alfred B. Evans Jr., Laura A. Henry and Lisa McIntosh Sundstrom (eds), *Russian Civil Society: A Critical Assessment* (Armonk, NY: M. E. Sharpe, 2005).

97 Cf. Leah Gilbert, 'Crowding out Civil Society: State Management of Social Organisations in Putin's Russia', *Europe-Asia-Studies*, Vol. 68, No. 9, 2016, pp. 1553–78.

98 Catherine Owen, 'A Genealogy of *Kontrol*' in Russia: From Leninist to Neoliberal Governance', *Slavic Review*, Vol. 75, No. 2, Summer 2016, pp. 331–53.

99 Carl Schreck, 'HRW Calls Russian "Foreign Agent" Law "Devastating" for Environmental Groups', *RFE/RL Russia Report*, 21 November 2017, https://www.rferl.org/a/russia-hrw-says-foreign-agent-law-devastating-environmental-groups/28868194.html.

100 Debra Javeline and Sarah Lindemann-Komarova, 'Indigenously Funded Russian Civil Society', Ponars Eurasia Policy Memo No. 496, November 2017, p. 6.

101 Sarah Lindemann-Komarova, 'My Universe Continues to Expand: Challenging the Western Narrative that Russia is Unfree', *The Nation*, 25 April 2017, https://www.thenation.com/article/my-universe-continues-to-expand/.

102 Marlene Laruelle, 'Russia's Militia Groups and their Use at Home and Abroad', *Russia.Nei.Visions*, No. 113 (Paris: IFRI, April 2019), p. 7.

103 Debra Javeline and Sarah Lindemann-Komarova, 'A Balanced Assessment of Russian Civil Society', *Journal of International Affairs*, Vol. 63, No. 2, Spring/Summer 2010, pp. 171–88.

104 These themes are explored in Vladimir Shlapentokh, *Contemporary Russia as a Feudal Society* (New York: Palgrave Macmillan, 2007); and Vladimir Shlapentokh and Anna Arutunyan, *Freedom, Repression, and Private Property in Russia* (Cambridge: Cambridge University Press, 2013).

105 Dmitri Furman, 'Imitation Democracies: The Post-Soviet Penumbra', *New Left Review*, No. 54, November–December 2008, pp. 29–47.

106 For a collection of his essays describing sovereign democracy and other issues, see Vladislav Surkov, *Texts* (Moscow: 'Europe' Publishing House, 2010).

107 Vladislav Surkov, 'Sovereignty: The Political Synonym for Competiveness', in Surkov, *Texts*, pp. 91–135.

3 PUTIN AND POLITICS

1 Carl Schmitt, *The Concept of the Political*, translated and with an introduction by George Schwab (Chicago, IL: University of Chicago Press, 1996), p. 26.

2 Carl Schmitt, *Political Theology*, transated by George Schwab (Chicago, IL: University of Chicago Press, 1985), p. 15, retranslated.

3 Naomi Klein, *The Shock Doctrine: The Rise of Disaster Capitalism* (London: Penguin, 2008).

4 Naomi Klein, *No Is Not Enough* (London: Allen Lane, 2017).

5 Ivan Morozov, *Zamurovannye: Khroniki Kremlevskogo tsentrala* (Moscow: Vagrius, 2009).

6 Marlene Laruelle, *Russian Nationalism: Imaginaries, Doctrines, and Political Battlefields* (London: Routledge, 2018).

7 For details, see Cameron Ross, 'Federalism and Defederalisation in Russia', in *Routledge Handbook of Russian Politics and Society*, edited by Graeme Gill and James Young (London: Routledge, 2012), pp. 140–52.

8. Jean-Francois Ratelle and Emil Aslan Souleimanov, 'A Perfect Counterinsurgency? Making Sense of Moscow's Policy of Chechenisation', *Europe-Asia Studies*, Vol. 68, No. 8, October 2016, pp. 1287–1314.

9. Maksim Kimerling, 'Gleb Pavlovsky: "kreml bol'she ne "teatr Karabasa-Barabasa"', *Fontanka.ru*, 7 January 2018, http://www.fontanka.ru/2018/01/05/032/.

10. Elena Milashina, 'Ubiistvo chesti', *Novaya gazeta*, 3 April 2017, pp. 12–13. See also Elena Milashina and Irina Gordienko, 'Lyudi teryayut strakh', *Novaya gazeta*, April 2017, pp. 12–13.

11. Kathrin Hille, 'Chechnya Faces Uphill Battle Wooing Tourists to Ski Resort', *Financial Times*, 30 January 2018, p. 7.

12. Robert Bruce Ware (ed.), *The Fire Below: How the Caucasus Shaped Russia* (New York: Bloomsbury, 2013).

13. Marlène Laruelle, 'Kadyrovism: Hardline Islam as a Tool of the Kremlin?', *Russie.Nei. Visions*, No. 99 (Paris: IFRI, March 2017), p. 8.

14. Amy Knight, 'Putin's Monster', *New York Review of Books*, 19 May 2017, http://www.nybooks.com/daily/2017/05/19/putins-monster-ramzan-kadyrov/.

15. Associated Press, 'Vladimir Putin Accuses Lenin of Placing a "Time Bomb" Under Russia', *Guardian*, 25 January 2016, https://www.theguardian.com/world/2016/jan/25/vladimir-putin-accuses-lenin-of-placing-a-time-bomb-under-russia. For the 'atomic bomb' quotation, see 'Zasedanie Soveta po nauke i obrazovaniyu', 21 January 2016, http://kremlin.ru/events/president/news/51190.

16. Timothy Snyder, 'Ivan Ilyin, Putin's Philosopher of Russian Fascism', *New York Review of Books*, http://www.nybooks.com/daily/2018/03/16/ivan-ilyin-putins-philosopher-of-russian-fascism/.

17. James H. Billington, *Russia in Search of Itself* (Washington, DC: Woodrow Wilson Center Press, 2004).

18. Vladimir Putin, 'Address to the Federal Assembly', 12 December 2012, http://eng.kremlin.ru/news/4739.

19. Alexei Miller, 'The Russian Revolution of 1917: History, Memory, and Politics', Valdai Paper No. 81, January 2018, http://valdaiclub.com/a/valdai-papers/valdai-paper-81-the-russian-revolution-of-1917/.

20. For a recent account, see Dominic Lieven, *Towards the Flame: Empire, War and the End of Tsarist Russia* (London: Penguin, 2016).

21. For an assessment, see Ivan Kurilla, 'History and Memory in Russia during the 100-Year Anniversary of the Great Revolution', Ponars Eurasia Policy Memo No. 503, January 2018.

22. Miller, 'The Russian Revolution of 1917', p. 9.

23. For discussion, see Anna Yarovaya, 'The First Steps towards Exonerating Russian Gulag Historian Yuri Dmitriyev', *oDR*, 2 March 2018, https://www.opendemocracy.net/od-russia/anna-yarovaya/the-first-steps-towards-exonerating-yuri-dmitriyev.

24. Alec Luhn, 'Hunt for Lost Gulag Graves Unearths Uncomfortable Truths in Russia', *Guardian*, 4 August 2017, p. 23.

25. Alexander Baunov, 'Who Will Win the Battle for the Bolshoi?', *Carnegie.ru*, 27 July 2017, http://carnegie.ru/2017/07/27/who-will-win-battle-for-bolshoi-pub-72669.

26. Luhn, 'Hunt for Lost Gulag Graves', p. 23.
27. Thomas Sherlock, 'Russian Politics and the Soviet Past: Reassessing Stalin and Stalinism under Vladimir Putin', *Communist and Post-Communist Studies*, Vol. 49, 2016, pp. 45–59.
28. Sherlock, 'Russian Politics and the Soviet Past', p. 47.
29. Jonathan Steele, 'Obituary of Arseny Roginsky', *Guardian*, 5 January 2018, p. 37.
30. An argument made by Sergei Solovyov, 'Attempts at Decommunization in Russia Upset De-Stalinization', *Russia in Global Affairs*, 17 January 2019, https://eng.globalaffairs.ru/number/Attempts-at-Decommunization-in-Russia-Upset-de-Stalinization-19917.
31. Wood, *Russia without Putin*.
32. Vladimir Putin, 'Opening of Wall of Sorrow Memorial to Victims of Political Repression', *Kremlin.ru*, 30 October 2017, http://en.kremlin.ru/events/president/news/55948.
33. E.g., Andrei Kolesnikov, 'A Past that Divides: Russia's New Official History', *Carnegie Moscow Centre*, 5 October 2017, http://carnegie.ru/2017/10/05/past-that-divides-russia-s-new-official-history-pub-73304.
34. 'Vladimir Putin Accuses Lenin of Placing a "Time Bomb" Under Russia'.
35. Kolesnikov, 'A Past That Divides'.
36. Vladimir Putin, 'Meeting of the Valdai International Discussion Club', 19 October 2017, http://en.kremlin.ru/events/president/news/55882.
37. Pål Kolstø, 'Crimea vs. Donbas: How Putin Won Russian Nationalist Support – and Lost it Again', *Slavic Review*, Vol. 75, No. 3, Fall 2016, pp. 702–725; Pål Kolstø, 'Marriage of Convenience? Collaboration between Nationalists and Liberals in the Russian Opposition 2011–12', *Russian Review*, Vo. 75, No. 4, 2016, pp. 645–63.
38. Such divided views come out in polls conducted by the Levada Centre, including consistent criticism that Putin had failed to deal with corruption. E.g., see poll published on 24 April 2017, 'Vladimir Putin: Otnoshenie i otsenki', http://www.levada.ru/2017/04/24/15835/print/.
39. Kseniya Kirillova, 'The Kremlin Guard: Russia's Pro-Government Youth Organizations', *Defense Report*, 30 April 2018, httpsh//defencereport.com.
40. Andrei Kolesnikov and Evgeniya Albats, 'Rosobrnadzor i Poltavchenko: Protiv Putina?', *New Times*, 2 October 2017, https://newtimes.ru/articles/detail/119423.
41. Neil MacFarquar, 'Putin's Re-election is Assured: Let the Succession Fight Begin', *New York Times*, 11 December 2017, https://www.nytimes.com/2017/12/11/world/europe/russia-vladimir-putin-election.html.
42. Ben Noble, 'Volodin's Duma', *Intersection*, 13 December 2016, http://intersectionproject.eu/article/politics/volodins-duma.
43. Irina Olimpieva, 'Why Russian Officials Want to Control the Social Sciences', *Moscow Times*, 11 July 2017, https://themoscowtimes.com/articles/why-russian-officials-want-to-control-the-social-sciences-58367.
44. Simon Kuper, 'What Putin Learnt from Berlusconi', *Financial Times*, 31 May 2013, https://www.ft.com/content/74ff0f94-c8bd-11e2-acc6-00144feab7de.

45　Fred Weir, 'Russia's Media Scene: Not Just a State Affair', *Christian Science Monitor*, 6 February 2018, https://www.csmonitor.com/World/Europe/2018/0206/Russia-s-media-scene-not-just-a-state-affair.

46　'Ezhegodnaya bol'shaya press-konferentsiya', , 14 February 2008, http://kremlin.ru/events/president/transcripts/24835.

47　Yuri Lobunov, 'Putin's 150 Promises', *Intersection*, 15 December 2017, http://intersectionproject.eu/article/politics/putins-150-promises.

48　Max Weber, 'Politics as a Vocation', in *From Max Weber: Essays in Sociology*, edited by H. H. Gerth and C. Wright Mills (New York: Oxford University Press, 1958), pp. 125–6.

49　For a recent analysis, see Archie Brown, *The Myth of the Strong Leader: Political Leadership in the Modern Age* (London: Vintage, 2015).

50　Carl Schreck, 'From "Not Us" to "Why Hide It?": How Russia Denied Its Crimea Invasion, Then Admitted It', *RFE/RL Russia Report*, 26 February 2019, https://www.rferl.org/a/from-not-us-to-why-hide-it-how-russia-denied-its-crimea-invasion-then-admitted-it/29791806.html.

51　Helena Goscilo and Vlad Strukov (eds), *Celebrity and Glamour in Contemporary Russia: Shocking Chic* (London: Routledge, 2010).

52　Valerie Sperling, 'Putin's Macho Personality Cult', *Communist and Post-Communist Studies*, Vol. 49, No. 1, 2016, p. 15.

53　Helena Goscilo, *Putin as Celebrity and Cultural Icon* (London: Routledge, 2014).

54　Owen, 'A Genealogy of *Kontrol'* in Russia'.

55　Vladimir Putin, 'Otkrytoe pis'mo Vladimira Putina k Rossiiskim izbiratelyam', *Izvestiya*, 25 February 2000, p. 5.

56　Tatyana Stanovaya, 'Putin's Post-Political Government', *Carnegie Moscow Centre*, 26 June 2017, http://carnegie.ru/commentary/71355.

57　These words are from the 'mission statement' of the journal *Stasis*, published by the European University at St Petersburg.

58　Cf. Andrew Monaghan, 'The Vertikal: Power and Authority in Russia', *International Affairs*, Vol. 88, No. 1, January 2012, pp. 1–16; Andrew Monaghan, 'Defibrllating the Vertikal? Putin and Russian Grand Strategy', Russia and Eurasia Programme Research Paper (London: Chatham House, October 2014).

59　Joel S. Hellman, 'Winners Take All: The Politics of Partial Reform in Postcommunist Transitions', *World Politics*, Vol. 50, No. 2, 1998, pp. 203–234.

60　Philip Hanson, 'The Russian Economic Puzzle: Going Forwards, Backwards or Sideways?' *International Affairs*, Vol. 83, No. 5, September–October 2007, pp. 869–89.

61　As described in Sakwa, *Putin Redux*.

62　Joachim Zweynert and Ivan Boldyrev, 'Conflicting Patterns of Thought in the Russian Debate on Modernisation and Innovation 2008–2013', *Europe-Asia Studies*, Vol. 69, No. 6, August 2017, p. 922.

63　Zweynert and Boldyrev, 'Conflicting Patterns', pp. 922–3.

64　Zweynert and Boldyrev, 'Conflicting Patterns', p. 924.

65　Zweynert and Boldyrev, 'Conflicting Patterns', p. 924.

4 POLITICS AND THE THIRD STATE

1. Samuel A. Greene, *Moscow in Movement: Power and Opposition in Putin's Russia* (Stanford, CA: Stanford University Press, 2014).
2. Dmitry Medvedev, 'Address to the Federal Assembly', 22 December 2011, http://news.kremlin.ru/news/14088.
3. Dan Healey, *Russian Homophobia from Stalin to Sochi* (London: Bloomsbury Academic, 2018), p. 199.
4. Joel Moses, 'Political Rivalry and Conflict in Putin's Russia', *Europe-Asia Studies*, Vol. 69, No. 6, August 2017, pp. 961–88.
5. Moscow Times, 'Yekaterinburg Mayor Evgeny Roizman on Why Russians Should Boycott the Elections', 29 January 2018, https://themoscowtimes.com/articles/-not-voting-is-a-matter-of-principle-60319.
6. Maksim Trudolyubov, 'Dva gosudarstva Vladimira Putina: Obychnoe i oprichnina', *Republic.ru*, 20 February 2018, https://republic.ru/posts/89598.
7. 'Russia Closes 93 Prisons in 7 Years Due to More Lenient Laws – Official', *RT.com*, 3 September 2018, https://www.rt.com/russia/437479-russia-closes-93-prisons/.
8. For a vivid description of how the system started in the Yelsin years, see Anna Arutunyan, *The Putin Mystique: Inside Russia's Power Cult* (Talton Edge: Skyscraper Publications, 2014), pp. 85–102.
9. Arutunyan, *The Putin Mystique*, p. 97.
10. Andrei Soldatov and Irina Borogan, *The New Nobility: The Restoration of Russia's Security State and the Enduring Legacy of the KGB* (New York: Public Affairs, 2010).
11. See Joshua Yaffa, 'Putin's Shadow Cabinet and the Bridge to Crimea', *New Yorker*, 29 May 2017, https://www.newyorker.com/magazine/2017/05/29/putins-shadow-cabinet-and-the-bridge-to-crimea.
12. 'Valerii Solovei: "Dazhe druz'ya prezidenta ne vsegda mogut vliyat' na prinyatie reshenii"', *New Times*, 25 April 2017, http://newtimes.ru/stati/temyi.
13. Clifford G. Gaddy and Barry W. Ickes, *Russia's Addiction: How Oil, Gas, and the Soviet Legacy have Shaped a Nation's Fate* (Washington, DC: Brookings Institution Press, 2016).
14. O. E. Bessonova, *Razdatochnya ekonomika Rossii: Evolyutsiya cherez transformatsiyu* (Moscow: Rosspen, 2006).
15. Simon Kordonskii, *Rossiya: Pomestnaya federatsiya* (Moscow: Evropa, 2010). Russia, of course, did not have feudalism in the technical sense, so the term is applied here symbolically in a manner familiar to Western readers.
16. Arutunyan, *The Putin Mystique*, p. 113.
17. Mark Galeotti, *The Vory: Russia's Super Mafia* (New Haven, CT: Yale University Press, 2018).
18. AFP, 'Russia's Feared Mafia Leaders in "Shock" as Vladimir Putin shows Who's Boss', 13 March 2019, https://www.scmp.com/news/world/russia-central-asia/article/3001483/russias-feared-mafia-leaders-shock-vladimir-putin.
19. For an assessment, see Karen Dawisha, 'Is Russia's Foreign Policy That of a Corporatist-Kleptocratic Regime?', *Post-Soviet Affairs*, Vol. 27, No. 4, 2011, pp. 331–65.

20 Luke Harding, *Mafia State: How One Reporter Became an Enemy of the Brutal New Russia* (London: Guardian Books, 2011).

21 Misha Glenny, *McMafia: Seriously Organised Crime* (London: Vintage, 2017).

22 These are described by Alena Ledeneva, *Can Russia Modernise? Sistema, Power Networks, and Informal Governance* (Cambridge: Cambridge University Press, 2013).

23 John Kennedy, 'Entrepreneurship and Limited Access: Rethinking Business-State Relations in Russia', *Post-Communist Economies*, published online 19 May 2017, http://www.tandfonline.com/doi/full/10.1080/14631377.2017.1314999.

24 For the experience of court users, see Kathryn Hendley, 'Contempt for Court in Russia: The Impact of Litigation Experience', *Review of Central and East European Law*, Vol. 42, 2017, pp. 134–68.

25 Kathryn Hendley, *Everyday Law in Russia* (Ithaca, NY: Cornell University Press, 2017).

26 Dmitry Travin, 'Pochemu president ne ogranichit davlenie silovykh struktur na biznes', *Republic*, 10 October 2017, https://republic.ru/posts/86874.

27 Transparency International, 'Corruption Perception Index 2018', https://www.transparency.org/cpi2018.

28 Vladimir Soloviev, *Empire of Corruption: The Russian National Pastime*, translated by Matthew Hyde (Tilburg: Glagoslav, 2014).

29 TASS, 'Top Prosecutor Shows Corruption in Russia Caused Losses of $2.5 bln over Past Three Years', 8 December 2017, http://tass.com/politics/979806.

30 Stanislav Markus, *Property, Predation and Protection: Piranha Capitalism in Russia and Ukraine* (Cambridge: Cambridge University Press, 2015).

31 Thomas Firestone, 'Criminal Corporate Raiding in Russia', *International Lawyer*, Vol. 42, No. 4, Winter 2008, pp. 1207–29; Anton Kazun, 'Violent Corporate Raiding in Russia: Preconditions and Protective Factors', *Demokratizatsiya: The Journal of Post-Soviet Democratization*, Vol. 23, No. 4, Fall 2015, pp. 459–84.

32 Alexander Lukin, 'Putin's Regime and Its Alternatives', *Strategic Analysis*, Vol. 42, No. 2, 2018, p. 137.

33 Viktor Martyanov, 'Soslovnoe gosudarstvo v modernom obshchestve ili bor'ba s rossiiskoi korruptsiei kak problema sokrashcheniya statusnoi renty', *Obshchestvennye nauki i sovremennost'*, No. 2, 2016, p. 95.

34 Lukin, 'Putin's Regime and its Alternatives', p. 141.

35 Gulnaz Sharafutdinova, *Political Consequences of Crony Capitalism inside Russia*, Contemporary European Politics and Society (Notre Dame, IN: University of Notre Dame Press, 2011).

36 Vladimir Putin, 'Presidential Address to the Federal Assembly', *Kremlin.ru*, 3 December 2015, http://en.kremlin.ru/events/president/news/50864.

37 Philip Hanson, 'Reiderstvo: Asset Grabbing in Russia', Russia and Eurasia PP 2014/03 (London: Chatham House, 2014), p. 3.

38 Quoted in 'Police Brutality in Russia: Cope for Hire', *Economist*, 18 March 2010, http://www.economist.com/node/15731344/print.

39 Vladimir Pastukhov, 'Legenda No 1917', *Novaya gazeta*, 22 August 2013. For an extended analysis, see Vladimir Pastukhov, *Restavratsiya vmesto reformatsii: Dvadtsat' let, kotorye potryasli Rossiyu* (Moscow: OGI, 2012).

40 Ben Aris, 'Meet the Stoligarchs, Putin's Pals who Control a Fifth of the Russian Economy', *BNE Intellinews*, 11 July 2016, http://www.intellinews.com/meet-the-stoligarchs-putin-s-pals-who-control-a-fifth-of-the-russian-economy-99918/.

41 Gessen, *The Man without a Face*.

42 Karen Dawisha, *Putin's Kleptocracy: Who Owns Russia?* (New York: Simon & Schuster, 2014).

43 Yurii Felshtinsky and Vladimir Pribylovsky, *The Age of Assassins: The Rise and Rise of Vladmir Putin* (London: Gibson Square, 2008), pp. 87–92.

44 Soldatov and Borogan, *The New Nobility*, p. 241.

45 For a typical analysis along these lines, see Maksim Kalashnikov, *Putin inkorporeited: Kak Putinu obustroit' Rossiyu* (Moscow: Algoritm/Eksmo, 2013).

46 For a good discussion, see Henry Foy, '"We Need to Talk about Igor": The Rise of Russia's Most Powerful Oligarch', *Financial Times*, 1 March 2018, https://www.ft.com/content/dc7d48f8-1c13-11e8-aaca-4574d7dabfb6.

47 Brian D. Taylor, *State Building in Putin's Russia: Policing and Coercion after Communism* (Cambridge: Cambridge University Press, 2011).

48 Boris Yamshanov and Viktor Vasenin, 'Neposredstvennaya zhizn': Predlozheniya ot Bastrykina – sozdat' ediniy sledstevnnyi komitet i vvesti otchety o raskhodakh chinovnikov', *Rossiiskaya gazeta*, 7 September 2010.

49 Karina Orlova, 'One Man's Land: Behind the FSB's Attack on Russia's Investigative Committee', *The American Interest*, 20 July 2016, https://www.the-american-interest.com/2016/07/20/who-is-behind-the-fsbs-attack-on-russias-investigative-committee/.

50 Anna Romanova and Boris Korban, 'Konets spetsnaza Sechina', *New Times*, 4 December 2017, https://newtimes.ru/articles/detail/132259.

51 Natal'ya Kozlova, 'Kak dela?', *Rossiiskaya gazeta*, 25 July 2017, p. 1.

52 Jack Farchy, 'Putin Creates New National Guard to Seal his Authority', *Financial Times*, 6 April 2016, https://www.ft.com/content/3f906d98-fc14-11e5-b3f6-11d5706b613b; Orlova, 'One Man's Land'.

53 Joshua Yaffa, 'The Double Sting: A Power Struggle between Russia's Rival Security Agencies', *New Yorker*, 27 July 2015, http://www.newyorker.com/magazine/2015/07/27/the-double-sting.

54 Kozlova, 'Kak dela?', p. 1.

55 Oleg Shchedrov, 'Russia's Medvedev Frustrated by Slow Reforms', *Reuters*, 31 July 2008, https://uk.reuters.com/article/us-russia-medvedev- business-idUKL161861520080731.

56 Leonid Ragozin, 'When Russian Officials "Nightmare" Your Business', *Bloomberg*, 29 January 2018, https://www.bloomberg.com/news/features/2018-01-29/when-russian-officials-nightmare-your-business-you-can-lose-everything-even-your-life.

57 Yury Saprykin, 'The Serebrennikov Case: A Theater of the Absurd', *Moscow Times*, 16 January 2018, https://themoscowtimes.com/articles/serebrennikov-case-theater-absurd-60193.

58 Andrey Arkhangelsky, 'Setting the Boundaries: Russia's New Cultural State Policy', *Carnegie Moscow Centre*, 21 September 2017.
59 Yulia Latynina, '"Duraki" nanosyat otvetnyi udar', *Novaya gazeta*, No. 92, 23 August 2017, pp. 4–5.
60 Xan Brooks, 'The Big Chill', *Guardian Review*, 13 January 2018, p. 15.
61 For background, see '*Denis Nikandrov*', *Crimerussia.ru*, 1 August 2016.
62 'Back To the "Wild Nineties"', *Khodorkovsky.com*, 1 August 2016, http://www.khodorkovsky.com/back-wild-nineties/.
63 'Sud ostavil pod arestom generala CK Denisa Nikandrova', *TVRain*, 4 August 2016, https://tvrain.ru/news/sud_priznal_zakonnymnezakonnym_arest-generala_sk_nikandrova.
64 Peter Hobson, 'Hunter Becomes Prey: The Fall of a Russian "Attack-Dog" Investigator', *Moscow Times*, 29 July 2016, https://www.themoscowtimes.com/2016/07/29/hunter-becomes-prey-the-fall-of-a-russian-attack-dog-investigator-a54772.
65 '*Denis Nikandrov*', *Crimerussia.ru*, 1 August 2016.
66 Sakwa, *Putin Redux*, p.100.
67 Hobson, 'Hunter Becomes Prey'.
68 *Denis Nikandrov*', *Crimerussia.ru*, 1 August 2016.
69 Tom Parfitt, 'Moscow Investigators Held Over Links to Mobster', *The Times*, 20 July 2016, p. 30.
70 See, e.g., Sakwa, *Putin Redux*, pp. 61–3, 94–101, 283–5; Bettina Renz, 'The Russian Power Ministries and Security Services', in *Routledge Handbook of Russian Politics and Society*, edited by Graeme Gill and James Young (London: Routledge, 2012), pp. 370–90; US State Department, 'Russia 2015 Human Right Report', sections 1c, 1d and 1e, pp. 4–19; Freedom House, 'Russia – Nations in Transit 2016', pp. 2, 4–5, 10–11.
71 Orlova, 'One Man's Land'.
72 'Abuse of Office, Bribes & Embezzlement: Top 5 Recent Russian Corruption Scandals', *RT.com*, 18 December 2017, https://www.rt.com/politics/413538-top-5-recent-russian-corruption/.
73 'Colonel Zakharchenko', *Khodorkovsky.com*, 3 October 2016, http://www.khodorkovsky.com/colonel-zakharchenko/.
74 Danila Galperovich, 'Russian Economic Minister's Arrest: Part of Crackdown on Government "Liberals"?', *VOA*, 19 November 2016, https://www.voanews.com/a/russian-economics-minister-arrest-part-of-crackdown-on-government-liberals/3602721.html.
75 Evgeniya Pismennaya, Ilya Arkhipov, Henry Meyer and Irina Reznik, 'A Corruption Trial Splits the Kremlin', *Bloomberg*, 11 October 2017, https://www.bloomberg.com/news/articles/2017-10-11/a-corruption-trial-splits-the-kremlin.
76 Vladimir Putin, 'Annual News Conference', *Kremlin.ru*, 14 December 2017, http://en.kremlin.ru/events/president/news/56378.
77 Ivan Davydov, 'The Fate of Putin's Minister', *Intersection*, 13 December 2017, http://intersectionproject.eu/article/politics/fate-putins-minister.

78 Konstantin Gaaze, 'Corruption Case Puts Sechin in the Spotlight', *Carnegie Moscow Centre*, 23 August 2017, http://carnegie.ru/commentary/72888.

79 Anton Shekhovtsov, 'Putin's Russia 4.0: What Can We Expect from It?', 14 January 2018, http://www.tango-noir.com/2018/01/14/putins-russia-4-0-what-can-we-expect-from-it/.

80 Kenneth Rapoza, 'To Some in Russia, Oil Chief more Feared than Putin', *Forbes.com*, 9 January 2018, https://www.forbes.com/sites/kenrapoza/2018/01/09/to-some-in-russia-oil-chief-more-feared-than-putin/#4c0780252f34.

81 Il'ya Rozhdestvenskii, 'Novye lubyanskie', *New Times*, 11 September 2017.

82 Olga Romanova, 'The Billionaire Adviser: A Story of Russia's Anti-Corruption Campaign', *Carnegie Moscow Centre*, 16 October 2017, http://carnegie.ru/commentary/73422.

83 Tatyana Stanovaya, 'The Kremlin Hierarchy Is Fast decaying', *Moscow Times*, 22 February 2019, https://www.themoscowtimes.com/2019/02/22/the-kremlin-hierarchy-is-fast-decaying-a64589.

84 Max Seddon, 'The Russophile Investor Languishing in a Moscow Cell', *Financial Times*, 23/24 February 2019, p. 11.

85 Ekaterina Trifonova, 'Sposoby "Ne Koshmarit' Biznes" uzhe Pridumany', *Nezavisimaya gazeta*, 20 March 2018, p. 3.

86 Vladimir Putin, 'Presidential Address to the Federal Assembly', *Kremlin.ru*, 20 February 2019, http://en.kremlin.ru/events/president/news/59863.

87 'Bulldogs under the Rug', *Economist*, 28 March 2019, https://www.economist.com/europe/2019/03/28/russias-new-purges-rattle-the-elite.

88 'More than 1,300 Russian Officials Fired for Corruption in 2018', *Moscow Times*, 27 March 2019, https://www.themoscowtimes.com/2019/03/27/more-than-1300-russian-officials-fired-for-corruption-in-2018-prosecutors-a64970.

89 Denis Vardanyan, 'Benefitsiary martovskoi pobedy', *New Times*, 5 February 2018, https://newtimes.ru/articles/detail/145138?utm_source=twitter.com&utm_medium=social&utm_campaign=thenewtimes&utm_content=instant.

90 Anton Troianovski, 'Q & A: Sanctioned Putin Ally Holds out Hope That Trump Will Boost Russia Ties', *Washington Post*, 10 February 2018, https://www.washingtonpost.com/news/worldviews/wp/2018/02/10/qa-sanctioned-putin-ally-holds-out-hope-that-trump-will-boost-russia-ties/?utm_term=.134eb9ae7981.

91 Vardanyan, 'Benefitsiary martovskoi pobedy'.

5 MANAGED CAPITALISM

1 Peter Reddaway and Dmitri Glinski, *The Tragedy of Russia's Reforms: Market Bolshevism against Democracy* (Washington, DC: The United States Institute of Peace Press, 2001).

2 Maksim Trudolyubov, *Chastnoe prostranstvo, vlast' i sobstevennost v Rossii* (Moscow: Novoe Izdatel'stvo, 2015), p. 12.

3 Barrington Moore, *Social Origins of Dictatorship and Democracy: Lord and Peasant in the Making of the Modern World* (Boston: Beacon Press, 1967), p. 418.

4. Aleksandr Rar, *Vladimir Putin: 'Nemets' v Kremle*, translated from the German by I. Rozanov (Moscow: Olma-Press, 2001); Alexander Rahr, *Wladimir Putin: Der 'Deutsche' im Kreml*, 2nd edn (Munich: Universitas Publishing House, 2000).

5. Jan-Werner Müller, 'What do Germans Think about When They Think about Europe?', *London Review of Books*, Vol. 34, No. 3, 9 February 2012, pp. 18–19.

6. Chris Miller, *Putinomics: Power and Money in Resurgent Russia* (Chapel Hill: University of North Carolina Press, 2018).

7. Douglass C. North, John Joseph Wallis and Barry R. Weingast, *Violence and Social Orders: A Conceptual Framework for Interpreting Recorded Human History* (Cambridge: Cambridge University Press, 2009).

8. Daron Acemoglu and James A. Robinson, *Why Nations Fail? The Origins of Power, Prosperity, and Poverty* (London: Profile Books, 2013).

9. Alexander Auzan, 'The Future of Russia's Institutions', in *Russia: Strategy, Policy and Administration*, edited by Irvin Studin (London: Palgrave Macmillan, 2018), p. 44.

10. Auzan, 'The Future of Russia's Institutions', p. 47.

11. Paul Kennedy, *The Rise and Fall of the Great Powers: Economic Change and Military Conflict from 1500 and 2000* (London: Unwin Hyman, 1988).

12. These and other legacies are listed by Christopher Mark Davis, 'Russia's Changing Economic and Military Relations with Europe and Asia from Cold War to the Ukraine Conflict: The Impacts of Power Balances, Partnerships, and Economic Warfare', Korea Institute for International Economic Policy (KIEP), *KIEP Studies in Comprehensive Regional Strategies Collected Papers (International Edition)* (Seoul: KIEP, 2016), p. 207.

13. Clifford G. Gaddy and Barry W. Ickes, 'Russia's Virtual Economy', *Foreign Affairs*, Vol. 77, No. 5, September–October 1998, pp. 53–67; Clifford G. Gaddy, and Barry W. Ickes, *Russia's Virtual Economy* (Washington, DC: Brookings Institution Press, 2002).

14. Gabe LaMonica, 'McCain Calls Russia a "Gas Station"', *CNN*, 22 April 2014, http://politicalticker.blogs.cnn.com/2014/04/22/mccain-calls-russia-a-gas-station/.

15. Konstantin Gaaze, 'The Accidental Formation of Russia's War Coalition', *Carnegie Moscow Centre*, 22 June 2017, http://carnegie.ru/commentary/71340.

16. *Strategiya 2020: Novaya model' rosta – novaya sotsial'naya politika*, http://2020strategy.ru/data/2012/03/14/1214585998/1itog.pdf.

17. Sergei Guriev, 'How Transitional Institutions Could Transform Russia's Economy', *Carnegie.ru*, 13 November 2017, http://carnegie.ru/commentary/74790.

18. Aleksei Krivoshapko and Mattias Vestman, 'Kak izmerit' gosudarstvo-2', *Vedomosti*, 15 November 2017, p. 6.

19. David Szakonyi, *Governing Business: The State and Business in Russia* (Philadelphia, PA: Foreign Policy Research Institute, 2018), p. 22.

20. For an introduction to the issue, see Thomas F. Remington, 'Economic Inequality in Russia: Sources and Consequences', *Russian Analytical Digest*, No. 187, 25 July 2016, pp. 4–7.

21. Shaun Walker, 'Unequal Russia: Is Anger Stirring in the Global Capital of Inequality?', *Guardian*, 25 April 2017, https://www.theguardian.com/inequality/2017/apr/25/unequal-russia-is-anger-stirring-in-the-global-capital-of-inequality.

22 These data from Philip Hanson, 'Notes on the Economies of Three Rival Powers: the US, China and Russia', paper for CREES annual conference, 1–3 June 2018.
23 'The Top 1% Controls a Third of the Wealth', *Meduza*, 23 January 2019, https://meduza.io/en/feature/2019/01/23/the-top-1-controls-a-third-of-the-wealth-and-the-poor-are-getting-poorer-how-russia-became-one-of-the-most-unequal-places-on-earth.
24 Igor Nikolaev, 'Report Outlines Socioeconomic Inequality in Russia's Regions', *Moskovsky Komsomolets*, 22 March 2017.
25 Evan Gershkovich, ' "A Point of No Return": Russia's Libertarians Lead Protest against "Sovereign Internet" ', *Moscow Times*, 10 March 2019, https://www.themoscowtimes.com/2019/03/10/point-of-no-return-russias-libertarians-lead-protest-against-sovereign-internet-a64758.
26 Andrei Soldatov and Irina Borogan, *The Red Web: The Struggle between Russia's Digital Dictators and the New Online Revolutionaries* (New York: Public Affairs, 2015).
27 Fred Weir, 'Kremlin Cyberpower?', *Christian Science Monitor*, 19 April 2018, https://www.csmonitor.com/World/Europe/2018/0419/Kremlin-cyberpower-How-fight-over-messaging-app-is-showing-its-limits.
28 'Direct Line with Vladimir Putin', 7 June 2018, http://en.kremlin.ru/events/president/news/57692.
29 Fred Weir, '"Fake News" in Russia: State Censorship Elicits an Outcry', *Christian Science Monitor*, 20 March 2019, https://www.csmonitor.com/World/Europe/2019/0320/Fake-news-in-Russia-State-censorship-elicits-an-outcry.
30 Auzan, 'The Future of Russia's Institutions', p. 49.
31 Andrey Movchan, 'How to Fix Russia's Broken Banking System', *Carnegie Moscow Centre*, 14 January 2018, http://carnegie.ru/2018/01/14/how-to-fix-russia-s-broken-banking-system-pub-75267.
32 Rick Noack, 'US Sanctions against Russia are also Hurting Germany – a Lot', *Washington Post*, 14 December 2017, https://www.washingtonpost.com/news/worldviews/wp/2017/12/14/u-s-sanctions-against-russia-are-also-hurting-germany-a-lot/?utm_term=.edf7c3efcabd.
33 Davis, 'Russia's Changing Economic and Military Relations', p. 211. For an extended analysis, see Christopher Davis, 'The Ukraine Conflict, Economic-Military Power Balances, and Economic Sanctions', *Post-Communist Economies*, Vol. 28, No. 2, 2016, pp. 167–98.
34 'Russian Economy under Putin', *RT.com*, 27 January 2018, https://www.rt.com/business/417135-putin-presidency-economic-growth-russia/.
35 Bruno Maçães, "Russia's New Gold Rush Could Shake up the International Monetary System', *Moscow Times*, 8 April 2019, https://www.themoscowtimes.com/2019/04/08/russias-new-gold-rush-could-shake-up-the-international-monetary-system-a65131.
36 Paul Goncharoff, 'China, Russia and Gold in the De-Dollarizing World', *Russiafeed.com*, 2 May 2018, http://www.russiaknowledge.com/2018/04/29/china-russia-and-gold-vs-the-dollarised-world/.
37 Alexei Kudrin, 'Tezisy doklada Alekseya Kudrina "Ob istochnikakh ekonomicheskogo rosta (v perspektive do 2025 g.)"', 31 May 2016, http://akudrin.ru/

news/tezisy-doklada-alekseya-kudrina-ob-istochnikah-ekonomicheskogo-rosta-v-perspektive-do-2025-g-predstavlennogo-na-zasedanii-prezidiuma-ekonomichesk-ogo-soveta-25-maya-2016-goda.

38 TASS, 'Kudrin: Russia Needs to Settle Political Discord with the West to Reach High Growth Rates', 4 October 2016, http://tass.com/economy/904080.

39 'Russia to Increase Military Spending While Slashing Welfare Budget', *Moscow Times*, 4 October 2016, https://themoscowtimes.com/news/russia-to-increase-military-spending-whilst-slashing-budget-55583.

40 Their thinking is outlined in A. Kudrin and I. Sokolov, 'Budzhetnyi manevr i strukturnaya perestroika rossiiskoi ekonomiki', *Voprosy ekonomiki*, No. 9, 2017, pp. 5–27. A good press report is in 'Kudrin raskryl detali strategii razvitiya Rossii', *RBC*, 6 September 2017, https://www.rbc.ru/economics/06/09/2017/59afc0b29a794728 01e00408.

41 Olga Kuzmina, interview with Valery Fedorov, Center on Global Interests, 2 June 2016, http:/globalinterests.org.

42 Stanislav Tkachenko, 'The Meaning of Alexey Kudrin's Return', *Russia Direct*, 13 June 2016, http://www.russia-direct.org/opinion/meaning-alexey-kudrins-return.

43 Georgy Bovt, 'Without Reforms, Economic Sclerosis Awaits', *Intersection*, 11 August 2017, http://intersectionproject.eu/article/economy/without-reforms-economic-sclerosis-awaits.

44 World Bank, *Doing Business 2018: Reforming to Create Jobs* (Washington, DC: International Bank for Reconstruction and Development / the World Bank, 2018), http://russian.doingbusiness.org/~/media/WBG/DoingBusiness/Documents/Annual-Reports/English/DB2018-Full-Report.pdf.

45 Leonid Grigoryev, 'National Economic Security Strategy and Economic Challenges', Valdai Club, 28 June 2017, http://valdaiclub.com/a/highlights/national-economic-security-strategy/.

46 Stephen K. Wegren, 'Food Security and Countersanctions', *Russian Analytical Digest*, No. 204, 19 June 2017, pp. 2–5.

47 Alexander Lukin and Pavel Lukin, 'Economic Policy in Post-Soviet Russia in Historical Context', *Russian History*, No. 46, 2019, p. 82.

48 Sergey Zhavoronkov, 'Two Lean Years: Russia's Budget for 2018–19', *Intersection*, 6 December 2017, http://intersectionproject.eu/article/economy/two-lean-years-russias-budget-2018-20.

49 Filip Brokes, 'Russia's May Decrees Pushed the Poorest Regions into Debt', *Intellinews.com*, 27 February 2018, http://www.intellinews.com/russia-s-may-decrees-pushed-the-poorest-regions-into-debt-137447/.

50 Putin, 'Annual News Conference', 14 December 2017.

51 'Russia's Natural Resources Make up 60% of GDP', *Moscow Times*, 14 March 2019, https://www.themoscowtimes.com/2019/03/14/russias-natural-resources-make-up-60-of-gdp-reports-a64800.

52 Brigitte Granville and Vladimir Mau, 'Putin's Economic Dilemma', *Russia in Global Affairs*, 20 June 2018, http://eng.globalaffairs.ru/book/Putins-Economic-Dilemma-19624.

53 Chris Weafer, 'Going Cold Turkey: Russia Wants an End to OPEC-Production Cuts', *Intellinews.com*, 30 May 2018, http://www.intellinews.com/macro-advisory-going-cold-turkey-russia-wants-an-end-to-opec-production-cuts-142499/.

54 Roland Götz, 'The Nord Stream 2 Dispute: Legal, Economic, Environmental and Political Arguments', *Russian Analytical Digest*, No. 221, 11 June 2018, pp. 7–10.

55 Henry Foy, 'Gazprom Gas Exports to Europe Rise 8% to New Record', *Financial Times*, 3 January 2017, https://www.ft.com/content/1e4428b9-224e-36cc-9bdd-c7ca21c4907c.

56 Alena Makhnevea, 'Evropa vstala na zashchitu gaza', *Vedomosti*, 9 September 2016, p. 11.

57 RT, 'How Long Can Europe Survive Without Russian Gas?', 16 December 2017, https://www.rt.com/business/413375-russia-gas-europe-lng-dependence/.

58 Simon Pirani, 'The Decline and Fall of the Russia-Ukraine Gas Trade', *Russian Analytical Digest*, No. 221, 11 June 2018, p. 3.

59 Jake Rudnitsky and Elena Mazneva, 'OPEC Deal Doesn't Stop Russia from Record Oil Output in 2017', *Bloomberg*, 2 January 2018, https://www.bloomberg.com/news/articles/2018-01-02/russia-pumps-oil-at-record-pace-in-same-year-of-global-cuts.

60 Serene Cheong, 'Russia-China Oil Friendship Makes Crude Costlier for Europe', *Bloomberg*, 3 January 2018, https://www.bloomberg.com/news/articles/2018-01-02/russia-s-oil-friendship-with-china-makes-crude-costly-for-europe.

61 Marin Katusa, *The Colder War: How the Global Energy Trade Slipped from America's Grasp* (London: John Wiley, 2014).

62 Matthew J. Bryza, 'Disarm Russia's Gas Weapon', 20 June 2014, http://www.naturalgaseurope.com/.

63 Donald Tusk, 'A United Europe can End Russia's Energy Stranglehold', *Financial Times*, 21 April 2014, https://www.ft.com/content/91508464-c661-11e3-ba0e-00144feabdc0.

64 Tatiana Romanova, 'Is Russian Energy Policy towards the EU Only about Geopolitics? The Case of the Third Liberalisation Package', *Geopolitics*, Vol. 21, No. 4, October–December 2016, 2016, pp. 857–79.

65 Danila Bochkarev, 'What Gazprom's Accepting EU Rules of the Game Means for EU Energy Security', Valdai Discussion Club, 7 June 2018, http://valdaiclub.com/a/highlights/what-gazprom-s-accepting-eu-rules-of-the-game-mean/.

66 Shaun Walker, 'Putin Blames EU as Russia Abandons Plans for South Stream Pipeline', *Guardian*, 1 December 2014, http://www.theguardian.com/business/2014/dec/01/russia-blames-eu-as-it-abandons-plans-for-south-stream-gas-pipeline.

67 Vladimir Putin, 'Annual Press Conference', *Kremlin.ru*, 17 December 2015, http://en.kremlin.ru/events/president/news/50971.

68 Obama imposed executive sanctions on 6 March and 18 December 2014, 1 April 2015, and 26 July and 29 December 2016.

69 Mikhail Alexseev, 'Why Trump's Bid to Improve US-Russian Relations Backfired', Ponars Eurasia, February 2018, http://www.ponarseurasia.org/memo/why-trumps-bid-improve-us-russian-relations-backfired-congress.

70 For an excellent analysis, see Konstantin Khudoley, 'Russia and the US: The Way Forward', *Russia in Global Affairs*, No. 4, 2017, http://eng.globalaffairs.ru/number/Russia-and-the-US-The-Way-Forward-19263.

71 Wolfgang Ischinger, 'Why Europeans Oppose the Russia Sanctions Bill', *Wall Street Journal*, 17 July 2017, https://www.wsj.com/articles/why-europeans-oppose-the-russia-sanctions-bill-1500232733.

72 Paul Sonne, 'US Criticizes Germany's Support of New Russian Natural Gas Line', *Wall Street Journal*, 13 December 2017, https://www.wsj.com/articles/u-s-criticizes-germanys-support-of-new-russian-natural-gas-line-1513122298.

73 RFE/RL Russia Report, 'US Senators Decry Decision to Hold Off on New Russian Sanctions', 31 January 2018, https://www.rferl.org/a/us-senators-attack-trump-decision-hold-off-russia-sanctions/29009067.html.

74 Sabra Ayres, 'Russia Feeling the Financial Bite of US Sanctions', *Los Angeles Times*, 10 April 2018, p. A3.

75 'Excerpts from Dmitry Medvedev's Interview with Vesti and Subbotu Programme', 28 April 2018, http://government.ru/en/news/32506/.

76 'Over 40% of Russians Believe Western Sanctions Likely to Remain for Years', *Sputnik*, 29 April 2018, https://sputniknews.com/russia/201804291064013398-sanctions-lift-poll/.

77 Vladimir Putin, 'Interview with China Media Group', 5 June 2018, http://en.kremlin.ru/events/president/news/57684.

78 Dmitrii Butrin, Pavel Tarasenko, Ekaterina Mareeva and Galina Dudina, 'Kompleks mer po sderzhivaniyu Donal'da Trampa', *Kommersant*, 8 August 2018, p. 1.

79 The summary is from 'Russian Newspaper Leaks Draft Text of US Senate's Defending American Security from Kremlin Aggression Act', *Meduza*, 8 August 2018, which links through to the draft Senate document entitled '2018d140 Menendez Russia Sanctions Bill', https://meduza.io/en/news/2018/08/08/russian-newspaper-leaks-draft-text-of-u-s-senate-s-defending-american-security-from-kremlin-aggression-act.

80 'Defending American Security from Russian Aggression Act of 2019', 13 February 2019, https://www.congress.gov/bill/116th-congress/senate-bill/482/text#toc-id8ECC7DE75C5F408089FFD9B1C838ECEB.

81 Ivan Timofeev, 'Fighting Sanctions: From Legislation to Strategy', Valdai Club, 18 June 2018, http://valdaiclub.com/a/highlights/fighting-sanctions-strategy/.

82 Richard Connolly, *Russia's Response to Sanctions: How Western Statecraft is Reshaping Political Economy in Russia* (Cambridge: Cambridge University Press, 2018).

83 Sergei Karaganov, 'Svoboda v vybore puti', *Rossiiskaya gazeta*, 7 June 2018, p. 8.

6 FROM PARTNER TO ADVERSARY: RUSSIA AND THE WEST

1 Andrei P. Tsygankov, *The Strong State in Russia: Development and Crisis* (Oxford: Oxford University Press, 2014).

2   Vladimir Putin, 'Presidential Address to the Federal Assembly', *Kremlin.ru*, 20 February 2019, http://en.kremlin.ru/events/president/news/59863.

3   Cf. Allen C. Lynch, 'The Influence of Regime Type on Russian Foreign Policy Toward "the West", 1992–2015', *Communist and Post-Communist Studies*, Vol. 49, No. 1, 2016, pp. 101–11.

4   For an overview, see Angela Stent, *Putin's World: Russia against the West and with the Rest* (New York: Twelve, 2019).

5   Zbigniew Brzezinski, 'The Premature Partnership', *Foreign Affairs*, Vol. 73, No. 2, March–April 1994, pp. 67–82.

6   Olga Malinova, 'Obsession with Status and Ressentiment: Historical Backgrounds of the Russian Discursive Identity Construction', *Communist and Post-Communist Studies*, Vol. 47, Nos 3–4, 2014, pp. 291–303.

7   Cited in Richard Lourie, *Putin: His Downfall and Russia's Coming Crash* (New York: Thomas Dunne Books, 2017), p. 81.

8   Regina Heller, 'Russia's Quest for Respect in the International Conflict Management in Kosovo', *Communist and Post-Communist Studies*, Vol. 47, No. 304, 2014, pp. 333–43.

9   Guy Mettan, *Creating Russophobia: From the Great Religious Schism to Anti-Putin Hysteria* (Atlanta, GA: Clarity Press, 2017). See also Andrei Tsygankov, *Russophobia: Anti-Russian Lobby and American Foreign Policy* (Basingstoke: Palgrave Macmillan, 2009).

10 Vladimir Putin, 'Speech and the Following Discussion at the Munich Conference on Security Policy', *Kremlin.ru*, 10 February 2007, http://eng.kremlin.ru/transcripts/8498.

11 http://www.eho.com.hr/news/on-23-november-1959-in-a-speech-in-strasbourg-de-gaulle-announced-his-vision-for-europe/9341.aspx.

12 For overviews, see Jeffrey Mankoff, *Russian Foreign Policy: The Return of Great Power Politics*, 2nd edn (Lanham, MD: Rowman & Littlefield, 2012); Alexander Sergunin, *Explaining Russian Foreign Policy Behavior: Theory and Practice* (Stuttgart: Ibidem-Verlag, 2016); Andrei P. Tsygankov, *Russia's Foreign Policy: Change and Continuity in National Identity*, 5th edn (Lanham, MD: Rowman & Littlefield, 2019).

13 'Soloviev's Exclusive Interview with President Putin: The New World Order and Russia's Place in It', *Vesti.ru*, 2 April 2018, https://www.vesti.ru/doc.html?id=3002370&cid=4441.

14 Mark Urnov, '"Greatpowerness" as the Key Element of Russian Self-Consciousness under Erosion', *Communist and Post-Communist Studies*, Vol. 47, Nos 3–4, 2014, pp. 308–9.

15 Urnov, '"Greatpowerness"', p. 320.

16 Charles Dick, *Russian Ground Forces Posture towards the West*, Research Paper, Russia and Eurasia Programme (London: Chatham House, April 2019).

17 Richard Sakwa, 'Russian Neo-Revisionism', *Russian Politics*, Vol. 4, No. 1, 2019, pp. 1–21.

18 Russian Federation Ministry of Defence, 'Voennaya doktrina Rossiiskoi Federatsii', 25 December 2014. An English translation is available at https://www.offiziere.ch/wp-content/uploads-001/2015/08/Russia-s-2014-Military-Doctrine.pdf.

19 'Strategiya natsional'noi bezopasnosti Rossiiskoi Federatsii', 31 December 2015, http://www.scrf.gov.ru/documents/1/133.html; also in *Rossiiskaya gazeta*, 31 December 2015, http://rg.ru/2015/12/31/nac-bezopasnost-site-dok.html. An English translation is available at http://www.ieee.es/Galerias/fichero/OtrasPublicaciones/Internacional/2016/Russian-National-Security-Strategy-31Dec2015.pdf.

20 Russian Federation Ministry of Foreign Affairs, 'Kontsepsiya vneshnei politiki Rossiiskoi Federatsii', 30 November 2016, http://www.mid.ru/foreign_policy/news/-/asset_publisher/cKNonkJE02Bw/content/id/2542248.

21 'Strategiya natsional'noi bezopasnosti', 31 December 2015.

22 Edwin Bacon and Bettina Renz with Julian Cooper, *Securitising Russia: The Domestic Politics of Putin* (Manchester: Manchester University Press, 2006).

23 Bernhard Stahl, Robin Lucke & Anne Felfeli, 'Comeback of the Transatlantic Security Community? Comparative Securitisation in the Crimea Crisis', *East European Politics*, Vol. 32, No. 4, 2016, p. 539.

24 White House, *National Security Strategy of the USA*, February 2015, https://obamawhitehouse.archives.gov/sites/default/files/docs/2015_national_security_strategy_2.pdf.

25 'Kontsepsiya vneshnei politiki', 30 November 2016.

26 Vladimir Putin, 'Presidential Address to the Federal Assembly', *Kremlin.ru*, 1 December 2016, http://en.kremlin.ru/events/president/news/53379.

27 These points, with the exception of the last one, were identified by Isabelle Facon, *Russia's National Security Strategy and Military Doctrine and Their Implications for the EU*, Directorate-General for External Policies, Policy Department (Brussels: European Parliament, 2017), pp. 6–7.

28 Igor Ivanov, 'Russia and Europe: From Romanticism to Pragmatism', RIAC, 29 January 2018, http://russiancouncil.ru/en/analytics-and-comments/analytics/russia-and-europe-from-romanticism-to-pragmatism/.

29 Svetlana Savranskaya and Tom Blanton, 'NATO Expansion: What Gorbachev Heard', National Security Archive, George Washington University, 12 December 2017, https://nsarchive.gwu.edu/briefing-book/russia-programs/2017-12-12/nato-expansion-what-gorbachev-heard-western-leaders-early.

30 'Key Foreign Policy Events of 2014', 30 December 2014; http://www.mid.ru/BDOMP/Brp_4.nsf/arh/F991672ECE65419FC3257DBE002382A6?OpenDocument.

31 Gordon Hahn, *Ukraine over the Edge: Russia, the West and the 'New Cold War'* (Jefferson, NC: McFarland Books, 2017).

32 Sam Charap and Timothy Colton, *Everyone Loses: The Ukraine Crisis and the Ruinous Contest for Post-Soviet Eurasia* (London: Routledge/Adelphi, 2016).

33 Richard Sakwa, *Frontline Ukraine: Crisis in the Borderlands*, paperback edition with a new Afterword (London: I.B. Tauris, 2016). See also Richard Sakwa, 'The Ukraine Syndrome and Europe: Between Norms and Space', *The Soviet and Post-Soviet Review*, No. 44, 2017, pp. 9–31.

34 Gerard Toal, *Near Abroad: Putin, the West and the Contest over Ukraine and the Caucasus* (Oxford: Oxford University Press, 2017).

35 Marlene Laruelle, *The 'Russian World': Russia's Soft Power and Geopolitical Imagination* (Washington, DC: Center on Global Interests, May 2015).

36 Vladimir Putin, 'Address by the President of the Russian Federation', *Kremlin.ru*, 18 March 2014, http://en.kremlin.ru/events/president/news/20603.
37 Robert Legvold, *Return to Cold War* (Cambridge: Polity, 2016).
38 Andrew Monaghan, *A 'New Cold War'? Abusing History, Misunderstanding Russia*, Chatham House Research Paper (London: Chatham House, May 2015).
39 Gustav Gressel and Fredrik Wesslau, *The Great Unravelling: Four Doomsday Scenarios for Europe's Russia Policy* (London: ECFR, 2017), p. 1.
40 Vladimir Putin, 'Meeting of the Valdai International Discussion Club', *Kremlin.ru*, 19 October 2017, http://en.kremlin.ru/events/president/news/55882.
41 For an excellent analysis, see Aleksei Malashenko, *Nado li boyatsya Islama?* (Moscow: Ves' Mir, 2017).
42 Sergey Lavrov, 'Foreign Minister Sergey Lavrov's Remarks and Answers to Media Questions at the Moscow Non-Proliferation Conference', 20 October 2017, http://www.mid.ru/en/diverse/-/asset_publisher/zwI2FuDbhJx9/content/vystuplenie-ministra-inostrannyh-del-rossijskoj-federacii-s-v-lavrova-na-moskovskoj-konferencii-po-nerasprostraneniu-moskva-20-oktabra-2017-goda?.
43 White House, *National Security Strategy of the United States*, December 2017, p. 25, https://www.whitehouse.gov/wp-content/uploads/2017/12/NSS-Final-12-18-2017-0905.pdf.
44 Department of Defense, *Summary of the 2018 National Defence Strategy of the USA: Sharpening the American Military's Competitive Edge* (Washington, DC: Department of Defense, 2017), p. 1.
45 Secretary of Defense, *Nuclear Posture Review*, February 2018, p. 1. The final version is available at https://media.defense.gov/2018/Feb/02/2001872886/-1/-1/1/2018-NUCLEAR-POSTURE-REVIEW-FINAL-REPORT.PDF.
46 Russian Ministry of Foreign Affairs, 'Comment by the Information and Press Department on the US Nuclear Posture Review', 3 February 2018, http://www.mid.ru/en/diverse/-/asset_publisher/zwI2FuDbhJx9/content/kommentarij-departamenta-informacii-i-pecati-mid-rossii-v-svazi-s-publikaciej-novoj-adernoj-doktriny-ssa.
47 Vladimir Putin, 'Presidential Address to the Federal Assembly', *Kremlin.ru*, 1 March 2018, http://en.kremlin.ru/events/president/news/56957.
48 Putin, 'Presidential Address', 20 February 2019.

7 RECREATING THE HEARTLAND: EURASIAN PARTNERSHIPS

1 Vladimir Putin, 'Meeting of the Valdai Discussion Club', *Kremlin.ru*, 19 September 2013, http://en.kremlin.ru/news/6007.
2 Bruno Maçães, *The Dawn of Eurasia: On the Trail of the New World Order* (London: Allen Lane, 2018), p. xvii and *passim*.
3 Maçães, *The Dawn of Eurasia*, p. 34.
4 Cf. Glenn Diesen, *Russia's Geoeconomic Strategy for a Greater Eurasia* (London: Routledge, 2017).

5   Vladimir Putin, 'Novyi integratsionnyi proekt dlya Evrazii: budushchee, kotoroe rozhdaetsya segodnya', *Izvestiya*, 3 October 2011, p. 1; http://premier.gov.ru/events/news/16622.

6   Maksim Karliuk, 'The Eurasian Economic Union: An EU-Inspired Legal Order and its Limits', *Review of Central and East European Law*, Vol. 42, 2017, pp. 50–72.

7   Eurasian Development Bank: Centre for Integration Studies, *Eurasian Economic Integration 2017*, Report 43 (St Petersburg: Eurasian Development Bank, 2017), p. 11.

8   Eurasian Devlopment Bank, *Eurasian Economic Integration 2017*, Report 43, p. 72.

9   Artyom Shraibman, 'The Boundaries of Friendship', *Carnegie Moscow Centre*, 12 July 2017, http://carnegie.ru/commentary/71510.

10 These of course were also Russian concerns. Yong Wang, 'Offensive for Defensive: The Belt and Road Initiative and China's New Grand Strategy', *The Pacific Review*, Vol. 29, No. 3, pp. 455–63.

11 For a good introduction, see Alexander Cooley, *The New Great Power Context in Central Asia* (Oxford: Oxford University Press, 2012).

12 Andrei Kokoshin, *Real'nyi suverenitet v sovremennoi miropoliticheskoi sistemy*, 3rd edn (Moscow: Evropa, 2006).

13 Vladimir Putin, 'Russia's Place in a Changing World', *Moskovskie novosti*, 27 February 2012, http://worldmeets.us/Moskovskiye.Novosti000001.shtml#axzz5xRYC0PpK.

14 Valdai Discussion Club, 'Towards the Great Ocean – 3: Creating Central Eurasia', Valdai Report No. 3, June 2015, http://valdaiclub.com/a/reports/toward_the_great_ocean_3_creating_central_eurasia/.

15 'Plenary Session of St Petersburg International Economic Forum', 17 June 2016, http://en.kremlin.ru/events/president/news/.

16 Selcuk Colakoglu, 'BRICS: A New Decision-Maker in Global Governance?', *Diplo*, 18 October 2017, https://www.diplomacy.edu/blog/brics-new-decision-maker-global-governance.

17 Pavel Koshkin, 'BRICS for a Multi-Polar World', *Russia Direct*, 5 July 2013, http://www.russia-direct.org/qa/brics-multi-polar-world.

18 'Putin Calls for BRICS to Assert Financial Independence from the West', *Business New Europe*, 10 July 2015, http://www.bne.eu/content/story/putin-calls-brics-assert-financial-independence-west.

19 Sergei Ryabkov, 'BRICS: Common Approaches and Concrete Measures', *International Affairs* (Moscow), special issue, BRICS: Russia Ufa 2015, pp. 5 and 7.

20 Sergei Lavrov, 'Address to Readers', *International Affairs* (Moscow), special issue, BRICS: Russia Ufa 2015, p. 3.

21 'Concept of the Russian Federation's Presidency in BRICS in 2015–16', http://en.brics2015.ru/russia_and_brics/20150301/19483.html.

22 Georgy Toloraya, 'Russian Vision of BRICS Global Role: Implications of the Ufa Summit', paper prepared for the 9th World Congress of ICCEES, Mukahari, Japan, 3–8 August 2015.

23 Vladimir Putin, 'Press-konferentsiya Vladimira Putina po itogam sammitov BRIKS i ShOS', *Kremlin.ru*, 10 July 2015, http://kremlin.ru/events/president/news/49909.

24 Alexander Lukin, 'Shanghai Cooperation Organization: Looking for a New Role', Valdai Papers, Special Issue, Valdai Discussion Club, 2015, p. 2, http://valdaiclub.com/publication/79220.html.

25 Lukin, 'Shanghai Cooperation Organization', p. 3.

26 RATS SCO, 'Press Release on the Results of the Shanghai Cooperation Organisation Heads of State Council Meeting', 20 June 2017, http://ecrats.org/en/news/6848.

27 Dmitry Suslov, 'A Pivot Towards Asia, Integration and Mega-Regions', Valdai Discussion Club, 9 June 2016, http://valdaiclub.com/news/a-pivot-towards-asia-integration-and-mega-regions-balancing-russia-s-apr-policy/.

28 Oliver Stuenkel, 'The Ufa Declaration: An Analysis', *Post-Western World*, 9 July 2015, http://www.postwesternworld.com/2015/07/09/the-declaration-analysis/.

29 Mathew Burrows and Robert A. Manning, *Kissinger's Nightmare: How an Inverted US-China-Russia May be a Game-Changer*, Valdai Paper No. 33 (Moscow: Valdai Club, 2015), p. 3, available at http://valdaiclub.com/files/11410/.

30 Sergei Karaganov, 'From East to West, or Greater Eurasia', *Rossiiskaya gazeta*, 24 October 2016.

31 Sergey Lavrov, 'In a Polycentric World, Russia Wants to Collaborate', *The Globe and Mail*, 17 November 2016, https://www.theglobeandmail.com/report-on-business/rob-commentary/in-a-polycentric-world-russia-wants-to-collaborate/article32877820/.

32 Russian Ministry of Foreign Affairs, Lavrov news conference, 17 January 2017, http://www.mid.ru/en/vistupleniya_ministra/-/asset_publisher/MCZ7HQuMdqBY/content/id/2599609.

33 Michael Cox, 'Not Just "Convenient": China and Russia's New Strategic Partnership in the Age of Geopolitics', *Asian Journal of Comparative Politics*, Vol. 1, No. 4, 2016, pp. 317–334.

34 Alexander Lukin, *China and Russia: The New Rapprochement* (Cambridge: Polity, 2018).

35 TASS, 'Kremlin Aide Highlights Cooperation with China as Russia's Foreign Policy Priority', 4 June 2018, http://tass.com/politics/1007915.

36 Vladimir Putin, 'Answers to Journalists' Questions Following Direct Line', 15 June 2017, http://en.kremlin.ru/events/president/news/54794.

37 Vladimir Putin, 'Interview with China Media Group', 5 June 2018, http://en.kremlin.ru/events/president/news/57684.

38 Pepe Escobar, 'Putin and Xi top the G6+1', *Asia Times*, 10 June 2018, http://www.atimes.com/article/putin-and-xi-top-the-g61/.

39 Vladimir Putin, 'After the Shanghai Cooperation Organisation Summit, Vladimir Putin Met with Russian Journalists', *Kremlin.ru*, 10 June 2018, http://en.kremlin.ru/events/president/news/57719.

40 Sergei Karaganov, 'Svoboda v vybore puti', *Rossiiskaya gazeta*, 7 June 2018, p. 8.

41 Bobo Lo, 'Frontiers New and Old: Russia's Policy in Central Asia', *Russie.Nei.Visions* No. 82 (Paris: IFRI Russia/NIS Centre, January 2015), p. 9.

42 Jeffrey Goldberg, 'The Obama Doctrine: The US President Talks Through his Hardest Decisions about America's Role in the World', *The Atlantic*, April 2016, http://www.theatlantic.com/magazine/archive/2016/04/the-obama-doctrine/471525/.

43 Valdai Discussion Club, 'War and Peace in the 21st Century: A New International Balance as the Guarantee of Stability', Materials for Discussion at the 12th Annual Meeting of the Valdai Discussion Club, Sochi, 19–22 October 2015, p. 4. The final report was published as 'War and Peace in the 21st Century: International Stability and Balance of the New Type', Valdai Discussion Club Report, January 2016, http://valdaiclub.com/publications/reports/international-stability-and-balance-of-the-new-type/.

44 Valdai Discussion Club, 'War and Peace in the 21st Century', p. 5.

45 Julian Borger, 'Barack Obama: Russia is a Regional Showing Weakness over Ukraine', *Guardian*, 25 March 2014, https://www.theguardian.com/world/2014/mar/25/barack-obama-russia-regional-power-ukraine-weakness.

46 Ian Traynor, 'Barack Obama: No Cold War over Crimea', *Guardian*, 26 March 2014, https://www.theguardian.com/world/2014/mar/26/obama-no-cold-war-crimea.

47 Cited by Adriel Kasonta, 'How to Make Enemies and Alienate Friends', *RIAC*, 5 February 2018, http://russiancouncil.ru/en/analytics-and-comments/columns/political-life-of-usa/how-to-make-enemies-and-alienate-friends/.

48 Dmitriy Frolovskiy, 'Jewish Businesses are on the Rise in Russia', *Jerusalem Post*, 14 February 2018, http://www.jpost.com/Opinion/Jewish-businesses-are-on-the-rise-in-Russia-542565.

49 Nikolay Kozhanov, 'Russia and the Kingdom of Saudi Arabia: Between Syria and OPEC', *Russian Analytical Digest*, No. 219, 3 May 2018, pp. 4–7.

8 THE WINDS OF CHANGE

1 The Levada Centre data can be found at http://www.levada.ru/23-07-2015/iyulskie-reitingi-odobreniya-i-doveriya.

2 Nikolay Petrov, 'Russia on the Eve of its Presidential Election', Ponars Eurasia Policy Memo No. 509, February 2018, http://www.ponarseurasia.org/sites/default/files/policy-memos-pdf/Pepm509_Petrov_Feb2018.pdf.

3 Vividly described by Marc Bennetts, *I'm Going to Ruin Their Lives: Inside Putin's War on Russia's Opposition* (London: Oneworld, 2016).

4 Survey conducted by RAS Institute of Sociology, reported by Pavel Aptekar', 'Rossiyanie zakhoteli peremen', *Vedomosti*, 19 December 2017, https://www.vedomosti.ru/opinion/articles/2017/12/19/745708-rossiyane-peremen.

5 Andrei Kolesnikov, 'Do Russians Want Change?', *Carnegie Moscow Centre*, 16 January 2018, http://carnegie.ru/commentary/75261.

6 Tatyana Stanovaya, 'Bezpoikonye okhraniteli: Kak ura-patrioty stali problemoi dlya putinskoi sistemy', *Republic.ru*, 2 August 2017, https://republic.ru/posts/85503.

7 The abuses are described in detail by Alisa Kustikova, '"Karusel": Stop – snyato!', *Novaya gazeta*, No. 95, 1 September 2017, pp. 7–15.

8 'Russian Election Boss Proposes Stepping up Public Monitoring of Polls', *RT.com*, 9 October 2017, https://www.rt.com/politics/406133-russian-elections-boss-proposes-to/.

9. 'Kemerovo Governor Warned not to use Administrative Resource in Election – Pamfilova', *Interfax*, 16 March 2018, http://interfax.com/newsinf.asp?id=817589.
10. Tatyana Stanovaya, 'Kremlin-Duma Reshuffle Offers False Hope to Russia', *Carnegie Moscow Centre*, 12 October 2016, http://carnegie.ru/commentary/64834.
11. Moscow Times, 'Opposition Roizman Drops out of Governor's Race, Calls for Election Boycott', 3 August 2017, https://www.themoscowtimes.com/2017/07/19/opposition-roizman-drops-out-governor-election-calls-for-boycott-a58428.
12. 'Russia Elections Chief Says Stronger Competition Needed at Regional Polls', *RT.com*, 2 August 2017, https://www.rt.com/politics/398300-russian-elections-chief-speaks-in/.
13. *On vam ne Dimon: Tainaya imperiya Dmitriya Medvedeva*, https://dimon.navalny.com/ and YouTube.
14. Nabi Abdullaev, 'The Murky Mechanics of Russia's Governor Reshuffle', *Moscow Times*, 9 October 2017, https://themoscowtimes.com/articles/the-murky-mechanics-of-russias-governor-reshuffle-59202.
15. Natalya Zubarevich, 'The Fall of Russia's Regional Governors', *Carnegie Moscow Centre*, 12 October 2017, http://carnegie.ru/commentary/73369.
16. Elena Mukhametshina and Ol'ga Churakova, 'Budushchego ne vidno', *Vedomosti*, 17 July 2017, p. 2.
17. Andrei Pertsev, 'Russia's Choice of Moral Rhetoric over Pragmatism is a Ticking Time Bomb', *Carnegie.ru*, 21 July 2017, http://carnegie.ru/commentary/71593.
18. Kathrin Hille, 'Alexei Navalny: A Genuine Alternative to Vladimir Putin?', *Financial Times*, 7 August 2017, https://www.ft.com/content/16df421e-72c1-11e7-aca6-c6bd07df1a3c.
19. Andrei Movchan, 'Programma Naval'nogo dlya mificheskogo naroda', *Vedomosti*, 13 December 2017, https://www.vedomosti.ru/opinion/articles/2017/12/13/745174-movchan.
20. Evgeniya Kuznetsova, in a report of the Centre for Economic and Political Reform, 'Eksperty zayavili o rezkom roste chisla protestov v Rossii', *RBK*, 10 July 2017, http://www.rbc.ru/politics/10/07/2017/596375709a7947363a3a9d94.
21. Yana Gorokhovskaia, 'In Moscow, Candidates Opposed to Putin are Running – and Winning', *Washington Post*, 4 January 2018, https://www.washingtonpost.com/news/monkey-cage/wp/2018/01/04/in-moscow-candidates-opposed-to-putin-are-running-and-winning-heres-why-that-matters/?utm_term=.1fb8ada042b5.
22. Yavlinsky, *The Putin Systsem*, p. xvii.
23. Yana Gorokhovskaia, 'Grassroots Capacity Building: Why Municipal Politics in Moscow are Important Signposts of Russia's Democratic Development', Ponars Eurasia Policy Memo No. 502, January 2018.
24. 'In Western Moscow, Putin Allies Lose an Election but Cling to Power', *Reuters*, 24 November 2017, https://uk.reuters.com/article/uk-russia-election-moscow/in-western-moscow-putin-allies-lose-an-election-but-cling-to-power-idUKKBN1DO10I.
25. Maria Eismont, 'New Politicians Are Searching for a New Agenda', *Vedomosti*, 23 November 2017 [in Russian], https://www.vedomosti.ru/opinion/columns/2017/11/23/742779-kak-dela.

26 Geogy Bovt, 'Why Moscow's Untouchable Mayor, Sergei Sobyanin, Is Doomed To Be Re-Elected', *Moscow Times*, 7 September 2018, https://www.themoscowtimes.com/2018/09/07/why-moscow-untouchable-mayor-sergei-sobyanin-is-doomed-to-be-re-elected-opinion-a62812.

27 Konstantin Gaaze, 'Zdravyi smysl protiv trekhlineiki: Kak v Rossii uchatsya govorit' o politike', *RBK*, 21 July 2017. The debate was aired on *Ekho Moskvy*, *TV Rain* (*Dozhd*) and the *Reuters* websites.

28 Leonid Bershidsky, 'Putin's No Good, but Where's the Alternative?', *Bloomberg*, 21 July 2017, https://www.bloomberg.com/view/articles/2017-07-21/putin-s-no-good-but-where-s-the-alternative.

29 Ilya Yablokov, *Fortress Russia: Conspiracy Theories in Post-Soviet Russia* (Cambridge: Polity, 2018).

30 Gordon M. Hahn, 'The Schism within Russia's Pro-Democracy Movement', *Russian and Eurasian Politics*, 17 July 2017, https://gordonhahn.com/2017/07/17/the-schism-among-russias-pro-democrats/.

31 Cf. Alexander Lukin, *The Political Culture of the Russian 'Democrats'* (Oxford: Oxford University Press, 2000). For an updated and extended version, see A. V. Lukin and P. V. Lukin, *Umom Rossiyu ponimat': Postsovetskaya politicheskaya kultura i otechestvennaya istoriya* (Moscow: Ves Mir, 2015).

32 Arutunyan, *The Putin* Mystique, p. 236.

33 Grigory Melkonyants, 'How to Monitor Russia's Next Election', *Moscow Times*, 7 February 2018, https://themoscowtimes.com/articles/how-to-monitor-the-russian-elections-60413.

34 Aleksey Gorbachev, 'Kreml' reanimiruet ideyu dvukhpartiinoi sistemy', *Nezavisimaya gazeta*, 18 October 2017, http://www.ng.ru/politics/2017-10-18/1_7097_kreml.html.

35 Levada Centre, 'Menee 60% Rossiyan vyrazili zhelanie poiti na vybory prezidenta', 4 December 2017, https://www.levada.ru/2017/12/04/menee-60-rossiyan-vyrazili-zhelanie-pojti-na-vybory-prezidenta/.

36 David Filipov, 'This Russian Presidential Contender has Zero Chance against Putin: But a Man Can Dream', *Washington Post*, 7 January 2018, https://www.washingtonpost.com/world/europe/this-russian-presidential-contender-has-zero-chance-against-putin-but-a-man-can-dream/2018/01/05/defcee7a-f0d1-11e7-95e3-eff284e71c8d_story.html?utm_term=.8f9a6a682d08.

37 Christopher Moldes, 'The Struggle for New Blood and the Future of Russia's Left', *oDR*, 20 February 2018, https://www.opendemocracy.net/od-russia/christopher-moldes/struggle-for-new-blood-and-future-of-russia-s-left.

38 Kathrin Hille, 'Putin's Poll Rivals Gain a Platform but Cannot Win', *Financial Times*, 13 February 2018, https://www.ft.com/content/3f333c08-0d70-11e8-8eb7-42f857ea9f09.

39 'Post-Putin: Imagining the Unimaginable', *Bearmarketbrief*, 2 October 2017, https://bearmarketbrief.com/2017/10/02/post-putin-imagining-the-unimaginable/

40 Nadezhda Azhgikhina, 'Grigory Yavlinsky's Program Gives Russian Society a Chance to Preserve its Dignity', *The Nation*, 2 February 2018, https://www.thenation.com/article/grigory-yavlinskys-program-gives-russian-society-a-chance-to-preserve-its-dignity/.

41 Masha Gessen, 'The Curious Case of the Television Star Running against Vladimir Putin', *New Yorker*, 12 February 2018, https://www.newyorker.com/news/our-columnists/the-curious-case-of-the-television-star-running-against-vladimir-putin.

42 Hille, 'Putin's Poll Rivals Gain a Platform'.

43 Gessen, 'The Curious Case of the Television Star'.

44 'Sobchak Calls Presidential Run a Step to Changing Russian System, Rejects Navalny Boycott', *RFE/RL*, 29 December 2017, https://www.rferl.org/a/russia-sobchak-interview-presidency-navalny/28946492.html.

45 'Presidential Candidate Yavlinsky's Public Support HQ Gets Three Co-Chairs', Interfax, 23 January 2018, http://www.interfax.com/newsinf.asp?id=805127.

46 Andrey Movchan, 'Navalny's Blinkered Economic Programme', *Carnegie Moscow Centre*, 23 January 2018, http://carnegie.ru/commentary/75326.

47 Putin, 'Vladimir Putin's Annual News Conference', 14 December 2017.

48 Andrew Roth, 'Putin Paints Rosy Picture of Economy Heading into 2018 Election', *Washington Post*, 11 January 2018, https://www.washingtonpost.com/world/europe/putin-paints-rosy-picture-of-economy-heading-into-2018-election/2018/01/10/1cce185a-e59c-11e7-927a-e72eac1e73b6_story.html?utm_term=.fb72f80867e0.

49 Data from VTsIOM, reported in TASS, 'Putin's 2017 Trust Rating Hits Record-High in December – Poll', 11 January 2018, http://tass.com/society/984606.

50 Putin, 'Presidential Address', 1 March 2018.

51 Organization for Security and Co-operation in Europe, 'Russia Presidential Election Well Administered, but Characterized by Restrictions on Fundamental Freedoms, Lack of Genuine Freedom, International Observers Say', OSCE Press Release, 19 March 2018, https://www.osce.org/odihr/elections/375661. This was also the finding of the full report issued in June.

52 *Kommersant*, 'Evropeiskie nablyudateli ne nashli konkurentsii na rossiiskikh vyborakh', 7 June 2018, https://www.kommersant.ru/doc/3651447.

53 Moscow Times, 'After Putin's Historic Grand Slam, What's Next for Russia?', 19 March 2018, https://themoscowtimes.com/articles/after-putins-historic-grand-slam-whats-next-for-russia-60870.

54 'Putin's Reelection: A Discussion with Kirill Rogov', Ponars, 7 June 2018, http://www.ponarseurasia.org/point-counter/article/putins-reelection-capturing-russias-electoral-patterns-discussion-kirill-rogov.

55 Vladimir Pastukhov, 'Tri prezidentskie karty', *Novaya gazeta*, 26 March 2018, https://www.novayagazeta.ru/articles/2018/03/24/75929-tri-prezidentskie-karty.

56 For a thoughtful analysis making some of these points, see Pavel Aptekar, Vladimir Ruvinskii and Mariya Zheleznova, 'Kogo pobedil Vladimir Putin', *Vedomosti*, 19 March 2018, p. 6.

57 Vladimir Putin, 'Vystuplenie na tseremonii vstupleniya v dolzhnost' Prezidenta Rossii', 7 May 2018, http://kremlin.ru/events/president/news/57416.

58   Kathrin Hille, 'Aide Alexei Kudrin Considered for Lead Role in Easing Tension and Restoring Growth', *Financial Times*, 2 May 2018, https://www.ft.com/content/c1721646-4d51-11e8-8a8e-22951a2d8493.

59   Alexei Kudrin, 'Perekhod ot lataniya dyr k razvitiyu', *Kommersant*, 24 April 2018, p. 2.

60   'Meeting with Accounts Chamber Chairman Alexei Kudrin', 4 June 2018, http://en.kremlin.ru/events/president/news/57643.

61   Leonid Bershidsky, 'Putin Turns Swathes of Russia into Flyover Country', *Bloomberg*, 7 March 2019, https://www.bloomberg.com/opinion/articles/2019-03-07/putin-s-development-plan-picks-favorites-among-russian-regions.

62   E.g., a RANEPA study argued that raising the pension age for men to 65 and for women to 63 would boost the GDP by 5.5 per cent by 2030 and 28 per cent by 2050, TASS, 'RBC: Government to Specify Scope of Pension Reform', 8 June 2018, http://tass.com/pressreview/1008666.

63   'Prezident podpisal Ukaz "O national'nykh tselyakh i strategicheskikh zadachakh razvitiya Rossiiskoi Federatsii na period do 2024 goda"', *Kremlin.ru*, 7 May 2018, http://kremlin.ru/events/president/news/57425.

64   Leonid Bershidsky, 'Russia Can't Decide Whether It's Rich or Poor', *Bloomberg*, 24 January 2019, https://www.bloomberg.com/opinion/articles/2019-01-24/russia-can-t-decide-whether-it-s-rich-or-poor.

65   Fred Weir, 'To Pay for a "Russia First" Agenda, Putin Takes Ax to Military Spending', *Christian Science Monitor*, 8 May 2018, https://www.csmonitor.com/World/Europe/2018/0508/To-pay-for-a-Russia-first-agenda-Putin-takes-ax-to-military-spending.

66   Denis Volkov, '"No Trust": What Russians Think about the Pension Reform', *Carnegie Moscow Centre*, 9 August 2018, https://carnegie.ru/commentary/77015.

67   Vladimir Putin, 'The President's Address to Russian Citizens', *Kremlin.ru*, 29 August 2018, http://en.kremlin.ru/events/president/news/58405.

68   'Popular Support for Putin's Foreign Policy on the Decline, Pollster Says', *Moscow Times*, 9 August 2018, https://www.themoscowtimes.com/2018/08/09/popular-support-for-putins-foreign-policy-is-dropping-a62482.

69   'Answers to Media Questions', *Kremlin.ru*, 18 March 2018, http://en.kremlin.ru/events/president/news/57085.

70   TASS, 'Putin Vows to Abide by Two-Term Limit on Consecutive Presidential Tenures', 25 May 2018, http://tass.com/politics/1006561.

71   Andrey Pertsev, 'Depoliticization in Russia: The Growth of the Protest Vote', *Carnegie Moscow Centre*, 14 September 2018, https://carnegie.ru/commentary/77254.

72   Data from VTsIOM, confirmed by Levada polls, 'Trust in Putin Slides to 13-year Low of 33.4% in January', *Intellinews.com*, 21 January 2019, http://www.intellinews.com/trust-in-putin-slides-to-13-year-low-of-33-4-in-january-155055/.

73   Editorial, *Vedomosti*, 17 January 2019.

74   Denis Volkov and Andrei Kolesnikov, 'The Perils of Change: Russians' Mixed Attitudes toward Reform', *Carnegie Moscow Centre*, February 2018, http://carnegieendowment.org/files/VolkovKolesnikov_RussianReform_article.pdf.

75   Putin, 'Presidential Address', 20 February 2019.

76 For fascinating reflections on the opposition, see Gleb Pavlovsky, 'Taking to the Street Left Russia's Opposition Out in the Cold', *Moscow Times*, 12 March 2019, https://www.themoscowtimes.com/2019/03/12/taking-to-the-street-left-russias-opposition-out-in-the-cold-a64778.

9 THE PUTIN PHENOMENON

1 Brian D. Taylor, *The Code of Putinism* (Oxford: Oxford University Press, 2018), p. 2 and *passim*.

2 Taylor, *The Code of Putinism*, p. 41.

3 Yulia Latynina, 'The Kremlin's Lack of Control has Made Me Flee Russia', *Moscow Times*, 22 September 2017, https://themoscowtimes.com/articles/why-I-fled-russia-yulia-latynina-59010.

4 The argument advanced by Vladimir Pastukhov, 'Neudacha okhotnika: Chego na samom dele dobivalsya Sechin, nachinaya delo Ulyukaeva', *Republic*, 23 September 2017.

5 Aleksei Firsov, 'Odinokii Viking: Kak formiruetsya publichnyi obraz Igorya Sechina', *Republic*, 16 September 2017, https://republic.ru/posts/86415.

6 Andrey Pertsev, 'New Role for United Russia', *Carnegie Moscow Centre*, 12 February 2018, http://carnegie.ru/commentary/75510.

7 Andrey Pertsev, 'Russia's Regions Strike Back', *Carnegie Moscow Centre*, 30 November 2017, http://carnegie.ru/commentary/74872.

8 Andrew Osborn, 'Putin Plan to Rejuvenate Russian Politics Makes Slow Progress', *Reuters*, 20 November 2017, https://www.reuters.com/article/us-russia-election-putin-analysis/putin-plan-to-rejuvenate-russian-politics-makes-slow-progress-idUSKBN1DK14E.

9 Irina Turnakova, 'Zagovoril Usmanov – zagovorit i Sechin', interview with Gleb Pavlovsky, *Fontanka.ru*, 19 May 2017, http://m.fontanka.ru/2017/05/19/154/.

10 Gleb Pavlovsky, 'Nobody's President? Putin Enters the Era of Transition', *Carnegie Moscow Centre*, 28 November 2017, http://carnegie.ru/commentary/74843.

11 Minchenko Consulting, *Doklad: Bol'shoe pravitel'stvo Vladimira Putina i 'Politburo-2.0'*, 21 August 2012, http://minchenko.ru/analitika/analitika_27.html.

12 Minchenko Consulting, *"Politburo 2.0" and Post-Crimean Russia*, abridged version, 22 October 2014, http://www.minchenko.ru/netcat_files/File/Politburo_2014_ENG1_pre_final1.pdf.

13 Konstantin Gaaze, 'Court and Politburo: Putin's Changing Inner Circle', *Carnegie Moscow Centre*, 22 September 2017, http://carnegie.ru/commentary/73193.

14 The distinction is analysed in George W. Breslauer, *Gorbachev and Yeltsin as Leaders* (Cambridge: Cambridge University Press, 2002).

15 For an informative discussion, see Walter Laqueur, *Putinism: Russia and Its Future with the West* (New York: Thomas Dunne & St. Martin's, 2015), in particular pp. 118–21. For a rather less enlightening discussion, see Michel Eltchaninoff, *Inside the Mind of Vladimir Putin* (London: Hurst, 2018).

16 For an excellent analysis of 'The Transformation', see Daniel Treisman, *The Return: Russia's Journey from Gorbachev to Medvedev* (London: Simon & Schuster, 2011), pp. 197–239.

17 Reddaway and Glinski, *The Tragedy of Russia's Reforms*.

18 Orthodox Christianity, 'Percentage of Russians Condemning Abortion Has Tripled in 20 Years', 12 January 2018, http://orthochristian.com/109867.html.

19 Nick Ivanov, 'The West Doesn't Realize How Moderate Vladimir Putin Really Is', *Russiafeed.com*, 23 January 2018, http://russiafeed.com/west-doesnt-realize-how-moderate-vladimir-putin-really-is/.

20 Kerry Brown, 'What Has Karl Marx Ever Done for China?', *The Diplomat*, 14 May 2018, https://thediplomat.com/2018/05/what-has-karl-marx-ever-done-for-china/.

21 Karl Marx, 'The Eighteenth Brumaire of Louis Bonaparte', in *Marx and Engels: Selected Works in One Volume* (London: Lawrence and Wishart, 1968), p. 99.

22 Marx, 'The Eighteenth Brumaire of Louis Bonaparte', p. 171.

23 Marx, 'The Eighteenth Brumaire of Louis Bonaparte', p. 180.

24 Elena Chebankova, 'Contemporary Russian Conservatism', *Post-Soviet Affairs*, Vol. 32, No. 1, 2016, pp. 28–54.

25 Sakwa, *Russia against the Rest*, pp. 98–104.

26 See Svetlana Alexievich, *Second-Hand Time* (London: Fitzcarraldo, 2016), for powerful first-hand testimonies of a system that appeared locked in 'timelessness' (*bezvremen'e*).

27 ECFR China Analysis, *Grand Designs: Does China Have a 'Grand Strategy'?*, October 2017, http://www.ecfr.eu/publications/summary/grands_designs_does_china_have_a_grand_strategy.

28 Andrew Monaghan, *Power in Modern Russia: Strategy and Mobilisation* (Manchester: Manchester University Press, 2017), p. 1.

29 Ludger Helms (ed.), *Poor Leadership and Bad Governance: Reassessing Presidents and Prime Ministers in North America, Europe and Japan* (Cheltenham: Edward Elgar, 2012). For the chapter on Russia, see Richard Sakwa, 'Leadership, Governance and Statecraft in Russia', pp. 149–72.

30 Brown, *The Myth of the Strong Leader*.

31 Monaghan, *Power in Modern Russia*, pp. 1–2.

32 Putin, 'Russia at the Turn of the Millennium', pp. 209–19.

33 These plans are outlined by Monaghan, *Power in Modern Russia*, pp. 19–32.

34 Monaghan, *Power in Modern Russia*, p. 6.

35 Vladimir Putin, 'Meeting of the Valdai International Discussion Club', *Kremlin.ru*, 24 October 2014, http://eng.kremlin.ru/news/23137.

36 Zygar, *All the Kremlin's Men*.

37 Freedom House, *Freedom in the World 2018: Democracy in Crisis*, https://freedomhouse.org/report/freedom-world/freedom-world-2018.

38 Anatoly Karlin, 'Freedom House: Human Rights Abuse against Satirists', *Unz Review*, 17 January 2018, http://www.unz.com/akarlin/freedom-house-human-rights-abuse-against-satirists/.

39 Eric van de Beek, 'Press Freedom in Russia: Putin as a Dog', *Russia Insider*, 11 November 2017, https://russia-insider.com/en/press-freedom-russia-putin-dog/ri21544.

10 PARADOXES OF PUTINISM

1 Immanuel Kant, 'What is Enlightenment?', in *Kant: Political Writings*, edited by Hans Reiss, translated by H. B. Nisbett (Cambridge: Cambridge University Press, 1991), p. 59.
2 Nikolas K. Gvosdev, 'Russia's Presidential Election Runs into Reality', *The National Interest*, 21 January 2018, http://nationalinterest.org/feature/russias-president-problems-will-remain-the-same-after-the-24159.
3 Described by Vladimir Gel'man in many works, latterly in his *Authoritarian Russia: Analyzing Post-Soviet Regime Changes* (Pittsburgh, CT: University of Pittsburgh Press, 2015); Vladimir Gel'man, 'The Vicious Circle of Post-Soviet Neopatrimonialism', *Post-Soviet Affairs*, Vol. 32, No. 5, 2016, pp. 455–73; Vladimir Gel'man, 'The Politics of Fear: How Russia's Rulers Counter their Rivals', *Russian Politics*, No. 1, 2016, pp. 27–45.
4 Neil MacFarquhar, 'Putin's Election is Assured: Let the Succession Begin', *New York Times*, 11 December 2017, https://www.nytimes.com/2017/12/11/world/europe/russia-vladimir-putin-election.html.
5 Wood, *Russia without Putin*.
6 Kirill Rogov, 'What Russia's New Government Tells us about Succession after Putin', *Carnegie Moscow Centre*, 28 May 2018, https://carnegie.ru/commentary/76456.
7 Daniel Treisman, 'Democracy by Mistake', *VOX CEPR Policy Portal*, 26 November 2017, https://voxeu.org/article/democracy-mistake.
8 Gleb Pavlovsky, 'Zastoya ne zhdite', *New Times*, 13 December 2017.
9 Konstantin Gaaze, 'Between Day and Night: Who Will Control Putin's Fourth Term', *Carnegie Moscow Centre*, 21 December 2017, http://carnegie.ru/commentary/75087.
10 Gaaze, 'Between Day and Night'.
11 'Gleb Pavlovsky: "kreml bol'she ne "teatr Karabasa-Barabasa"'.
12 Vladislav Surkov, 'Odinochestvo polukrovki', *Russia in Global Affairs*, 9 April 2018, http://www.globalaffairs.ru/global-processes/Odinochestvo-polukrovki-14-19477.
13 Vladislav Surkov, 'Dolgoe gosudarstvo Putina: O tom, chto sdes' voobshche proiskhodit', *Nezavisimaya gazeta*, 11 February 2019, http://www.ng.ru/ideas/2019-02-11/5_7503_surkov.html.
14 Alexander Dugin, 'It's Time for Super-Putin: Dugin on Surkov's Putin Analysis', translated by Kristina Russ, *Geopolitika.ru*, 16 February 2019, https://www.geopolitica.ru/en/article/its-time-super-putin-dugin-surkovs-putin-analysis.
15 Gleb Pavlovsky, 'Russian Politics under Putin: The System Will Outlast the Master', *Foreign Affairs*, May/June 2016, https://www.foreignaffairs.com/articles/russia-fsu/2016-04-18/russian-politics-under-putin.
16 Andrei Shleifer and Daniel Treisman, 'A Normal Country', *Foreign Affairs*, Vol. 83, No. 2, March–April 2004, pp. 20–39; Andrei Shleifer, *A Normal Country: Russia After Communism* (Cambridge, MA: Harvard University Press, 2005).

BIBLIOGRAPHY

Abdullaev, Nabi, 'The Murky Mechanics of Russia's Governor Reshuffle', *Moscow Times*, 9 October 2017, https://themoscowtimes.com/articles/the-murky-mechanics-of-russias-governor-reshuffle-59202.

Acemoglu, Daron, and James A. Robinson, *Why Nations Fail? The Origins of Power, Prosperity, and Poverty* (London: Profile Books, 2013).

AFP, 'Russia's Feared Mafia Leaders in "Shock" as Vladimir Putin shows Who's Boss', 13 March 2019, https://www.scmp.com/news/world/russia-central-asia/article/3001483/russias-feared-mafia-leaders-shock-vladimir-putin.

Alexseev, Mikhail, 'Why Trump's Bid to Improve US-Russian Relations Backfired', Ponars Eurasia, February 2018, http://www.ponarseurasia.org/memo/why-trumps-bid-improve-us-russian-relations-backfired-congress.

Alexievich, Svetlana, *Second-Hand Time* (London: Fitzcarraldo, 2016).

Amos, Howard, 'Vladimir Putin's Man in the Balkans', *Politico*, 21 June 2017, http://www.politico.eu/article/vladimir-putin-balkans-point-man-nikolai-patrushev/.

Andrews, Josephine T., *When Majorities Fail: The Russian Parliament, 1990–1993* (Cambridge: Cambridge University Press, 2002).

Aptekar', Pavel, 'Rossiyanie zakhoteli peremen', *Vedomosti*, 19 December 2017, https://www.vedomosti.ru/opinion/articles/2017/12/19/745708-rossiyane-peremen.

Aptekar', Pavel, Vladimir Ruvinskii and Mariya Zheleznova, 'Kogo pobedil Vladimir Putin', *Vedomosti*, 19 March 2018, p. 6.

Arkhangelsky, Andrey, 'Setting the Boundaries: Russia's New Cultural State Policy', *Carnegie Moscow Centre*, 21 September 2017.

Aris, Ben, 'Meet the Stoligarchs, Putin's Pals who Control a Fifth of the Russian Economy', *BNE Intellinews*, 11 July 2016, http://www.intellinews.com/meet-the-stoligarchs-putin-s-pals-who-control-a-fifth-of-the-russian-economy-99918/.

Arutunyan, Anna, *The Putin Mystique: Inside Russia's Power Cult* (Talton Edge: Skyscraper Publications, 2014).

Associated Press, 'Vladimir Putin Accuses Lenin of Placing a "Time Bomb" under Russia', *Guardian*, 25 January 2016, https://www.theguardian.com/world/2016/jan/25/vladmir-putin-accuses-lenin-of-placing-a-time-bomb-under-russia.

Atwal, Maya, and Edwin Bacon, 'The Youth Movement Nashi: Contentious Politics, Civil Society, and Party Politics', *East European Politics*, Vol. 28, No. 3, 2012, pp. 256–66.

Auzan, Alexander, 'The Future of Russia's Institutions', in *Russia: Strategy, Policy and Administration*, edited by Irvin Studin (London: Palgrave Macmillan, 2018), pp. 43–55.

Ayres, Sabra, 'Russia Feeling the Financial Bite of US Sanctions', *Los Angeles Times*, 10 April 2018, p. A3.

Azhgikhina, Nadezhda, 'Grigory Yavlinsky's Program Gives Russian Society a Chance to Preserve Its Dignity', *The Nation*, 2 February 2018, https://www.thenation.com/article/grigory-yavlinskys-program-gives-russian-society-a-chance-to-preserve-its-dignity/.

Bacon, Edwin, *Inside Russian Politics* (London: Biteback Publishing, 2017).

Bacon, Edwin, 'Policy Change and the Narratives of Russia's Think Tanks', *Palgrave Communications*, 7 August 2018, https://www.nature.com/articles/s41599-018-0148-y.

Bacon, Edwin, and Bettina Renz, with Julian Cooper, *Securitising Russia: The Domestic Politics of Putin* (Manchester: Manchester University Press, 2006).

Balzer, Harley, 'Vladimir Putin on Russian Energy Policy', n.d., *The National Interest*, http://nationalinterest.org/article/vladimir-putin-on-russian-energy-policy-600.

Banfield, Edward C., *The Moral Basis of a Backward Society* (New York: Free Press, 1958).

Barbashin, Anton, and Hannah Thorburn, 'Putin's Brain: Alexander Dugin and the Philosophy behind Putin's Invasion of Crimea', *Foreign Affairs*, 31 March 2014, https://www.foreignaffairs.com/articles/russia-fsu/2014-03-31/putins-brain.

Barry, Ellen, 'Rally Defying Putin's Party Draws Tens of Thousands', *New York Times*, 10 December 2011, https://www.nytimes.com/2011/12/11/world/europe/thousands-protest-in-moscow-russia-in-defiance-of-putin.html.

Bassin, Mark, *The Gumilev Mystique: Biopolitics, Eurasianism, and the Construction of Community in Modern Russia* (Ithaca, NY: Cornell University Press, 2016).

Beek, Eric van de, 'Press Freedom in Russia: Putin as a Dog', *Russia Insider*, 11 November 2017, https://russia-insider.com/en/press-freedom-russia-putin-dog/ri21544.

Bennetts, Marc, *I'm Going to Ruin Their Lives: Inside Putin's War on Russia's Opposition* (London: Oneworld, 2016) (originally published as *Kicking the Kremlin*, 2014).

Bershidsky, Leonid, 'Putin's No Good, but Where's the Alternative?', *Bloomberg*, 21 July 2017, https://www.bloomberg.com/view/articles/2017-07-21/putin-s-no-good-but-where-s-the-alternative.

Bershidsky, Leonid, 'Russia Can't Decide Whether It's Rich or Poor', *Bloomberg*, 24 January 2019, https://www.bloomberg.com/opinion/articles/2019-01-24/russia-can-t-decide-whether-it-s-rich-or-poor.

Bershidsky, Leonid, 'Putin Turns Swathes of Russia into Flyover Country', *Bloomberg*, 7 March 2019, https://www.bloomberg.com/opinion/articles/2019-03-07/putin-s-development-plan-picks-favorites-among-russian-regions.

Bessonova, O. E., *Razdatochnya ekonomika Rossii: Evolyutsiya cherez transformatsiyu* (Moscow: Rosspen, 2006).

Billington, James H., *Russia in Search of Itself* (Washington, DC: Woodrow Wilson Center Press, 2004).

Blakkisrud, Helge, and Kolstø, Pål (eds), *Russia before and after Crimea: Nationalism and Identity, 2010–2017* (Edinburgh: Edinburgh University Press, 2014).

Bochkarev, Danila, 'What Gazprom's Accepting EU Rules of the Game Means for EU Energy Security', Valdai Discussion Club, 7 June 2018, http://valdaiclub.com/a/highlights/what-gazprom-s-accepting-eu-rules-of-the-game-mean/.

Borger, Julian, 'Barack Obama: Russia Is a Regional Showing Weakness over Ukraine', *Guardian*, 25 March 2014, https://www.theguardian.com/world/2014/mar/25/barack-obama-russia-regional-power-ukraine-weakness.

Bortnikov, Alexander, 'FSB rasstavlyaet aktsenty', *Rossiiskaya gazeta*, 19 December 2017, https://www.rg.ru/2017/12/19/aleksandr-bortnikov-fsb-rossii-svobodna-ot-politicheskogo-vliianiia.html.

Bovt, Georgy, 'Without Reforms, Economic Sclerosis Awaits', *Intersection*, 11 August 2017, http://intersectionproject.eu/article/economy/without-reforms-economic-sclerosis-awaits.

Bovt, Geogy, 'Why Moscow's Untouchable Mayor, Sergei Sobyanin, Is Doomed to Be Re-Elected', *Moscow Times*, 7 September 2018, https://www.themoscowtimes.com/2018/09/07/why-moscow-untouchable-mayor-sergei-sobyanin-is-doomed-to-be-re-elected-opinion-a62812.

Bransten, Jeremy, 'Public Chamber Criticized as "Smokescreen"', *RFE/RL Russian Political Weekly*, Vol. 5, No. 13, 1 April 2005.

Breslauer, George W., *Gorbachev and Yeltsin as Leaders* (Cambridge: Cambridge University Press, 2002).

Brokes, Filip, 'Russia's May Decrees Pushed the Poorest Regions into Debt', *Intellinews.com*, 27 February 2018, http://www.intellinews.com/russia-s-may-decrees-pushed-the-poorest-regions-into-debt-137447/.

Brown, Archie, *The Myth of the Strong Leader: Political Leadership in the Modern Age* (New York: Vintage, 2015).

Brown, Kerry, 'What Has Karl Marx Ever Done for China?', *The Diplomat*, 14 May 2018, https://thediplomat.com/2018/05/what-has-karl-marx-ever-done-for-china/.

Bryza, Matthew J., 'Disarm Russia's Gas Weapon', 20 June 2014, http://www.naturalgaseurope.com/.

Brzezinski, Zbigniew, 'The Premature Partnership', *Foreign Affairs*, Vol. 73, No. 2, March–April 1994, pp. 67–82.

Burrows, Mathew, and Robert A. Manning, *Kissinger's Nightmare: How an Inverted US-China-Russia May be a Game-Changer*, Valdai Paper No. 33 (Moscow: Valdai Club, 2015), available at http://valdaiclub.com/files/11410/.

Carnaghan, Ellen, *Out of Order: Russian Political Values in an Imperfect World* (University Park: Pennsylvania State University Press, 2007).

Charakopos, Michael, and Athanasios Dagoumas, 'State Capitalism in Time: Russian Natural Gas at the Service of Foreign Policy', *Europe-Asia Studies*, Vol. 70, No. 3, April 2018, pp. 441–61.

Charap, Sam, and Timothy Colton, *Everyone Loses: The Ukraine Crisis and the Ruinous Contest for Post-Soviet Eurasia* (London: Routledge/Adelphi, 2016).

Chebankova, Elena, 'The Evolution of Russia's Civil Society under Vladimir Putin: A Cause for Concern or Grounds for Optimism?', *Perspectives on European Politics and Society*, Vol. 10, No. 3, September 2009, pp. 394–416.

Chebankova, Elena, *Civil Society in Putin's Russia* (London: Routledge, 2013).

Chebankova, Elena, 'Contemporary Russian Liberalism', *Post-Soviet Affairs*, Vol. 30, No. 5, 2014, pp. 341–69.

Chebankova, Elena, 'Contemporary Russian Conservatism', *Post-Soviet Affairs*, Vol. 32, No. 1, 2016, pp. 28–54.

Chebankova, Elena, 'Ideas, Ideology and Intellectuals in Search of Russia's Political Future', *Daedalus*, Vol. 146, No. 2, Spring 2017, pp. 76–88.

Cheong, Serene, 'Russia-China Oil Friendship Makes Crude Costlier for Europe', *Bloomberg*, 3 January 2018, https://www.bloomberg.com/news/articles/2018-01-02/russia-s-oil-friendship-with-china-makes-crude-costly-for-europe.

Cherkesov, Viktor, 'Nevedomstvennye razmishleniya o professii: Moda na KGB?', *Komsomolskaya Pravda*, 29 December 2004, p. 6.

Cherkesov, Viktor, 'Vmesto poslesloviya: Chekistov byvshikh ne byvaet', *Komsomolskaya Pravda*, 29 December 2004, p. 7.

Clover, Charles, *Black Wind, White Snow: The Rise of Russia's New Nationalism* (London: Yale University Press, 2016).

Cohen, Jean L., *Civil Society and Political Theory* (Boston, MA: MIT Press, 1994).

Colakoglu, Selcuk, 'BRICS: A New Decision-Maker in Global Governance?', *Diplo*, 18 October 2017, https://www.diplomacy.edu/blog/brics-new-decision-maker-global-governance.

Connolly, Richard, *Russia's Response to Sanctions: How Western Statecraft Is Reshaping Political Economy in Russia* (Cambridge: Cambridge University Press, 2018).

Cooley, Alexander, *The New Great Power Context in Central Asia* (Oxford: Oxford University Press, 2012).

Cox, Michael, 'Not Just "Convenient": China and Russia's New Strategic Partnership in the Age of Geopolitics', *Asian Journal of Comparative Politics*, Vol. 1, No. 4, 2016, pp. 317–34.

Cox, Robert W., 'Civil Society at the Turn of the Millennium: Prospects for an Alternative World Order', *Review of International Studies*, Vol. 25, No. 1, January 1999, pp. 3–28.

D'Arcais, Paolo Flores, 'Anatomy of Berlusconismo', *New Left Review*, No. 68, 2011, pp. 121–40.

Davydov, Ivan, 'The Fate of Putin's Minister', *Intersection*, 13 December 2017, http://intersectionproject.eu/article/politics/fate-putins-minister.

Davis, Christopher Mark, 'Russia's Changing Economic and Military Relations with Europe and Asia from Cold War to the Ukraine Conflict: The Impacts of Power Balances, Partnerships, and Economic Warfare', Korea Institute for International Economic Policy (KIEP), *KIEP Studies in Comprehensive Regional Strategies Collected Papers (International Edition)* (Seoul: KIEP, 2016), pp. 195–286.

Davis, Christopher Mark, 'The Ukraine Conflict, Economic-Military Power Balances, and Economic Sanctions', *Post-Communist Economies*, Vol. 28, No. 2, 2016, pp. 167–98.

Dawisha, Karen, 'Is Russia's Foreign Policy That of a Corporatist-Kleptocratic Regime?', *Post-Soviet Affairs*, Vol. 27, No. 4, 2011, pp. 331–65.

Dawisha, Karen, *Putin's Kleptocracy: Who Owns Russia?* (New York: Simon & Schuster, 2014).

Delyagin, Mikhail, 'Liberal'naya verkhushka unichtozhaet Rossiyu v ugodu zapada', 9 January 2018, https://izborsk-club.ru/14642.

Department of Defense, *Summary of the 2018 National Defence Strategy of the USA: Sharpening the American Military's Competitive Edge* (Washington, DC: Department of Defense, 2017).

Dick, Charles, *Russian Ground Forces Posture towards the West*, Research Paper, Russia and Eurasia Programme (London: Chatham House, 2019).

Diesen, Glenn, *Russia's Geoeconomic Strategy for a Greater Eurasia* (London: Routledge, 2017).

'Doklad Mariny Sal'e i Yuriya Gladkova o deyatel'nosti V. V. Putina na postu glavy komiteta po vneshnim svyazyam merii Sankt-Peterburga', copyright 'Okalman', 28 November 2007, http://www.compromat.ru/main/putin/saliedokl.htm.

Dugin, Alexander, 'It's Time for Super-Putin: Dugin on Surkov's Putin Analysis', translated by Kristina Russ, *Geopolitika.ru*, 16 February 2019, https://www.geopolitica.ru/en/article/its-time-super-putin-dugin-surkovs-putin-analysis.

ECFR China Analysis, *Grand Designs: Does China have a 'Grand Strategy'?* (October 2017), http://www.ecfr.eu/publications/summary/grands_designs_does_china_have_a_grand_strategy.

Eckstein, Harry, Frederic J. Fleron Jr., Erik P. Hoffmann and William M. Reissinger, *Can Democracy Take Root in Post-Soviet Russia? Explorations in State-Society Relations* (Lanham, MD: Rowman & Littlefield, 1998).

Egorov, Ivan, 'Kto upravlyaet khaosom', *Rossiiskaya Gazeta*, 11 February 2015, p. 1.

Eismont, Maria, 'New Politicians Are Searching for a New Agenda', *Vedomosti*, 23 November 2017 [in Russian], https://www.vedomosti.ru/opinion/columns/2017/11/23/742779-kak-dela.

Eltchaninoff, Michel, *Inside the Mind of Vladimir Putin* (London: Hurst, 2018).

Escobar, Pepe, 'Putin and Xi top the G6+1', *Asia Times*, 10 June 2018, http://www.atimes.com/article/putin-and-xi-top-the-g61/.

Eurasian Development Bank: Centre for Integration Studies, *Eurasian Economic Integration 2017*, Report 43 (St Petersburg: Eurasian Development Bank, 2017).

Evans, Alfred B. Jr, Laura A. Henry and Lisa McIntosh Sundstrom (eds), *Russian Civil Society: A Critical Assessment* (Armonk, NY: M. E. Sharpe, 2005).

Facon, Isabelle, *Russia's National Security Strategy and Military Doctrine and Their Implications for the EU*, Directorate-General for External Policies, Policy Department (Brussels: European Parliament, 2017).

Farchy, Jack, 'Putin Creates New National Guard to Seal his Authority', *Financial Times*, 6 April 2016, https://www.ft.com/content/3f906d98-fc14-11e5-b3f6-11d5706b613b.

Felshtinsky, Yurii, and Vladimir Pribylovsky, *The Age of Assassins: The Rise and Rise of Vladimir Putin* (London: Gibson Square, 2008).

Filipov, David, 'This Russian Presidential Contender has Zero Chance against Putin: But a Man Can Dream', *Washington Post*, 7 January 2018, https://www.washingtonpost.com/world/europe/this-russian-presidential-contender-has-zero-chance-against-putin-but-a-man-can-dream/2018/01/05/defcee7a-f0d1-11e7-95e3-eff284e71c8d_story.html?utm_term=.8f9a6a682d08.

Firestone, Thomas, 'Criminal Corporate Raiding in Russia', *International Lawyer*, Vol. 42, Issue 4, Winter 2008, pp. 1207–29.

Firsov, Aleksei, 'Odinokii Viking: Kak formiruetsya publichnyi obraz Igorya Sechina', *Republic*, 16 September 2017, https://republic.ru/posts/86415.

Foglesong, David S., 'Putin: From Soulmate to Archenemy', *Raritan*, Vol. 38, No. 1, Summer 2018, pp. 18–41.

Foy, Henry, 'Gazprom Gas Exports to Europe Rise 8% to New Record', *Financial Times*, 3 January 2017, https://www.ft.com/content/1e4428b9-224e-36cc-9bdd-c7ca21c4907c.

Foy, Henry, '"We Need to Talk about Igor": The Rise of Russia's Most Powerful Oligarch', *Financial Times*, 1 March 2018, https://www.ft.com/content/dc7d48f8-1c13-11e8-aaca-4574d7dabfb6.

Fraenkel, Ernst, *The Dual State: A Contribution to the Theory of Dictatorship*, translated from the German by E. A. Shils, in collaboration with Edith Lowenstein and Klaus Knorr (New York: Oxford University Press, 1941; reprinted by The Lawbook Exchange, Ltd, 2006).

Freedom House, *Freedom in the World 2018: Democracy in Crisis*, https://freedomhouse.org/report/freedom-world/freedom-world-2018.

Frolovskiy, Dmitriy, 'Jewish Businesses are on the Rise in Russia', *Jerusalem Post*, 14 February 2018, http://www.jpost.com/Opinion/Jewish-businesses-are-on-the-rise-in-Russia-542565.

Frum, David, *Trumpocracy: The Corruption of the American Republic* (New York: Harper, 2018).

Furman, Dmitri, 'Imitation Democracies: The Post-Soviet Penumbra', *New Left Review*, No. 54, November–December 2008, pp. 29–47.

Gaaze, Konstantin, 'The Accidental Formation of Russia's War Coalition', *Carnegie Moscow Centre*, 22 June 2017, http://carnegie.ru/commentary/71340.

Gaaze, Konstantin, 'Corruption Case Puts Sechin in the Spotlight', *Carnegie Moscow Centre*, 23 August 2017, http://carnegie.ru/commentary/72888.

Gaaze, Konstantin, 'Court and Politburo: Putin's Changing Inner Circle', *Carnegie Moscow Centre*, 22 September 2017, http://carnegie.ru/commentary/73193.

Gaaze, Konstantin, 'Between Day and Night: Who Will Control Putin's Fourth Term', *Carnegie Moscow Centre*, 21 December 2017, http://carnegie.ru/commentary/75087.

Gaddy, Clifford G., and Barry W. Ickes, *Russia's Addiction: How Oil, Gas, and the Soviet Legacy Have Shaped a Nation's Fate* (Washington, DC: Brookings Institution Press, 2016).

Gaddy, Clifford G., and Barry W. Ickes, 'Russia's Virtual Economy', *Foreign Affairs*, Vol. 77, No. 5, September–October 1998, pp. 53–67.

Gaddy, Clifford G., and Barry W. Ickes, *Russia's Virtual Economy* (Washington, DC: Brookings Institution Press, 2002).

Gaidar, Yegor, *Days of Defeat and Victory*, translated by Jane Miller (Seattle: University of Washington Press, 1999).

Galeotti, Mark, *The Vory: Russia's Super Mafia* (New Haven, CT: Yale University Press, 2018).

Galperovich, Danila, 'Russian Economic Minister's Arrest: Part of Crackdown on Government "Liberals"?', *VOA*, 19 November 2016, https://www.voanews.com/a/russian-economics-minister-arrest-part-of-crackdown-on-government-liberals/3602721.html.

Gel'man, Vladimir, *Authoritarian Russia: Analyzing Post-Soviet Regime Changes* (Pittsburgh, CT: University of Pittsburgh Press, 2015).

Gel'man, Vladimir, 'The Vicious Circle of Post-Soviet Neopatrimonialism', *Post-Soviet Affairs*, Vol. 32, No. 5, 2016, pp. 455–73.

Gel'man, Vladimir, 'The Politics of Fear: How Russia's Rulers Counter Their Rivals', *Russian Politics*, No. 1, 2016, pp. 27–45.

Gessen, Masha, *The Man without a Face: The Unlikely Rise of Vladimir Putin* (New York: Riverhead Books, 2012).

Gessen, Masha, 'The Curious Case of the Television Star Running against Vladimir Putin', *New Yorker*, 12 February 2018, https://www.newyorker.com/news/our-columnists/the-curious-case-of-the-television-star-running-against-vladimir-putin.

Gershkovich, Evan, ' "A Point of No Return": Russia's Libertarians Lead Protest against "Sovereign Internet" ', *Moscow Times*, 10 March 2019, https://www.themoscowtimes.com/2019/03/10/point-of-no-return-russias-libertarians-lead-protest-against-sovereign-internet-a64758.

Gilbert, Leah, 'Crowding out Civil Society: State Management of Social Organisations in Putin's Russia', *Europe-Asia-Studies*, Vol. 68, No. 9, 2016, pp. 1553–78.

Glennon, Michael J., *National Security and Double Government* (Oxford: Oxford University Press, 2016).

Glenny, Misha, *McMafia: Seriously Organised Crime* (London: Vintage, 2017).

Goble, Paul, 'Putin Hasn't Destroyed Russia but Rather Russia Has Destroyed Him, Konchalovsky Says', *Window on Eurasia: New Series*, 3 August 2017, http://windowoneurasia2.blogspot.co.uk/2017/08/putin-hasnt-destroyed-russia-but-rather.html.

Goncharoff, Paul, 'China, Russia and Gold in the De-Dollarizing World', *Russiafeed.com*, 2 May 2018, http://www.russiaknowledge.com/2018/04/29/china-russia-and-gold-vs-the-dollarised-world/.

Gorokhovskaia, Yana, 'Grassroots Capacity Building: Why Municipal Politics in Moscow Are Important Signposts of Russia's Democratic Development', Ponars Eurasia Policy Memo No. 502, January 2018.

Gorokhovskaia, Yana, 'In Moscow, Candidates Opposed to Putin are Running – and Winning', *Washington Post*, 4 January 2018, https://www.washingtonpost.com/news/monkey-cage/wp/2018/01/04/in-moscow-candidates-opposed-to-putin-are-running-and-winning-heres-why-that-matters/?utm_term=.1fb8ada042b5.

Goldberg, Jeffrey, 'The Obama Doctrine: The US President Talks through His Hardest Decisions about America's Role in the World', *The Atlantic*, April 2016, http://www.theatlantic.com/magazine/archive/2016/04/the-obama-doctrine/471525/.

Gorbachev, Aleksey, 'Kreml' reanimiruet ideyu dvukhpartiinoi sistemy', *Nezavisimaya gazeta*, 18 October 2017, http://www.ng.ru/politics/2017-10-18/1_7097_kreml.html.

Goscilo, Helena, *Putin as Celebrity and Cultural Icon* (London: Routledge, 2014).

Goscilo, Helena, and Vlad Strukov (eds), *Celebrity and Glamour in Contemporary Russia: Shocking Chic* (London: Routledge, 2010).

Götz, Roland, 'The Nord Stream 2 Dispute: Legal, Economic, Environmental and Political Arguments', *Russian Analytical Digest*, No. 221, 11 June 2018, pp. 7–10.

Gramsci, Antonio, 'Notes on Italian History', in *Selections From the Prison Notebooks of Antonio Gramsci*, edited and translated by Quintin Hoare and Geoffrey Nowell Smith (London: Lawrence & Wishart, 1971), pp. 104–20.

Granville, Brigitte, and Vladimir Mau, 'Putin's Economic Dilemma', *Russia in Global Affairs*, 20 June 2018, http://en.globalaffairs.ru/book/Putins-Economic-Dilemma-19624.

Greene, Samuel A., *Moscow in Movement: Power and Opposition in Putin's Russia* (Stanford, CA: Stanford University Press, 2014).

Gressel, Gustav, and Fredrik Wesslau, *The Great Unravelling: Four Doomsday Scenarios for Europe's Russia Policy* (London: ECFR, 2017).

Grigoryev, Leonid, 'National Economic Security Strategy and Economic Challenges', Valdai Club, 28 June 2017, http://valdaiclub.com/a/highlights/national-economic-security-strategy/.

Gumilev, Lev, *Ethnogenesis and the Biosphere* (Moscow: Progress Publishers, 1990).

Guriev, Sergei, 'How Transitional Institutions could Transform Russia's Economy', *Carnegie.ru*, 13 November 2017, http://carnegie.ru/commentary/74790.

Gvosdev, Nikolas K., 'Russia's Presidential Election Runs into Reality', *The National Interest*, 21 January 2018, http://nationalinterest.org/feature/russias-president-problems-will-remain-the-same-after-the-24159.

Hahn, Gordon M., *Russia's Revolution from Above, 1985–2000: Reform, Transition, and Revolution in the Fall of the Soviet Communist Regime* (New Brunswick, NJ: Transaction Publishers, 2002).

Hahn, Gordon M., *Ukraine over the Edge: Russia, the West and the 'New Cold War'* (Jefferson, NC: McFarland Books, 2017).

Hahn, Gordon M., 'The Schism within Russia's Pro-Democracy Movement', *Russian and Eurasian Politics*, 17 July 2017, https://gordonhahn.com/2017/07/17/the-schism-among-russias-pro-democrats/.

Hale, Henry E., 'Why Not Parties? Electoral Markets, Party Substitutes, and Stalled Democratization in Russia', *Comparative Politics*, Vol. 37, No. 2, 2005, pp. 147–66.

Hale, Henry E., *Why Not Parties in Russia? Democracy, Federalism and the State* (Cambridge: Cambridge University Press, 2006).

Hale, Henry E., *Patronal Politics: Eurasian Regime Dynamics in Comparative Perspective* (New York: Cambridge University Press, 2015).

Hale, Henry E., 'The Continuing Evolution of Russia's Political System', in *Developments in Russian Politics 9*, edited by Richard Sakwa, Henry Hale and Stephen White (London: Palgrave Macmillan, 2018), pp. 205–16.

Hanson, Philip, 'The Russian Economic Puzzle: Going Forwards, Backwards or Sideways?' *International Affairs*, Vol. 83, No. 5, September–October 2007, pp. 869–89.

Hanson, Philip, 'Reiderstvo: Asset Grabbing in Russia', Russia and Eurasia PP 2014/03 (London: Chatham House, 2014).

Hanson, Philip, 'Notes on the Economies of Three Rival Powers: the US, China and Russia', paper for CREES annual conference, 1–3 June 2018.

Harding, Luke, *Mafia State: How One Reporter Became an Enemy of the Brutal New Russia* (London: Guardian Books, 2011).

Healey, Dan, *Russian Homophobia from Stalin to Sochi* (London: Bloomsbury Academic, 2018).

Hedlund, Stefan, *Russian Path Dependence* (London: Routledge, 2005).

Heller, Regina, 'Russia's Quest for Respect in the International Conflict Management in Kosovo', *Communist and Post-Communist Studies*, Vol. 47, No. 304, 2014, pp. 333–43.

Hellman, Joel S., 'Winners Take All: The Politics of Partial Reform in Postcommunist Transitions', *World Politics*, Vol. 50, No. 2, 1998, pp. 203–34.

Helms, Ludger (ed.), *Poor Leadership and Bad Governance: Reassessing Presidents and Prime Ministers in North America, Europe and Japan* (Cheltenham: Edward Elgar, 2012), pp. 149–72.

Hendley, Kathryn, *Everyday Law in Russia* (Ithaca, NY: Cornell University Press, 2017).

Hendley, Kathryn, 'Contempt for Court in Russia: The Impact of Litigation Experience', *Review of Central and East European Law*, Vol. 42, 2017, pp. 134–68.

Hill, Fiona, and Clifford Gaddy, *Mr. Putin: Operative in the Kremlin*, new and expanded edition (Washington, DC: Brookings Institution Press, 2015).

Hille, Kathrin, 'Alexei Navalny: A Genuine Alternative to Vladimir Putin?', *Financial Times*, 7 August 2017, https://www.ft.com/content/16df421e-72c1-11e7-aca6-c6bd07df1a3c.

Hille, Kathrin, 'Chechnya Faces Uphill Battle Wooing Tourists to Ski Resort', *Financial Times*, 30 January 2018, p. 7.

Hille, Kathrin, 'Putin's Poll Rivals Gain a Platform but Cannot Win', *Financial Times*, 13 February 2018, https://www.ft.com/content/3f333c08-0d70-11e8-8eb7-42f857ea9f09.

Hille, Kathrin, 'Aide Alexei Kudrin Considered for Lead Role in Easing Tension and Restoring Growth', *Financial Times*, 2 May 2018, https://www.ft.com/content/c1721646-4d51-11e8-8a8e-22951a2d8493.

Hobson, Peter, 'Hunter Becomes Prey: The Fall of a Russian "Attack-Dog" Investigator', *Moscow Times*, 29 July 2016, https://www.themoscowtimes.com/2016/07/29/hunter-becomes-prey-the-fall-of-a-russian-attack-dog-investigator-a54772.

Horvath, Robert, 'Putin's "Preventive Counter-Revolution": Post-Soviet Authoritarianism and the Spectre of Velvet Revolution', *Europe-Asia Studies*, Vol. 63, No. 1, January 2011, pp. 1–25.

Horvath, Robert, *Putin's 'Preventative Counter-Revolution': Post-Soviet Authoritarianism and the Spectre of Velvet Revolution* (London: Routledge, 2013).

Huntington, Samuel, *Political Order in Changing Societies* (New Haven, CT: Yale University Press, 1968).

INSOR, *Demokratiya: Razvitie rossiiskoi modeli* (Moscow: Ekon-Inform 2008).

INSOR, *Rossiya XXI veka: Obraz zhelaemogo zavtra* (Moscow: Ekon-Inform, 2010).

INSOR, *Attaining the Future: Strategy 2012* (Moscow: Ekon-Inform, 2011).

Intellinews, 'Trust in Putin Slides to 13-year Low of 33.4% in January', 21 January 2019, http://www.intellinews.com/trust-in-putin-slides-to-13-year-low-of-33-4-in-january-155055/.

Ischinger, Wolfgang, 'Why Europeans Oppose the Russia Sanctions Bill', *Wall Street Journal*, 17 July 2017, https://www.wsj.com/articles/why-europeans-oppose-the-russia-sanctions-bill-1500232733.

Ivanov, Igor, 'Russia and Europe: From Romanticism to Pragmatism', RIAC, 29 January 2018, http://russiancouncil.ru/en/analytics-and-comments/analytics/russia-and-europe-from-romanticism-to-pragmatism/.

Ivanov, Nick, 'The West Doesn't Realize How Moderate Vladimir Putin Really Is', *Russiafeed.com*, 23 January 2018, http://russiafeed.com/west-doesnt-realize-how-moderate-vladimir-putin-really-is/.

Javeline, Debra, and Sarah Lindemann-Komarova, 'A Balanced Assessment of Russian Civil Society', *Journal of International Affairs*, Vol. 63, No. 2, Spring/Summer 2010, pp. 171–88.

Javeline, Debra, and Sarah Lindemann-Komarova, 'Indigenously Funded Russian Civil Society', Ponars Eurasia Policy Memo No. 496, November 2017.

Jones, Owen, *The Establishment: And How They Get Away with It* (London: Penguin, 2015).

Kalashnikov, Maksim, *Putin inkorporeited: Kak Putinu obustroit' Rossiyu* (Moscow: Algoritm/Eksmo, 2013).

Kant, Immanuel, 'What is Enlightenment?', in *Kant: Political Writings*, edited by Hans Reiss, translated by H. B. Nisbett (Cambridge: Cambridge University Press, 1991), pp. 54–63.
Karaganov, Sergei, 'From East to West, or Greater Eurasia', *Rossiiskaya gazeta*, 24 October 2016.
Karaganov, Sergei, 'Svoboda v vybore puti', *Rossiiskaya gazeta*, 7 June 2018, p. 8.
Karlin, Anatoly, 'Freedom House: Human Rights Abuse against Satirists', *Unz Review*, 17 January 2018, http://www.unz.com/akarlin/freedom-house-human-rights-abuse-against-satirists/.
Karliuk, Maksim, 'The Eurasian Economic Union: An EU-Inspired Legal Order and Its Limits', *Review of Central and East European Law*, Vol. 42, 2017, pp. 50–72.
Kasonta, Adriel, 'How to Make Enemies and Alienate Friends', *RIAC*, 5 February 2018, http://russiancouncil.ru/en/analytics-and-comments/columns/political-life-of-usa/how-to-make-enemies-and-alienate-friends/.
Kasparov, Garry, with Mig Greengard, *Winter Is Coming: Why Vladimir Putin and the Enemies of the Free World Must Be Stopped* (London: Atlantic Books, 2015).
Katusa, Marin, *The Colder War: How the Global Energy Trade Slipped from America's Grasp* (London: John Wiley & Sons, 2014).
Kazun, Anton, 'Violent Corporate Raiding in Russia: Preconditions and Protective Factors', *Demokratizatsiya: The Journal of Post-Soviet Democratization*, Vol. 23, No. 4, Fall 2015, pp. 459–84.
Kennedy, John, 'Entrepreneurship and Limited Access: Rethinking Business-State Relations in Russia', *Post-Communist Economies*, published online 19 May 2017, http://www.tandfonline.com/doi/full/10.1080/14631377.2017.1314999.
Kennedy, Paul, *The Rise and Fall of the Great Powers: Economic Change and Military Conflict from 1500 and 2000* (London: Unwin Hyman, 1988).
Khodorkovskii, Mikhail, *Stat'i, dialogi, intervyu* (Moscow: Eksmo, 2010).
Khodorkovskii, Mikhail, and Nataliya Gevorkyan, *Tyur'ma i volya* (Moscow: Howard Roark, 2012).
Khudoley, Konstantin, 'Russia and the US: The Way Forward', *Russia in Global Affairs*, No. 4, 2017, http://en.globalaffairs.ru/number/Russia-and-the-US-The-Way-Forward-19263.
Kimerling, Maksim, 'Gleb Pavlovsky: "kreml bol'she ne "teatr Karabasa-Barabasa"', *Fontanka.ru*, 7 January 2018, http://www.fontanka.ru/2018/01/05/032/.
Kirillova, Kseniya, 'The Kremlin Guard: Russia's Pro-Government Youth Organizations', *Defense Report*, 30 April 2018, https://defencereport.com.
Klein, Naomi, *The Shock Doctrine: The Rise of Disaster Capitalism* (London: Penguin, 2008).
Klein, Naomi, *No Is Not Enough* (London: Allen Lane, 2017).
Knight, Amy, 'Putin's Monster', *New York Review of Books*, 19 May 2017, http://www.nybooks.com/daily/2017/05/19/putins-monster-ramzan-kadyrov/.
Kokoshin, Andrei, *Real'nyi suverenitet v sovremennoi miropoliticheskoi sistemy*, 3rd edn (Moscow: Evropa, 2006).
Kolesnikov, Andrei, 'Do Russians Want Change?', *Carnegie Moscow Centre*, 16 January 2018, http://carnegie.ru/commentary/75261.
Kolesnikov, Andrei, and Evgeniya Albats, 'Rosobrnadzor i Poltavchenko: Protiv Putina?', *New Times*, 2 October 2017, https://newtimes.ru/articles/detail/119423.
Kolstø, Pål, 'Crimea vs. Donbas: How Putin Won Russian Nationalist Support – and Lost It Again', *Slavic Review*, Vol. 75, No. 3, Fall 2016, pp. 702–25.
Kolstø, Pål, 'Marriage of Convenience? Collaboration between Nationalists and Liberals in the Russian Opposition 2011–12', *The Russian Review*, Vol. 75, No. 4, 2016, pp. 645–63.
Kolstø, Pål, and Helge Blakkisrud (eds), *The New Russian Nationalism: Imperialism, Ethnicity and Authoritarianism 2000–2015* (Edinburgh: Edinburgh University Press, 2017).

Kommersant, 'Evropeiskie nablyudateli ne nashli konkurentsii na rossiiskikh vyborakh', 7 June 2018, https://www.kommersant.ru/doc/3651447.

Kononenko, Vadim, and Arkady Moshes (eds), *Russia as a Network State: What Works in Russia When Institutions Do Not?* (Basingstoke: Palgrave Macmillan, 2010).

Kordonskii, Simon, *Rossiya: Pomestnaya federatsiya* (Moscow: Evropa, 2010).

Koshkin, Pavel, 'BRICS for a Multi-Polar World', *Russia Direct*, 5 July 2013, http://www.russia-direct.org/qa/brics-multi-polar-world.

Kotkin, Stephen, *Uncivil Society: 1989 and the Implosion of the Communist Establishment* (New York: Random House, 2009).

Kozhanov, Nikolay, 'Russia and the Kingdom of Saudi Arabia: Between Syria and OPEC', *Russian Analytical Digest*, No. 219, 3 May 2018, pp. 4–7.

Kozlova, Natal'ya, 'Kak dela?', *Rossiiskaya gazeta*, 25 July 2017, p. 1.

Krivoshapko, Aleksei, and Mattias Vestman, 'Kak izmerit' gosudarstvo-2', *Vedomosti*, 15 November 2017, p. 6.

Kubyshkin, Aleksandr, and Aleksandr Sergunin, 'The Problem of the "Special Path" in Russian Foreign Policy', *Russian Politics and Law*, Vol. 50, No. 6, November–December 2012, pp. 7–18.

Kudrin, Alexei, 'Tezisy doklada Alekseya Kudrina "Ob istochnikakh ekonomicheskogo rosta (v perspektive do 2025 g.)"', 31 May 2016, http://akudrin.ru/news/tezisy-doklada-alekseya-kudrina-ob-istochnikah-ekonomicheskogo-rosta-v-perspektive-do-2025-g-predstavlennogo-na-zasedanii-prezidiuma-ekonomicheskogo-soveta-25-maya-2016-goda.

Kudrin, Alexei, 'Perekhod ot lataniya dyr k razvitiyu', *Kommersant*, 24 April 2018, p. 2.

Kudrin, A., and I. Sokolov, 'Budzhetnyi manevr i strukturnaya perestroika rossiiskoi ekonomiki', *Voprosy ekonomiki*, No. 9, 2017, pp. 5–27.

Kuper, Simon, 'What Putin Learnt from Berlusconi', *Financial Times*, 31 May 2013, https://www.ft.com/content/74ff0f94-c8bd-11e2-acc6-00144feab7de.

Kustikova, Alisa, '"Karusel": Stop – snyato!', *Novaya gazeta*, No. 95, 1 September 2017, pp. 7–15.

Kurilla, Ivan, 'History and Memory in Russia during the 100-Year Anniversary of the Great Revolution', Ponars Eurasia Policy Memo No. 503, January 2018.

Kuznetsova, Evgeniya, 'Eksperty zayavili o rezkom roste chisla protestov v Rossii', *RBK*, 10 July 2017, http://www.rbc.ru/politics/10/07/2017/596375709a7947363a3a9d94.

LaMonica, Gabe, 'McCain Calls Russia a "Gas Station"', *CNN*, 22 April 2014, http://politicalticker.blogs.cnn.com/2014/04/22/mccain-calls-russia-a-gas-station/.

Laqueur, Walter, *Putinism: Russia and its Future with the West* (New York: Thomas Dunne & St. Martin's, 2015).

Laruelle, Marlene (ed.), *Eurasianism and the European Far Right: Reshaping the Europe-Russia Relationship* (Lanham, MD: Lexington Books, 2015).

Laruelle, Marlene, *The 'Russian World': Russia's Soft Power and Geopolitical Imagination* (Washington, DC: Center on Global Interests, 2015).

Laruelle, Marlene, 'The Izborsky Club, or the New Conservative Avant-Garde in Russia', *Russian Review*, Vol. 75, No. 4, 2016, pp. 626–44.

Laruelle, Marlène, 'Kadyrovism: Hardline Islam as a Tool of the Kremlin?', *Russie.Nei.Visions*, No. 99 (Paris: IFRI, March 2017).

Laruelle, Marlene, 'The Kremlin's Ideological Ecosystems: Equilibrium and Competition', Ponars Eurasia Policy Memo No. 493, November 2017, http://www.ponarseurasia.org/sites/default/files/policy-memos-pdf/Pepm493_Laruelle_Memo_Nov2017_0.pdf.

Laruelle, Marlene, *Russian Nationalism: Imaginaries, Doctrines, and Political Battlefields* (London: Routledge, 2018).

Laruelle, Marlene, 'Russia's Militia Groups and their Use at Home and Abroad', *Russia.Nei. Visions*, No. 113 (Paris: IFRI, April 2019).
Latynina, Yulia, '"Duraki" nanosyat otvetnyi udar', *Novaya gazeta*, No. 92, 23 August 2017, pp. 4–5.
Latynina, Yulia, 'The Kremlin's Lack of Control has Made Me Flee Russia', *Moscow Times*, 22 September 2017, https://themoscowtimes.com/articles/why-I-fled-russia-yulia-latynina-59010.
Lavrov, Sergei, 'Address to Readers', *International Affairs* (Moscow), special issue, BRICS: Russia Ufa, 2015, pp. 3–4.
Lavrov, Sergey, 'In a Polycentric World, Russia Wants to Collaborate', *The Globe and Mail*, 17 November 2016, https://www.theglobeandmail.com/report-on-business/rob-commentary/in-a-polycentric-world-russia-wants-to-collaborate/article32877820/.
Lavrov, Sergey, 'Foreign Minister Sergey Lavrov's Remarks and Answers to Media Questions at the Moscow Non-Proliferation Conference', 20 October 2017, http://www.mid.ru/en/diverse/-/asset_publisher/zwI2FuDbhJx9/content/vystuplenie-ministra-inostrannyh-del-rossijskoj-federacii-s-v-lavrova-na-moskovskoj-konferencii-po-nerasprostraneniu-moskva-20-oktabra-2017-goda?.
Lawrence, Patrick, 'Discerning Vladimir Putin', *Raritan*, Vol. 38, No. 1, Summer 2018, pp. 1–15.
Ledeneva, Alena, *Can Russia Modernise? Sistema, Power Networks, and Informal Governance* (Cambridge: Cambridge University Press, 2013).
Legvold, Robert, *Return to Cold War* (Cambridge: Polity, 2016).
Levada Centre, 'Menee 60% Rossiyan vyrazili zhelanie poiti na vybory prezidenta', 4 December 2017, https://www.levada.ru/2017/12/04/menee-60-rossiyan-vyrazili-zhelanie-pojti-na-vybory-prezidenta/.
Lieven, Dominic, *Towards the Flame: Empire, War and the End of Tsarist Russia* (London: Penguin, 2016).
Lewin, Moshe, *The Gorbachev Phenomenon: A Historical Interpretation* (Berkeley: University of California Press, 1988).
Lindemann-Komarova, Sarah, 'My Universe Continues to Expand: Challenging the Western Narrative that Russia is Unfree', *The Nation*, 25 April 2017, https://www.thenation.com/article/my-universe-continues-to-expand/.
Lo, Bobo, 'Frontiers New and Old: Russia's Policy in Central Asia', *Russie.Nei.Visions*, No. 82 (Paris: IFRI Russia/NIS Centre, January 2015), p. 9.
Lobunov, Yuri, 'Putin's 150 Promises', *Intersection*, 15 December 2017, http://intersectionproject.eu/article/politics/putins-150-promises.
Lourie, Richard, *Putin: His Downfall and Russia's Coming Crash* (New York: Thomas Dunne Books, 2017).
Lukin, Alexander, *The Political Culture of the Russian 'Democrats'* (Oxford: Oxford University Press, 2000).
Lukin, Alexander, 'Shanghai Cooperation Organization: Looking for a New Role', Valdai Papers, Special Issue, Valdai Discussion Club, 2015, http://valdaiclub.com/publication/79220.html.
Lukin, Alexander, *China and Russia: The New Rapprochement* (Cambridge: Polity, 2018).
Lukin, Alexander, 'Putin's Regime and its Alternatives', *Strategic Analysis*, Vol. 42, No. 2, 2018, pp. 134–53.
Lukin, Alexander, and Pavel Lukin, *Umom Rossiyu ponimat': Postsovetskaya politicheskaya kultura i otechesvennaya istoriya* (Moscow: Ves Mir, 2015).
Lukin, Alexander, and Pavel Lukin, 'Economic Policy in Post-Soviet Russia in Historical Context', *Russian History*, No. 46, 2019, pp. 53–83.

Lynch, Allen C., 'The Influence of Regime Type on Russian Foreign Policy toward "the West", 1992–2015', *Communist and Post-Communist Studies*, Vol. 49, No. 1, 2016, pp. 101–111.

MacFarquhar, Neil, 'Putin's Election is Assured: Let the Succession Begin', *New York Times*, 11 December 2017, https://www.nytimes.com/2017/12/11/world/europe/russia-vladimir-putin-election.html.

Maçães, Bruno, *The Dawn of Eurasia: On the Trail of the New World Order* (London: Allen Lane, 2018).

Maçães, Bruno, "Russia's New Gold Rush Could Shake up the International Monetary System", *Moscow Times*, 8 April 2019, https://www.themoscowtimes.com/2019/04/08/russias-new-gold-rush-could-shake-up-the-international-monetary-system-a65131.

Makhnevea, Alena, 'Evropa vstala na zashchitu gaza', *Vedomosti*, 9 September 2016, p. 11.

Malashenko, Aleksei, *Nado li boyatsya Islama?* (Moscow: Ves' Mir, 2017).

Malinova, Olga, 'Obsession with Status and Ressentiment: Historical Backgrounds of the Russian Discursive Identity Construction', *Communist and Post-Communist Studies*, Vol. 47, Nos 3–4, 2014, pp. 291–303.

Mankoff, Jeffrey, *Russian Foreign Policy: The Return of Great Power Politics*, 2nd edn (Lanham, MD: Rowman & Littlefield, 2012).

Markus, Stanislav, *Property, Predation and Protection: Piranha Capitalism in Russia and Ukraine* (Cambridge: Cambridge University Press, 2015).

Martin, Kimberly, 'The "KGB State" and Russian Political and Foreign Policy Culture', *Journal of Slavic Military Studies*, Vol. 30, No. 2, 2017, pp. 131–51.

Marx, Karl, 'The Eighteenth Brumaire of Louis Bonaparte', in *Marx and Engels: Selected Works in One Volume* (London: Lawrence and Wishart, 1968), pp. 97–180.

Martyanov, Viktor, 'Soslovnoe gosudarstvo v modernom obshchestve ili bor'ba s rossiiskoi korruptsiei kak problema sokrashcheniya statusnoi renty', *Obshchestvennye nauki i sovremennost'*, No. 2, 2016.

McFaul, Michael, *Russia's Unfinished Revolution: Political Change from Gorbachev to Putin* (Ithaca, NY: Cornell University Press, 2001).

McFaul, Michael, *From Cold War to Hot Peace: The Inside Story of Russia and America* (London: Allen Lane, 2018).

Medushevskii, Andrei, *Politicheskaya istoriya russkoi revolyutsii: Normy, instituty, formy sotsial'noi mobilizatsii v XX veke* (Moscow: Tsentr gumanitarnykh initsiativov, 2017).

Medvedev, Dmitry, 'Address to the Federal Assembly', 22 December 2011, http://news.kremlin.ru/news/14088.

Melkonyants, Grigory, 'How to Monitor Russia's Next Election', *Moscow Times*, 7 February 2018, https://themoscowtimes.com/articles/how-to-monitor-the-russian-elections-60413.

Mettan, Guy, *Creating Russophobia: From the Great Religious Schism to Anti-Putin Hysteria* (Atlanta, GA: Clarity Press, 2017).

Mickiewicz, Ellen, *No Illusions: The Voices of Russia's Future Leaders* (New York: Oxford University Press, 2014).

Milashina, Elena, 'Ubiistvo chesti', *Novaya gazeta*, April 2017, pp. 12–13.

Milashina, Elena, and Irina Gordienko, 'Lyudi teryayut strakh', *Novaya gazeta*, April 2017, pp. 12–13.

Miller, Alexei, 'The Russian Revolution of 1917: History, Memory, and Politics', Valdai Paper No. 81, January 2018, http://valdaiclub.com/a/valdai-papers/valdai-paper-81-the-russian-revolution-of-1917/.

Miller, Chris, *Putinomics: Power and Money in Resurgent Russia* (Chapel Hill: University of North Carolina Press, 2018).

Minchenko Consulting, *Doklad: Bol'shoe pravitel'stvo Vladimira Putina i 'Politburo-2.0'*, 21 August 2012, http://minchenko.ru/analitika/analitika_27.html.

Minchenko Consulting, *"Politburo 2.0" and Post-Crimean Russia*, abridged version, 22 October 2014, http://www.minchenko.ru/netcat_files/File/Politburo_2014_ENG1_pre_final1.pdf.

Moldes, Christopher, 'The Struggle for New Blood and the Future of Russia's Left', *oDR*, 20 February 2018, https://www.opendemocracy.net/od-russia/christopher-moldes/struggle-for-new-blood-and-future-of-russia-s-left.

Monaghan, Andrew, 'The Vertikal: Power and Authority in Russia', *International Affairs*, Vol. 88, No. 1, January 2012, pp. 1–16.

Monaghan, Andrew, 'Defibrllating the Vertikal? Putin and Russian Grand Strategy', Russia and Eurasia Programme Research Paper (London: Chatham House, October 2014).

Monaghan, Andrew, 'A "New Cold War"? Abusing History, Misunderstanding Russia', Chatham House Research Paper (London: Chatham House, May 2015).

Monaghan, Andrew, *Power in Modern Russia: Strategy and Mobilisation* (Manchester: Manchester University Press, 2017).

Moore, Barrington, *Social Origins of Dictatorship and Democracy: Lord and Peasant in the Making of the Modern World* (Boston, MA: Beacon Press, 1967).

Morozov, Ivan, *Zamurovannye: Khroniki Kremlevskogo tsentrala* (Moscow: Vagrius, 2009).

Moscow Times, 'Opposition Roizman Drops out of Governor's Race, Calls for Election Boycott', 3 August 2017, https://www.themoscowtimes.com/2017/07/19/opposition-roizman-drops-out-governor-election-calls-for-boycott-a58428.

Moscow Times, 'Yekaterinburg Mayor Evgeny Roizman on Why Russians Should Boycott the Elections', 29 January 2018, https://themoscowtimes.com/articles/-not-voting-is-a-matter-of-principle-60319.

Moscow Times, 'After Putin's Historic Grand Slam, What's Next for Russia?', 19 March 2018, https://themoscowtimes.com/articles/after-putins-historic-grand-slam-whats-next-for-russia-60870.

Moses, Joel, 'Political Rivalry and Conflict in Putin's Russia', *Europe-Asia Studies*, Vol. 69, No. 6, August 2017, pp. 961–88.

Movchan, Andrei, 'Programma Naval'nogo dlya mificheskogo naroda', *Vedomosti*, 13 December 2017, https://www.vedomosti.ru/opinion/articles/2017/12/13/745174-movchan.

Movchan, Andrey, 'How to Fix Russia's Broken Banking System', *Carnegie Moscow Centre*, 14 January 2018, http://carnegie.ru/2018/01/14/how-to-fix-russia-s-broken-banking-system-pub-75267.

Movchan, Andrey, 'Navalny's Blinkered Economic Programme', *Carnegie Moscow Centre*, 23 January 2018, http://carnegie.ru/commentary/75326.

Mukhametshina, Elena, and Ol'ga Churakova, 'Budushchego ne vidno', *Vedomosti*, 17 July 2017, p. 2.

Müller, Jan-Werner, 'What do Germans Think about When they Think about Europe?', *London Review of Books*, Vol. 34, No. 3, 9 February 2012, pp. 18–19.

Myers, Steven Lee, *The New Tsar: The Rise and Reign of Vladimir Putin* (London: Simon & Schuster, 2015).

NATO, 'Founding Act on Mutual Relations, Cooperation and Security between NATO and the Russian Federation', 27 May 1997, http://www.nato.int/cps/en/natohq/official_texts_25468.htm.

NATO-Russia Council, *Nato-Russia Council, Rome Declaration, 28 May 2002*, http://www.nato.int/nrc-website/media/59487/2002.05.28_nrc_rome_declaration.pdf.

Neumann, Iver B., *Russia and the Idea of Europe* (London: Routledge, 1996).

Nikolaev, Igor, 'Report Outlines Socioeconomic Inequality in Russia's Regions', *Moskovsky Komsomolets*, 22 March 2017.

Noack, Rick, 'US Sanctions against Russia are also Hurting Germany – a Lot', *Washington Post*, 14 December 2017, https://www.washingtonpost.com/news/worldviews/wp/2017/12/14/u-s-sanctions-against-russia-are-also-hurting-germany-a-lot/?utm_term=.edf7c3efcabd.

Noble, Ben, 'Volodin's Duma', *Intersection*, 13 December 2016, http://intersectionproject.eu/article/politics/volodins-duma.

North, Douglass C., John Joseph Wallis and Barry R. Weingast, *Violence and Social Orders: A Conceptual Framework for Interpreting Recorded Human History* (Cambridge: Cambridge University Press, 2009).

Olimpieva, Irina, 'Why Russian Officials Want to Control the Social Sciences', *Moscow Times*, 11 July 2017, https://themoscowtimes.com/articles/why-russian-officials-want-to-control-the-social-sciences-58367.

Organization for Security and Co-operation in Europe, 'Russia Presidential Election Well Administered, but Characterized by Restrictions on Fundamental Freedoms, Lack of Genuine Freedom, International Observers Say', OSCE Press Release, 19 March 2018, https://www.osce.org/odihr/elections/375661. Orlova, Karina, 'One Man's Land: Behind the FSB's Attack on Russia's Investigative Committee', *The American Interest*, 20 July 2016, https://www.the-american-interest.com/2016/07/20/who-is-behind-the-fsbs-attack-on-russias-investigative-committee/.

Orthodox Christianity, 'Percentage of Russians Condemning Abortion Has Tripled in 20 Years', 12 January 2018, http://orthochristian.com/109867.html.

Osborn, Andrew, 'Putin Plan to Rejuvenate Russian Politics Makes Slow Progress', *Reuters*, 20 November 2017, https://www.reuters.com/article/us-russia-election-putin-analysis/putin-plan-to-rejuvenate-russian-politics-makes-slow-progress-idUSKBN1DK14E.

Owen, Catherine, 'A Genealogy of *Kontrol*' in Russia: From Leninist to Neoliberal Governance', *Slavic Review*, Vol. 75, No. 2, Summer 2016, pp. 331–53.

Pautova, Larissa, 'In Stability We Trust? A Brief Sketch of Everyday Semantics', *Russia in Global Affairs*, 6 June 2017, http://en.globalaffairs.ru/number/In-Stability-We-Trust-18762.

Plokhy, Serhii, *Lost Kingdom: A History of Russian Nationalism from Ivan the Great to Vladimir Putin* (London: Allen Lane, 2017).

Parfitt, Tom, 'Moscow Investigators Held Over Links to Mobster', *The Times*, 20 July 2016, p. 30.

Parland, Thomas, *The Rejection in Russia of Totalitarian Socialism and Liberal Democracy: A Study of the Russian New Right* (Helsinki: University of Helsinki Societas Scientiarum Fennica, 1993).

Pastukhov, Vladimir, *Restavratsiya vmesto reformatsii: Dvadtsat' let, kotorye potryasli Rossiyu* (Moscow: OGI, 2012).

Pastukhov, Vladimir, 'O Naval'nom, Strelkove, liberal'noi auditoria i Otkrytou Rossii bez kavychek', *Republic.ru*, 31 July 2017.

Pastukhov, Vladimir, 'Neudacha okhotnika: Chego na samom dele dobivalsya Sechin, nachinaya delo Ulyukaeva', *Republic*, 23 September 2017.

Pastukhov, Vladimir, 'Tri prezidentskie karty', *Novaya gazeta*, 26 March 2018, https://www.novayagazeta.ru/articles/2018/03/24/75929-tri-prezidentskie-karty.

Pavlovsky, Gleb, 'Russian Politics under Putin: The System Will Outlast the Master', *Foreign Affairs*, May/June 2016, https://www.foreignaffairs.com/articles/russia-fsu/2016-04-18/russian-politics-under-putin.

Pavković, Aleksandar, 'Sacralisation of Contested Territory in Nationalist Discourse: A Study of Milošević's and Putin's Public Speeches', *Critical Discourse Studies*, Vol. 14, No. 4, 2017, pp. 497–513.

Pavlovsky, Gleb, 'Nobody's President? Putin Enters the Era of Transition', *Carnegie Moscow Centre*, 28 November 2017, http://carnegie.ru/commentary/74843.

Pavlovsky, Gleb, 'Zastoya ne zhdite', *New Times*, 13 December 2017.

Pavlovsky, Gleb, 'Taking to the Street Left Russia's Opposition Out in the Cold', *Moscow Times*, 12 March 2019, https://www.themoscowtimes.com/2019/03/12/taking-to-the-street-left-russias-opposition-out-in-the-cold-a64778.

Petro, Nicolai N., 'Are We Reading Russia Right?', *The Fletcher Forum of World Affairs*, Vol. 42, No. 2, Summer 2018, pp. 1–24.

Petrov, Nikolay, 'Russia on the Eve of its Presidential Election', Ponars Eurasia Policy Memo No. 509, February 2018, http://www.ponarseurasia.org/sites/default/files/policy-memos-pdf/Pepm509_Petrov_Feb2018.pdf.

Pertsev, Andrei, 'Russia's Choice of Moral Rhetoric over Pragmatism is a Ticking Time Bomb', *Carnegie.ru*, 21 July 2017, http://carnegie.ru/commentary/71593.

Pertsev, Andrey, 'President and Patriarch: What Putin Wants from the Orthodox Church', *Carnegie Moscow Centre*, 19 December 2017, http://carnegie.ru/commentary/75058.

Pertsev, Andrey, 'Russia's Regions Strike Back', Carnegie Moscow Centre, 30 November 2017, http://carnegie.ru/commentary/74872.

Pertsev, Andrey, 'New Role for United Russia', Carnegie Moscow Centre, 12 February 2018, http://carnegie.ru/commentary/75510.

Pertsev, Andrey, 'Depoliticization in Russia: The Growth of the Protest Vote', *Carnegie Moscow Centre*, 14 September 2018, https://carnegie.ru/commentary/77254.

Pirani, Simon, 'The Decline and Fall of the Russia-Ukraine Gas Trade', *Russian Analytical Digest*, No. 221, 11 June 2018, pp. 2–5.

Pismennaya, Evgeniya, Ilya Arkhipov, Henry Meyer and Irina Reznik, 'A Corruption Trial Splits the Kremlin', *Bloomberg*, 11 October 2017, https://www.bloomberg.com/news/articles/2017-10-11/a-corruption-trial-splits-the-kremlin.

Pivovarov, Yurii S., *Russkaya politika v ee istoricheskom i kul'turnom otnosheniyakh* (Moscow: Rosspen, 2006).

Pivovarov, Yurii S., 'Russkaya vlast' i publichnaya politika : Zametki istorika o prichinakh neudachi demokraticheskogo tranzita', *Polis*, No. 1, 2006, pp. 12–32.

Pivovarov, Yurii S., 'Mezhdu kazachestvom i knutom: K stoletiyu russkoi konstitutsii i russkogo parlamenta', *Polis*, No. 2, 2006, pp. 5–26.

Pivovarov, Yurii S., *Russkoe nastoyashchee i sovetskoe proshloe* (Moscow: Tsentr gumanitarnykh initsiativ, 2017).

Pivovarov, Yurii S., and A. I. Fursov, 'Russkaya sistema i reformy', *Pro i Contra*, Vol. 4, No. 4, Autumn 1999, pp. 176–97.

'Putin', directed by Andrei Kondrashov, part 2, published online 15 March 2018, https://www.youtube.com/watch?v=YI43tQx4hos.

Putin, Vladimir, with Nataliya Gevorkyan, Natalya Timakova and Andrei Kolesnikov, *First Person: An Astonishingly Frank Self-Portrait by Russia's President Vladimir Putin*, translated by Catherine A. Fitzpatrick (London: Hutchinson, 2000). The original Russian version is Vladimir Putin, *Ot pervogo litsa: Razgovory s Vladimirom Putinym*, with Nataliya Gevorkyan, Natal'ya Timakova and Andrei Kolesnikov (Moscow: Vagrius, 2000).

Putin, Vladimir, 'Russia at the Turn of the Millennium', in Putin, *First Person*, pp. 209–19. The text was originally published as Vladimir Putin, 'Rossiya na rubezhe tysyacheletiya', *Rossiiskaya gazeta*, 31 December 1999.

Putin, Vladimir, 'Otkrytoe pis'mo Vladimira Putina k Rossiiskim izbiratelyam', *Izvestiya*, 25 February 2000, p. 5.

Putin, Vladimir, 'Annual Address to the Federal Assembly of the Russian Federation', 25 April 2005, http://www.kremlin.ru/events/president/transcripts/22931.

Putin, Vladimir, 'Speech and the Following Discussion at the Munich Conference on Security Policy', 10 February 2007, http://en.kremlin.ru/transcripts/8498.

Putin, Vladimir, 'Novyi integratsionnyi proekt dlya Evrazii: budushchee, kotoroe rozhdaetsya segodnya', *Izvestiya*, 3 October 2011, p. 1, http://premier.gov.ru/events/news/16622.

Putin, Vladimir, 'Russia's Place in a Changing World', *Moskovskie novosti*, 27 February 2012, http://worldmeets.us/Moskovskiye.Novosti000001.shtml#axzz5xRYC0PpK.

Putin, Vladimir, 'Address to the Federal Assembly', *Kremlin.ru*, 12 December 2012, http://en.kremlin.ru/news/4739.

Putin, Vladimir, 'Meeting of the Valdai Discussion Club', *Kremlin.ru*, 19 September 2013, http://en.kremlin.ru/news/6007.

Putin, Vladimir, 'Presidential Address to the Federal Assembly', *Kremlin.ru*, 12 December 2013, http://en.kremlin.ru/news/6402.

Putin, Vladimir, 'Address by the President of the Russian Federation', *Kremlin.ru*, 18 March 2014, http://en.kremlin.ru/events/president/news/20603.

Putin, Vladimir, 'Meeting of the Valdai International Discussion Club', *Kremlin.ru*, 24 October 2014, http://en.kremlin.ru/news/23137.

Putin, Vladimir, 'Press-konferentsiya Vladimira Putina po itogam sammitov BRIKS i ShOS', *Kremlin.ru*, 10 July 2015, http://kremlin.ru/events/president/news/49909.

Putin, Vladimir, 'Presidential Address to the Federal Assembly', *Kremlin.ru*, 3 December 2015, http://en.kremlin.ru/events/president/news/50864.

Putin, Vladimir, 'Annual Press Conference', *Kremlin.ru*, 17 December 2015, http://en.kremlin.ru/events/president/news/50971.

Putin, Vladimir, 'Presidential Address to the Federal Assembly', *Kremlin.ru*, 1 December 2016, http://en.kremlin.ru/events/president/news/53379.

Putin, Vladimir, 'Answers to Journalists' Questions Following Direct Line', 15 June 2017, http://en.kremlin.ru/events/president/news/54794.

Putin, Vladimir, 'Meeting of the Valdai International Discussion Club', *Kremlin.ru*, 19 October 2017, http://en.kremlin.ru/events/president/news/55882.

Putin, Vladimir, 'Opening of Wall of Sorrow Memorial to Victims of Political Repression', *Kremlin.ru*, 30 October 2017, http://en.kremlin.ru/events/president/news/55948.

Putin, Vladimir, 'Annual News Conference', *Kremlin.ru*, 14 December 2017, http://en.kremlin.ru/events/president/news/56378.

Putin, Vladimir, 'Presidential Address to the Federal Assembly', *Kremlin.ru*, 1 March 2018, http://en.kremlin.ru/events/president/news/56957.

Putin, Vladimir, 'Vystuplenie na tseremonii vstupleniya v dolzhnost' Prezidenta Rossii', *Kremlin.ru*, 7 May 2018, http://kremlin.ru/events/president/news/57416.

Putin, Vladimir, 'Interview with China Media Group', 5 June 2018, http://en.kremlin.ru/events/president/news/57684.

Putin, Vladimir, 'Direct Line with Vladimir Putin', *Kremlin.ru*, 7 June 2018, http://en.kremlin.ru/events/president/news/57692.

Putin, Vladimir, 'After the Shanghai Cooperation Organisation Summit, Vladimir Putin Met with Russian Journalists', *Kremlin.ru*, 10 June 2018, http://en.kremlin.ru/events/president/news/57719.

Putin, Vladimir, 'The President's Address to Russian Citizens', *Kremlin.ru*, 29 August 2018, http://en.kremlin.ru/events/president/news/58405.

Putin, Vladimir, 'Presidential Address to the Federal Assembly', *Kremlin.ru*, 20 February 2019, http://en.kremlin.ru/events/president/news/59863.

Putnam, Robert, *Making Democracy Work* (Princeton, NJ: Princeton University Press, 1993).
Rahr, Alexander, *Wladimir Putin: Der 'Deutsche' im Kreml*, 2nd edn (Munich: Universitas Publishing House, 2000).
Rar, Aleksandr, *Vladimir Putin:'Nemets' v Kremle*, translated from the German by I. Rozanov (Moscow: Olma-Press, 2001).
Ragozin, Leonid, 'When Russian Officials "Nightmare" your Business', *Bloomberg*, 29 January 2018, https://www.bloomberg.com/news/features/2018-01-29/when-russian-officials-nightmare-your-business-you-can-lose-everything-even-your-life.
Rapoza, Kenneth, 'To Some in Russia, Oil Chief more Feared than Putin', *Forbes.com*, 9 January 2018, https://www.forbes.com/sites/kenrapoza/2018/01/09/to-some-in-russia-oil-chief-more-feared-than-putin/#4c0780252f34.
Ratelle, Jean-Francois, and Emil Aslan Souleimanov, 'A Perfect Counterinsurgency? Making Sense of Moscow's Policy of Chechenisation', *Europe-Asia Studies*, Vol. 68, No. 8, October 2016, pp. 1287–314.
RATS SCO, 'Press Release on the Results of the Shanghai Cooperation Organisation Heads of State Council Meeting', 20 June 2017, http://ecrats.org/en/news/6848.
RFE/RL Russia Report, 'US Senators Decry Decision to Hold Off on New Russian Sanctions', 31 January 2018, https://www.rferl.org/a/us-senators-attack-trump-decision-hold-off-russia-sanctions/29009067.html.
Richard, Hélène, ' "Be Partisan and Bet it all on Red": When the US Swung a Russian Election', *Le Monde Diplomatique*, March 2019, https://mondediplo.com/2019/03/04russia.
Reddaway, Peter, and Dmitri Glinski, *The Tragedy of Russia's Reforms: Market Bolshevism against Democracy* (Washington, DC: The United States Institute of Peace Press, 2001).
Remington, Thomas F., 'Economic Inequality in Russia: Sources and Consequences', *Russian Analytical Digest*, No. 187, 25 July 2016, pp. 4–7.
Renz, Bettina, 'The Russian Power Ministries and Security Services', in *Routledge Handbook of Russian Politics and Society*, edited by G. Gill and J. Young (London: Routledge, 2012), pp. 370–90.
Richter, James, 'The Ministry of Civil Society? The Public Chambers in the Regions', *Problems of Post-Communism*, Vol. 56, No. 6, November–December 2009, pp. 7–20.
Rivera, David W., and Sharon Werning Rivera, 'The Militarization of the Russian Elite under Putin', *Problems of Post-Communism*, Vol. 65, No. 4, 2018, pp. 221–32.
Roberts, Sean P., *Putin's United Russia Party* (London: Routledge, 2012).
Robinson, Neil, *The Political Economy of Russia* (Lanham, MD: Rowman & Littlefield, 2012).
Robinson, Neil, 'Russian Neo-Patrimonialism and Putin's "Cultural Turn" ', *Europe-Asia Studies*, Vol. 69, No. 2, 2017, pp. 348–66.
Rogov, Kirill, 'What Russia's New Government Tells us about Succession after Putin', *Carnegie Moscow Centre*, 28 May 2018, https://carnegie.ru/commentary/76456.
Romanova, Anna, and Boris Korban, 'Konets spetsnaza Sechina', *New Times*, 4 December 2017, https://newtimes.ru/articles/detail/132259.
Romanova, Olga, 'The Billionaire Adviser: A Story of Russia's Anti-Corruption Campaign', *Carnegie Moscow Centre*, 16 October 2017, http://carnegie.ru/commentary/73422.
Romanova, Tatiana, 'Is Russian Energy Policy towards the EU Only about Geopolitics? The Case of the Third Liberalisation Package', *Geopolitics*, Vol. 21, No. 4, October–December 2016, pp. 857–79.
Rosenberg, Steve, 'Russia PM Vladimir Putin Accuses US over Poll Protests', *BBC News*, 8 December 2011, https://www.bbc.com/news/world-europe-16084743.

Ross, Cameron, 'Federalism and Defederalisation in Russia', in *Routledge Handbook of Russian Politics and Society*, edited by Graeme Gill and James Young (London: Routledge, 2012), pp. 140–52.

Roth, Andrew, 'Putin Paints Rosy Picture of Economy Heading into 2018 Election', *Washington Post*, 11 January 2018, https://www.washingtonpost.com/world/europe/putin-paints-rosy-picture-of-economy-heading-into-2018-election/2018/01/10/1cce185a-e59c-11e7-927a-e72eac1e73b6_story.html?utm_term=.fb72f80867e0.

Roxburgh, Angus, *The Strongman: Vladimir Putin and the Struggle for Russia* (London: I.B. Tauris, 2011).

RT, 'How Long Can Europe Survive Without Russian Gas?', 16 December 2017, https://www.rt.com/business/413375-russia-gas-europe-lng-dependence/.

Rudnitsky, Jake, and Elena Mazneva, 'OPEC Deal Doesn't Stop Russia from Record Oil Output in 2017', *Bloomberg*, 2 January 2018, https://www.bloomberg.com/news/articles/2018-01-02/russia-pumps-oil-at-record-pace-in-same-year-of-global-cuts.

Russian Federation Ministry of Foreign Affairs, 'Kontsepsiya vneshnei politiki Rossiiskoi Federatsii', 30 November 2016, http://www.scrf.gov.ru/documents/2/25.html.

Russian Ministry of Foreign Affairs, Lavrov news conference, 17 January 2017, http://www.mid.ru/en/vistupleniya_ministra/-/asset_publisher/MCZ7HQuMdqBY/content/id/2599609.

Russian Ministry of Foreign Affairs, 'Comment by the Information and Press Department on the US Nuclear Posture Review', 3 February 2018, http://www.mid.ru/en/diverse/-/asset_publisher/zwI2FuDbhJx9/content/kommentarij-departamenta-informacii-i-pecati-mid-rossii-v-svazi-s-publikaciej-novoj-adernoj-doktriny-ssa.

Ryabkov, Sergei, 'BRICS: Common Approaches and Concrete Measures', *International Affairs* (Moscow), special issue, BRICS: Russia Ufa 2015.

Sakwa, Richard, *Putin: Russia's Choice*, 2nd edn (London: Routledge, 2008).

Sakwa, Richard, 'The Dual State in Russia', *Post-Soviet Affairs*, Vol. 26, No. 3, July–September 2010, pp. 185–206.

Sakwa, Richard, *The Crisis of Russian Democracy: The Dual State, Factionalism and the Medvedev Succession* (Cambridge: Cambridge University Press, 2011).

Sakwa, Richard, 'Leadership, Governance and Statecraft in Russia', in *Poor Leadership and Bad Governance: Reassessing Presidents and Prime Ministers in North America, Europe and Japan*, edited by Ludger Helms (Cheltenham: Edward Elgar, 2012), pp. 149–172.

Sakwa, Richard, *Putin and the Oligarch: The Khodorkovsky – Yukos Affair* (London: I.B. Tauris, 2014).

Sakwa, Richard, *Putin Redux: Power and Contradiction in Contemporary Russia* (London: Routledge, 2014).

Sakwa, Richard, 'From the Dual to the Triple State?', in *The Challenges for Russia's Politicized Economic System*, edited by Susanne Oxenstierna (London: Routledge, 2015), pp. 128–44.

Sakwa, Richard, *Frontline Ukraine: Crisis in the Borderlands*, paperback edition with a new afterword (London: I.B. Tauris, 2016).

Sakwa, Richard, 'The Age of Eurasia?', in *The Politics of Eurasianism: Identity, Culture and Russia's Foreign Policy*, edited by Mark Bassin and Gonzalo Pozo (Lanham, MD: Rowman & Littlefield, 2016), pp. 205–24.

Sakwa, Richard, 'The Trials of Khodorkovsky in Russia', in *Political Trials in Theory and History*, edited by Jens Meierhenrich and Devin O. Pendas (Cambridge: Cambridge University Press, 2016), pp. 369–93.

Sakwa, Richard, 'The Ukraine Syndrome and Europe: Between Norms and Space', *The Soviet and Post-Soviet Review*, No. 44, 2017, pp. 9–31.

Sakwa, Richard, *Russia against the Rest: The Post-Cold War Crisis of World Order* (Cambridge: Cambridge University Press, 2017).

Sakwa, Richard, 'Russian Neo-Revisionism', *Russian Politics*, Vol. 4, No. 1, 2019, pp. 1–21.

Sakwa, Richard, Henry Hale and Stephen White, *Developments in Russian Politics 9* (London: Palgrave Macmillan, 2018).

Saprykin, Yury, 'The Serebrennikov Case: A Theater of the Absurd', *Moscow Times*, 16 January 2018, https://themoscowtimes.com/articles/serebrennikov-case-theater-absurd-60193.

Savranskaya, Svetlana, and Tom Blanton, 'NATO Expansion: What Gorbachev Heard', National Security Archive, George Washington University, 12 December 2017, https://nsarchive.gwu.edu/briefing-book/russia-programs/2017-12-12/nato-expansion-what-gorbachev-heard-western-leaders-early.

Schmitt, Carl, *Political Theology*, translated by George Schwab (Chicago: University of Chicago Press, 1985).

Schmitt, Carl, *The Concept of the Political*, translated and with an introduction by George Schwab (Chicago, IL: University of Chicago Press, 1996).

Schreck, Carl, 'HRW Calls Russian "Foreign Agent" Law "Devastating" for Environmental Groups', *RFE/RL Russia Report*, 21 November 2017, https://www.rferl.org/a/russia-hrw-says-foreign-agent-law-devastating-environmental-groups/28868194.html.

Schreck, Carl, 'From "Not Us" to "Why Hide It?": How Russia Denied its Crimea Invasion, then Admitted it', *RFE/RL Russia Report*, 26 February 2019, https://www.rferl.org/a/from-not-us-to-why-hide-it-how-russia-denied-its-crimea-invasion-then-admitted-it/29791806.html.

Secretary of Defense, *Nuclear Posture Review*, February 2018, https://media.defense.gov/2018/Feb/02/2001872886/-1/-1/1/2018-NUCLEAR-POSTURE-REVIEW-FINAL-REPORT.PDF.

Seddon, Max, 'The Russophile Investor Languishing in a Moscow Cell', *Financial Times*, 23/24 February 2019, p. 11.

Sergunin, Alexander, *Explaining Russian Foreign Policy Behavior: Theory and Practice* (Stuttgart: Ibidem-Verlag, 2016).

Sharafutdinova, Gulnaz, *Political Consequences of Crony Capitalism inside Russia*, Contemporary European Politics and Society (Notre Dame, IN: University of Notre Dame Press, 2011).

Shchedrov, Oleg, 'Russia's Medvedev Frustrated by Slow Reforms', *Reuters*, 31 July 2008, https://uk.reuters.com/article/us-russia-medvedev-business-idUKL161861520080731.

Shekhovtsov, Anton, *Russia and the Western Far Right: Tango Noir* (London: Routledge, 2017).

Shekhovtsov, Anton, 'Putin's Russia 4.0: What Can We Expect from It?', 14 January 2018, http://www.tango-noir.com/2018/01/14/putins-russia-4-0-what-can-we-expect-from-it/.

Sherlock, Thomas, 'Russian Politics and the Soviet Past: Reassessing Stalin and Stalinism under Vladimir Putin', *Communist and Post-Communist Studies*, Vol. 49, 2016, pp. 45–59.

Shevtsova, Liliya, 'Beremennye revolyutsiei', *Radio Svoboda*, 17 October 2017, https://www.svoboda.org/a/28791261.html.

Shlapentokh, Vladimir, *Contemporary Russia as a Feudal Society* (New York: Palgrave Macmillan, 2007).

Shlapentokh, Vladimir, and Anna Arutunyan, *Freedom, Repression, and Private Property in Russia* (Cambridge: Cambridge University Press, 2013).

Shleifer, Andrei, and Daniel Treisman, 'A Normal Country', *Foreign Affairs*, Vol. 83, No. 2, March–April 2004, pp. 20–39.

Shleifer, Andrei, *A Normal Country: Russia After Communism* (Cambridge, MA: Harvard University Press, 2005).

Shraibman, Artyom, 'The Boundaries of Friendship', *Carnegie Moscow Centre*, 12 July 2017, http://carnegie.ru/commentary/71510.

Shuster, Simon, 'Rewriting Russian History: Did Boris Yeltsin Steal the 1996 Presidential Election?', *Time*, 24 February 2012, http://content.time.com/time/world/article/0,8599,2107565,00.html.

Smirnov, Valerii, *Front Putina: Protiv kogo?* (Moscow: Algoritm, 2011).

Snyder, Timothy, 'Ivan Ilyin, Putin's Philosopher of Russian Fascism', *New York Review of Books*, http://www.nybooks.com/daily/2018/03/16/ivan-ilyin-putins-philosopher-of-russian-fascism/.

Soldatov, Andrei, and Irina Borogan, *The New Nobility: The Restoration of Russia's Security State and the Enduring Legacy of the KGB* (New York: Public Affairs, 2010).

Soldatov, Andrei, and Irina Borogan, *The Red Web: The Struggle between Russia's Digital Dictators and the New Online Revolutionaries* (New York: Public Affairs, 2015).

Sonne, Paul, 'US Criticizes Germany's Support of New Russian Natural Gas Line', *Wall Street Journal*, 13 December 2017, https://www.wsj.com/articles/u-s-criticizes-germanys-support-of-new-russian-natural-gas-line-1513122298.

Soloviev, Vladimir, *Empire of Corruption: The Russian National Pastime*, translated by Matthew Hyde (Tilburg: Glagoslav, 2014).

Solovyov, Sergei, 'Attempts at Decommunization in Russia Upset De-Stalinization', *Russia in Global Affairs*, 17 January 2019, https://en.globalaffairs.ru/number/Attempts-at-Decommunization-in-Russia-Upset-de-Stalinization-19917.

Sperling, Valerie, 'Putin's Macho Personality Cult', *Communist and Post-Communist Studies*, Vol. 49, No. 1, 2016, pp. 13–23.

Stahl, Bernhard, Robin Lucke and Anne Felfeli, 'Comeback of the Transatlantic Security Community? Comparative Securitisation in the Crimea Crisis', *East European Politics*, Vol. 32, No. 4, 2016, pp. 525–46.

Stanovaya, Tatyana, 'Putin's Post-Political Government', *Carnegie Moscow Centre*, 26 June 2017, http://carnegie.ru/commentary/71355.

Stanovaya, Tatyana, 'Bezpoikonye okhraniteli: Kak ura-patrioty stali problemoi dlya putinskoi sistemy', *Republic.ru*, 2 August 2017, https://republic.ru/posts/85503.

Stanovaya, Tatyana, 'Kremlin-Duma Reshuffle Offers False Hope to Russia', *Carnegie Moscow Centre*, 12 October 2016, http://carnegie.ru/commentary/64834.

Stanovaya, Tatyana, 'The Kremlin Hierarchy is Fast decaying', *Moscow Times*, 22 February 2019, https://www.themoscowtimes.com/2019/02/22/the-kremlin-hierarchy-is-fast-decaying-a64589.

Steele, Jonathan, 'Obituary of Arseny Roginsky', *Guardian*, 5 January 2018, p. 37.

Stent, Angela, *Putin's World: Russia against the West and with the Rest* (New York: Twelve, 2019).

Stone, Oliver, 'The Putin Interviews', Showtime, 12–15 June 2017; part 1, https://www.youtube.com/watch?v=QvlKSbYkTXI and follow links.

'Strategiya natsional'noi bezopasnosti Rossiiskoi Federatsii', 31 December 2015, English translation available at http://www.ieee.es/Galerias/fichero/OtrasPublicaciones/Internacional/2016/Russian-National-Security-Strategy-31Dec2015.pdf; also in *Rossiiskaya gazeta*, 31 December 2015, http://rg.ru/2015/12/31/nac-bezopasnost-site-dok.html.

Strategiya 2020: Novaya model' rosta – novaya sotsial'naya politika, http://2020strategy.ru/data/2012/03/14/1214585998/1itog.pdf.

Studin, Irvin, 'Introduction: Ten Theses on Russia in the Twenty-First Century', in *Russia: Strategy, Policy and Administration*, edited by Irvin Studin (London: Palgrave Macmillan, 2018), pp. 1–14.

Stuenkel, Oliver, 'The Ufa Declaration: An Analysis', *Post-Western World*, 9 July 2015, http://www.postwesternworld.com/2015/07/09/the-declaration-analysis/.

Surkov, Vladislav, 'Suverenitet – eto politicheskii sinonim konkurentosposobnosti', speech of 7 February 2006, *Politicheskii klass*, 31 March 2006, pp. 15–21.

Surkov, Vladislav, *Texts* (Moscow: 'Europe' Publishing House, 2010).

Surkov, Vladislav, 'Odinochestvo polukrovki', *Russia in Global Affairs*, 9 April 2018, http://www.globalaffairs.ru/global-processes/Odinochestvo-polukrovki-14-19477.

Surkov, Vladislav, 'Dolgoe gosudarstvo Putina: O tom, chto sdes' voobshche proiskhodit', *Nezavisimaya gazeta*, 11 February 2019, http://www.ng.ru/ideas/2019-02-11/5_7503_surkov.html.

Suslov, Dmitry, 'A Pivot towards Asia, Integration and Mega-Regions', Valdai Discussion Club, 9 June 2016, http://valdaiclub.com/news/a-pivot-towards-asia-integration-and-mega-regions-balancing-russia-s-apr-policy/.

Szakonyi, David, *Governing Business: The State and Business in Russia* (Philadelphia, PA: Foreign Policy Research Institute, 2018).

TASS, 'Kudrin: Russia Needs to Settle Political Discord with the West to Reach High Growth Rates', 4 October 2016, http://tass.com/economy/904080.

TASS, 'Top Prosecutor Shows Corruption in Russia Caused Losses of $2.5 bln over Past Three Years', 8 December 2017, http://tass.com/politics/979806.

TASS, 'Putin's 2017 Trust Rating Hits Record-High in December – Poll', 11 January 2018, http://tass.com/society/984606.

TASS, 'Putin Vows to Abide by Two-Term Limit on Consecutive Presidential Tenures', 25 May 2018, http://tass.com/politics/1006561.

TASS, 'Kremlin Aide Highlights Cooperation with China as Russia's Foreign Policy Priority', 4 June 2018, http://tass.com/politics/1007915.

TASS, 'RBC: Government to Specify Scope of Pension Reform', 8 June 2018, http://tass.com/pressreview/1008666.

Taylor, Brian D., *State Building in Putin's Russia: Policing and Coercion after Communism* (Cambridge: Cambridge University Press, 2011).

Taylor, Brian D., *The Code of Putinism* (Oxford: Oxford University Press, 2018).

Tkachenko, Stanislav, 'The Meaning of Alexey Kudrin's Return', *Russia Direct*, 13 June 2016, http://www.russia-direct.org/opinion/meaning-alexey-kudrins-return.

Timofeev, Ivan, 'Fighting Sanctions: From Legislation to Strategy', Valdai Club, 18 June 2018, http://valdaiclub.com/a/highlights/fighting-sanctions-strategy/.

Toal, Gerard, *Near Abroad: Putin, the West and the Contest over Ukraine and the Caucasus* (Oxford: Oxford University Press, 2017).

Toloraya, Georgy, 'Russian Vision of BRICS Global Role: Implications of the Ufa Summit', paper prepared for the 9th World Congress of ICCEES, Mukahari, Japan, 3–8 August 2015.

Tolstoy, Andrey, and Edmund McCaffrey, 'Mind Games: Alexander Dugin and Russia's War of Ideas', *World Affairs Journal*, March 2015, http://www.worldaffairsjournal.org/93030.

Transparency International, 'Corruption Perception Index 2018', https://www.transparency.org/cpi2018.

Travin, Dmitry, 'Ordinary Russians Have No One to Tell Them How Miserable Their Lives Are Becoming', *Moscow Times*, 10–16 November 2016, p. 5.

Travin, Dmitry, 'Pochemu president ne ogranichit davlenie silovykh struktur na biznes', *Republic*, 10 October 2017, https://republic.ru/posts/86874.

Traynor, Ian, 'Barack Obama: No Cold War over Crimea', *Guardian*, 26 March 2014, https://www.theguardian.com/world/2014/mar/26/obama-no-cold-war-crimea.

Treisman, Daniel, *The Return: Russia's Journey from Gorbachev to Medvedev* (London: Simon & Schuster, 2011).

Treisman, Daniel (ed.), *The New Autocracy: Information, Politics, and Policy in Putin's Russia* (Washington, DC: Brookings, 2017).
Treisman, Daniel, 'Democracy by Mistake', *VOX CEPR Policy Portal*, 26 November 2017, https://voxeu.org/article/democracy-mistake.
Trifonova, Ekaterina, 'Sposoby "Ne Koshmarit' Biznes" uzhe Pridumany', *Nezavisimaya gazeta*, 20 March 2018, p. 3.
Troianovski, Anton, 'Q & A: Sanctioned Putin Ally Holds out Hope That Trump Will Boost Russia Ties', *Washington Post*, 10 February 2018, https://www.washingtonpost.com/news/worldviews/wp/2018/02/10/qa-sanctioned-putin-ally-holds-out-hope-that-trump-will-boost-russia-ties/?utm_term=.134eb9ae7981.
Trudolyubov, Maksim, *Chastnoe prostranstvo, vlast' i sobstevennost v Rossii* (Moscow: Novoe Izdatel'stvo, 2015), translated as Trudolyubov, Maxim, *The Tragedy of Property: Private Life, Ownership and the Russian State* (Cambridge: Polity, 2018).
Trudolyubov, Maksim, 'Dva gosudarstva Vladimira Putina: Obychnoe i oprichnina', *Republic.ru*, 20 February 2018, https://republic.ru/posts/89598.
Trudolyubov, Maxim, 'The Hidden, Self-Reliant Russia', Kennan Institute, 16 August 2018, https://www.wilsoncenter.org/blog-post/the-hidden-self-reliant-russia.
Tsygankov, Andrei P., *Russophobia: Anti-Russian Lobby and American Foreign Policy* (Basingstoke: Palgrave Macmillan, 2009).
Tsygankov, Andrei P., *The Strong State in Russia: Development and Crisis* (Oxford: Oxford University Press, 2014).
Tsygankov, Andrei P., 'In the Shadow of Nikolai Danilevskii: Universalism, Particularism, and Russian Geopolitical Theory', *Europe-Asia Studies*, Vol. 69, No. 4, 2017, pp. 571–93.
Tsygankov, Andrei P., *Russia's Foreign Policy: Change and Continuity in National Identity*, 5th edn (Lanham, MD: Rowman & Littlefield, 2019).
Turnakova, Irina, 'Zagovoril Usmanov – zagovorit i Sechin', interview with Gleb Pavlovsky, *Fontanka.ru*, 19 May 2017, http://m.fontanka.ru/2017/05/19/154/.
Tusk, Donald, 'A United Europe can End Russia's Energy Stranglehold', *Financial Times*, 21 April 2014, https://www.ft.com/content/91508464-c661-11e3-ba0e-00144feabdc0.
Umland, Andreas, 'Why Aleksandr Dugin's "Neo-Eurasianism" Is Not Eurasianist', *The Politicon*, 1 June 2018, http://thepoliticon.net/essays/546-why-aleksandr-dugins-neo-eurasianism-is-not-eurasianist.html.
Urban, Mark, *The Skripal Files: The Life and Near Death of a Russian Spy* (London: Macmillan, 2018).
Urban, Michael, *Cultures of Power in Post-Communist Russia: An Analysis of Elite Political Discourse* (New York: Cambridge University Press, 2010).
Urnov, Mark, '"Greatpowerness" as the Key Element of Russian Self-Consciousness under Erosion', *Communist and Post-Communist Studies*, Vol. 47, Nos 3–4, 2014, pp. 305–22.
US Congress, 'Defending American Security from Russian Aggression Act of 2019', 13 February 2019, https://www.congress.gov/bill/116th-congress/senate-bill/482/text#toc-id8ECC7DE75C5F408089FFD9B1C838ECEB.
Valdai Discussion Club, 'Towards the Great Ocean – 3: Creating Central Eurasia', Valdai Report No. 3, June 2015.
Valdai Discussion Club, 'War and Peace in the 21st Century: A New International Balance as the Guarantee of Stability', Materials for Discussion at the 12th Annual Meeting of the Valdai Discussion Club, Sochi, 19–22 October 2015, p. 4. The final report was published as 'War and Peace in the 21st Century: International Stability and Balance of the New Type', Valdai Discussion Club Report, January 2016, http://valdaiclub.com/publications/reports/international-stability-and-balance-of-the-new-type/.

Vardanyan, Denis, 'Benefitsiary martovskoi pobedy', *New Times*, 5 February 2018, https://newtimes.ru/articles/detail/145138?utm_source=twitter.com&utm_medium=social&utm_campaign=thenewtimes&utm_content=instant.

Russian Federation Ministry of Defence, Russian Federation Ministry of Defence, 'Voennaya doktrina Rossiiskoi Federatsii', 25 December 2014, English translation available at https://www.offiziere.ch/wp-content/uploads-001/2015/08/Russia-s-2014-Military-Doctrine.pdf.

Volkov, Denis, '"No Trust": What Russians think about the Pension Reform', *Carnegie Moscow Centre*, 9 August 2018, https://carnegie.ru/commentary/77015.

Volkov, Denis, and Andrei Kolesnikov, 'The Perils of Change: Russians' Mixed Attitudes toward Reform', *Carnegie Moscow Centre*, February 2018, http://carnegieendowment.org/files/VolkovKolesnikov_RussianReform_article.pdf.

Walker, Shaun, 'Putin Blames EU as Russia Abandons Plans for South Stream Pipeline', *Guardian*, 1 December 2014, http://www.theguardian.com/business/2014/dec/01/russia-blames-eu-as-it-abandons-plans-for-south-stream-gas-pipeline.

Walker, Shaun, 'Unequal Russia: Is Anger Stirring in the Global Capital of Inequality?', *Guardian*, 25 April 2017, https://www.theguardian.com/inequality/2017/apr/25/unequal-russia-is-anger-stirring-in-the-global-capital-of-inequality.

Walker, Shaun, *The Long Hangover: Putin's New Russia and the Ghosts of the Past* (New York: Oxford University Press, 2018).

Wang, Yong, 'Offensive for Defensive: The Belt and Road Initiative and China's New Grand Strategy', *Pacific Review*, Vol. 29, No. 3, pp. 455–63.

Ware, Robert Bruce (ed.), *The Fire Below: How the Caucasus Shaped Russia* (New York: Bloomsbury, 2013).

Weafer, Chris, 'Going Cold Turkey: Russia Wants an End to OPEC-Production Cuts', *Intellinews.com*, 30 May 2018, http://www.intellinews.com/macro-advisory-going-cold-turkey-russia-wants-an-end-to-opec-production-cuts-142499/.

Weber, Max, 'Politics as a Vocation', in *From Max Weber: Essays in Sociology*, edited by H. H. Gerth and C. Wright Mills (New York: Oxford University Press, 1958), pp. 77–128.

Wegren, Stephen K., 'Food Security and Countersanctions', *Russian Analytical Digest*, No. 204, 19 June 2017, pp. 2–5.

Weir, Fred, 'Kremlin Cyberpower?', *Christian Science Monitor*, 19 April 2018, https://www.csmonitor.com/World/Europe/2018/0419/Kremlin-cyberpower-How-fight-over-messaging-app-is-showing-its-limits.

Weir, Fred, 'Russia's Media Scene: Not Just a State Affair', *Christian Science Monitor*, 6 February 2018, https://www.csmonitor.com/World/Europe/2018/0206/Russia-s-media-scene-not-just-a-state-affair.

Weir, Fred, 'To Pay for a "Russia First" Agenda, Putin Takes Ax to Military Spending', *Christian Science Monitor*, 8 May 2018, https://www.csmonitor.com/World/Europe/2018/0508/To-pay-for-a-Russia-first-agenda-Putin-takes-ax-to-military-spending.

Weir, Fred, '"Fake News" in Russia: State Censorship Elicits an Outcry', *Christian Science Monitor*, 20 March 2019, https://www.csmonitor.com/World/Europe/2019/0320/Fake-news-in-Russia-State-censorship-elicits-an-outcry.

White, David, *The Russian Democratic Party Yabloko* (Aldershot: Ashgate, 2006).

White House, *National Security Strategy of the USA*, February 2015, https://obamawhitehouse.archives.gov/sites/default/files/docs/2015_national_security_strategy_2.pdf.

White House, *National Security Strategy of the United States*, December 2017, https://www.whitehouse.gov/wp-content/uploads/2017/12/NSS-Final-12-18-2017-0905.pdf.

Wilson, Andrew, *Virtual Politics: Faking Democracy in the Post-Soviet World* (New Haven, CT: Yale University Press, 2005).

Wood, Tony, *Russia without Putin: Money, Power and the Myths of the New Cold War* (London: Verso, 2018).

World Bank, *Doing Business 2018: Reforming to Create Jobs* (Washington, DC: International Bank for Reconstruction and Development / the World Bank, 2018), http://russian.doingbusiness.org/~/media/WBG/DoingBusiness/Documents/Annual-Reports/English/DB2018-Full-Report.pdf.

Yablokov, Ilya, *Fortress Russia: Conspiracy Theories in Post-Soviet Russia* (Cambridge: Polity, 2018).

Yaffa, Joshua, 'The Double Sting: A Power Struggle between Russia's Rival Security Agencies', *New Yorker*, 27 July 2015, http://www.newyorker.com/magazine/2015/07/27/the-double-sting.

Yaffa, Joshua, 'Putin's Shadow Cabinet and the Bridge to Crimea', *New Yorker*, 29 May 2017, https://www.newyorker.com/magazine/2017/05/29/putins-shadow-cabinet-and-the-bridge-to-crimea.

Yamshanov, Boris, and Viktor Vasenin, 'Neposredstvennaya zhizn': Predlozheniya ot Bastrykina – sozdat' edinyi sledstevnnyi komitet i vvesti otchety o raskhodakh chinovnikov', *Rossiiskaya gazeta*, 7 September 2010.

Yanov, Alexander, *The Russian Challenge and the Year 2000* (Oxford: Blackwell, 1987).

Yarovaya, Anna, 'The First Steps towards Exonerating Russian Gulag Historian Yuri Dmitriyev', *oDR*, 2 March 2018, https://www.opendemocracy.net/od-russia/anna-yarovaya/the-first-steps-towards-exonerating-yuri-dmitriyev.

Yavlinsky, Grigory, *The Putin System: An Opposing View* (New York: Columbia University Press, 2019).

Zhavoronkov, Sergey, 'Two Lean Years: Russia's Budget for 2018–19', *Intersection*, 6 December 2017, http://intersectionproject.eu/article/economy/two-lean-years-russias-budget-2018-20.

Zubarevich, Natalya, 'The Fall of Russia's Regional Governors', *Carnegie Moscow Centre*, 12 October 2017, http://carnegie.ru/commentary/73569.

Zudin, Aleksei Yu., 'Rezhim V. Putina: Kontury novoi politicheskoi sistemy', *Obshchestvennye nauki i sovremennost'*, No. 2, 2003, pp. 67–83.

Zweynert, Joachim, and Ivan Boldyrev, 'Conflicting Patterns of Thought in the Russian Debate on Modernisation and Innovation 2008–2013', *Europe-Asia Studies*, Vol. 69, No. 6, August 2017, pp. 912–39.

Zygar, Mikhail, *All the Kremlin's Men: Inside the Court of Vladimir Putin* (New York: Public Affairs, 2016), the English version of *Vsya kremlevskaya rat': Kratkaya istoriya sovremennoi rossii* (Moscow: Intellektual'naya Literatura, 2016).

INDEX

21st Century Russia: The Shape of a Desirable Future 32

Abdullatipov, Ramazan 194
ABM. *See* Anti-Ballistic Missile treaty
Abramovich, Roman 93
Abyzov, Mikhail 110–11
administrative regime 10, 20–1, 23–4, 27, 43–8, 50, 56, 59, 94–5, 99, 101, 189, 195, 224–5, 231, 233, 244
  compensates for 43
  democracy is 56
  divergence between 46
  governance goals 231
  independent bourgeoisie, rise of 44
  legitimacy of 24
  monocentric practices of 21
  political accountability 225
  power of 59, 231
  rationality 233
  regime–state 23
  return of politics, 195
  tutelary role of 10
Afghanistan 14, 153, 164, 174, 178, 183, 186
AFK Sistema 93, 106, 108
Agency for Strategic Initiatives 110
Alekperov, Vagit 93
algorithmic governance 46, 52
Alikhanov, Anton 112
All Russia (*Vsya Rossiya*) 19
All-Russian Centre for the Study of Public Opinion (VTsIOM) polling agency 128
All-Union Communist Party (Bolsheviks) (VKP(b)) 23

amoral familism 52
anomie concept 52
Anti-Ballistic Missile (ABM) treaty 154
anti-corruption issues 103
anti-Gazprom law 137
anti-hegemonic alignment 143, 150, 176
anti-Maidan groups 73
anti-religious extremism 190
APEC. *See* Asia-Pacific Economic Cooperation (APEC)
Arab Spring 86, 227, 238
Arashukov, Rauf 109
argumentative governance 46
ASEAN. *See* Association of South-East Asian Nations (ASEAN)
Asia-Pacific Economic Cooperation (APEC) 174
Association of South-East Asian Nations (ASEAN) 143
Ataturk, Kemal 242
The Atlantic 184
authoritarian neoliberalism 79, 228
Auzan, Alexander 115, 118, 122–3
Avetisyan, Artem 110
Azarov, Dmitry 112

Bacon, Edwin 51
Bagehot, Walter 45
Baikal-Amur Mainline (BAM) 114
Baker, James 159
ballistic missile defence (BMD) 165
Baltic Pipeline System 2 135
BAM. *See* Baikal-Amur Mainline (BAM)
Banfield, Edward 52
Baring Vostok Capital Partners 110
Barkashov, Alexander 61

Barsukov, Mikhail 34
Bastrykin, Mikhail 101–2, 104–5
Belarus 9, 132, 134–5, 169, 171, 173, 176, 178, 180, 232, 237
Belt and Road Initiative (BRI) 168
Belyaninov, Andrei 106, 172
Belykh, Nikita 105–6, 192–3
Berezovsky, Boris 35, 116
Beria syndrome 108
Berlin Wall 3
Berlusconi, Silvio 44, 75
besieged fortress 197
bipolar model 219
BMD. *See* ballistic missile defence
Bolshevik revolution 18, 39, 66–7, 69–70, 72, 222
Bonaparte, Louis 224
Borodin, Pavel 5
Bortnikov, Alexander 37
bourgeois rule 17, 44, 47, 51, 70, 93, 98, 113, 220, 224, 226
Bratstvo (Brotherhood) pipeline system 134
Brazil, Russia, India, China and South Africa (BRICS) members 125
Brezhnev, Leonid 3, 11, 30, 75, 80, 84, 198
BRI. *See* Belt and Road Initiative
Bryza, Matthew 136
Brzezinski 167
business:
    across borders 171
    bilateral 141
    environment 95
    factional balancing 94
    government support for 190
    merger 145
    model of unification 150
    Putin meeting with 139
    quasi-feudal relationship 93
    security matters into 35
    small/medium sector 203
    'raids' by 20
    technocratic style 80
    tycoons 28
    in United States 140

CAATSA. *See* Countering America's Adversaries through Sanctions Act
Calvey, Michael 110

captive nations 150
Cardin, Ben 139
CBR. *See* Central Bank of Russia (CBR)
CEC. *See* Central Election Commission
CEE. *See* Central and Eastern Europe
Central and Eastern Europe (CEE) 137
Central Bank of Russia (CBR) 123, 125, 129, 207
Central Election Commission (CEC) 191
Centre for Strategic Research (CSR) 33, 128–9, 207
CFE. *See* Conventional Forces in Europe (CFE)
Chaika, Yuri 101, 105, 192
Chebankova, Elena 43, 53
Chechen war 6, 14–15, 34, 65, 78, 99, 147, 149, 154
Chechenisation 63
Chechnya, Kadyrovite 6, 19, 36, 63–5, 68, 197, 204, 216, 240
Chekism 35
Chemezov, Sergei 111–12, 219
Cherkesov, Viktor 35
Chernomyrdin, Viktor 19
Chicherin, Boris 32
China 16, 21, 103, 107, 121–2, 125, 135–6, 143, 149–50, 157, 164, 167–8, 171–84, 187, 224, 232, 238, 24
China-Pakistan Economic Corridor (CPEC) 179
Chubais, Anatoly 28, 34–5, 61, 126, 222
Churov, Vladimir 191
CIS. *See* Commonwealth of Independent States (CIS)
Civic Chamber 46–8, 53
Clinton, Bill 149, 152
Clinton, Hillary 17, 36, 149, 152, 168, 178
CoE. *See* Council of Europe
Cold War 1, 3, 8, 13, 16, 81, 136, 139, 142, 145, 154, 160–1, 163–4, 168, 181, 187–8, 215, 237
    post-Cold War 12–17, 85, 146–52, 161–2, 184, 215, 232
Collective Security Treaty Organisation (CSTO) 155
colour revolutions 70, 73, 227
Committee for State Security (KGB) 2
Commonwealth of Independent States (CIS) 8, 155

communal apartment (*kommunalka*) 2
communist revanche 19
Communist Party of China (CPC) 183
Communist Party of the Russian
    Federation (CPRF) 6, 19, 27–8, 38, 56,
    60, 67, 88–9, 199–200, 211, 223, 238
Communist Party of the Soviet Union
    (CPSU) 2, 4, 8, 20, 23, 25, 99
competitive coexistence 154
Conference on Security and Cooperation
    in Europe (CSCE) 148
Congress of People's Deputies (CPD) 4–5,
    8, 25–6, 38
conjugation (*sopryazhenie*) 173
conservative-guardianship strategy 80
Contingent Reserve Arrangement
    (CRA) 176
Conventional Forces in Europe (CFE) 14
correlation of forces 157
Corruption:
    anti-corruption campaigner 33, 76, 88,
        103, 198
    meta-corruption 46, 92–100, 96, 99–
        101, 192, 194
    prosecutions 101
    (Russian) Investigative Committee
        (RIC) 104
    security services 95
    venal 47, 95–96, 99, 100, 192, 194,
        231, 235
Corruption Perceptions Index (CPI) 96
Council of Europe (CoE) 149
Countering America's Adversaries through
    Sanctions Act (CAATSA)
CPC. *See* Communist Party of China
CPD. *See* Congress of People's
    Deputies (CPD)
CPEC. *See* China-Pakistan Economic
    Corridor
CPRF. *See* Communist Party of the Russian
    Federation (CPRF)
CPSU. *See* Communist Party of the Soviet
    Union (CPSU)
CRA. *See* Contingent Reserve
    Arrangement
Crimea 36, 41, 74, 77, 88, 93, 118, 124, 126,
    159–60, 168, 171, 185, 189, 191, 197,
    202, 206, 211, 223
crushing sanctions 141

CSCE. *See* Conference on Security and
    Cooperation in Europe
CSTO. *See* Collective Security Treaty
    Organisation

Danilevsky, Nikolai 39–40
DASKAA. *See* Defending American
    Security from Kremlin Aggression
    Act 138, 141, 162
Davis, Christopher 124
Dawisha, Karen 99
de Benoist, Alain 39
de Gaulle, Charles 151, 215, 242
decommunisation 69, 72, 221
Defending American Security
    from Kremlin Aggression Act
    (DASKAA) 141–2
Defending Elections from Threats
    by Establishing Redlines Act
    (DETER) 141
Delyagin, Mikhail 39
democracy:
    and economic development 18, 51
    formalities observed under Putin 7
    imitation democracy 56
    managed democracy 17
    sovereign democracy 21–2, 56
*Democracy: Development of the Russian
    Model* 32
democratic revolution 13, 27, 70, 92, 221
democrats 26, 28, 141, 198
demokratizatsiya (democratisation) 3
Den' (*The Day*) 38
Deposit Insurance Agency 123
Deripaska, Oleg 35, 93, 140
derzhavnik (great power defender) 61
destalinisation 69, 221
DETER. *See* Defending Elections from
    Threats by Establishing Redlines
    Act 141
dialogue partner 175
dirigiste democracy 21
dirigiste inflexion 42
distributed denial of service (DDoS)
    attacks 37
doctoral (*kandidatskaya*) dissertation 5
domestic security policy 37
doomsday scenarios 161
dramaturgiya 47

Druzhba (Friendship) oil pipeline 134–5
Drymanov, Alexander 104
dual state model 18, 32, 44–52, 59–60, 82, 92, 94, 109, 195, 220–1, 224, 233–4, 238–9, 241, 244–6
duality. *See* dual state
Dugin, Alexander 39, 41, 242
Duma election 19, 27, 49, 76, 86–9, 191, 205, 212
Durov, Pavel 121–2
Dyumin, Alexei 220
Dzerzhinsky, Felix 69

East Siberia–Pacific Ocean (ESPO) line 136
Eastern Partnership (EaP) 151
Eckstein, Harry 52
economic liberals 31–3, 107
Economic Security and Countering Corruption (GUEBiPK) 102
Economic Security Service (SEB) 101
economic statism 83
ECtHR. *See* European Court of Human Rights (ECtHR)
EDB. *See* Eurasian Development Bank
elections:
  parliamentary election 6, 17, 38, 112, 204, 217
  presidential election 11, 18–19, 28, 34, 49, 89, 92, 129, 140–1, 190–1, 198–206
  regional elections 192, 211
electoral system 87, 89
elites 10, 20, 46, 49, 69, 84–5, 117, 199, 218, 222, 227, 241, 244
enlightened despotism model 46
era of stagnation (*zastoi*) 11
ESPO. *See* East Siberia–Pacific Ocean (ESPO) line
ethics of responsibility 77
ethnogenesis 40
Eucken, Walter 114
eudaemonic trap 10
Eurasia 143, 147–8, 167–8, 172–6, 178–81, 187
Eurasian Development Bank (EDB) 169
Eurasian Economic Union (EEU) 42, 155, 167, 168–75, 181–3

Eurasian integration 41–2, 143, 157, 167, 168–75, 234
Eurasianists 26, 30–1, 39–42, 81, 100, 136, 151, 168, 226–7
Europe and Humanity (1920) 39
European Bank for Reconstruction and Development (EBRD) 110
European Court of Human Rights (ECtHR) 61
European University in St Petersburg (EUSP) 74, 103
Everyday Saints and Other Stories 11
Exodus to the East 39

faction 30–2, 36, 38–9, 77, 99–100, 105, 172, 222
factional conflict 82, 100–1, 105, 245
factionalism 43, 60, 78, 81, 100–112, 240
Fatherland (*Otechestvo*) party 19
Federal Customs Service (FCS) 106, 172
Federal Penitentiary Service (FSIN) 109, 195
Federal Security Service (FSB) 5, 7, 34–7, 69, 76, 80, 93, 98–102, 104, 106–7, 109, 111, 121, 142, 239
Federal Service for Drug Control (FSKN) 102
Federation Council (FC) 27, 47, 62, 109
Fedorov, Valery 128
Felshtinsky, Yurii 199
Feoktistov, Oleg 102, 107, 109
fiat system 126
financial 'laundromats' 95
First Chief Directorate (PGU) 2
fiscal rule 133
foreign agents law 190
foreign direct investment (FDI) 110
fortuna 77
Foundation for the Struggle against Corruption (FBK) 33
Foundations of Geopolitics (*Osnovy Geopolitika*) 41
Fourth Political Theory 41
free trade area (FTA) 169
FSB. *See* Federal Security Service (FSB)
FSKN. *See* Federal Service for Drug Control
FTA. *See* free trade area

Fungal, Sergei 111
Furman, Dmitry 56

Gaaze, Konstantin 207, 240–1
Gaidar, Yegor 19
Galeotti, Mark 94
GAZ. *See* Gorky Automobile Plant
Gazprom 5, 86, 98, 109, 134–5, 137, 141, 234
GDR. *See* German Democratic Republic (GDR)
Georgia 13, 36, 64, 71, 151–4
GEP. *See* Greater Eurasian Partnership
German Democratic Republic (GDR) 3
Germany 7–8, 13, 40, 53, 67, 71, 103, 114, 122, 124, 129, 134–5, 139, 147, 152, 172
Gessen, Masha 99
Gini coefficient 121
glasnost' (openness) 3
Glazyev, Sergei 41, 128–9
gold-backed currency 125, 126, 133
Golikova, Tatyana 207
Gorbachev, Mikhail 1, 3–4, 9, 12–13, 15, 25, 30, 33, 35, 65, 82, 86, 146–7, 151, 159, 163, 181, 230, 239, 242
Gorky Automobile Plant (GAZ) 199
gosudarstvenniki 84
Graham, Lindsey 141
Gramsci, Antonio 43–4, 225–6
Great Patriotic War 7, 9
Greater Eurasian Partnership (GEP) 167, 173, 175–176, 180–1
Grossraum 41
Grudinin, Pavel 200, 204
guardianship tradition (*okhraniteli*) 34
Gudkov, Dmitry 196, 199
Gumilev, Lev 40
Guriev, Sergei 119

Hahn, Gordon 197
Hale, Henry 45
Hamiltonian strategy 123
Hanson, Philip 97–8
Healey, Dan 87
Heartland 167
Hedlund, Stefan 53
Heidegger, Martin 41
Hellman, Joel 83

heterogeneous bloc 81
historic bloc 225
Hitler, Adolf 8, 17, 67
Hobbesian model 54–5
Holocaust Memorial Day 186
Holodomor 8
horizontal forces 16, 20, 24, 74, 78, 82–3, 127, 149, 171, 181, 216–17
Huntington, Samuel 18, 241
hybrid warfare 136, 158

Ichkeria 6, 63
ICT. *See* information and communication technology
ideational-interest groups 100
Ilyin, Ivan 65
IMF. *See* International Monetary Fund (IMF)
information and communication technology (ICT) 209
informational autocracy 49
Inozemtsev, Vladislav 198
Institute of Contemporary Development (*Institut sovremmennogo razvitiya*, INSOR) 32
Interior Security Department (USB) 102
International Monetary Fund (IMF) 125
internet service providers (ISPs) 121
intra-systemic factionalism 111–12, 234, 240
Ishaev, Viktor 111
ISPs. *See* internet service providers (ISPs)
The Italian. *See* Kochuikov, Andrei
Izborskii Klub 39
Izvestiya 80

Jinping, Xi 172, 182–3
Judaism 12
Jurgens, Igor 85

Kadyrov, Akhmad 63–5
Kalashov, Zakhariy (*Shakro Molodoi, Young Shakro*) 104
Karaganov, Sergei 143, 180, 183, 187
Kashin, Oleg 197
Kasparov, Garry 34
katechon 55
Katusa, Marin 136
Kennedy, Paul 116

KGB. *See* Committee for State Security (KGB)
Khasbulatov, Ruslan 26
Khodorkovsky, Mikhail 28, 32–3, 46–7, 93, 100, 104, 107, 192, 237
Khorashavin, Aleksandr 106
Khudilainen, Alexander 89
Kirienko, Sergei 78, 112, 211, 222
Kirill, Patriarch 11–12, 103
Kirishi oil refinery 135
Kissinger, Henry 5, 180–1
Klein, Naomi 60
kleptocracy 38, 93, 134, 234, 239, 241
Knight, Amy 65, 201
Kochuikov, Andrei 104
Kogogin, Sergei 111
Kolesnikov, Boris 102
kommunalka 12
kompromat (compromising materials) 101
Konchalovsky, Andrei 17
kontraktniki 153
Kordonsky, Simon 29, 94
kormlenie (tax farming) 93
Korshunov, Oleg 109
Korzhakov, Alexander 34–5, 99
Kosovo 149, 160, 163
Kovalchuk, Mikhail 111–12
Kovalchuk, Yuri 112, 220
Kremlin 1–10, 17–19, 24, 27, 43–4, 48, 65, 69, 71, 75, 78, 87–8, 92, 109–110, 113–114, 118, 121–2, 129, 139–41, 150, 152–3, 183, 185, 190, 194, 201, 204–6, 217–18, 223, 227, 232, 241
Krym Nash (Crimea is Ours) 88
Kudrin, Alexei 32–3, 35, 74, 128–9, 131, 204, 207–10, 230
Kukly political puppet show 55
Kurginyan, Sergei 39
Kyrgyzstan 169–71, 174, 178

laissez faire capitalism 114
Lamonov, Alexander 104
Laruelle, Marlene 31
Latynina, Yulia 103, 216–17
Lavrov, Sergei 177
LDPR. *See* Liberal Democratic Party of Russia (LDPR)
legal populism 46
Legvold, Robert 160

Leontiev, Mikhail 39
Leontyev, Konstantin 40
Levchenko, Sergei 88
Leviathan 54–5, 103
Liberal Democratic Party of Russia (LDPR) 27, 29, 38, 56, 60, 89, 111, 199–200, 238
liberal internationalist period 153
liberals. *See individual entries*
limited-access orders 83, 115
Litvinenko, Vladimir 5, 216
Liyuan, Peng 172
Lo, Bobo 183
logic of *enlargement* 1
Lokot, Anatoly 88
luck 77
Lukin, Alexander 96, 178, 192
Luzhkov, Yuri 19

Machiavelli, Niccolo 77
Mackinder, Halford 167
mad printing press 75
mafiya, the 95
Magnitsky Act 44, 138, 143
Magnitsky, Sergei 44, 101, 138
Maidan revolution 151
Maksimenko, Mikhail 104–5
Malofeev, Konstantin 31
Manafort, Paul 140
Manturov, Denis 111–12, 207
manual management 17
Markin, Vladimir 104
Mathilda 191
May Decrees (2012) 132 (2018) 208–9
McCain, John 117
mechanical stability 59, 211, 213
media 19–20, 25, 38, 39, 49, 75–6, 102, 105, 122, 156, 162, 189, 191, 200, 203, 205, 212, 246
Medinsky, Vladimir 69, 103
Medvedev, Dmitry 18, 21, 32–3, 39, 44, 63, 82, 85–7, 95–6, 100–3, 105, 107, 110–11, 120, 140, 154, 192–3, 204, 207, 209, 218, 220, 225, 234, 237–8, 240–4
changed governors 193
clash with Putin 85
condemned sanctions 140
defined evolutionary path 85
increased retirement age 209

liberal statist 33
modern reform 87
national humiliation 111
political reform 63
presidency 32, 95-6, 100-2, 240
prime minister 86, 207
privatisationprogramme 107
Menendez, Bob 141
meso-factionalism 111
meta-corruption 46, 92, 96, 99-101, 192, 194
MFA. *See* Ministry of Foreign Affairs
Mikhailov, Sergei 112
Military Doctrine 155
Millennium Manifesto 9
Miller, Alexei 67, 98
Milonov, Vitaly 74
Ministry of Foreign Affairs (MFA) 159
Ministry of Internal Affairs (MVD) 35, 100, 102, 106
Mironenko, Sergei 74
Mironov, Ivan 61
Mobile TeleSystems (MTS) 108
modernisation programme 153
Modi, Narendra 179
modus vivendi 95
Monaghan, Andrew 160, 229-30
Mongol yoke 152
Moore, Barrington 113
Mordashov, Alexei 93
Moscow 3, 5-6, 8, 11, 1219, 26, 30, 35, 38-40, 55, 62-4, 67, 69, 71, 76, 88, 103-6, 108, 118-19, 133-6, 143, 148-9, 154, 155, 157-8, 162-6, 174, 176, 182, 184-7, 196, 200, 204, 206, 212, 218, 220, 223, 238, 240-1
Moscow School of Social and Economic Sciences (MSSES) 103
MSSES. *See* Moscow School of Social and Economic Sciences (MSSES)
MTS. *See* Mobile TeleSystems (MTS)
Mussolini, Benito 55, 244

Nabiullina, Elvira 125, 207
NAM. *See* Non-Aligned Movement
Napoleon III 55, 223, 224-5, 227
National Defence Strategy 164
National Economic Security Strategy to 2030 130

National Guard (NG, *Rosgvardiya*) 35-6
National Liberation Movement (NOD) 73
national patriots 38
National Security Strategy 155-6, 164
NATO. *See* North Atlantic Treaty Organisation
NATO-Russia Council (NRC) 14
Navalny, Alexei 33, 88-9, 96, 105, 190, 192-3, 195-200, 202, 205-6, 210, 212, 222
  intention for Presidency 192-5
  member of Yabloko 33
  Moscow mayoral election 88-9, 96, 105, 190,
  political competitiveness 196-206
  sentence against 193
Nazarbayev, Nursultan 40, 172, 176
NDB. *See* New Development Bank
neformaly (informal associations) 10
Nelyubov' 103
Nemtsov, Boris 64, 217, 222
neo-containment policy 142
neo-Eurasianists 40
neo-Gorbachevite cycle 230
neo-isolationism 162
neo-mercantilism 162
neo-patrimonialism 44-57, 94, 98-9, 221
neo-revisionism 155
neo-traditionalists 14, 26, 31, 38-9, 43, 55-6, 71, 73, 83, 100, 200, 226-7, 230
New Development Bank (NDB) 173
New Economic Policy 143
New Eurasianists 41
new political thinking (NPT) 3
new realism strategy 154
New Strategic Arms Reduction Treaty (START) 165
Nikandrov, Denis 104-5
Nikitin, Gleb 112
NOD. *See* National Liberation Movement (NOD)
Non-Aligned Movement (NAM) 150
normality 3, 55, 56, 60, 187, 195, 244
North Atlantic Treaty Organisation (NATO) 12, 13-14, 32, 36-7, 142, 147, 149, 150, 154, 155-7, 159, 160, 163, 165, 185, 223

INDEX   313

North, Douglass 115
Novgorod, Nizhny 112, 199–200, 208, 226
NPT. *See* new political thinking (NPT)
NRC. See NATO–Russia Council

OAK. *See* United Aircraft Corporation (OAK)
Obama, Barack 138, 152, 164, 184–6
obiter dicta 80
Oblast, Kemerovo 192
Oblast, Kirov 192
Oblast, Nizhny Novgorod 200
OBOR. *See* One Belt, One Road
OCCRP.*See* Organised Crime and Corruption Reporting Project (OCCRP)
OCGs. *See* organised criminal groups (OCGs)
ODIHR. *See* Office of Democratic Elections and Human Rights
Office of Democratic Elections and Human Rights (ODIHR) 204
okhraniteli bloc 71
oligarchs 7, 17, 20, 26, 28, 33–5, 43, 45, 60, 83, 92–3, 98, 113, 116, 131, 139–41, 222, 230, 234–5, 242
Olimpieva, Irina 75
One Belt, One Road (OBOR) 168
OPEC. *See* Organisation of Petroleum Exporting Countries
open-access orders 83, 115
opposition 19, 27, 34, 60, 75, 76, 86, 88–9, 134, 158, 187, 190, 193, 195–7, 199–203, 206, 211–12, 239
oprichnina 92
Orange Revolution in Ukraine 36, 48, 150
Organisation for Security and Cooperation in Europe (OSCE) 204
Organisation of Petroleum Exporting Countries (OPEC) 107, 136
Organised Crime and Corruption Reporting Project (OCCRP) 95
organised criminal groups (OCGs) 95, 104
OSCE. *See* Organisation for Security and Cooperation in Europe
OSK. *See* United Shipbuilding Corporation (OSK)
Otechestvo-Vsya Rossiya (OVR) 19
Ovsyannikov, Dmitry 112

PA. *See* Presidential Administration (PA)
PACE. *See* Parliamentary Assembly of the Council of Europe
pacification 14, 54, 83, 224
paleoliberals 114
Pamfilova, Ella 191–2
para-constitutionalism 47–8, 92
parapolitics 48, 92
Parland, Thomas 38
Parliamentary Assembly of the Council of Europe (PACE) 184
parliamentary election 6, 17, 38, 112, 204, 217
partial reform equilibrium 83, 123
Partido Revolucionario Institucional (PRI) 75
Partnership and Cooperation Agreement (PCA) 15
Party gold 99
Pastukhov, Vladimir 20, 98, 205
patronal politics 45, 47, 235
Patrushev, Nikolai 36–7, 120
Pavlovsky, Gleb 43, 64, 85, 219, 240–1
payment versus payment (PVP) system 125
PCA. *See* Partnership and Cooperation Agreement
perennial candidate 201
Perepilichny, Alexander 109
perestroika (restructuring) 3–4, 10, 20, 25, 30, 33, 53, 67–8, 86, 198, 201
Permanent Joint Council (PJC) 14
Peskov, Dmitry 109
Philippe, Louis 224
Pichugin, Alexei 61
Pivovarov, Yuri 74
PJC. *See* Permanent Joint Council
Plokhy, Serhii 43
Poklonskaya, Natalya 191
Poland 7–8, 134–6, 165–6
police 35, 68–9, 88, 98, 101, 103
Politburo 2.0 219
political institutions 18, 32, 47, 49, 51, 59, 115, 119
political parties 32, 47, 56, 192, 199, 239
political prisoners 61, 73, 97
Political Theology 60
Politics as a Vocation 77
Politkovskaya, Anna 64, 216
polycentrism 157

Pompeo, Mike 164
ponyatiya 23, 29, 101
popular capitalism 123
populist 162
Potomsky, Vadim 88
power *vertical* 24, 54, 101, 109, 219
PPP. *See* purchasing power parity (PPP) terms
Prague Spring in 1968 30
preparation (*podgotovka*) 117
presidency 1, 8, 18, 20, 26, 27, 29, 32–3, 44–7, 63, 86–7, 95–6, 100, 154, 187, 192–3, 200, 210, 234, 237, 240, 244
Presidential Administration (PA) 2
Presidential Council for the Development of Civil Society and Human Rights 122
presidential election 11, 18, 28, 34, 49, 89, 92, 129, 140–1, 190–1, 199–206
Prevention and Elimination of the Consequences of Computer Attacks (GosSOPKA) 37
PRI. *See* Partido Revolucionario Institucional (PRI)
Pribylovsky, Vladimir 99
Primakov, Evgeny 19, 149–50, 154, 215, 222
The Prince 77
private capitalism 122
profit-seeking model 83
Prokhanov, Alexander 38–9
Prokhorov, Mikhail 88, 105, 200
Prosecutor General's Office (PGO) 34
protests
　in 2011–12 88; 189, 199
　in 2018 206
　in 2019 212
　against electoral fraud 154; 196
　anti-corruption 76
　electoral fraud 36, 73
　fraud and ballot stuffing 86
　on social issues 210
　social and political 195
　social media and 212–13
　street 122
protest movement 63, 195, 198
Pukhly (Pudgy) 109
purchasing power parity (PPP) terms 124–5

Putin, Vladimir Spiridonovich 2
Putin, Vladimir Vladimirovich
　2018 election 198–206
　abolition of direct elections 62–3
　about 2
　adherence to two presidential terms 1
　anti-revolution 70–6
　as deputy head of PA 5
　as deputy mayor 2, 4, 7
　as international affairs advisor 4
　and past 65–70
　as prime minister 6, 19
　Asian gambit 180–5
　authoritarianism 12
　came to power 99
　campaigning 203
　centrism 34, 77
　challenges of 206–13
　complex political identity 1
　confrontation era 158–66
　cronies 239
　cult of personality 55
　democracy paradox 16–22
　de-offshorisation campaign 96, 109
　derangement syndrome 215
　desegmentation 62
　energy superpower 153
　faction manager 77
　factional spectrum 31
　financial crisis 117–18
　foreign policy concept 155–6
　fourth term 185–95
　FSB head 5
　heartland strategy 167–74
　heir-apparent to Yeltsin 11
　improve labour productivity 132
　in GDR 3
　industrial strategy 117
　KGB service 2–5, 7
　kommunalka to the Kremlin 1–6
　Kremlin official responsible for the regions 1–6
　labour productivity 132
　leadership strategy 11, 77–8; 185
　maintenance of dominant political party 75
　maximising natural resources 5
　Munich Security Conference (2007) 151
　oligarch capitalism 113, 116

INDEX 315

ordoliberalism 114
organised religion and 11
paradoxes of stability system 80
people 215–20
peripheral authoritarianism 24
personality cult 78
phenomenon 215–20
political personality 7–8
post–Atlantic world 175–80
post-Cold War era 12
power 215–20
presidential campaign 111
problem of ideology 79
pro-natalist policies 126
public-private partnership 118
Putinite 'vertical of power' 20
reform plans 116–17
regime reset 191
relationship with EU 158
restoring financial stability 123
retirement age 132
return to politics 195–8
rule as eclectic mix of systems 11
on Russia's development as democratic state 9
secretary to the Security Council 2
security strategy 155
social market economy 114
social responsibility 118
stability system 56
stability-focused regime management 114–15
statecraft 31, 77–8
statist capitalism 119
strategy 229–32
struggle against terrorism 14
success in parliamentary election (December 1999) 6
Ukrainian authorities 12
understanding of politics 79
weakening of balancing act 111
winds of change 185–98
Putina, Maria Ivanovna 2
Putinisation of energy thesis 136
Putinism:
  consensus 226
  defender of international status 82
  domestic politics 82–3
  dual state 59
  exception 60
  factional model 82
  four great 'blocs' 81
  hegemonic system 60
  horizontal structure 83
  inertial motion 81
  micro-factionalism 234
  paradoxes 233–46
  post-communist social transformation 60
  powering 132–8
  predominance of single group 81
  rule 234
  social contract 82–3
  sovereignty 59
  stability system 83
  stable equilibrium 82
  stasis 81–4
  succession 236–46
  tutelary system 83
  vertical of power 82
Putnam, Robert 52
PVP. *See* 'payment versus payment' (PVP) system

quasi-feudal relationship 93

radical liberals 33–4, 127, 150
raiding (*reiderstvo*) 96–7, 99, 115–16, 127, 217
ratio decidendi 80
RCEP. *See* Regional Comprehensive Economic Partnership
Realpolitik approach 42
Regional Comprehensive Economic Partnership (RCEP) 173
regional elections 192, 211
Reiderstvo 97–8
rent managers 97
rent-extraction model 83
rent-management system 83, 116, 124, 129
resilience 80, 120, 130, 133, 142–3
Responsibility to Protect (R2P) 156
revisionist powers 164
Robinson, Neil 50, 115
ROC. *See* Russian Orthodox Church (ROC)
Rocher, Yves 193
Rogozin, Dmitry 207

Roizman, Evgeny 88–9
rokirovka 85–6, 207
Romanova, Olga 103
Rose Revolution in Georgia 36, 71
Roskomnadzor 121–2
Rosneft 5, 93, 98, 100–1, 106–8, 217, 234, 244–5
Rossiiskii 40
Rostec (Rostekhnologii) 111–12, 115, 195, 226, 234
Rotenberg, Arkady 93, 98, 195, 220
RSFSR. *See* Russian Soviet Federative Socialist Republic (RSFSR)
Rumyantsev, Alexander 111
Russia:
    banking system in 123
    banning banks 141
    bourgeois entrepreneurs 113
    budget revenue 132–3
    civil society 51–2
    constitutional coup 26
    constitutional crisis 26
    digital revolution challenges 121
    dirigiste strategies 120
    duality 44–51
    economic gap challenge 122–3
    energy issue 134
    European energy relations 136
    failure of ideas 84
    foreign agents 54
    foreign funding 54
    foreign policy 145, 151–8
    gas transport 134
    GDP 119, 125
    global 185–8
    gold reserves 125
    heartland policy 143
    independence 25
    interlocking network 24
    managed capitalism 114
    media control 76
    memorial attack 69
    meta-factions 29–44
    model 117
    national champions 117, 126
    national identity 100
    NGOs 53–4
    oil prices 133
    path dependency problem 119
    politics in post-cold war era 16
    politics of exception 63
    post–cold war orders 146–51
    post-communist practices 25, 114
    post-revolutionary demobilisation 76
    property rights 113
    reform 51–7
    regime-state 23–9
    rent in 121
    rent-management system 116
    sanctions imposed on 124, 130–1
    Saudi Arabia, coordination between 133
    security services 122
    social capital theory 52
    state security 117
    strategic partnership with 15
    structural reforms in 126
    student activism 76
    two political systems 47
    using sovereign fund 124
    without Putin 242–6
Russia and Europe (1869) 39
Russia at the Turn of the Millennium 9
Russian Declaration of State Sovereignty 8
Russian Far East (RFE) 111
Russian Investigative Committee (RIC) 34
Russian new right 38
Russian Orthodox Church (ROC) 11, 31, 67, 87, 242
Russian Popular Front (*Obshcherossiiskii narodnyi front*, ONF) 48–9
Russian Soviet Federative Socialist Republic (RSFSR) 25
Russian spring 86
Russian system (*Russkaya sistema*) 53
Russian World (*Russkii Mir*) 160
Russkii 40
Russkii Mir (Russian World) 41
Russo-Atlantic relations 13
Russophobia 150
Russo-Western relations 150
Rutskoi, Alexander 26
Ryabkov, Sergei 177
Ryzhkov, Vladimir 202

Saakashvili, Mikheil 71, 203
sacred lands 194
Salye, Marina 5

Sarkisyan, Tigran 169
Sauer, Derk 75
Schlosberg, Lev 88
Schmitt, Carl 59
Schulman, Yekaterina 241
SCO. See Shanghai Cooperation Organisation
Sechin, Igor 86, 93, 98, 100–2, 106–8, 217, 219–20, 240, 244
Second Cold War 12, 142, 145–6
securitisation 136
security service (*siloviki*):
  against opponents 237
  factions 240
  FSB 106
  internet freedom 49, 211
  mission to defend country 100
  modern investigation methods 122
  powerful force 98–9
  SEB 101
  war 240
SEEC. See Supreme Eurasian Economic Council
Serebrennikov, Kirill 103
Shaimiev, Mintimir 19
Shakhrai, Sergei 5
Shanghai Cooperation Organisation (SCO) 143, 150, 173, 175–6, 178, 181, 183
Shanin, Teodor 103
Shaninka. See MSSES
Shevardnadze, Edward 71
Shevchenko, Maksim 39
Shirshina, Irina 88–9
Shlyapuzhnikov, Alexei 106
Shmeleva, Elena 111
shock absorber 169
shock doctrine 60
Shoigu, Sergei 220
Shport, Vyacheslav 111
Silk Road Economic Belt (SREB) 168
siloviki bloc 34–8, 43, 69, 81, 95, 98, 100, 107, 109, 111, 191, 227, 237, 240
sistema 24, 47, 53–4, 93, 106, 108, 231
small- and medium-enterprise (SME) sector 119
SME. See small- and medium-enterprise (SME) sector
Sobchak, Anatoly 4–5, 79, 196, 201–2, 205
Sobchak, Ksenia 196, 201–2, 205

social contract 10, 54–5, 82–3, 93, 114, 127, 210, 222
social *control* (supervision) 53
social liberals 32–3
SOEs. See state-owned enterprises (SOEs)
Solntsevskaya Bratva (Solntsevo Brotherhood) 104
Soskovets, Oleg 34
Sovereign Wealth Fund 124–5, 230–4
Soviet Union
  Cold War and 8
  collapse (*krushenie*) 9, 11, 17–18, 24, 26, 38, 40, 51–2, 97, 99, 109, 124, 153, 164, 186, 200, 212, 221–2, 232, 243
  dissolution of 8–9
  Germany's invasion of 7
  Gorbachev's attempts to hold 9
  regime legitimacy 10
  velvet revolutions 8
special path (*Sonderweg*) 42
spetsinformatsiya(technical information) system 124
spiritual values 194
SPS. See Union of Right Forces
SREB. See Silk Road Economic Belt
Sretensky Monastery 11, 69, 220
Stalin, Joseph 8, 23–4, 37, 55, 68–9, 71–2, 198, 222, 242
Stalinism 68–70, 72
Starikov, Nikolai 39
START. See New Strategic Arms Reduction Treaty
stasis 31, 51, 81–4
state:
  fragmentation 32
  prerogative state 245
state capitalism 122–3
state-owned enterprises (SOEs) 119
stoligarchs 98, 116
Stone, Oliver 3–4, 7
strategic atrophy 164
strategic partners 185
Strategy 2010 116–17
Strategy 2020 reform plan 118, 127
Strelkov (Girkin), Igor 197
Studin, Irvin 46
Sugrobov, Denis 102–3
Supreme Eurasian Economic Council (*SEE* C) 169

Surkov, Vladislav 21, 31, 56, 78, 85, 110–11, 199, 242
　aligned with Medvedev 85
　democratic statist 56
　domestic political affairs 78, 111
　head of domestic affairs 21
　new type of state 242
　normality in Russia 56
　Russian politics 242
　sovereign democracy 31, 56
　years of solitude 242

Taibbi, Matt 215
Talbott, Strobe 149
Taylor, Brian 216
Telegram 121–2
TEN. *See* Trans-Europe Network (TEN)
TEP. *See* Third Energy Package (TEP)
terrorism 14, 37, 141, 151, 164, 179
Third Energy Package (TEP) 136
Third state
　administrative rents 97
　corruption 95–7
　deep state 92, 95
　dual state 94
　dualism 92
　Duma elections 89
　factional balancing 94
　gubernatorial elections 92
　power system 99
　regime system 85–92, 94
　rent management system 94
　security apparatus 93
　security forces role 98
　social contract 93
　stability system 99
　upper and underworld 94
Tikhon, Bishop 11, 220
Tillerson, Rex 106, 139
Timchenko, Gennady 54, 98, 220
Titov, Boris 129, 131, 201, 205
Tocquevillean myth 54
Tokaev, Kassym-Jomart 237
Toloraya, Georgy 177
traditional values 194
Trans-Europe Network (TEN) 135
transformation 1, 12, 13, 14, 15, 146, 147, 148, 151
Travin, Dmitry 34

Trudolyubov, Maksim 92, 113
Tuapse oil refinery 244
Tulip Revolution 36
Turkmenistan 134, 174
Tusk, Donald 136

Uchitel, Alexei 191
Ukraine 8–9, 11–13, 36, 43, 48, 71, 73–4, 78, 89, 96, 124, 134–8, 151, 153–4, 159–61, 163, 169, 174–5, 185, 187, 197, 210, 223
Ulyukaev, Alexei 107–9, 217, 240
Union of Right Forces (SPS) 105
Union of Soviet Socialist Republics (USSR) 8–9, 13, 23, 34, 65, 71, 124, 154, 172, 181, 197, 229
United Aircraft Corporation (OAK) 117
United Nations Security Council (UNSC) 9, 149, 155, 163, 179
United Russia 20, 38, 161
　creation 20, 38
United Shipbuilding Corporation (OSK) 117
United States:
　adoption of Russian children 44
　bilateral summit cancellation 141
　Moscow bombings 63
　Magnitsky Act 44
　oil and gas industries 136
　and Russia 126, 167, 202
Unity 6, 19
UNSC. *See* United Nations Security Council
Urlashov, Evgeny 88–9
Usmanov, Alisher 121, 219
USSR. *See* Union of Soviet Socialist Republics
Ust-Luga oil terminal 135

Vader, Darth 106
Vaino, Anton 111–12, 220
value-added tax (VAT) 209
VAT. *See* value-added tax
venal corruption 96, 99–100, 192, 194
virtual politics 47
virtual private networks (VPN) 37, 122
VKontakte (VK) 121
Volodin, Vyacheslav 2, 44, 75, 78, 88–9, 111–12, 191, 194, 217

Voloshin, Alexander 35
vory v zakone (thieves in law) 94
VPN. *See* virtual private network (VPN) services

Wall of Sorrow 69–70
war weariness 209
web anonymisers 37
Weber, Max 46, 77
Weimar Russia 53
West Germany 134
Westernisers 30
Wood, Tony 69, 236
World Trade Organisation (WTO) 118
WTO. *See* World Trade Organisation (WTO)

Yabloko party 24, 27, 33, 56, 60, 88–90, 191–2, 196–7, 199, 201
Yakovlev, Vladimir 4–5, 80
Yakunin, Vladimir 31
Yalta and Potsdam agreements of 1945 8
Yamal–Europe gas pipeline 134
Yanov, Alexander 53
Yarovaya, Irina 121, 192
Yavlinsky, Grigory 24–5, 33, 192, 199, 201–2, 205

Yeltsin, Boris 1, 4–8, 10, 12, 15–16, 18–21, 24–8, 33, 35, 38, 40, 43–6, 52, 60, 62–3, 85, 92, 106, 113, 116, 145, 147, 149, 163, 198, 200, 202, 220, 222, 237–8, 240, 242
Yevtushenkov, Vladimir 106
Yew, Lee Kuan 237
young technocrats 194
Yukos oil company 28, 32, 46–7, 61, 78, 83, 100, 104, 116, 126, 222, 233, 241
Yumashev, Valentin 34

Zakharchenko, Dmitry 106
Zavtra (*Tomorrow*) 38
zemshchina state 92
zero-sum strategy 14
Zhirinovsky, Vladimir 27, 38, 199–200, 204–5
Zinichev, Yevgeny 220
Zolotov, Viktor 36, 102
Zubov, Andrei 74
Zudin, Alexei 20
Zvyagintsev, Andrei 103–4
Zygar, Mikhail 43, 231
Zyuganov, Gennady 6, 18–19, 27–8, 199–201